Winning in the Futures Market

Also by George Angell

COMPUTER-PROVEN COMMODITY SPREADS
SURE-THING OPTIONS TRADING
HOW TO TRIPLE YOUR MONEY EVERY YEAR
WITH STOCK INDEX FUTURES
AGRICULTURAL OPTIONS

GEORGE ANGELL

Winning in the Futures Market

Second Edition

DOUBLEDAY & COMPANY, INC.
GARDEN CITY, NEW YORK
1987

This book was originally published under the title
Winning in the Commodities Market

Library of Congress Cataloging-in-Publication Data
Angell, George.
  Winning in the futures market.

  Rev. ed. of: Winning in the commodities market. 1st
ed. 1979.
  Includes index.
  1. Commodity exchanges. 2. Financial futures.
I. Angell, George. Winning in the commodities market.
II. Title.
HG6046.A573 1987   332.64′4   86–6280
ISBN 0-385-19949-X

For Deborah Shapiro

Acknowledgments

Although it is never possible to thank everyone who teaches you something about the market, or life, I'd like to mention a few people who either helped me acquire the knowledge contained within this book or helped make the book a possibility. In one way or another, they all deserve my gratitude.

First and foremost, I'd like to thank my first editor at Doubleday, Joseph Gonzalez, who picked the original manuscript out of the slush pile and helped turn it into a modestly successful book. In addition, I owe gratitude to my subsequent editors, Ferris Mack and Harold Kuebler, and Ferris' ever-helpful assistant, Lani Mysak.

For specific information contained within the book, I am indebted to Richard D. Donchian, one of the wisest men on Wall Street, who has been in the investment business over fifty years. I'd also like to thank Bill Ohama, of E. F. Hutton in Los Angeles, for sharing his three- and four-dimensional charting concepts with me. These innovative charting concepts, which first appeared in print in the first edition of this book, are now accepted as standard charting practice in many investment circles. Bill deserves thanks for introducing a charting concept that has become an accepted part of technical analysis.

For his tireless work in programming, testing, and developing the LSS

3-day Cycle Method, Duane Davis, of Turner Data Systems in Irvine, California, deserves thanks. Without Duane's help, the LSS system could have never been proved, and hence never been made available to those who have learned the system and used the software. I recommend Duane to anyone seeking professional programming help in developing or testing a trading system.

Lastly, for showing me how to beat the market, I'm indebted to my friend, Barry Haigh. Barry taught me how to double up and go the other way in the market—a lesson that every futures trader should take to heart.

Contents

Introduction

"Half bid on fifty! Half bid on fifty!" a man in a red trading jacket yells. He waves his arms in the air, pivots, and begins to jump. "Half bid on fifty!" he yells louder.

"Sell fifty at double!" another man, halfway across the jammed trading pit, yells back. "Sell 'em at double!" His cry is met by a chorus of buyers. "Half bid! Half bid! Half bid!" The roar is deafening.

One soon relents. "Double bid on fifty!" the red-jacketed man yells into the crowd. "Double bid!" His cry is met by a resounding "Sold!" The two men pause and, taking note of each other with a flick of a finger, write the transaction down on trading cards each holds in his hands. The transaction, which involves stock index futures valued at $4.5 million, takes no more than twenty seconds to complete.

Seconds pass. And the market begins to run.

The bid rises to sixty. Sixty-five offered. Seventy bid, seventy-five offered. Seventy-five bid. Soon the sellers give up altogether. The rally is underway. Eighty, ninety, even bid!

Ten minutes after buying fifty contracts valued at close to $4.5 million, the buyer begins selling into the rally. He offers then at fifteen, twenty, and twenty-five. The buyers take the whole fifty contracts. For his ten minutes work, he is rewarded with a $15,000 profit.

Welcome to the world of stock index futures trading—the fastest-growing and most exciting area of today's new futures market. The scene is the floor of the Chicago Mercantile Exchange. The futures contract is the Standard & Poor's 500, the undisputed leader in the burgeoning world of stock index futures. Down on the floor of the Merc, where some three hundred traders daily engage in the rough-and-tumble world of stock index futures, a thousand more around them trade contracts valued at billions of dollars on such divergent commodities and financial instruments as Deutschemark and Eurodollar futures, live cattle and pork bellies, Treasury bills and live hogs. Here, where emotions run high and fistfights are not uncommon, big traders often win and lose six-figure bets within hours. The stakes are high. And nowhere are the sudden, explosive moves that make millionaires of some and bankrupts of others more common than amid the frenzy in the S&P pit.

One trader bit another in the S&P pit last year. The stricken trader didn't notice until the blood spurted onto his shirt. Amid the free-for-all that passes for the S&P pit, angry verbal—occasionally physical—exchanges are commonplace. Most of them amount to nothing, however, and are part and parcel of the momentary frenzy when the market runs. To keep the traders, who sometimes stand in the same place six hours a day, comfortable, the designers of the new exchange provided air ducts in the tiers upon which the traders stand. Few notice the cooled air; they don't go there every day and risk fortunes for the amenities. Yet, given the high tension associated with the enterprise of trading stock index futures, most of them take breaks during the day. For relaxation, many traders go downstairs to the private Merc club that borders the Chicago River. There they watch the price ticker on the wall with phones by their tables. They also eat and drink. And worry.

While not the most widely traded of all futures contracts—the Chicago Board of Trade's U.S. Treasury bond contract holds that distinction—the Standard & Poor's 500 contract, which only commenced trading in April 1982, has won wide support and demonstrated consistent growth throughout the futures industry. Unheard of just five years ago, the concept of stock index trading has caught on like wildfire. Today, in addition to the leading S&P 500 futures contract, there are five other futures contracts based on stock indexes as well as several stock index options traded. A futures contract pegged to a statistical index, a stock index futures is nothing more than a legal fiction. The contract can't be settled by delivery, since delivering one share each of the 500 in the S&P 500, or the more than 1,700 shares that constitute the Big Board's composite stock index, would be an impracticality, if not an impossibility. As a result, the designers of stock index futures developed the notion of *cash settlement.* This means that no underlying shares ever change hands; instead, a payment from loser to winner is made in cash—a simple bookkeeping entry.

Stock index futures trading is but the latest development in the boom in financial futures. Beginning with the introduction of currency futures and, later, a host of financial futures in the early and mid seventies, the growth of this sector of the futures market has outpaced the more traditional agricultural products by a wide margin. Today, you can trade any number of financial futures that were unheard of just a few years ago. There are futures contracts on bank CD's, Treasury bonds, bills, and notes, Eurodollars, foreign currencies, freight rates, the consumer price index, and a handful of stock market averages, including the newest, NASDAQ-100 futures, on the booming over-the-counter market. Not surprisingly, as a result of the introduction of these new products, the focus of the futures industry has been changing. The trend is away from the mainstay agricultural products, although the agricultural sector is still a vital segment of the futures market, and toward the less tangible financial products. Moreover, as evidenced by the acceptance of the new markets by the leading banks and financial institutions that have wholeheartedly embraced the new products, the futures market transformation has widened the audience considerably. What was once a strictly U.S.-based market has suddenly become a thriving international marketplace, in keeping with the trend toward globalization of the world economy.

What's next? It is hard to say. But recent events suggest more changes ahead. When the first edition of this book appeared, in 1979, a wholesale rush into the commodity markets was just beginning. As investors eagerly sought a refuge from double-digit inflation, one commodity after another was bid up to unrealistic heights—with the predictable crash coming on its heels. It is not that such impressive fortunes were made during those years of the late seventies and early eighties, but that so few were able to see the bubble beginning to burst. Eight-hundred-dollar gold? Fifty-dollar silver? The speculative binge had to end. Today, to show you how things can change, the once high-flying grain markets are in the doldrums—indeed, new life-of-contract lows are commonplace in the agricultural pits—but the cycle is getting ready to come around again. After all, the oldest rule of the contrarian investor is to buy when everyone is pessimistic. Who could ask for a better opportunity than today's futures market? Or should one limit that to today's agricultural commodities market? The booming financial futures aren't suffering from a lack of participation.

But even the decline in certain segments of the market have had beneficial effects upon the average investor. Take commission rates, for example. As recently as four or five years ago, the typical speculator wouldn't think twice about paying seventy-five or a hundred dollars for a round-turn commission. No more. Today, even the wire houses, which traditionally charged the highest fees, will negotiate commissions down to the twenty-to-thirty-dollar level. This lower cost of operating in the futures market heightens the opportunities. And widespread discounting has been just one new trend.

Another significant trend, with widespread implications for the future, involves the introduction of new products. As we've mentioned, the boom in financial futures has taken up the slack where the agricultural commodities declined in interest. Now, in addition to new financial futures, we have the introduction of entirely new products—primarily *options on futures*—which have introduced still more complex, yet potentially profitable, ways of operating in the market. To understand them, of course, requires new knowledge. Here again, perhaps this book can be of some help.

What's the main attraction of the new options? Safety, on the one hand; enhanced income, on the other. It all depends on whether you want to buy or write options. One thing is entirely new, however: with the introduction of options on futures, one can now, for the very first time, operate in the futures market with strictly limited risk. That means no margin calls. No surprises due to limit moves. Unless you've been on the wrong side of the futures market once too often, you probably don't realize what an advantage this limited-risk concept is.

For the advanced student of the markets, options offer a truly creative way to match one's wits with one's need for risk versus reward. In addition to simply buying and writing options, one can trade them against futures, use them to spread one month against another, establish hedges against one's cash position, and a host of other complex—and profitable—strategies. Options can be used as an insurance policy or to enhance your profit. It is how you use them that decides whether they increase or decrease your risk and overall net exposure.

First introduced as a pilot program by the Commodity Futures Trading Commission (CFTC), the industry's regulator, back in 1981, options on futures were at first limited to U.S. Treasury bonds, gold, and a couple of other commodities. Today, with the introduction of the new farm commodity options, the second-generation option is available. In time, there will probably be options available on just about every futures contract. Since the trading principles are essentially the same—whether you trade soybeans or silver—you might as well understand how these new options work. In updating this new edition, we've devoted an entire chapter to these contracts that have only recently arrived on the futures scene.

Looking ahead, one can only guess at the future. Will we have "beans in the teens" once again? Will inflation cause the metals markets to boom? Will interest rates decline—or rise? Whatever happens, you can be sure the economic events of the future will be reflected in these highly leveraged markets. And new fortunes will be won. Just as some things constantly change, others stay the same. Whether you're following stock index futures or soybean futures, the goal is still the same: price protection if you're a hedger and price appreciation if you're a speculator. But what's the best plan to follow?

In this new edition, we've concentrated on updating the traditional concepts while offering the latest in trading developments. Included you will find the names and addresses of some of today's hottest money managers, the how and why of trading the new options on futures, and a look at the proprietary LSS day-trading system that was especially developed for the volatile S&P index—which, by the way, has some interesting quirks not found among more "traditional" commodities. Ideally, you'll be able to pick and choose among a variety of approaches and find the one that's best for you.

For the novice, you still have to go through basic training. In the pages that follow, you will learn the meaning of a futures contract, how margin works, the ins and outs of dealing with a broker, how to place an order, and much more. In time, this will all become second nature. But if you haven't been exposed to this information before, you have to pick it up somewhere. So here's a good place to start.

For the seasoned trader, the quest for information becomes ever more essential. Where's the market going? Well, that depends. After all, it isn't by accident that 10 percent of the participants in the futures markets make 100 percent of the profits. If you confronted a seasoned professional with the news that he earned a fortune in the futures market by being lucky, he'd laugh—and justifiably so—in your face. The few who make the consistent money in the futures market do so because they *know* how the market works. They know all the tricks, the false moves, the human mistakes—everything. In short, they know how to read the market. The more you learn, the more you'll see how so much of what goes on in the futures market fits a pattern.

It is discerning the meaning of that pattern that takes work. And that means doing a lot of work. Despite all the information published on the futures markets in recent years, a number of myths persist. The fact is that the informed minority tends to reap the enormous profits available in the futures markets, and the uninformed majority willingly contribute to their fortunes. No doubt, this is due in part to the nature of the markets; in a zero-sum game, such as futures trading, there simply aren't sufficient profits for everyone to win. But certainly a clearer viewpoint of the actual playing of the futures game can help you win your fair share of the time.

Much of the new material in the second edition covers short-term, day-trading techniques. For some, unfamiliar with the ups and downs of futures trading, the short term might be considered a week or two. But in the futures market, where, due to the leverage, the pace seems so accelerated, a week can seem like a lifetime—especially if one finds oneself on the wrong side of the market. The fact is, the would-be long-term trader won't be alive, financially speaking, unless he concentrates on surviving over the short haul. So try to learn how to earn modest short-term profits first—and only then attempt to make a long-term market killing.

In the first edition of this book, I recounted how I had parlayed a small amount of money in copper futures into a significantly larger amount by pyramiding in a bull market fueled by devaluation scares. I've only recently realized just how lucky I was. Had I been buying a few weeks later,

I'd probably still be paying off the losses—and this happened back in 1973! So much for beginner's luck.

One common pitfall, into which many first-time traders stumble, is doing the right thing in the market for the wrong reasons. Richard Dennis, who has made over $100 million in the futures market before the age of forty, tells the story of the successful floor trader who was envied by everyone down on the floor at the Chicago Board of Trade. Day after day, this fortunate trader was able to extract profits out of the market. But then, one day, his winning streak came to an end. It developed, according to Dennis, that this trader had been engaged in a very risky form of trading and it took time for the law of averages to catch up to him—which it did with a vengeance.

Paradoxically, initial success can prove one's undoing. Over a period of five or six months' time, a friend carefully built up his equity to over $70,000 down on the floor of the Chicago Mercantile Exchange by writing puts and calls on Deutschemark options. The strategy seemed to work so well that he was willing to sell (write) options to any and every buyer. Then, one day, the market, which had been marking time in a narrow trading range, came to life. He lost the entire seventy grand in three days!

Another friend, from Cleveland, had an even better run. Starting with just eight thousand dollars, he managed to parlay the money into more than $350,000 in copper futures during the long, sustained bear market several years ago. His strategy was simple: Sell. Take the paper profits, sell more contracts short, and hold on. This was his strategy. Toward the end of his incredible success, he even had a $50,000 day. But you know what happened. He overstayed the market and was lucky to get out with a few thousand dollars. Stories like these occur all the time. In the big run-up in silver prices several years ago, a physician friend had the good fortune to buy silver contracts right at the bottom. He had several hundred thousands of dollars in profits by the time silver reached $50 an ounce. "What were you thinking when it was at $50 an ounce?" I asked him once. "That it would go to $100 an ounce," he replied. He rode it back down. Another casualty of the market. There's an infinite number of stories similar to these.

While they are interesting, such stories, to be truly useful, must be instructive. What were the mistakes demonstrated here that, given another chance, could have been rectified? Certainly, one quality that separates the professionals from their hapless cousins is discipline. The discipline to act forthrightly. But there are other helpful qualities as well. A good trader needs a combination of money, intelligence, and—most important of all—what legendary trader W. D. Gann used to call "nerve." Pure courage. For best results, one should have a blend of these qualities. Certainly, money alone isn't enough. The floors of the exchanges are crowded with would-be Jesse Livermores. The money will get you in the door, but it won't make you successful. "To make a small fortune in the commodities market," goes a well-known saying, "start with a large one."

How about intelligence? Can't hurt, right? Well, yes and no. It depends upon what you mean. In recent years, the markets have been attracting the theoretical types—guys with computer-like brains crammed with statistical data but few street smarts. As a rule, the guys with the street smarts from the South Side of Chicago make a fortune off these theoretical types. The overly cerebral trader tends to become paralyzed when it comes time to act. In commenting on the kind of intelligence required to successfully trade commodity futures contracts, one winning trader put it this way: "We get out of the market when we see the smoke coming under the door. Not after we realize the whole house is on fire."

Enough for the war stories.

What do you need to know to get started? To be careful. And to make your mistakes before you commit serious funds to the market. Also, try to learn as much as you can. Lastly, don't fall for simple solutions. "There is always an easy solution to every human problem," H. L. Mencken once said, "neat, plausible, and wrong." This advice is doubly true where the futures market is concerned.

Today's futures markets are a financial frontier. They are as challenging, unbridled, and dangerous as the Old West. Yet they offer a world of opportunity to the individual with the wit, discipline, and courage to set out to conquer this undisputedly difficult financial terrain. "It's a business," explained one successful trader, "where the cream rises." What more could one ask for? So if you are any good, you'll know that you have achieved victory not over others, although only a minority can win, but, much more important, over yourself—an attribute that will stand you in good stead from the first to the last. Let's get started.

Winning in the
Futures Market

1

What You Need to Know

THE FUNDAMENTALS
OF COMMODITY FUTURES TRADING

Walk down the aisle of any modern supermarket and you will see dozens of commodities from every region of the country and the world. Bacon from hogs raised in Nebraska, cereals made from oats grown in Illinois, bread made from wheat grown in Kansas. Chicken from California, beef from Texas, orange juice from Florida, cocoa from Ghana, coffee from Brazil, sugar from Honduras, corn from Iowa, potatoes from Maine. The list goes on and on. Each and every one of us consumes a number of commodities vital to our existence every day. But comparatively few have a knowledge of the regulatory mechanism that assures us there will be coffee on the shelves, potatoes in the produce department, and fresh beef in the meat refrigerator when we do our weekly shopping.

For most of us, the knowledge of *why* or *how* this regulatory mechanism works is not as important as knowing that it *does* work. But without the existence of the commodity futures markets, many of these commodities so vital to our everyday life would frequently be in scarce supply, if available at all, and their prices would certainly be much higher, due primarily to the high risks inherent in the production and processing of the commodities themselves.

Droughts, freezes, rains, sudden changes in government policies, and a multitude of other hazards can wreak havoc on even the best-conceived production program. Likewise, the users of raw commodities—whether they be manufacturers, of tubing who use hundreds of thousands of pounds of copper as a raw material each year, or chocolate manufacturers dependent on a ready supply of cocoa from Africa—must deal with the uncertainties of supply and demand, and price their goods accordingly. In a competitive world, not to strive to produce a product as cheaply as possible can seriously threaten the existence of a business. Manufacturers and processors know this. But what they cannot know is the prevailing price of a commodity at the time they need it. For the same reason, a farmer, rancher, or producer may know the costs of running his farm, ranch, or mining operation. But this knowledge cannot guarantee him the price he wants for his grain, livestock, or precious metal. Supply and demand alone will dictate the price he will receive for his commodity. To offset the risks of the open marketplace, farmers, ranchers, producers, processors, and other principals involved in the production and processing of raw commodities turn to the commodity futures markets.

The futures markets, as the name implies, are markets in which commodities or financial instruments to be delivered at some time in the future are bought and sold. For example, a wheat farmer in Nebraska might utilize the futures market to sell his crop while his wheat is still in the ground. Why? To achieve price protection. By the time the wheat is harvested in the fall, perhaps five or six months in the future, the price of wheat may have fallen sharply. To protect against a possible decline in wheat prices, therefore, the farmer *hedges* his crop in the futures market. Specifically, he *sells* wheat futures. By doing do, he establishes a selling price that provides him a profit on his farming operations.

Once he sells wheat futures, the farmer's selling price is established and he can go about his farming operations indifferent to wheat prices. Falling wheat prices would mean a profit on the futures position; rising prices, the opposite: a loss on the futures position but perhaps an offsetting gain on his cash wheat at the harvest. Regardless of whether his profit derives primarily from the sale of the cash wheat or the decline—and hence profitability —of his short futures position, the outcome is essentially the same. By enabling him to hedge, the futures market has served a risk-transference mechanism. And the hedger's fixed selling price is achieved.

Now let's look at the opposite side of the equation. Consider the case of a hypothetical *user* of wheat grain—say, a bread manufacturer—who wants to purchase wheat at some future time. The processor may also want to guarantee himself a purchasing price that will enable him to achieve a normal business profit. Indeed, if wheat prices rise substantially over the next five or six months, the bread manufacturer will find his profit margins threatened. To ensure an ample supply of wheat at a price consistent with his own marketing objectives, the processor will go into the futures market and *purchase* contracts for delivery at some time in the future. Guaranteed a price, the processor can continue to operate on a profitable basis regardless of the subsequent movement in wheat prices.

There is a third individual who also participates in the buying and selling of commodity futures contracts. Neither a producer nor a user of the physical commodity, this individual enters the market with only one goal in mind: to make a profit from correctly anticipating the direction of prices. This is the *speculator*. By assuming the risks that the producers and processors decide to avoid, the speculator stands to make money if his judgment proves correct, and stands to lose money if his judgment proves wrong. For example, returning to our illustration of the Nebraska wheat farmer, we can see that a speculator who anticipates a rise in the price of wheat would gladly purchase the wheat contracts the farmer wishes to sell. By doing so, the speculator guarantees the wheat farmer his selling price; in the bargain, the speculator stands to profit if the wheat market trades higher. And if the speculator's judgment proves wrong? In this instance, he would sell out his position at a lower price—albeit at a loss—to someone else who, for whatever reason, wants to buy wheat futures.

The speculator likewise plays an important role in taking the other side of transactions in which hedgers are purchasing futures contracts. For instance, a speculator might sell wheat futures contracts if he anticipates lower prices. (The buying and selling between hedger and speculator does not, however, take place in a one-to-one fashion. Rather, a market *local,* who trades for his own account, might *scalp* a small profit by, let's say, selling September wheat futures to a hedger who is buying at $2.87 a bushel and then *covering,* or buying them back, from a speculator at $2.86½ a bushel. The one-half-cent profit would be the scalper's profit on the trade. And both hedger and speculator will have achieved their objectives of being respectively long and short the market.) The speculator, whether he is a local on the floor or a public trader on the outside, doesn't provide the worthwhile service of providing market liquidity out of altruism, however. He is out to make a profit. He anticipates, let's say, a price decline, and he sells wheat contracts in hopes of buying them back lower, a strategy known as *selling short.* Thus, when the speculator sells futures contracts, unlike the farmer he does so with the expectation of buying them lower. He can only earn a profit, therefore, if prices decline. Should prices rise, and the speculator is short, he *must* cover his short position by purchasing contracts at a higher price. By definition, the speculator doesn't have the underlying commodity in his possession. Thus, he cannot deliver wheat or any other commodity upon maturity of the futures contract.

Because producers and processors do not correspond in a one-to-one ratio, the speculator's role in the futures market is absolutely vital to the smooth functioning of this economic system. Without the speculator to provide liquidity to the markets, each farmer or user of a particular commodity or financial instrument would have to contract with a buyer on an individual basis. Since seeking out a buyer and a seller for each large unit of the commodity or financial instrument produced and used would be an extremely difficult process involving considerable imbalances in the price due to changing supply and demand, the futures market provides a centralized arena where the risks involved in producing and using commodities can be transferred from those unwilling to assume them (the producers and users) to those who are willing to assume them (the speculators). This is the primary function of the commodity futures market. Because the risks are considerable, so, too, are the profits and losses that a speculator can expect to win or lose.

The Futures Contract

The unit of exchange in the commodities markets is known as the futures contract. A futures contract provides for the future delivery of various agricultural or industrial commodities at a specified date, time, and place. The contractual obligations, depending upon whether one is a buyer or a seller, may be satisfied either by taking or making delivery of an approved grade of the commodity or by making an offsetting sale or purchase of an equivalent commodity futures contract on the same exchange prior to the designated date of delivery. Just as securities are bought and sold in round lots of one hundred shares each, commodities are bought and sold in standardized contractual units. Each futures contract for each commodity is identical to every other; however, the specifications of futures contracts are different for each commodity. Thus, every contract of frozen concentrated orange juice is 15,000 pounds, every cotton contract is 50,000 pounds, and every contract of lumber consists of 130,000 board feet of wood. Similarly, the quality of every contract of a given commodity is the same. Most futures contracts call for a certain grade of the commodity, which is usually the grade most in demand for commercial use. For the seller making delivery of the commodity, the grade specified in the contract must be delivered. Should the seller offer a grade inferior to that specified in the commodity contract, the buyer has the right of refusal, or he can accept the inferior grade at a discount price. In normal practice, a speculator, who intends to neither make nor take delivery of the physical commodity, will not concern himself with the grade of commodity called for in the contract. But he will most certainly want to know the size of the contract in order to calculate his profits or losses.

The key advantage of having standardized contracts is that they are completely interchangeable. Moreover, contract standardization also helps to minimize confusion when it comes to determining the value of a price move. To determine the value of a price move of a commodity, you should know the following:

The contract size
The unit in which the futures contract is quoted
The minimum price fluctuation
The value of the minimum price fluctuation
The daily trading limit
The value of the daily trading limit

Let's look at these terms one at a time. *The contract size* refers to the standardized unit that constitutes one contract. We have mentioned the size of the orange juice, cotton, and plywood contracts above. Others, to name just a handful, are listed below:

COMMODITY	CONTRACT SIZE
Copper	25,000 pounds
Cattle	40,000 pounds
Coffee "C"[1]	37,500 pounds
Silver	5,000 troy ounces
Sugar	112,000 pounds
Gold	100 troy ounces

Knowing the size of the unit you are trading is vital to understanding futures trading. For, as you shall soon see, the contract size dictates the value of a one-cent or one-dollar move in the price of the underlying commodity. The *unit in which the futures contract is quoted* is also an important factor to consider. As you become familiar with futures trading, you will see that the grains are quoted in cents per bushel, the meats in cents per pound, the metals in either cents or dollars per ounce, and the currencies in cents per unit of currency. Here again, understanding the unit in which the futures contract is quoted becomes second nature once you become familiar with the markets. Continuing with our representative sample of commodities, the units in which they are quoted are as follows:

COMMODITY	UNIT QUOTED
Copper	cents per pound
Cattle	cents per pound
Coffee "C"	cents per pound
Silver	cents per troy ounce
Sugar	cents per pound
Gold	dollars per ounce

The *minimum price fluctuation* is generally a function of the unit in which the commodity is quoted. Thus, the grains can fluctuate a minimum

---

[1] On the New York Coffee and Sugar Exchange three coffee contracts are traded—the "B," "C," and "U" contracts. The "B" and "U" contracts, which are Brazilian and African coffees, respectively, are relatively inactive and used mainly by the commercial trade. The "C" contract, which consists of 37,500 pounds of coffee originating from Mexico, El Salvador, Guatemala, or Colombia, enjoys the widest speculative participation.

of 1/8 or 1/4 of a cent per bushel (depending on the exchange); the meats, a minimum of 2.5/100 of a cent per pound; the metals, a minimum of 1/10 of one cent per ounce of silver, 10 cents per ounce of gold, or 10/100 of a cent per pound of copper. To sum up:

COMMODITY	MINIMUM FLUCTUATION
Copper	10/100 of a cent per pound
Cattle	2.5/100 of a cent per pound
Coffee "C"	1/100 of a cent per pound
Silver	1/10 of a cent per ounce
Sugar	1/100 of a cent per pound
Gold	10 cents per ounce

The *value of the minimum price fluctuation* is the dollar-and-cents equivalent of the minimum price fluctuation multiplied by the contract size of the commodity you are trading. The size of a contract of frozen concentrated orange juice, for instance, is 15,000 pounds and is quoted in hundredths of a cent per pound. The minimum price fluctuation of an orange juice contract is 5/100 of a cent per pound. By multiplying the minimum price fluctuation by the size of the contract, you obtain the value of the minimum price fluctuation—or, in this case, $7.50. The following are some representative minimum fluctuation values:

COMMODITY	MINIMUM PRICE FLUCTUATION VALUE
Copper[2]	10 points or $25
Cattle (live)[3]	2½ points or $10
Coffee "C"	one point or $3.75
Silver	1/10 of a cent or $5.00
Sugar	one point or $11.20
Gold	10 cents or $10

Except for the grains, whose minimum fluctuations are quoted in quarters (or eighths, as at the MidAmerica Exchange), the minimum price-fluctuation value is generally referred to as a point. Exceptions do exist, however, and the minimum fluctuation value of commodities such as orange juice, copper, or cattle will be more than one point. To arrive at the value of a point, take the total contract size and divide by 10,000. For example, the copper contract consists of 25,000 pounds, which, divided by 10,000, gives you the value of one point, or $2.50. The minimum price-fluctuation value of copper is 10/100 of a cent per pound times 25,000 pounds, which equals $25, or 10 points.

The *daily trading limit* measures the maximum amount a commodity can move above or below the previous day's close in a single trading

---

[2] In commodities in which the minimum "tick" is greater than one point—such as copper or cattle—the price will always move in multiples of that minimum tick.

[3] In the larger feeder cattle contract, 2½ points equals $10.50.

session. The limits are set by the exchanges to allow trading to cool down before the next session begins. The following day, of course, the commodity can once again resume its previous momentum and move an equivalent of the daily trading limit. The *value of the daily trading limit* measures the maximum amount you can win or lose on one contract of a commodity in a single trading session. It should be noted that the trading limits are changed from time to time to correspond with the volatility in a market. The following are some representative trading limits and their dollar values:

COMMODITY	DAILY LIMIT	VALUE OF DAILY LIMIT
Copper	3 cents	$750
Cattle	1½ cents	$600
Coffee "C"	4 cents	$1,500
Silver	20 cents	$1,000
Sugar	1 cent	$1,120
Gold	ten dollars	$1,000

Contract Specifications

Before you attempt to trade any commodity, you will want to acquaint yourself fully with the specifications of the contract as well as the trading rules, daily limits, and hours established by the exchange. Typical commodity contract information includes the following:

Name of commodity
Name of the exchange
The trading hours
Size of contract and contract grade or grades
Delivery months
How prices are quoted
Minimum fluctuation
Dollar value of minimum tick (i.e., fluctuation)
Dollar value of one-cent move
Daily trading limits
The commission schedule

Let's use pork bellies as an example. As a knowledgeable pork belly trader, you'll want to be familiar with the fact that the opening bell rings at precisely 9:10 A.M. central time, and the closing bell sounds at 1:00 P.M. Each pork belly contract calls for 38,000 pounds of frozen pork bellies traded for delivery in the months of February, March, May, July, and August. Quoted in cents per pound (or dollars per hundredweight), the minimum tick is .00025 of a dollar, equal to $9.50. The daily trading limit on pork bellies is two cents above or below the previous day's close—the equivalent of $760 per contract.

Margin

Each futures contract that is bought and sold on a commodity futures exchange must be backed by a good-faith deposit known as *margin.* As money deposited with your broker prior to initiating your first trade, margin serves to guarantee the performance of your side of the contract. This "earnest" money, which is not in any way a down payment, ensures the integrity of every futures contract. Thus, if you lose money on a trade, the margin guarantees that the person who "took the other side" of your trade will be paid; conversely, margin also ensures that you will be paid profits you have coming to you.

Each day, following the close of trading, your brokerage house must settle its accounts with a central regulatory body for each exchange known as the *clearinghouse.* The clearinghouse is a party to all trades and simply redistributes the money from the losers to the winners daily. Your margin deposit, therefore, serves to guarantee your financial integrity with your brokerage house, which, in turn, is responsible to the clearinghouse for performance of all futures contracts its customers trade.

Unlike the stock market, where the balance of the money owed on a security must be borrowed, and hence interest paid by the buyer, futures trading does not involve any loans or partial payments. Therefore, you will never be asked to pay interest on margin money. In addition, margin money, not being a down payment, is not actually a cost. Thus, if your trading is successful and no losses are incurred in your account, you can expect to receive back your margin money along with your profits. Commission costs, of course, will be deducted from this amount.

There are two types of margin: *initial margin* and *maintenance margin.* Initial margin is the amount you will be requested to deposit with your broker before you commence trading; maintenance margin is the amount which must be maintained in your account after trading begins. When the equity in your account falls below the maintenance level, you will be issued a *margin call.* This is a written or oral request from your broker to deposit additional funds with him to maintain sufficient margin in your account. Should you fail to meet a margin call, your position will automatically be liquidated by the brokerage house and you will no longer be in the market. This is done to protect the broker from additional adverse movements in the market. After all, once your margin money is gone, the broker is responsible for any deficits on your outstanding positions.

When you enter into an agreement with a commission house to trade commodity futures contracts, you are asked to sign a customer's agreement form. This form spells out the agreement between customer and broker, including the rules pertaining to margin. It is this form that gives the brokerage house the right to sell out your position in the event that margin is severely impaired and you do not meet a margin call. A typical form reads as follows:

It is understood and agreed that we reserve the right to close out transactions without notice when the margins on deposit with us (1) are exhausted, or (2) are inadequate in our judgment to protect us against price fluctuations, or (3) are below the minimum margin requirements under the rules and regulations of the exchange relating thereto.

The implications of the customer's agreement form are clear and unequivocal. You, the customer, are responsible for all losses resulting from your trading activities. This means if the market moves against you in a five- or six-day limit move, you are responsible for the losses above and beyond your initial margin money. There are ways to take preventive actions to avoid runaway losses. But you should be mindful that your risk whenever you trade commodity futures is not limited to the initial margin requirement.

To illustrate how margin works, let's consider a trade in which you want to purchase a contract of 5,000 ounces of silver. We'll assume that the initial margin for silver is $2,500 and the maintenance margin is $2,000. This means the market can only impair your margin by $500 before you will be asked to bring your account back to the maintenance level by depositing additional margin with your broker. Should you be issued a margin call, and fail to respond, your position will automatically be liquidated.

The size of the margin requirement for each particular commodity is set by the exchanges. In general, margin size is tied to two general factors: the volatility of the commodity in question, and that of the futures market as a whole. During periods of high volatility, therefore, expect margin requirements to be high; during periods of lessened volatility the exchanges generally lower the requirements. Most brokerage houses ask for more margin than the minimum required by the exchanges. This is to protect themselves from overzealous traders who are apt to run up a deficit and leave the broker to make good on his commitment to the clearinghouse.

The reasons for changing the margin requirements are several. First, their movement upward or downward is used to discourage or encourage speculation, depending upon the liquidity of a commodity at a given time. Since higher margins mean that a speculator must have greater resources at his disposal, those traders with a smaller financial base will drop out of a market when margins are raised. Secondly, margins are often raised to protect the integrity of futures contracts and to protect the speculator against himself. In volatile markets, sudden moves can impair capital quickly, and larger margins serve to protect the equity behind each futures contract. Moreover, since the broker is ultimately responsible to the clearinghouse for the performance of each contract traded by its clients, the higher margins help to ensure that sufficient money will be available to pay the winners.

Commissions

While margins are not a true cost in trading commodity futures contracts, commissions most certainly are. Each time you buy and sell a commodity futures contract—only one *round-turn commission* is paid on the two transactions—you must pay your broker a fee for his services. This fee, considering the commission you would pay on practically any other type of investment, is quite low: about one half a percentage point of the total value of the contract. Admittedly, the percentage rises when you compare the commission with the margin deposit. But the cost is still small.

In recent years, commissions in the futures markets have been discounted considerably. Whereas, nine or ten years ago, fixed commission rates were the rule in futures, today's futures trader can negotiate any commission he likes, assuming he can find a brokerage firm willing to meet his price. The amount one pays in commissions will be dependent upon a number of factors, including the size of the account, the volume of the trading, the amount of money one is willing to leave in cash (on which the house can earn interest), and other considerations. In general, the discount houses don't provide brokers and advice; rather, they serve as order takers for experienced traders. With some persistence, the knowledgeable futures trader using a discounter can expect to pay somewhere between $11 and $17 per round turn. At the full-service wire houses, however, you are going to have to pay considerably more—perhaps as much as $40 to $50.

To the commodities speculator, relatively low commission costs mean greater opportunities for profit, since even a small gain on a trade will overcome the cost of a round-turn commission.

Unlike stock trading, in which a commission must be paid both when you buy and when you sell, commodity trading involves just one commission, when you offset your trade. Thus, if you are a buyer initially, the round-turn commission will be subtracted from your equity position when you sell your contract; conversely, if you are a short seller initially, the commission cost will be deducted from your equity when you cover or liquidate your position by buying back your contract. In either instance, one commission is paid for each completed trade.

Delivery Months

Commodity futures contracts are traded for delivery in specified months throughout the year. As each delivery month approaches, the speculators, who have only been participating in the markets to profit from changes in price, *offset* their contracts and exit the market, and the actual buyers and sellers of the physical commodity are left to *take* and *give delivery* as the contract matures. To offset a contract means simply to take the other side. That is, the buyers must sell and the sellers must buy. Once this process is completed, one is said to have liquidated his position and is completely out of the market.

For those who use the commodity futures markets to give or take delivery of the actual commodity, however, the approach of the delivery month has a different meaning. Not interested in liquidating his position, the user (remember our illustration of the bread manufacturer?) will hold his contract until delivery. Conversely, the producer (the grain farmer) will likewise hold his contracts and deliver against them when they come due in the delivery month.

There are two parties to every futures contract: the buyer and the seller. The buyer contracts to purchase a specified amount of a given commodity at a specified time; the seller contracts to sell a specified amount of a given commodity at a specified time. Both buyer and seller also contract to make this transaction at a specified price—namely, the prevailing price they agreed upon when they bought or sold the futures contract. Because all futures contracts are standardized for each commodity, the original buyer need not purchase from the original seller. Indeed, a futures contract may have changed hands hundreds of times over the life of the contract. But *the seller of a contract, who holds the contract at the end of the last trading day, must deliver the physical commodity specified in the contract to the buyer,* who holds the other side, at the close of trading on the last trading day. The seller, therefore, always gives delivery and the buyer always takes delivery. This is a very important concept. It is also the reason why *you must never hold a commodity futures contract beyond the first day of the delivery month unless you intend to give or take delivery.*

The typical commodity has about six delivery months per year. The month that is about to mature is known as the *nearby,* and the months that are further off are known as the *distant, deferred,* or *far-out* months. There are a variety of reasons why you would pick one contract month over another, but for our present purposes it is vital to know why a speculator, who neither produces nor uses the physical commodity, must not participate in a contract trading during the delivery month.

The exception to this rule is stock index futures contracts. The stock indices have a so-called *cash settlement* provision. This means that upon maturity of the contract, the nearby futures position is marked to the market of the closing price of the underlying cash index, and the buyers and sellers have their accounts settled according to this final cash index price—and no delivery occurs.[4] As a result of this no-delivery provision, stock index futures traders need not be concerned about holding contracts into the delivery month. In reality, the stock index futures tend to have the

[4] "Marked to the market" is a term that refers to the settling of accounts each day by the clearinghouse. Following the close of trading, winning traders have their accounts credited and losing traders have their accounts debited under the marked-to-the-market method.

greatest participation right up to the last week of trading. At that point, most traders "roll over" into the adjacent contract.

In most other contracts, however, in which an underlying commodity or financial instrument actually exists, the rule is to avoid trading in the delivery month. In addition to the possibility of having to deal with a delivery situation, there is also the removal of trading limits on delivery-month contracts. As a result, there is an unlimited risk involved when trading in the delivery month when no limits are imposed.

In stock index futures there are no limits. The market can move as far and as fast as it wants. Because of the natural interaction of buyers and sellers, however, the markets have rarely moved more than 600 points during a single trading session. But even this amount is considerable. A 600-point move in Standard & Poor's 500 futures amounts to $3,000 on a single contract.

Let's look at a situation where actual delivery might occur. Again, you must remember that this rarely happens by mistake. As a rule, only a small minority of hedgers, who actually require the underlying commodity, will ever concern themselves with delivery. Let's say it is July and you've purchased heating-oil contracts on the New York Mercantile Exchange for delivery the following September. If you liquidate your heating-oil position prior to maturity of the contracts in September, you will have a profit or loss depending upon where you are able to sell them. If, for instance, you purchase September heating-oil futures for 73 cents on the 42,000-gallon contract and are able to sell them at 77 cents, the four-cent profit, $1,680 per contract, will be yours to keep—minus your commission costs. If, on the other hand, you end up selling your contracts at a lower price, the difference between where you bought and where you sold will constitute your loss.

So far, the example has been relatively straightforward. Now let's assume you purchase September heating-oil contracts and you hold them until maturity. What happens? Quite simply, you'll be asked to take delivery of the heating oil. First, you will have to put up the cash for the oil. If you contracted to pay 73 cents per gallon, your bill will amount to 42,000 times as much, or $30,660 for each heating-oil contract representing 42,000 gallons of No. 2 heating oil. If you purchased ten contracts, the bill will be ten times as much, and so on. The buyer takes delivery and the seller gives delivery. Typically, the transaction involves a receipt for the oil, which will be stored in a local area, depending on the terms of the contract. As the buyer, you will be required to pay storage and insurance fees for the oil. Once delivery occurs, you will have to arrange to resell—or retender—the heating oil. That is, unless you are in the heating-oil business and can send one of your tank trucks over to pick it up.

If you are a *seller* of heating-oil contracts and fail to "cover," or buy back your contracts, prior to expiration, you will be expected to "give delivery." How can you give delivery of something you don't already own?

Simply put, you cannot. So if a scarcity of heating oil exists, you'll be hard put to come up with the oil for delivery. And this is why you never want to find yourself in such a situation. When a shortage occurs, the buyers will bid up the market on the short sellers. Not wanting to buy back contracts at a higher price, the short sellers may hold onto their positions in hope of a price break. When the break doesn't occur, the short sellers are said to be "squeezed"—a panic situation for the shorts. To avoid even the remote possibility of having something like this occur when you are short, you must be willing to take losses quickly when you are wrong. For an experienced futures trader, taking losses becomes second nature. Even under favorable circumstances, you have to remember that about half of your trades will result in losses. The idea is to take them quickly and don't even entertain the thought of holding them for more than a few days, let alone into the delivery month, when you will be required to give or take delivery.

Fortunately, despite stories you may have heard to the contrary, an unwitting speculator almost never is faced with giving or taking delivery of a commodity. Less than 2 percent of all futures contracts ever traded are held through the last trading day. The rest are offset prior to that time, and the profits or losses between winning and losing speculators and hedgers are divided up as the maturity date approaches.

If you are a speculator, with no interest in the physical commodity, the mechanics of taking or giving delivery will have little meaning for you. It is sufficient to know that you should never, with a few possible exceptions, trade a contract during the delivery month. As long as you follow this simple rule you will never have to face taking delivery of a commodity you don't want or need. No commodity can be delivered until the contract comes to maturity. As a result, if you are holding September 1986 heating-oil contracts during August 1986, you have no reason to suspect that you might be forced to take delivery prior to the maturity date. It just won't happen. You can, of course, hold futures contracts right up to the last trading day. But the risk of receiving what is known as a *delivery notice*, issued by one who is "short the futures contract," advising that the actual commodity is being delivered, is not worth the risk.

You should also know that commodity futures contracts are traded for delivery as far off as fourteen months in the future. There may be a September 1987 heating-oil contract trading, therefore, at the same time that a September 1986 heating-oil contract is trading. They are for the exact same commodity, but for delivery a year apart. Their respective futures prices will, of course, reflect the time difference involved.

The grade delivered against a futures contract must be the grade specified in the contract. You cannot deliver Hard Red Winter wheat, traded on the Kansas City Board of Trade, for instance, against the so-called Spring wheat traded in Minneapolis. In addition, the delivery of a commodity must be made at a location specified in the contract. In most instances, this will be a licensed warehouse near Chicago or New York, and the commodity must be covered by a warehouse receipt.

Hedging

Hedging is a process that producers and processors engage in to eliminate the risks associated with price fluctuations. It is a means of transferring the risk of drastic inventory price changes to other participants in the futures markets. A farmer or processor hedges his cash commodity by taking a position in the futures market opposite to his position in the cash market. For example, a farmer who has wheat in the ground (is long cash wheat) will sell wheat futures to hedge his crop. A commercial baker, on the other hand, who must purchase wheat at some future date (is short wheat) will buy wheat futures to hedge his inventory position.

Hedging has been referred to as a form of "price insurance" for the users and producers of commodities—or a strategy for the management of risks. People hedge to achieve protection against an existing price risk. Based on the premise that business profits should reflect managerial skill, rather than marketplace happenstance, hedging occasionally *limits* profits which might have developed as a result of favorable market forces, but, more important, it secures a reasonable amount of certainty in a highly uncertain economic world. In return for achieving this certainty, a producer or user of a commodity will gladly give up a portion of potential windfall profits.

While the hedging is frequently looked upon as a form of price insurance, the term is slightly inaccurate. Insurance is based upon risk sharing. A hedger doesn't actually *share* the risk with anyone. Rather, he *shifts* the risk onto other traders who are willing to assume them: speculators, who take on another's risk in pursuit of a profit. Thus, hedgers and speculators represent a symbiotic relationship, both mutually benefiting from their activities in the marketplace. Unfortunately, not all traders benefit equally, however, and some, of course, benefit not at all. For the risks are such that quite a few futures speculators (the estimates are as high as 85 to 95 percent) lose their money in the market. That hedgers lose money in their futures operations is also true; but, in this instance, the loss has served a valuable function, and the hedger, who has conducted his hedging strategy correctly, *always* makes or saves money in the cash market when he takes a loss in futures. Thus, the role of speculator and hedger is marked by a significant difference.

The commodity futures markets will appear more comprehensible if we remember that futures markets were developed to meet the needs of farmers, whose products (such as grain) are harvested in one short period of time, and buyers of their products (such as millers and grain processors), who use these commodities throughout the year. Thus, the rationale of futures market is to provide an arena where producers and purchasers—the hedgers—of agricultural, processed, refined, and manufactured products can shift the risk of price fluctuations to risk-takers—namely, the speculators.

The Two Types of Hedges

Because of the divergent needs of buyers and processors of commodities, hedging, as we have seen, is used as both a marketing tool and a purchasing tool. For the producer or owner of a commodity traded in the futures market, hedging is used to fix the price of a crop before harvest. This type of hedge is known as a *selling hedge.* For the users of a commodity, the futures market can be used to fix the price of commodities needed at a later date or the price of products to be sold at a later date. When used for this purpose, the hedge is said to be a *buying hedge.*

The Buying Hedge. The buying hedge is used by all those who must buy physical commodities: grain-elevator operators, processors, cattle raisers, feedlot operators, manufacturers, and exporters. Since buyers, like sellers, are subject to price fluctuations in the marketplace when purchasing cash commodities, they use the futures market to assure their costs *before* they actually need the commodity. For example, consider a clothing manufacturer who sells cotton shirts and slacks. The manufacturer knows he can make a reasonable profit on his clothing line if he can continue to purchase cotton at, say, fifty cents per pound, the prevailing market price. Above that price, however, the manufacturer's profit margins will be cut severely, since he has also contracted with a major retailer to sell his fabric at a specified price. In September, therefore, the manufacturer will go into the futures market and purchase contracts of cotton for delivery the following May. Let's assume that within that time span a bull market develops, causing prices to soar to one dollar a pound. How fares the clothing manufacturer? Although the cash cotton now costs twice as much as it did formerly, the profit on the futures contracts offset the losses in the cash markets. The transactions will appear as follows:

The Buying Hedge—Cotton

CASH	FUTURES
September 1:	
Sells 500,000 pounds of cotton clothing to retailers, with markup estimated at 50-cent cotton cost	Buys 500,000 pounds (10 contracts) of May cotton futures at 50 cents
May 1:	
Buys 500,000 pounds of cash cotton at $1.00 per pound	Sells 500,000 pounds (10 contracts) of May cotton futures at $1.00 per pound
loss: 50 cents per pound	*gain:* 50 cents per pound

NET RESULT: $0.00

By using futures, the manufacturer hedged himself and came out even. The initial order, which was based on 50-cents-per-pound cotton, can now be fulfilled, and a normal profit margin for the clothing manufacturer is assured. Had the buying hedge not been placed, however, the cost of the cotton (which would have been twice the anticipated expenses) might have caused the company to sustain substantial losses.

While this illustration is highly simplified, it does show that the buying hedge is a valuable tool for anyone facing the necessity of buying a cash commodity in the future.

The Selling Hedge. As a marketing tool, the selling hedge serves to guarantee a grower or producer a predetermined price for his crop or financial instrument—which, in the grower's case, might still be in the ground at the time the hedge is placed. The objective of the selling hedge is to protect the value of existing inventory or the value of a crop yet to be harvested. Since the hedger who will use a selling hedge actually owns the cash commodity, he will go to the futures market as a seller.

For example, a thrift or lending institution might hedge in the U.S. Treasury bond futures market to protect itself against rising interest rates. Because bond futures move *inversely* to interest rates, rising rates will translate into declining bond prices. A major thrift that purchases bonds would therefore run the risk of declining bond prices reflecting negatively upon its portfolio performance. To protect its "cash" position—namely, the bank's bond portfolio—the thrift institution might sell U.S. Treasury bond contracts.

Assuming that the thrift would like to lock in the yields of its bond portfolio, it might want to sell U.S. Treasury bond futures against its position. If rates decline and bond prices fall, the decline in the value of the bank's portfolio will be offset by a comparable gain in the short futures position. Let's assume June Treasury bonds decline during the period the hedge is in place. The transactions might appear as follows:

The Selling Hedge—Treasury Bonds

CASH	FUTURES
March 1:	*March 1:*
Bank purchases the equivalent of 12 long-term U.S. Government Treasury bonds yielding 11.3% for a net price of 74 (value: $74,000 each)	Bank sells 12 June U.S. Treasury bond futures contracts at a price of 74-14 (value: $74,437 each)
June 1:	*June 1:*
Bank sells the equivalent of 12 long-term U.S. Government Treasury bonds yielding 11.8%	Bank purchases (covers) 12 June U.S. Treasury bond futures contracts at a price of 71-29

for a net price of 71 (value: $71,000 each)	(value: $71,906 each)
loss: $3,000 per bond, or $36,000	*gain:* $2,532 per contract, or $30,372

NET LOSS: $5,628

The hedger, in this example, recovered a portion of his real loss in the selling hedge. If Treasury bonds had risen, and interest rates had declined, the loss on the futures selling hedge would have been offset, in part if not completely, by the long bond portfolio. In this simplified example, the hedger is protected regardless of the subsequent movement of interest rates, and hence bond prices. Thus, the selling hedge, or short hedge, is a valuable tool for anyone owning a commodity or financial instrument vulnerable to a drop in price. And it works essentially the same way if prices rise.[5]

The Role of the Speculator

Now that we've seen how hedging is used as a management tool by some participants in the market, we can more easily appreciate the role of the speculator, who willingly assumes the risk that the hedger wishes to avoid. The speculator is a unique kind of individual. He tends to enjoy the risk taking that speculation involves, and, more often than not, is quick to size up a situation and take market action based on his best judgment. The successful speculator, therefore, is at ease with uncertainty, and rather than running from risk, he sees the underlying opportunity it presents. This is not to say he is reckless. He is not. Indeed, in contrast to the inveterate gambler, who has no respect for money and is willing to bet on anything regardless of the odds, the successful speculator tries very hard to ascertain what his chances are in coming out ahead in a given market strategy and attempts to employ defensive tactics to see him through a given trade. On the other hand, the speculator is not an investor, either. The futures markets won't allow him the privilege of waiting around five or six months to size up a situation. The market must be performing according to his expectations or he takes his profits or losses and gets out. The reason for this is simply the rapidity at which profits are won or lost in the futures markets. At one-cent move against a speculator's position in sugar will cost him $1,120 per contract. Since such a move can take place in five minutes' time, it isn't hard to see why one must be sharply attuned to the possibilities and volatility of the market if one is to avoid possible ruin.

Contrary to popular belief, the speculator isn't responsible for the wide price swings experienced in the futures markets in recent years—in fact, if

[5] For a more complete discussion of hedging and hedging strategies, see Chapter 4.

anything, speculators have helped to damp price swings. As proof of this, consider the so-called "thin," or illiquid, markets, which are characterized by limited speculative participation, and you'll see the difference. Severe and sudden price dislocations triggered by a small imbalance in supply or demand occur frequently in markets that are dominated by a handful of market principals. The Arab oil embargo of several years back is an excellent example. With a small number of individuals holding control of all the supply or demand of a market, you are bound to get price manipulation. But, as a rule, this doesn't happen in the futures markets, where a wide variety of speculators are all competing together and where the steady interaction of buyers and sellers tends to keep prices more reasonable. When prices rise, there are always those brave short sellers selling into rallies in anticipation of a subsequent fall. Conversely, any decline in futures prices will find buyers willing to soften the fall. That speculators do their buying and selling solely in their own self-interest is beside the point. The fact is that speculative activity in the market rarely results in either extremely inflated or depressed prices. Rather, speculative activity tends to result in a price based solely on the market forces of supply and demand.

It is important to understand that risk is always present in the production of goods. Moreover, the risk would be present whether futures markets existed or not. For example, as a soybean crop grows, is harvested, and then is marketed, the risks of price changes must be assumed by those individuals who own the soybeans or have commitments to buy them. Speculation permits these risks to be borne by others who are willing to assume them—separating the risk-bearing ability from production and marketing ability.

In pursuit of his own profit, the speculator will buy or sell a commodity futures contract. The object is to buy low and sell high—although not necessarily in that order. For a trader may as easily sell short a futures contract, in hopes of buying it back at a lower price, as he may buy a contract in hopes of price appreciation. The order in which the speculator buys and sells is of little importance. That the market moves in his favor, however, is of vital importance. Short-selling is a common occurrence in the futures market, and every trader should be as comfortable selling "short" as he is buying "long." How can you sell something you don't own? is the most common question asked concerning this practice. But you participate in short sales of everyday items all the time without being aware of it. For example, when you purchase a magazine subscription through the mail, you are "long" the magazines (which, incidentally, have not been produced yet), and the magazine publisher is "short" the copies he owes you. That is, he has sold you something he doesn't yet own: the unproduced magazines. But you, being the buyer, don't mind, because you have a reasonably good idea that he will fulfill his contractual obligation with you and deliver the magazines. Now assume for a moment that the magazine publisher writes you a letter and says he is sorry but the magazine is going out of business—and returns your money. He has then covered his "short" position with you. Instead of the magazine he couldn't deliver, he returns your money. A similar situation occurs when a speculator sells short a commodity futures contract. Not being in the egg, orange juice, or cattle business, the speculator has no intention of delivering the commodity he sold short. Instead, he intends to liquidate his contract by buying it back. If he can buy it back for less than he originally sold it, he stands to make a profit. However, he must liquidate or offset his short sale by buying it back regardless of the movement of the market. Therefore, if the market has risen since he sold short his futures contract, he will be forced to repurchase it at a higher price than he sold it, resulting in a net loss. As you can see, the speculator will only sell short when he anticipates lower prices. The hedger, on the other hand, will sell short simply to establish a price for his crop that is in the ground. The difference is significant.

What else does a speculator do besides go "long" and "short" individual commodities? Being risk conscious, the speculator will use a number of techniques to minimize the chances that the market will move against him. A common practice among speculators is to place a *spread* between different contract months of the same commodity or between different commodities. For example, an iced-broilers trader might buy April broilers and sell December broilers. Since one month might gain faster on another month in an up market or fall faster than another in a down market, the trader stands to make a profit as the spread widens or narrows. But his risk is limited because both the April and the December contracts will tend to move up or down in somewhat the same manner. That is, what he makes on one contract will be lost, but to a greater or lesser extent, on the other contract. The "spread," or price difference, between where a spread is placed and where it is taken off, or "lifted," is what determines the speculator's profit or loss. Spread trading is a highly desirable technique to understand and use in many markets. Some speculators trade spreads exclusively. To make this very important concept concrete, let's again turn to an illustration from everyday life. Assume you go to an automobile dealer to purchase a new car. You decide to buy a car, but the dealer doesn't have the model and color that you want in stock, so he takes an order from you and promises the automobile you desire in two months' time. You leave a deposit with him and go home and await the arrival of your car. Now consider the dealer's situation. He is "short" one car to you—the one he promised to deliver in two months. But he is "long" one car from the manufacturer to whom he immediately passed along your order. Thus, he is in a spread position. His profit will come from the difference between what he charged you (the retail cost) and what he must pay the manufacturer (the wholesale cost). Unfortunately, spread trading is not quite this simple. You rarely start out with a built-in profit between your long and short positions. Rather, the respective movements of the two contract months will determine your profit or loss. Nevertheless, the illustration of being both "long" and "short" a commodity, in the instance of the automobile dealer, is an accurate one.

Spreads, of course, are not limited to a single commodity. You may spread soybean oil against soybean meal, hogs against pork bellies, plywood against lumber, or a handful of other related commodities against one another. But the principle remains the same. At this point, it is important to know that this is one of several ways that speculators attempt to profit from the futures market.

Speculators are also classified, in addition to their trading activities, in terms of the size of their participation in the markets—namely, as large traders or small traders. Large traders, according to the rules of the Commodity Futures Trading Commission (CFTC), are those traders who, in most commodities, hold a minimum of twenty-five contracts, long or short, at any one time. Known as reportable positions, these holdings must be reported to the CFTC whenever this many or more contracts are held in a speculative account. The authorities have also set a limit on the maximum number of contracts a speculator may hold of a single commodity at the same time. These are known as position limits. But, for the vast majority of traders, these limits are merely academic, because few traders ever approach the number of contracts to which one is limited under this rule. For example, an oats trader must report his position when he holds over forty contracts, and must not hold over four hundred contracts. For cattle, the reportable position is twenty-five contracts, and the limit is four hundred fifty contracts. For soybeans, forty contracts is the reportable limit, and six hundred contracts the position limit. And so on. Hedgers are not limited in the number of contracts they may hold.

Opening the Account

Now that you have some knowledge of how and why commodity futures contracts are traded, the mechanics of opening the trading account should be easy to master. You can open an account to trade commodities through any brokerage house dealing in futures. These brokerage houses may be either so-called "wire" houses, which deal in stocks, bonds, commodities, and other investments, or one of the smaller houses dealing exclusively in commodities futures. In either instance, the brokerage house will be a *futures commissions merchant,* which means it can take orders from the public and charge commissions for buying or selling commodity futures contracts through one or more of the memberships it holds on the various exchanges.

When you open your account, you will be asked to sign a customer's agreement form. As we have seen on pages 8–9, this will outline in detail the responsibilities you are expected to fulfill when you trade futures. It is important to recognize that your financial obligations are not limited to the amount of money you initially deposit as margin. Rather, you are responsible for the full value of the movement of all commodities in which you hold an open position. This agreement also gives the brokerage house the right to liquidate any position you have in which you fail to meet maintenance margin. Prior to liquidating your position, however, the brokerage house will notify you of the need for additional margin. Should you fail to meet this margin call and should the market continue to impair your margin, your position will automatically be liquidated by the brokerage house. Should the account be liquidated at a net deficit, meaning you have lost all your margin money and then some, you will be expected to pay the additional funds to bring the account up to a zero balance.

Brokerage houses, you must remember, are responsible to the clearinghouses for all positions held by their customers. If the customer fails to make good on a loss, the brokerage house will have to cover the transaction. To avoid this, brokerage houses insist on ample margin before you make your first trade. Typically, the average brokerage house won't open a commodity account for less than $5,000. Several years ago, when the markets were considerably less volatile, the amount of funds needed to open an account was much less. But $5,000 is a good average figure. Some brokerage houses, of course, require more—often as much as $25,000. Unlike the securities markets, where you have five business days to pay for a stock you purchase, the futures markets are operated on a strict cash basis. Profits or losses for every contract are calculated daily at the close of trading. As a result, funds to pay the winners are also available daily. To ensure the integrity of every contract, margin to cover losses must be deposited prior to initiating a trade.

Once the papers are signed and the funds are deposited to cover your margin requirements, you are ready to make your first trade. In placing your order with your broker, you simply have to tell him what commodity you wish to trade, whether you wish to buy long or sell short, and the delivery month—or months, if you are trading spreads. In addition, you will want to tell him how you want the order executed—that is, at what price to enter the market (a limit order) or give him a general order to buy or sell at the prevailing price, known as a *market order.*[6] Lastly, when you place your initial order, you may wish to place a *stop order,* which will determine where you exit the market based on price action.

Let's say you anticipate a fall in bond prices and want to sell ten contracts of September Treasury bonds at the prevailing market price. You would instruct your broker as follows: "Sell ten September Treasury bonds at the market." With this information, he can convey the order to the floor broker in the bond pit in Chicago. Generally, within minutes, the *fill* order

---

[6] By definition, when a commodity is bought or sold "at the market," the floor broker must execute the order promptly at the most favorable price possible. When a *limit* order is imposed by the customer, however, the floor broker is prevented from paying more than the limit on a buy order, or selling less than the limit on a sell order.

will be returned with the price at which the ten bond contracts were sold. For example, the broker may tell you, "You sold ten September bonds at 80–14." This means you are "short" ten Treasury bond contracts for delivery in September. The price, 80–14, refers to 80 and 14/32. Each tick in U.S. Treasury bonds is equal to a value of $31.25 per contract. If the price falls that same morning, five days later, a month later, or even six months later—as long as it falls prior to the expiration date of the September contract—you will have a profit. Conversely, every time the price of bonds rises by 1/32, you stand to lose $31.25 per contract, or $312.50 for the ten contracts. Let's assume, however, that prices fall to 75–14 in six weeks' time. You now have a five-basis-point profit and instruct your broker to "cover" your short positions. He does so by buying back ten September bond contracts at the market. You will now have a profit of $5,000 per contract, or $50,000 on the ten contracts minus the commission costs, roughly $200.

Remember, there are many variations on the theme presented above. In shorting Treasury bond futures, you may have used a *limit order,* indicating you wanted a price of, say, 80–23 or higher. When using limit orders, however, you must realize that occasionally you won't be able to get the price you want and you may miss a market. The commodity markets are very flexible when it comes to orders. A futures broker can take just about any order that the floor can understand. And if the floor can't handle the order the way you want, you can have your broker watch the price changes and call in the order at the appropriate time. Many traders use *stop orders* to protect themselves when they place a trade. In the above example, the trader was short bond futures and feared a price rise. He would, therefore, place a stop order above the market to liquidate his position if prices rose. The stop would automatically become a market order once the price touched the stop. Some orders, known as *day orders,* are limited to a single trading session. If these so-called *fill-or-kill orders* are not executed within a relatively short period of time, they are automatically canceled and the trader must again put in his order the next day. When placing an order, make sure you indicate "day only" or "fill-or-kill," or whatever. Otherwise, you may find an order coming back weeks later. There are also *time orders*—market on open, for instance, or market on close—which, if not acted upon within a given period of time, become void. Flexibility is clearly the key when it comes to placing orders.

Each time you make a trade, you will receive both a verbal and written confirmation of your trade. Secondly, you will receive a profit-and-loss statement for each trade based upon what you bought and sold and what the net result was. At the end of each month, you will receive a monthly statement indicating all open and closed net positions and your present equity level. Paper profits and losses, which occur before open positions are closed out and profits or losses realized, are commonplace in commodity trading, but the profits and losses represent real dollars. If, at the end of a trading day, you have a profit on a position, you are entitled to take that profit. The only requirement is that you leave enough money in your account to satisfy your brokerage house minimum and to keep your positions fully margined. Because of the propensity of the futures markets to make sudden changes, however, most traders leave the money in the account lest an adverse move leave them undermargined.

The Commodity Exchanges

A commodity futures exchange is an orderly marketplace where contracts are bought and sold. The exchanges, which are regulated by the Commodity Futures Trading Commission, are not in the business of buying and selling commodity futures, but in providing a suitable environment for commodity futures trading to take place. The principal North American exchanges are in New York, Chicago, Kansas City, Minneapolis, and Winnipeg. Overseas, there are futures exchanges in London, Paris, Tokyo, Liverpool, and other cities. At the heart of a commodity exchange is the trading floor. Sometimes as large as a football field, the trading floor is a combination of member stations, market information centers, a sophisticated telecommunications network, and—most dramatic of all—the trading pit area where member-brokers transact their business. Each exchange —there are more than a dozen in the United States—has a governing body elected by the membership. This board of governors hires the staff that oversees the day-to-day administrations of the exchange.

The Clearinghouse

The clearinghouse[7] is the foundation of an exchange's financial integrity. It is a party to all transactions in that it pays the profits of the winners and deducts the losses of the losers at the close of trading each day. Thus, when you deposit a margin check with your broker, he, in turn, must deposit sufficient funds with the clearinghouse to cover your trading activities. Because the clearinghouse insists that all clearing members maintain sufficient margin, no one has ever lost money through default of a clearing member. Since the clearinghouse treats its members as the buyers and sellers of commodity futures contracts, it does not deal directly with the trading public. Every member of a commodity exchange is not necessarily a clearing member. But every member, like every speculator, must ultimately clear its trades through a clearinghouse member.

The clearinghouse becomes the opposite party on every transaction. This is significant because it means the customer need not be concerned about who took the opposite side of his trade. For instance, if you made a

[7] The clearinghouse of each exchange is, in turn, regulated by the Commodity Futures Trading Commission, which performs audits on the clearinghouse's books to see that all financial guidelines and commitments are being honored.

short sale of March sugar in June, the buyer would be the clearinghouse. By September, you may have a profit on that March sugar contract and wish to buy it back and take your profits. Again, the seller, who will take the other side of that trade, will be the clearinghouse. Of course, the clearinghouse will merely serve as an intermediary. The important point is that the original parties to a trade will no longer have an obligation to each other. Each party may liquidate (sell a contract previously bought or buy back a contract previously sold) his contracts without any contact with the individual with whom he originally traded.

Reading the Newspaper Reports

Now that you understand the basics of commodity futures trading, it is an easy matter to understand the columns of figures that appear on the daily futures page in your newspaper. For purposes of illustration, let's say you are interested in October hogs and you refer to *The Wall Street Journal* for Tuesday, August 20, 1985. Under the heading "Livestock & Meat," the hogs column would have appeared as follows:

HOGS (CME) 30,000 LBS.; CENTS PER LB.

	OPEN	HIGH	LOW	SETTLE	CHANGE	LIFETIME HIGH	LIFETIME LOW	OPEN INTEREST
Oct	36.20	36.85	36.10	36.65	+.17	51.75	36.10	9,023

In addition to the above information, price quotations for six other trading months, August 1985 through July 1986, were also provided. But we will concentrate on the October 1985 contract price information right now. First, the heading tells you that the prices below are for live hogs traded on the Chicago Mercantile Exchange (CME). The standard contract consists of thirty thousand pounds and is quoted in cents per pound. The open denotes the first trading price of the day, 36.20 cents (or $36.20 per hundredweight). The high was the highest price reached for the contract during the day, and the low denotes the lowest price at which live hogs traded. Hogs closed the day at 36.65 cents per pound, or $36.65 per hundredweight, .17 points above the previous day's close. The change always signifies the change from one close to another. During the life of the October contract, which extends from the first day of trading, over one year ago, until August 20, 1985, October hogs achieved a high price of 51.75 and a low of 36.10, the low made on this day. Closing prices are sometimes referred to as settlement prices. However, when you have split closes (which occur when two or more floor traders finalize a transaction at slightly different prices just moments before the final bell) such as 36.45–36.50, a settlement price (usually halfway between the two prices) will be established following the termination of trading.

Most newspapers also print volume and open-interest statistics. These figures are usually one day behind the prices, except for estimated figures. For example, *The Wall Street Journal* printed two volume statistics for August 20, 1985. The first was the estimated number of transactions for that date (3,788) and the second was the total number of transactions that actually occurred (7,288) on the previous trading day, Monday, August 19, 1985. The estimated sales are frequently different from the actual confirmed number of sales, which will appear the following day. The number of sales refers to all the contract months.

Open interest measures the number of unliquidated, outstanding contracts on a given day. These figures, for all the contract months, are also a day behind the prices and appear below the price tables. For August 19, 1985, live hogs had an open interest of 19,051, down 216 contracts from the previous day. Of this number, the October contract accounted for 9,023—by far the most active month. Open interest measures trader participation in the market. When you buy or sell short, you contribute to the open interest. When you offset your position by liquidating your position, whether long or short, you cause the open interest to fall. The size of the open interest indicates the degree of liquidity in a market and is a valuable tool used by traders in forecasting price movements.

For weekly prices and volume, *Barron's,* which also publishes a column on the commodity markets, is a useful periodical to read. The most comprehensive newspaper pertaining to the commodity markets is the New York *Journal of Commerce*. This newspaper publishes an in-depth analysis of most commodities daily, as well as an extensive list of cash prices and futures traded overseas.

The Value of Commodity Trading

Futures speculation serves to permit risks to be undertaken by those who are willing and able to assume them by separating the risk-bearing function (borne by the speculator) from the production and marketing function (borne by the hedger). A farmer, who may excel at growing corn, wheat, or soybeans, yet who may not be inclined to let indeterminable market conditions dictate his profit or loss, can transfer the risk involved in growing commodities to those who will voluntarily accept those risks: the speculators. Both participants, therefore, operating in their own self-interest, derive value from their trading operations in the futures markets. In this manner, speculator and hedger complement one another—and both stand to benefit from the relationship.

Because of the continuous interaction of speculators and hedgers in the marketplace, futures markets provide what is perhaps the most orderly and equitable method of price determination that man has yet devised. Supply and demand, as determined by the activities of traders buying and selling, establish so-called "equilibrium" price levels, below which sellers will not sell and above which buyers will not buy. Once this tenuous equilibrium is upset by a change in sentiment among traders, either buying or selling will predominate and prices will push higher or slip lower. Since this is a constant situation, commodity prices are considerably volatile. And volatility accompanied by high leverage makes for potential high profitability.

Just how profitable can commodity futures trading be? Well, if, over the past twelve to eighteen months, you put up $2,500 in margin to sell short December gold futures near the life-of-contract high and purchased near the life-of-contract low, near $300 an ounce, you'd have made a profit of $18,800. Had you been selling silver futures, you would have done even better: about $30,000 per contract separated the high price of $12 an ounce from the low price, which was under $6 an ounce. During the same period, the nearby contract of S&P futures moved over a $20,000 range on a one-contract basis. The bearish tone in agricultural commodities would have enabled the aggressive short seller to profit in just about all the grains and meats. A single contract of soybeans, during this period, ranged in value of over $8,000. While these examples are perhaps unrealistic, because they are drawn from contract highs and lows, they do show the kind of volatility available to the commodity futures speculator. Considering that the average margin required to purchase or sell a futures contract is generally between $1,800 and $2,500, persistent high volatility promises to return a minimum of several times the margin deposit over the life of the contract. There are few investments—or speculations—that offer this potential for gain.

Buying and Selling Futures Contracts—
The Advantages

Why trade commodity futures? The answer is simple. You can make a lot of money fast! Moreover, substantial profits are available to those who begin trading with a relatively small amount of money. The reason for the potential bonanza in commodity trading is the existence of leverage. This means you put up a small amount of money to control an asset (a commodity futures contract) worth many times the value of your initial margin deposit. Thus, a move in the value of the entire asset will have a proportionately large effect in terms of the value of the margin deposit. In a typical futures contract, an increase in value of just 5 percent can result in a profit of 100 percent to the holder of that commodity futures contract. It is this principle that has enabled speculators to win big fortunes trading commodity futures contracts.

Leverage

Leverage is the key to the huge profitability of trading futures contracts. It is the single most important factor that enables a trader to make a large gain on his money with a relatively small investment. And, paradoxically, it is also the reason why a majority of traders end up losing their trading capital.

To see the power of leverage, let's compare an outright stock purchase for cash with a highly leveraged situation in which a speculator goes long a futures contract. In both examples, we will assume that a trader has $1,000 at his disposal. First, let's consider the stock investor who purchases one hundred shares of common stock selling for $10 a share. For the moment, we will ignore commission costs. If the price of the stock subsequently rises 10 percent to $11 per share, the hundred shares will have a market value of $1,100, and the percentage profit will then be equal to the percentage rise in the value of the stock, or 10 percent.

But if we use the same $1,000 as margin for a commodity futures contract, and the market value increases a like amount, the outcome will be far different. Let's assume you purchase one contract of silver selling for $5.00 an ounce and use the $1,000 as margin money. Since that $1,000 now controls an asset—based on the standard contract size of 5,000 troy ounces—worth exactly $25,000 (5,000 ounces at $5.00 an ounce), you have put up only 4 percent of the total value of the commodity you control. This is a highly leveraged situation. Now, what happens if the price of silver rises? If we assume the same 10 percent rise in the price of silver that we previously examined in the illustration of the hundred shares of stock, the price of the silver must rise from $5.00 an ounce to $5.50 an ounce. The total contract value will now be $27,500 instead of $25,000—a 10 percent increase in value. But the initial equity will have grown by the difference of $2,500, representing a 150 percent increase. This is because the futures speculator participates in the total value of the futures contract —even though he initially puts up only a small percentage of the total value of the contract. Such is the power of leverage. Significantly, you have this powerful tool for profits working for you every time you buy or sell a commodity futures contract.

Liabilities

There are drawbacks, however, to the fantastic potential for profits inherent in futures trading. Because of the small percentage of equity a futures trader has in each contract he trades, even a modest adverse movement will result in losses. Once a margin call is issued, a trader has only two choices: to meet the call by putting up more margin, or to allow his broker to liquidate the position. There is always the possibility that prices might soon reassert themselves in a more favorable direction, but this, of course, can never be counted on. As a result, losses can mount suddenly. In the illustration of the silver market above, for example, a loss of $2,500 would have resulted had the market declined by 10 percent.

The speculator must also be mindful of another aspect of the risk involved. And this concerns the degree of liability. When you trade futures, you are responsible for the total value of a move of any position you hold. Therefore, if you have $2,500 in margin money backing a contract and the market moves against you by $5,000 before you manage to liquidate your position, you owe an additional $2,500 beyond your initial $2,500. Normally, a margin call that is not met will result in a liquidation of your position well before your account shows a deficit. But if you get caught on the wrong side of the market when a series of limit moves occur, you may have no opportunity to liquidate your position and thus sustain a loss in excess of your margin funds. When this occurs, your account will show a deficit and you will be required to pay the difference.

Should You Speculate?

The first rule of speculation pertains to your own temperamental capacity for risk taking. The question whether you should speculate or not deserves serious consideration, for not everyone has the temperament to endure a high level of risk day after day. Futures trading is an extremely competitive undertaking characterized by opportunities for fast profits and equally fast losses. Because of the speed with which profits can be won or losses sustained, traders must be quick to make trading decisions and quick to act upon them. Those who don't master the art of successful timing or the equally essential art of money management, generally lose their money trading commodity futures. Moreover, it should be noted that this includes most speculators. Small speculators, who frequently enter the market with just a few thousand in initial trading capital, tend to have the largest attrition rate.

It is important, especially when you are first getting started, to limit your exposure in the market. If you are in over your head, psychological and emotional factors will soon begin to influence your trading and you are apt to lose money as a result. An adage in the markets says, "Sell down to the sleeping point." That is, sell off enough of your position until you are comfortable sleeping nights.

In determining whether commodity futures speculation is for you, it helps to know the odds of coming out a winner on any given trade in advance. Obviously, this is rarely possible. But, for most, chances are probably about 50-50 of winning or losing on any single trade. You can, of course, improve the odds in your favor by trading only limited-risk spreads or utilizing other strategies presented in this book. But due to so-called "technical" price reactions and other temporary aberrations in the market, as many as 85 to 90 percent of all futures traders have been known to lose over time. Considering these odds, you should be prepared to lose all your trading capital when you decide to speculate. Chances are you won't. But it is a distinct possibility. There are three reasons why these percentages should not sound as discouraging as they seem. First, many traders, despite their protestations to the contrary, are not serious about making money in the market. Rather, they enjoy the excitement of buying and selling, watching price ticks in the boardroom, and the risk-taking involved in trading commodities. Some of these traders are inveterate gamblers; some lack the discipline to approach the market as the business it truly is. In addition, some aren't aware of or choose to ignore the sensible trading strategies outlined in this book. All these traders provide the profits for the minority that win consistently. Secondly, you can lose 90 percent of your trades and still profit *if* you cut your losses and let your profits ride. Acquiring the skill and discipline to do this, however, is often not easy. Thirdly, you must remember that hedgers use the futures markets to ensure themselves a profit margin in their normal business dealings. As a result, they may be quite willing to sustain losses in the futures markets when these losses are offset by gains in the cash markets. Their losses, of course, will provide the minority of successful speculators with ample profits.

Commodity trading requires a combination of bravery and cowardice, of egotism and humility. Just as soon as you think you have the game beat, you're bound to get your comeuppance in the form of a string of losses. So don't take what you consider to be your invincibility too seriously. All traders, even the best, have losses. It is learning to survive that counts.

The risks notwithstanding, commodity futures trading offers one of the most exciting and potentially profitable speculations in the world today. For the person willing to learn the basic rules and sustain the risks involved, the rewards can be enormous.

2

What You Must Do to Win

THE BASIC STRATEGIES

Playing the commodity game to win requires, among other things, a knowledge of the trading rules. We are not talking here about the mechanics of trading, or the rules that are spelled out in the bylaws of the respective commodity exchanges. Rather, we are referring to those commonsense rules of trading that every trader sooner or later wishes he had observed before he had undertaken a commodity position. Chances are, your broker won't take the time to stress the importance of these rules. Most brokers are too busy drumming up business to conduct educational sessions with their clients. In addition, some of the rules go against the advice of many brokers, who, after all, only profit from commissions that are generated when you undertake a trade. Seasoned traders, of course, are apt to be familiar with these basic strategies. In fact, for some the guidelines set down here are often so well engrained that they are second nature. But, for others, they may not be that familiar. Knowing the rules isn't a big problem. There are comparatively few, and they can easily be memorized overnight. But implementing them could present some difficulties. The reason for this is that our emotions frequently play a dominant part in our trading decisions. To counteract the influence of emotions, therefore, you may even wish to compose a checklist when you make a trade. It will serve to keep you honest and help you on the path to profits.

Study the Market You Are Trading

You have got to do your own homework. If you rely on hot tips, rumors, and the like, chances are, you won't last long as a commodity trader. Even competent advice, such as that which you might purchase through a good advisory service, has its limitations, since you are the one who must ultimately act on the advice. For instance, your advisory service might suggest you go long the June Value Line index futures. But unless you act on this advice quickly and protect your position with a judiciously placed stop-loss order, you may end up missing the market or suffering a loss. Always remember that you alone are ultimately responsible for the success or failure of your trading account.

Before you trade, familiarize yourself thoroughly with the commodities you intend to trade. There are many excellent textbooks, publications of various commodity exchanges, and USDA pamphlets that explain both the commodity markets and individual commodities. These should serve as a starting point. You then have to decide on an approach to the markets— that is, will you be a chart trader, use a mechanical system, employ limit orders, moving averages, oscillators, or on-balance volume studies to find a good commodity trade?

Next, you should draw up a balance sheet for your trading activities. On one side of this balance sheet you will list all the factors conducive to a price advance in the commodity you are following; on the other side, you will list all the factors conducive to a price decline. The whole balance sheet should be revised regularly and a new estimate of the situation made. If new information becomes available, the balance sheet should be revised to reflect the new information. This task will serve to keep you alerted to any developments unfavorable to your position.

Depending upon your point of view, the balance-sheet approach should help you create a trading plan. The trading plan will be a written document listing such information as the commodities you intend to trade, whether you are long, short, or spread, entry prices, target exit prices, margin requirements, and your general game plan. Having this information available before you take a position in the market will enable you to monitor and, if need be, modify your position as time goes on. Not to have such a plan results in haphazard trading that often culminates in losses.

Try to Avoid Market Orders

The instructions you give your broker will have a material effect upon your trading results. When you instruct your broker to buy or sell *at the market,* you have given him a *market order,* which will be executed at the best prevailing price on the floor of the commodity exchange. However, except when you want to liquidate or initiate a position immediately, regardless of price, the market order is not the most helpful. This is because futures prices are established by an auction market in which traders make *bids* and corresponding *offers*. The *bid* is the price offered for immediate acceptance of a specific amount of a commodity. The *offer,* or *asked,* price is that price at which a seller offers to deliver a specific amount of a commodity for immediate acceptance. Knowing this, you risk getting a higher price when you buy, and a lower price when you sell at the market. For example, let's assume you want to buy five contracts of gold on the Comex (Commodity Exchange) in New York. If you instruct your broker to "buy five October Comex gold at the market," you will be filled, more often than not, at the higher *asked* price. Let's say the bid and asked at the time your order reaches the floor is 358.20 bid and 358.60 asked. This 40-point spread between the bid and asked represents 40 cents per ounce of gold, or a total of $40 per contract. If you are filled at the asked price, therefore, you will pay $40 more per contract than the bid price. Multiplied by five contracts, this represents a total of $200 to you. Might you have been filled at the lower bid price and saved the extra $200? Perhaps. If sellers entered the market and buyers were unwilling to pay more than the prevailing $358.20 bid, the price would have had to fall if the sellers were determined to get filled. The point is, a market order represents an order that is to be filled immediately *regardless of price.* Very often, therefore, you will see the market rise in response to a flood of buy orders, only to subsequently fall as soon as the buying extinguishes itself. It is a very frustrating experience to place a market buy order and get filled at the top of the market. When selling, of course, the reverse situation applies. You then get filled at the bid price when you place a market order.

To avoid this frustration, it is best to place a *limit order,* which, naturally enough, is an instruction with strings attached. For example, in our illustration above, you might have instructed your broker to buy your gold at "358.20 or better," which would have required the market to meet the present bid price or lower. Unless the market is willing to meet your terms when you place a limit order, you stay out of the market altogether. For many traders, this method is ideal. After all, if the market isn't performing according to expectations, it is often better to stay out. You will occasionally miss markets when you employ limit orders, but if you are determined to get aboard at any price, you can always switch back to market orders.

By far, the most common limit order is known as a *stop.* A stop is an order to buy or sell at the prevailing price *after* the market touches the limit price specified. For example, you buy a commodity at, say, 39 cents per pound, and you place a *stop-loss order* or *sell-stop* at, say, 37.75 cents per pound. This means that once the 37.75 price is touched, your stop-loss automatically becomes a market order. Now you may or may not be able to get out of the market at 37.75, depending upon the speed and direction of prevailing prices. But your position will then be liquidated at the best price possible.

You can also use stop orders to initiate a position above or below the present market price. Let's assume you expect prices to *break out* of their present trading range at, say, 50 cents per pound. You can place a *buy-stop* order at 50 cents, which will become a market order to buy once prices reach that level. A *sell-stop* order, of course, will achieve the opposite result, making you short a commodity once a specific price is reached. These types of orders are also known as MIT orders, the acronym standing for *market if touched.*

Stops are especially useful to *technically oriented traders*—those who place importance upon price behavior—as opposed to *fundamentally oriented traders,* who emphasize supply-and-demand changes. Being price-oriented, the technical trader is apt to use limit orders to enter the market, to exit the market, and to protect his position via stop orders. For example, a gold trader, anticipating higher prices, might place a buy order at $375 an ounce, a sell order to take profits at $400 an ounce, and a stop-loss order to limit losses at $371 an ounce. The three orders could be entered at the same time and the market ignored until either (a) the position is sold at a $2,500 profit at $400 an ounce, or (b) the position is sold at a $4.00-an-ounce loss when the stop is triggered at $371. Of course, the third possibility exists that the contract will expire before either of these alternatives occurs. In this instance, you should follow the rule we discussed in Chapter 1 concerning liquidating your position prior to the first day of the delivery month.

In summary, use market orders only when you have a compelling reason to get into or out of a market right away. Otherwise, use limit orders.

Let Profits Ride

This rule, mentioned in Chapter 1, deserves renewed emphasis here. Most traders have a tendency to take small profits when they occur. But this frequently results in demoralization as you take a small piece out of a roaring bull market and later have to chase the market to get back aboard. In addition, it has the disadvantage of resulting in high commission costs. Strive to have the courage of your convictions when the market is proving you right. By avoiding the temptation to "play" the market on the basis of fluctuations in price, you will have the satisfaction of knowing that you stayed with a market and enjoyed full participation in the profits to be made.

Traders who take the long-term approach to the commodity markets ("long-term," in this instance, meaning anywhere from six months to a year or more) are known as *position traders.* Brokers don't like position traders, because they rarely generate significant commissions. Imagine how a broker must feel when his client makes $150,000 and he makes

$150. But the position traders are the ones who make the big money in commodity trading. Floor traders also make huge amounts, but their relationship to the market is somewhat different from that of an outside speculator. Among other things, they enjoy significantly reduced commission costs not available to any outside speculator.

Trade the Breakout of the Daily, Weekly, and Monthly Range

A *breakout* is defined as a movement, either up or down, away from an area where prices had consolidated. The *range* is the difference between the high and the low prices of the futures during a given period. As a rule, a breakout from any area of concentrated price activity is significant because it means that a preponderance of buyers or sellers have begun to dominate the market following a period of more or less equal strength between the two. It is this buying power or selling pressure that causes the markets to move higher or lower. To trade the breakout means, therefore, to take a position with the trend on the breakout. If you are an oats trader and you notice that oats have traded within a range of $1.25 a bushel and, say, $1.35 a bushel for a period of about thirty days, a breakout above $1.35 to, say, $1.38, may be a clue that the bulls have finally taken possession of the market and prices are headed higher. This would be the clue to buy. Trading ranges may be easily established for varying periods of time. The daily trading range extends from the high of one day to the low of the same day. A weekly trading range extends from the high of the week to the low of the week. Chart trading is particularly valuable when you are looking for a breakout, because the formations are easily identifiable on the chart.

Never Put Your Entire Position on at One Price

A good trader will always want to trade with the *trend*. The trend can be defined as the direction that prices are taking. Accordingly, you want to be sure you are long when prices are rising, and short when prices are falling. To make sure that prices are going in your direction when you enter a market, therefore, it is best to "test the waters" before you make a solid and substantial commitment in the form of a large position. To accomplish this, you should put on only a portion of your position at a single price. Once the market proves you correct by moving in the direction you anticipated, you may then add to your position. By using this method, you will always be using some of your paper profits on your initial positions to finance additional contracts. For example, you may want to start with several contracts of soybeans at, say 598. At 598½, you may wish to buy an additional contract or two, and still another contract at 599, 599½, and

600. This approach will help you have market momentum working for you.

Don't Overcommit

The size of your commitment must be governed by your total trading equity and the amount of risk you are willing to sustain. There is a well-known saying in the markets that goes: "Bulls make money, bears make money, but hogs get slaughtered." Remember this. Greed will cause you to lose every time. To protect your trading capital, you should limit your risk to a predetermined percentage of your equity. Moreover, this risk commitment should be spelled out in your trading plan. You might have $10,000 in equity and want to limit your risk to just 8 percent on each trade. You will then want to limit your potential loss to $800 on each trade, including commissions. Since there are times, as when a string of limit moves occur, when you won't be able to fully protect your position to this predetermined percentage, you should use extra caution to limit losses when they occur. You should also plan the size of your commitment with this potential for loss in mind. For example, exclusive of commissions, a 10-cent adverse move in soybeans will impair your capital by $500—if you hold one contract. Two contracts will do the same amount of financial damage with only a 5-cent move. If you hold four contracts, the market can move against you by only 2½ cents before you will be out $500. And with eight contracts, you are limited to a 1¼-cent move. Moreover, at these levels, commission costs are quite significant.

Traders on a budget will do well to consider trading mini-contracts traded on the MidAmerica Exchange, in Chicago. The MidAmerica offers futures contracts on the grains, livestock, and metals that are only a fraction of the size of the normal contracts. These *job lot* contracts, which offer the speculator or hedger a smaller unit of trading than the regular contracts, also require less margin. In addition, commissions are less, as are the risks. Typical grain contracts of soybeans, wheat, or corn are 1,000 bushels in size, just one fifth the size of the larger contracts traded on the Chicago Board of Trade, and the live hogs contract is 15,000 pounds, just one half the size of the hogs contract traded on the Chicago Mercantile Exchange.

When You Are Not Sure, Stand Aside

The beginning trader is tempted to trade or hold a position every day, and that is a costly tendency. Trades should be selected for definite reasons, not because you presently don't have any activity in your trading account. Unless you can enter into a trade anticipating a potential profit several times the anticipated risk, you should not be in that trade. Depending on market behavior and the number of commodities you follow, you may stay with a single position for six months or stay out of the market for six months. With over thirty-five commodities to choose from, there will always be an abundance of opportunities in the market. You must decide which ones you will take and which ones you will ignore. When a trading opportunity appears, however, and you are reasonably sure you have a promising market situation, you must act quickly. To fail to act when the moment is right will only result in unnecessary losses.

Be a Technician, Not a Fundamentalist

There are two schools of price-forecasting methods in the commodity futures markets: fundamental analysis and technical analysis. Fundamentalists are oriented toward forecasting the market in terms of supply-and-demand factors. Technicians stress price behavior and the movement of such technical indicators as open interest, volume, moving averages, and oscillators. The fundamentalist says that the key to the direction of prices rests with understanding the supply-and-demand forces in the market. In pursuit of this knowledge, the fundamentalist will read crop reports, cold-storage reports, U.S. weather reports, and a host of other information that may shed some light on the supply-and-demand situation. But the technician, who takes the opposite viewpoint, ignores the fundamental information in favor of watching price behavior. The technician maintains that whatever is taking place in the commodity will be reflected in price action.

Paradoxically, the two approaches do not invalidate one another. Rather, they complement one another. But the key difference is time. The fundamentalist, given sufficient opportunity to analyze the market properly, will inevitably come up with the correct answer as to the future direction of prices. But it takes time to figure the market out, and it takes time for the market to prove one correct. In either instance, the technician may readily see the coming move by analyzing price behavior. More important, the technical analyst, not being "wedded," in a sense, to a particular market interpretation, is much more flexible to move in and out of the market as he sees fit. The fundamentalist, on the other hand, is apt to stay with a market, despite adverse price behavior, because he "knows" that a given supply-and-demand situation must ultimately be reflected in price. Ask yourself which kind of trader you want to be. One who will let his interpretation, based on a haphazard analysis of limited resources, dictate his choices? Or one who lets the market decide what action to take? For traders with limited resources, which includes just about everybody, the latter approach seems more reasonable.

Dean Rusk, the former Secretary of State, once said that he had an idea that some crisis was brewing when the futures markets started to get active. The markets gave him a clue to an oncoming crisis even before a problem area manifested itself and became the subject of newspaper headlines. What Rusk was talking about was reading the language of the market—trying to interpret what the market was saying. Few indicators are so sensitive to forthcoming political, social, and economic events as the commodity futures markets.

Technical analysis is presently the best method we have for deciphering what the market will do tomorrow. Because technical analysis is an art, rather than a science, no single theory or interpretation is correct all the time. To make up for this margin of error, the technician looks for a variety of indicators to pinpoint critical areas of the market. Technical analysis can show when a market is weak or strong and when it is likely to reverse itself. Similarly, the fundamental analyst can tell you when a market is strong or weak, and he can also tell you the reason why. But due to the difference in the two forecasting techniques, the fundamentalist will generally lag behind the technician in making his predictions. As a result, the two will rarely agree on the same course of action in the market at the same time. Whereas the fundamentalist is looking at a supply-and-demand situation that exists today, the technician is busy analyzing the price action that is saying something about tomorrow. After all, the futures market is, quite literally, a game of futures. The market is always anticipating, never looking back. It is learning to read the language of the market that will enable you to win profits. Technical analysis is a guide to learning that language.

Build a Trading Pyramid

Proper money management is vital to success at commodity trading. To take full advantage of the opportunities when they present themselves, you must know how to put your positions on and how to stay with them. We have already mentioned the importance of not putting all your positions on at the same price. It is necessary that the market begin to move your way first. One method of accomplishing this task is to construct a trading pyramid. The trading pyramid consists of a base, with decreasing increments added to form the top of the structure. It is designed to keep the average price of all the positions you acquire low and to protect you against a subsequent reversal in the price trend. In the illustration below, each "X" stands for one contract. We will consider first the so-called *normal pyramid*. The normal pyramid is built with a large initial position, or base, with smaller and smaller increments added as follows:

THE NORMAL PYRAMID

Size of fourth addition	X
Size of third addition	X X X
Size of second addition	X X X X X
Size of first addition	X X X X X X X
Size of initial position	X X X X X X X X X

As you can see, as the market moved in your favor, you put on fewer and fewer positions. Having started with nine positions, you eventually held twenty-five. To see the value of the trading pyramid, we will look at an *inverted pyramid* in which contracts are acquired in the wrong fashion. In an inverted pyramid, which many traders use to their ultimate regret, greater and greater commitments are added to a small base. By buying more contracts as the market progresses in your favor, you only serve to make yourself more vulnerable to an adverse move. The average price is higher and the risk is far greater. Again, using an "X" to represent each contract, the inverted pyramid would appear as follows:

THE INVERTED PYRAMID

Size of fourth addition	X X X X X X X X X
Size of third addition	X X X X X X X
Size of second addition	X X X X X
Size of first addition	X X X
Size of initial position	X

Beginning with just one position, the trader in this illustration took on successively larger units as the market moved in a favorable direction. Due to the large commitment near the top, however, just a small reaction in prices would result in a loss for the trader. This is because the average price is always relatively close to the last position added, due to the size of the commitment.

Never Add to a Losing Position

Some commodity traders, many of whom began their investment careers in the stock market, have a tendency to engage in a practice known as *averaging*. When you average, you buy more of a commodity or a stock as the price declines. In the stock market, averaging is not necessarily a dangerous practice, since you can theoretically own a stock for a lifetime or longer. But in the commodity futures markets, where the life of a contract rarely exceeds eighteen months, averaging is much more risky. In the futures market, you don't have the luxury of time. You cannot wait many months, or even years, for the price direction to turn in your favor. Moreover, due to the high leverage involved in buying or selling futures contracts, an adverse move can easily jeopardize your equity. To prevent a small loss from growing into a large loss, therefore, never add to a losing position. Unless you have an excellent reason to think the market will change direction, you should cut your losses at the earliest possible moment.

Don't Form New Opinions During Trading Hours

Maybe you aren't given to emotional feelings about your investments, but most of us are. We see the market suddenly going higher and we forget that our charts and technical indicators tell us to stay out and we want to jump aboard. Or the market goes against us and we forget our decision to place close stops and watch it for a while—until we are in real trouble. Emotions act this way. And when they are present to the exclusion of reason, we are apt to make serious mistakes in the market. If you want to see the impact that emotions have on your market decisions, you should try *trading on paper* for a while. This means you select a commodity to trade and write the commodity, contract month, entry price, margin, and other assorted data down on paper and follow the commodity in the newspaper. You don't actually take a position in the market. Then you take your checkbook down to a commodity broker, open an account for $5,000 and select a real trade. You will probably notice the difference immediately. Try to do your market planning before and after market hours. Have a contingency plan, complete with mental or actual stop-loss orders in case the market doesn't go your way, and try to stick with your plan. Be flexible, but only during nonmarket hours.

Take a Trading Break

Trading success, like luck, tends to run in cycles. There will be periods when you can't seem to make a mistake. And there will be periods when everything you do results in losses. When you feel yourself going into a losing period, it is better to step back from the market than to press your luck. A trading break helps you to take a detached view of the market, and tends to give you a fresh look at yourself and the way you want to trade for the next several weeks or months. When you take a trading break, it is best to disassociate yourself from the market altogether. Go on vacation. Get away completely. Professional floor traders frequently use this technique following a string of losses. When they return, they are less apt to be thinking of recouping losses or proving themselves right in a market that has just thoroughly beaten them. Many other traders, especially professional floor traders who benefit from low commissions, have a rule that they never hold a position over a weekend. This permits them to get completely out of the market by each Friday afternoon and begin the week with a fresh start.

Start Small

If you are new to commodity trading, you will do better to start small until you become fully acquainted with the markets. The kind of knowledge you learn from actually trading cannot be easily conveyed in a book or magazine article, and every trader has to experience the markets firsthand before he feels comfortable in the role of commodity trader.

As we've previously mentioned, the MidAmerica Exchange offers minicontracts in the grains, metals, and live hogs. These smaller contracts are ideal for beginning traders and are as easy to trade and understand as the larger contracts. They feature lower margins and commissions in addition to reduced risk and corresponding opportunities for profit.

Due to the great deal of leverage inherent in any commodity transaction, you need not feel that your position is insignificant even if you trade only one contract at a time. A single contract of gold traded on the Comex in New York can appreciate in value by $2,500 a day—or $12,500 a week. Considering the low margin it requires to buy or sell any commodity futures contract, the percentage potential for appreciation can be well over 100 percent per week. Through *pyramiding,* a method by which additional new contracts are margined with the winnings of previously held contracts, a small position can grow into a large position almost overnight. It is this great pyramiding power that makes commodity futures such an attractive speculation.

Trade the Divergence Between Related Commodities

Because related commodities frequently move in unison, when you spot a wide divergence in a group, it could signal a trading opportunity. For example, if all grains except soybeans are moving higher, you might look for an opportunity to sell soybeans as soon as the grains in general appear to be weakening. The reverse of this would also be true: look to buy the strongest commodity in the group during periods of weakness. The Ohama 3-D Technique, which is covered in a subsequent chapter, is a method for spotting such divergences in the market. This method has had remarkable success in pinpointing tops and bottoms in related commodity futures.

Don't Follow the Crowd

"When everyone thinks alike, everyone is likely to be wrong," wrote Humphrey Neill, the father of contrary-opinion trading. Neill believed that the crowd, whether in politics or economics, always made its greatest mistakes at the point in history when events were about to change dramatically. Neill's studies, first published in 1954, revealed that (a) a "crowd" yields to instincts which an individual acting alone represses, (b) people tend to follow the "herd" instinct, (c) people are susceptible to *suggestion,* to *commands,* to *customs,* to *emotional motivation,* and (d) that a crowd never reasons, but follows its emotions and accepts without proof what is "suggested" or "asserted." Applied to the commodity futures markets, contrary-opinion theory revealed that indeed most traders were on the wrong side of the market at the major turning points. At market tops, the degree of bullish sentiment tended to be rampant; and at market bottoms, the bearish sentiment seemed equally rampant. At the tops it seemed that bullish traders were all holding their positions and hoping for more buyers to enter the market and push prices higher. Conversely, at market bottoms the bears had all sold and were awaiting additional sellers to push prices lower. But without new buyers entering a market at a top and without new sellers entering at a bottom, prices had only one way to go—the opposite direction. Studies have shown that at the extremes of the market, when 90 percent or more hold a similar attitude, the market *must* reverse itself. As a result, contrary-opinion traders establish positions opposite to prevailing opinion. Studies have shown that the greater the percentage of people holding an opinion, the stronger the signal is to establish a contrary position. Contrary-opinion traders are always looking for a one-sided market sentiment in order to take the opposite side. If you remember that the crowd is invariably wrong at the extremes in the market, you will likely do better by taking a position opposite to the majority opinion than to follow the crowd.

Don't Trade Too Many Commodities at Once

While you may want to follow a handful of commodities, you shouldn't try to trade more than two or three at once. Moreover, you should try to specialize in one area and concentrate on a group of commodities—such as the soybean complex, or the meats, or the metals. Diversification in the futures market isn't such a good idea, since the demands of doing a good analytical job are too great. Better to put all your energies into two or three commodities than try to keep track of two dozen. If the interest-rate futures market appeals to you, for instance, follow the T-bills, T-bonds, and the Ginnie Maes. But don't get involved with orange juice, which is affected by other factors in the economy. You will find that after a certain exposure to a market you will develop a feeling for how that market performs. This will enable you to keep your hand on the pulse of the market and trade it more effectively. But don't let this specialization keep you from opportunities that may exist elsewhere. From time to time, you may want to switch your trading interest as one commodity cools off and another begins to become active. There is a story, perhaps apocryphal, of a soybean trader, who, having lost all his money trading soybeans, was walking off the floor of the Board of Trade one day when he spotted a friend in the corn pit. Hearing his friend lament the fact that he would now have to sell his seat on the exchange, the corn trader said, "Look, you can come over here and trade corn." But the soybean trader replied, "I could, but I don't know anything about corn." Make sure your knowledge of your specialization stands you in better stead than did this trader's knowledge of soybeans. Traders tend to develop a certain affinity for certain commodities. If you find you are having a lot of success, in say, cotton, don't confuse yourself by jumping into stock index futures. Put all your eggs in one basket and let your profits ride.

Isolate Your Trading from Your Desire for Profit

A common pitfall for many traders plagued by losses is the desire to recoup those losses as fast as possible. But the market isn't concerned with your losses, and the market isn't about to behave in a certain way just to accommodate your desire. So forget about the past and concentrate on doing what the market tells you now. It is only in this frame of mind that you can expect to be a success at futures trading.

Block Out Other Opinions

You can greatly increase your profits by not listening to the advice of others. If you have a market technique that works for you, stay with your present method of trading and block out other opinions. There is no single trading system or method that works all the time, but some methods do work better than others, and some work for longer periods of time. When you find such a method, stay with it.

Five Basic Trading Rules

At this point, you may be eager to get started trading commodities. You know the basics and may feel you can better learn by actually taking a position in the market. But before you do, read over the following fundamental rules. Not to follow these rules will almost certainly result in substantial losses. If you are uncertain about a rule, continue to read the subsequent chapters. These rules are fundamental to any success in commodity futures trading.

RULE NUMBER 1. *Always use price charts.* Always begin a trade in commodities by acquainting yourself with the price history of the commodity. In the chapter on technical analysis and price charting, the interpretation of price configurations is discussed at length. But, for our present purposes, you should know that price charts are available from a number of advisory services that specialize in providing this information to the trader. Many traders prefer to keep their own charts. Regardless of how you obtain your charts, always refer to them when making a trade. They will tell you, for instance, at what prices the commodity has traded in recent months, whether you are approaching a new high or low, where the so-called "support" and "resistance" levels exist, and much, much more. No sophisticated commodity futures trader ever enters the market without referring to price charts. It is simply not done. Because timing is so critical to success in the market, the charts enable you to place your orders to buy and sell at precise levels.

It bears repeating that when you trade commodity futures, you are making a very risky transaction. Due to the leverage inherent in futures trading, a comparatively small movement in the value of the underlying commodity will be magnified many times in the value of the move relative to your overall margin position. Thus, with 5 percent of the value of the contract covered by margin, a 5 percent increase or decrease in the value of the commodity will represent a 100 percent increase or decrease of your margin money.

When you trade commodities, therefore, you don't have the luxury of a second chance. Price charts help you set up clearly defined entry and exit points. Moreover, due to the limited amount of time involved when you trade commodities, you don't have the luxury of adopting a wait-and-see attitude. The price charts will help you decide what action to take. Thus, it behooves you to study the nature of the commodity's price history.

What can you learn from price history? Many things. First, you can tell the character of a market. Does a commodity tend to make sudden moves and be quite volatile? Or is it a trending commodity? Orange juice, for instance, has had a price history characterized by long periods of inaction periodically broken by freeze warnings and the like which have caused the market to soar. Moreover, due to the seasonal nature of the market, the sudden price rises—and falls—have tended to occur at specific times during the year. A chart, of course, illustrating past price action can be very valuable in pinpointing the period when a commodity is about to make a significant move.

Commodity price charts also illustrate other indicators beyond price. A chart may give you the open interest for the entire commodity and for a particular contract month, the volume or number of contracts traded on a given day, moving averages, prices, and a number of other important variables—depending on the charts you purchase. You can also use your charts to plot oscillators or other indices you find valuable.

RULE NUMBER 2. *Do what the market tells you.* When trading commodity futures contracts, you must never, never fight the market. This means you must not try to trade against the trend. If the trend is up, buy long; if the trend is down, sell short. This sounds simple but is difficult to achieve in practice. Traders tend to ignore what the market tells them until it is too late. Thus, most traders will become buyers at the very top of the market and, conversely, sellers at the very bottom. While it is extremely difficult to pick tops and bottoms, trends are somewhat easier to pinpoint. Moving averages and a number of other mechanical systems work particularly well in trending markets. The basic idea the trend trader works with is that he is looking to take a piece out of the middle of the market—and not select the absolute bottom or top. Your charts, and the price action itself, will let you know whether you are trading with the trend. In addition, there are charting techniques that help you define a market trend. Never fight the trend. A few years ago, a group of European speculators attempted to pick the top of the cocoa market, much to their subsequent chagrin. They lost millions before they decided that their judgment was wrong.

How long does a market tend to trend? It depends. Markets go through periods of consolidations when they are up one day and down the next. These are generally sideways-moving markets. But the base formed by these sideways-moving markets often precedes a significant rise that could take many months to reach its culmination. As a rule, markets fall much faster than they rise, with the result that the greatest profits and losses occur in falling markets.

Traders tend to stay with trending markets for different lengths of time. A small number of traders, known as position traders, prefer to wait for a full move, which could take months, a year, or even more to develop. Position traders hold on as long as necessary. At the other extreme, you have the day trader, who may take either side of the market several times a day in pursuit of small gains. In either instance, it is the trend, long or short, that motivates the trader to take a position.

RULE NUMBER 3. *Never meet a margin call.* Margin calls are issued when the equity in your account falls below the maintenance level. That the market has been allowed to move this far against you, without your having taken protective action, is a sign that you are not trading correctly. Try to take losses as quickly as possible and liquidate your positions before they grow serious. When you fail to do this, you invite trouble.

The strategy is to place close stops near the market that will liquidate your position *before* a margin call is issued. If, however, several limit moves against you cause a margin call to be issued, instruct your broker to liquidate your position and take the loss. Many traders attempt to avoid this loss by meeting the margin call in hopes that the market will soon reassert itself in a more favorable direction. This is a mistake. In many markets, you could easily lose a fortune before the market turns your way again.

RULE NUMBER 4. *Cut your losses and let your profits ride.* This rule, perhaps better than any other, sums up the secret of successful commodity trading. Despite what you hear about how you can never go broke taking a profit, the simple fact is that you can very easily. Traders who take their profits every time they make a hundred dollars in the market are the same ones who watch their losses mount into the thousands before they ultimately throw in the towel. You can win at commodity trading if you are right only 10 percent of the time—as long as you follow this rule. Big profits on 10 percent of your trades will easily offset small losses on the other 90 percent.

To implement this rule, use stop-loss orders. When you buy, place stop-loss orders under the market; when you sell, place stop-loss orders above the market. Where do you place the stops? There are two methods. One is based on technical analysis in which you place the stops above and below so-called *resistance* and *support* levels respectively. A resistance level occurs where a preponderance of selling over buying causes prices to stop rising; a support level occurs when a preponderance of buying over selling causes prices to stop falling. Your charts should help you locate these areas. The other method is to liquidate your position when you have lost a certain percentage of your equity. For instance, if your total initial margin is $3,000, you may want to liquidate your position when you have lost, say, 20 percent of your equity, or $600.

To allow your profits to accumulate, you can use *trailing stops.* Trailing stops follow prices as they move up, in the case of a long position; and conversely, follow prices as they fall, in the case of a short position. For example, let's say you are a soybean buyer at $5.92 a bushel and you want to maintain a long position in the market with a stop 12 cents below the market. Let's assume that the market now moves up to $6.22. Your trailing stop is then moved to $6.10, up from the original $5.80. To protect your paper profit, the stop will continue to trail the price. Now prices move to $6.24 and the stop moves up two cents to $6.12 per bushel. Now assume the market makes another rally and prices move to $6.38. The trailing stop will now move up to $6.26. If prices plummet, your stop-loss order at $6.26 will get you out of the market at that level with plenty of your paper profits still intact.

Many traders make the mistake of taking profits too quickly. They like to believe that if the market continues to rally, they can always buy in again. But there are two problems connected with this type of thinking. The first is that each entry and exit from the market requires that a full round-turn commission be paid. The second involves the nature of the market. In a roaring bull market, with plenty of buyers bidding higher and higher prices, you aren't going to get in again at a very satisfactory price. And, of course, moving in and out of the market too frequently, you may be forced to give up a great part of the move and have commissions eat up much of what you do make.

Lastly, you can adhere to this rule by never getting into a trade in which the potential profits don't appear to be much greater than the risks. By looking for trades in which the potential profits outweigh the risks, you will be setting up a situation in which you stand to make a profit over a period of time. Again, this is not to say there won't be losses; there may be many. But the profits you do take will be considerable and will more than compensate for the losses incurred. For additional strategies on winning profits and cutting losses, consult Chapter 5.

RULE NUMBER 5. *Trade only the most active commodities.* This rule has a simple premise behind it. You take on an unnecessary risk when you trade a "thin," or inactive, market. Buyers and sellers interacting establish prices. Unless there are a sufficient number of each, there is no one ready to give you your profit when you want to take it. Moreover, in such markets, a handful of large traders can dominate and more or less establish prices by themselves. A corollary to this rule is to trade the most active trading month—unless, as in spread trading, you have a good reason not to. The most active trading month will generally be the nearby month, but not when the nearby month is the delivery month. For example, in mid-January, the nearby oats contract is for March delivery. But in March, the oats trader will switch to the May contract.

What commodities should you trade? That should be an individual decision based on many factors. But the most active ones which offer the best trading opportunities are the following:

Soybeans	Silver
Soybean Meal	Heating Oil
Soybean Oil	Deutschemark
Wheat	Swiss Franc
Corn	British Pound
Feeder Cattle	Eurodollars
Live Cattle	GNMA
Live Hogs	Treasury bonds
Pork Bellies	Treasury bills
Cotton	S&P 500
Copper	Major Market Index
Gold	NYSE Composite Index

3

Spread Trading

LIMITED-RISK STRATEGIES

The most common objection you will hear about commodity futures trading is that it is too risky. While the potential profits you may earn trading commodities are considerable, so also are the risks. A string of limit moves against a trader in almost any commodity can easily result in financial disaster. To offset these risks, some traders use strategies that clearly limit their market exposure while enabling them to participate in the highly leveraged futures markets. The most common strategy employed to achieve this goal is to trade what are known as *spreads*. Spreads (also called *straddles)* are market transactions in which you stand to profit not from the rise or fall of a single commodity futures contract, but from the relative price *differences* between two futures contracts. When you *place,* or *put on,* a spread, you buy one contract while simultaneously selling another. Thus you are long and short in two related commodity futures at the same time. The relative changes between the two prices at which you purchased and sold your two contracts will determine your profit or loss. For example, you might spread corn and wheat by buying one contract of December wheat and simultaneously selling a contract of December corn. This is known as an *intercommodity spread,* in which different commodities on the same exchange are bought and sold in the same contract month.

Since you will only spread commodities that are related, their prices will tend to move in the same direction. Therefore, what you gain on one contract you will lose on another. However, although related commodities and contract months tend to move together, they do not always move in unison with one another. That is, one might move up or down faster than the other. The relative difference between the point at which you initiate a spread and the point at which you liquidate it, therefore, will determine the success of the trade. The absolute direction of prices will not be as important as the fact that the spread widens or narrows over time.

Let's consider an example. Assume you have put on a spread between December wheat and December corn by buying wheat at $2.99 per bushel and simultaneously selling corn at, say, $2.29. You have thus put on the spread at December wheat 70 cents over December corn. Now let's assume that the grains are bullish and over time the price of both wheat and corn rises—but at a different rate. Six months later, let's say wheat prices in the December contract have risen to $3.92 per bushel for a 93-cent gain, while corn prices have only risen 81 cents per bushel to $3.10. The spread has now widened from 70 cents wheat over corn to 82 cents wheat over. The difference between these spreads constitutes your profit—namely, 12 cents. You would have made a total of 93 cents on your long wheat position and lost a total of 81 cents on your short corn position. The difference between what you gained and what you lost is your profit.

You may think that a 12-cent profit (equal to $600) is quite inadequate in a situation where you might have earned 93 cents (or $4,650 per contract) simply by taking an outright position in the wheat and ignoring the spread trade altogether. But the risks are commensurate. Had you been long wheat and prices had fallen 93 cents, you would have lost $4,650 plus commissions. The spread trader, on the other hand, might have earned a profit or sustained only a modest loss depending upon whether the spread widened or narrowed. For example, using the example of our December wheat/corn spread, let's assume that prices fell but wheat declined by only 26 cents to $2.73 per bushel (a $1,300 loss) while corn fell 48 cents to $1.81 per bushel (a $2,400 gain). The spread has again widened from 70 cents December wheat over to 92 cents December wheat over. The 22-cent difference in the spread now constitutes the profit: $1,100. Had the trader only been long December wheat, he would have sustained a sizable 26-cent, or $1,300, loss on this same transaction. The ability to profit in up or down markets as long as the spread moves in your direction is a key advantage of spread trading.

The purpose of spreading is to reduce risk, since changes in the *difference* between the two prices of your long and short positions are usually more gradual than they would be if you owned an outright position. Moreover, the margin requirements are usually much smaller for spreads than they are for net-long or net-short positions. Significantly, you cannot spread unrelated commodities without encountering difficulties. For example, you wouldn't spread soybeans against orange juice. The two commodities are too far apart in their price movements to lend themselves to a good spread situation. In addition, your broker would make it a bit harder by insisting on margin equal to two outright net positions and full round-turn commission costs. But you could spread July against March soybeans, or soybeans against soybean oil or soybean meal, because the price movements of these different contracts and commodities are related.

A spread trader concerns himself with the changes that occur in the differences or spread between the price of the two contracts—not in the absolute direction of prices. For two contracts can make a soaring price rise, and a spread trader can still lose money if the spread moves against him. Thus, traders who take a spread position in futures markets are not necessarily concerned with upward or downward price movement. They are attempting to benefit from price disparities that grow up between related commodities.

Three Basic Types of Spreads

All commodity spreads can be classified under one of the following three headings:

1. *Interdelivery (or intramarket) spreads.* This is the most common type of spread and consists of buying one month and selling another month in the same commodity. An example of an interdelivery spread would be long December corn / short September corn.

2. *The intercommodity spread.* This spread consists of buying a futures month in one commodity and selling a related futures month in another commodity. An example of this type of spread would be long December gold / short December silver.

3. *The intermarket spread.* This spread involves buying a commodity deliverable on one exchange and selling the same commodity deliverable on another exchange. Long Chicago December wheat / short Kansas City December wheat would be an illustration of an intermarket spread.

Premium Spreads

To understand spreads, you must understand the pricing mechanism in the futures markets. We know that a spread consists of one long position and one short position that are purchased and sold simultaneously in the market. But how do we decide to purchase one contract and sell another? This decision rests with the kind of market we are operating in and what we anticipate will happen.

Typically, in so-called "normal" markets, distant contract months will sell at a *premium* (i.e., a higher price) than nearby months. A commodity that is going to be delivered in December of one year will sell for more than a commodity that is to be delivered in March of the same year. This is so because the person who must hold onto the commodity until delivery in December will be faced with more expenses than the person who holds the commodity only a month or two. Storage, insurance, and interest costs must be paid for the months prior to delivery. Such so-called *carrying charge* markets, therefore, might have a pricing structure similar to the five contract months in soybean meal listed below:

MONTH	SETTLEMENT PRICE
January	164.20
March	164.70
May	167.00
July	168.80
August	169.00

In a carrying-charge market, one in which the distant contracts sell for more than nearbys, the commodity is generally not in tight demand. However, when the commercials and speculators are willing to pay more for a nearby contract, the market is said to be trading at a *premium* and the reverse is true. Significantly, this also means that a bull market is about to develop. When this tightness in supply or demand occurs, the commercials, who require the commodity in their daily business affairs, will immediately begin to bid up the price of the nearby month, and the distant months will fall behind despite the carrying charges, which will seem insignificant in comparison with the trade's need for the cash commodity. The result will be a *premium spread,* which occurs in what is known as an *inverted market.* It is important to understand that there is a limit on the premium which a distant month will command over a nearby in a carrying-charge market. But there is no limit to the amount by which a nearby month can exceed a more distant month in an inverted market. The following list of cocoa prices illustrates the price structure of an inverted market:

MONTH	SETTLEMENT PRICE
March	142.30
May	132.00
July	127.60
September	125.10
December	121.80

A premium spread or inverted market is the usual bull market signal. Ideally, you see the bullish situation developing before the nearby goes to a premium, and you put your bull spread on early in the move. But this, of course, is not always possible. So you might just have to play the situation as best you can. Due to seasonal influences and other transitory factors, a commodity may trade at a premium and return to carrying charges or a normal market configuration a number of times during a year. It is the spreader's task to take advantage of these temporary imbalances in price by purchasing one month and selling another, betting that the spread will widen or narrow.

What can send a normal market into disarray? A number of factors—such as impending shortages or surpluses, a new government crop-loan program, a freeze or drought, or simply the threat of these occurrences—can cause a premium spread to develop. Spreads are set up to capitalize on such imbalances in the normal price structure.

The "General Rule"

The "General Rule" says that near months will gain ground relative to distant months in a bull market and lose ground in a bear market. The reason for this is that a bull market usually reflects a current tight supply situation, which puts a premium on more immediately available supplies. As a result, we can formulate the following guidelines for spread traders:

1. *To put on a bull spread, buy the nearby and sell the distant contract month.* In bull markets, the nearby contracts will rise faster than the distant contracts, resulting in profitable opportunities for the spread trader. The size of the premium will depend on how badly buyers want the commodity and how reluctant owners of the commodity are to part with it. Their hesitancy to sell may be influenced by an expectation that price will climb even higher. In many commodities, the *interdelivery spread,* in which one contract month of the same commodity is spread against another contract month, can be used as a proxy for an outright long or short position.

2. *To put on a bear spread, sell the nearby and buy the distant contract month.* In bear markets, the surplus or lessened demand for a commodity will cause the month closest to the cash or *spot* month to decline rapidly in comparison to more distant months when more normal conditions may prevail. As a result, the spread trader who shorts the nearby and buys the far-out month will stand to profit from a widening in the spread.

3. *Before you put on a bull or bear spread according to the rules above, always make sure the "General Rule" applies.* There are a number of commodities for which the "General Rule" does not apply, and even in those commodities where it does apply there are a number of exceptions. First, the "General Rule" can be considered applicable to the following commodities:

Corn	Cocoa
Soybeans	Orange Juice
Soybean Meal	Copper
Soybean Oil	Pork Bellies
Wheat	

Commodities conforming to the *inverse* of the "General Rule" would include potatoes and platinum. In these commodities, among several others, the distant months gain relative to the more nearby contracts in a rising market, and lose relative to the nearby contract in a declining market. In these markets, therefore, you should reverse your strategy. As a proxy for an outright long position in a market where the inverse of the "General Rule" is called for, you would spread a long deferred contract against a short nearby contract. And as a proxy for an outright short position, you would spread a short deferred contract against a long nearby contract.

The Advantages of Spreads

The most important advantage of trading spreads is that of limited risk. When you hold an outright net position, your risk is virtually unlimited; when you hold a spread position, however, your liability is strictly limited. The reason for this is related to the nature of a spread. In general, when you trade a spread, the loss on one leg of the position will be offset by a gain on the other leg. Rarely will two related markets move in such a manner that the short leg will be subject to a loss at the same time that the long leg is also in a loss position. For this to occur, the market in which you are short would have to rise while the market in which you are long would have to fall. As long as you spread related commodities, this won't be a problem.

Because of the limited risk associated with spread trading, commodity exchanges have less rigorous margin requirements for this form of trading. As a rule, spread margins are 25 to 75 percent below normal margins on outright positions. Thus, a spread on a commodity that might require $2,000 in margin for a net long or short position would probably have a margin requirement ranging from $500 to $1,500. Because of the lower margins for spreads, you can often obtain a more attractive risk/reward ratio by trading them. For instance, let's compare a commodity whose spread margin is $500 and whose normal margin is $1,500. All other things being equal, the spread trade offers a more attractive opportunity unless the single outright position offers at least three times the profit potential.

Spreads also enjoy an advantage in terms of commission costs. For the cost of brokerage for both legs of a spread are significantly below the cost of the round-turn on two separate contracts. Expect to pay just a little more than a single round-turn commission when you trade a spread.

A knowledge of spreads can also be valuable in trading outright positions. For example, a failure of the nearby month to gain ground on distant months in a bull market may be an indication of market weakness. You need not be a spread trader to take advantage of a situation like this. Moreover, as you gain proficiency in recognizing price distortions in the market, you will know which contracts to buy or sell to receive maximum benefit from your trading—regardless of whether you are a spread trader or not.

Lastly, given the limited-risk aspect, spreads are ideal for the small trader. You probably won't make a market killing by trading spreads, but chances are you won't be wiped out financially, either. Professionals, who make their living from the markets, are enthusiastic spread traders. This should give you an indication of the value of this form of trading.

The Limited-risk Spread

Just as outright positions are associated with varying degrees of risk, so, too, are spreads. Some spreads are safer than others because a carrying-charge market is limited in the distance that one month will trade over another. For example, if the carrying charge on a given commodity is, say, 2 cents per month, there is little likelihood that one distant month will exceed another by more than this premium. A month that experienced a higher premium would rapidly be brought back in line with the cost of carrying charges by speculative selling. However, should a bull market develop in that same commodity as a result of tight supplies, the immediate need for the cash commodity would cause the nearby month to rise more rapidly than the distant months, creating a potentially profitable situation for the spread trader. In this instance, you would have a highly volatile nearby month and a much less volatile distant month. By buying the nearby and selling the distant month, you would have a bull spread that would provide profits in direct proportion to the ability of the nearby to gain ground at the expense of the distant month.

Such a spread is limited in risk because the carrying charges will dictate the maximum price distance that one contract will trade in terms of another. For example, let's assume you have a potential May/December corn spread and the full carrying charge is 11 cents. This means that the December contract will never trade for more than 11 cents over the May contract. It may trade closer to May, but it won't trade more than 11 cents apart. Now let's assume the trader puts on the May/December corn spread when May is 6 cents under December. What is the maximum risk? Five cents. The worst thing that can happen is that the market goes to full carry, or 11 cents December over May. Since the market is already valuing the May contract at 6 cents under December, the risk is limited to just five more cents.

On the other hand, there is no limit on how far the May contract may trade over the December contract. Thus, if May rises sharply and the corn spread becomes a premium spread, the potential for profit is very great. For example, if May goes to just 8 cents over December, the spread will have a gain of 14 cents.

Using January 15 as the day we initiate the spread and April 15 as the day we liquidate the spread, let's look at the detailed accounting for this hypothetical spread below:

DATE	ACTION TAKEN	
January 15	Bought one contract May corn at $2.57	Sold one contract December corn at $2.63
April 15	Sold one contract May corn at $2.93	Bought one contract December corn at $2.85
Result:	$.36 gain on May corn = $1,800	$.22 loss on December corn = $1,100

$1,800   profit on the May contract

− 1,100   loss on the December contract.

$ 700   profit on this spread, exclusive of commissions

Once a $50 spread commission is subtracted from the total equity, the $650 net profit would represent a 173 percent profit on the initial spread margin of $375. The risk, once the spread was initiated at May 6 cents under December, was always limited to 5 cents, or $250 plus the commission cost of $50.

Due to the built-in safety with a limited-risk spread, a trader can rest easy even if the market breaks several daily trading limits. The risk is always limited to full carrying charges. In the same market, the outright position trader would not enjoy the same degree of safety and, indeed, may face catastrophic losses should the market move against him.

As with any commodity trade, the limited-risk spread can go wrong if you aren't fully aware of what you are doing. To qualify as a limited-risk spread, each of the following requirements must be met:

1. A long position is taken in a nearby contract against the short sale of a more distant contract of the same commodity. Thus, you will have a bull spread.

2. The commodity must be one which may be accepted on delivery when the nearby (long) contract matures, and be eligible without reinspection for delivery when the more distant month, which was sold short, matures.

3. The commodity must be physically available for delivery without dependence upon transportation.

4. The short sale in the more distant month should be made at a premium over the price of the nearby month. This premium should cover a portion of the carrying costs. Since the carrying costs usually limit the amount by which the distant contract may trade over the nearby contract, the risk exposure is limited and can be calculated.

The most popular limited-risk spreads will occur in the following commodities: wheat, corn, oats, soybeans, soybean meal, soybean oil, pork bellies, orange juice, and cotton. Highly perishable commodities, those which cannot be carried from month to month, are bad limited-risk spreads and should not be traded according to the above rules. These commodities would include: eggs, broilers, cattle, and hogs, among others. The element of storage is vital to placing a limited-risk spread. Non-storable commodities do not adhere to the "General Rule" and are, therefore, inappropriate for this spread. Let's illustrate the reason for this nonapplicability with the example of live cattle. Live cattle, by definition, are a completely nonstorable commodity. When feedlot cattle reach market weight, they must be marketed and cannot await better prices by being put into storage. As a consequence of the intrinsic nature of this commodity, different months in live cattle are, in a sense, different commodities. February live cattle, for instance, are quite different from August live cattle. The two different contract months will be priced according to the market's perception of the supply-and-demand picture at the time the contract matures. It is not unusual for a Cattle on Feed report to carry bullish implications for a near month and bearish implications for a distant month. In such a case, the futures market can often react by moving in opposite directions for the near and deferred contracts. While it is conceivable that a trader can make excellent profits by correctly spreading this commodity, the risks are often commensurate with taking on two outright positions.

One other circumstance that may result in a limited-risk spread not working out is when the federal government imposes price ceilings on nearby deliveries. While the nearbys would then be limited by these ceilings, the distant months would not. As a result, in anticipation of tight supplies in the future as well, the distant months will go to a premium over the nearbys. This, of course, would result in disaster for the spread trader who is long a contract month that cannot rise and short a month that is rising rapidly. Barring this government intervention, however, the limited-risk spread is an excellent means of participating in the futures markets.

Arbitrage

Strictly speaking, *arbitrage* means to buy in one market and sell simultaneously in another. The international commodities—silver, copper, cocoa, and sugar—traded in New York and London offer the most common arbitrage opportunities. But one also hears of domestic arbitrage between such markets as New York silver against Chicago silver.

For international arbitrage, you will have a few problems that the spreader of domestic commodities does not have. The most significant is that you will be required to post full margin and pay full commissions in both New York and London. Secondly, there are differences in how the same commodities are quoted in New York and London. London sugar is quoted in pounds sterling per long ton; New York sugar is quoted in cents per pound. London copper is quoted in pounds sterling per long ton; New York copper is quoted in cents per pound. A third dissimilarity relates to varying contract sizes in the different commodities. With the exception of sugar, which is traded in a 112,000-pound contract in both countries, the contract sizes for coffee, copper, and silver are different. To compensate for these differences, the arbitrager must trade an unequal number of contracts in each country. The goal of this practice is to equalize as nearly as possible the contract sizes. The list below indicates the respective contract sizes and how best to arbitrage them:

COMMODITY	CONTRACT SIZE NEW YORK	CONTRACT SIZE LONDON	CORRECT ARBITRAGE MIX
Cocoa	10 metric tons	10 metric tons (22,046 pounds)	1 New York/ 1 London
Copper	25,000 pounds	25 metric tons (55,115 pounds)	2 New York/ 1 London
Coffee	37,500 pounds	5 metric tons (11,023 pounds)	1 New York/ 3 London
Silver	5,000 troy ounces	10,000 troy ounces	2 New York/ 1 London
Sugar	112,000 pounds	50 long tons (112,000 pounds)	1 London/ 1 New York

A fourth factor relates to changes in currency fluctuations while you are holding commodity futures contracts in two countries. Devaluation of the pound against the dollar, or vice versa, could possibly have a beneficial or adverse effect upon your trading capital. As a rule, in evaluating the effects of a currency dislocation on your futures position, you should remember that the net result of purchasing commodity futures contracts is to be "short" the currency with which you purchased those contracts; conversely, being short commodity futures contracts is to be "long" the currency of the country those contracts are quoted in. The reason for this is relatively simple. Commodities are quite frequently looked upon as a "store of value." When the value of a currency becomes suspect, regardless of what government officials or monetary authorities have to say on the subject, active efforts will be made by thousands of holders of that currency to sell it and buy something which is expected to increase in value— like a commodity. Since the supply of any given commodity is relatively fixed at any one moment in time, a flight from paper money into commodities will see an abundance of currency chasing a relative scarcity of commodities. The result will be higher commodity prices and a lowering in value of the worth of the currency. Given this phenomenon, a rule can be stated as follows: In times of currency instability, *the direction of the price of commodities is always opposite to that of the currency from which the speculators are in flight.* Examples of this occurrence are not hard to find. Speculators who feared devaluation of the British pound and the U.S. dollar in recent years sold those currencies and purchased gold or stronger currencies, such as the Swiss franc. The readjustment that occurred—gold soaring to unprecedented heights, the dollar devalued—was inevitable.

Currency fluctuations can upset even the most well-planned arbitrage situation. To conduct your day-to-day arbitrage operations, therefore, you should have the following formula to convert the London prices into dollars and cents:

$$\frac{\text{London price} \times \text{Exchange rate}}{\text{Number of pounds in London contract}} = \text{New York price}$$

For example, let's assume you wish to convert the London copper price into its equivalent in New York when the exchange rate is \$1.9630 per pound sterling and the respective copper prices quoted in London and New York are £768.5/ton and \$.6705/lb. To compare the two, multiply the London price by the exchange rate and divide by the number of pounds in a metric ton (the unit in which London copper is quoted), as follows:

$$\frac{£768.5 \times 1.9630}{2,204.62} = .6842$$

This answer reveals that London copper is selling at a premium of 137 points over New York, the .6842 representing the equivalent of \$.6842/lb. in London.

Given this information, you are in a position to evaluate the arbitrage possibilities inherent in the two markets. In this hypothetical example, if you know that London tends to trade at a broader premium than 137 points over New York, you have the makings of a good arbitrage situation. Buy London copper and sell New York copper, would be the appropriate response if this fact were indeed true. If the price differential has been known to narrow below 137 points London over New York, the correct strategy would be to sell London and buy New York, to profit from the narrowing divergence.

The arbitrager should always remember that currency fluctuations and possible devaluation are omnipresent realities in the modern world. To guard against losing your capital due to currency debasement, try to be long commodities in the country where you anticipate the devaluation will occur, and sell short commodities in a country in which you anticipate a strengthening in the currency. Commodity prices will tend to move in the direction opposite to that of a country's currency.

The Two-day Rule

The two-day rule is simply a timing tool to help you enter and exit a spread position at an appropriate time. When entering a spread position, the rule says: *Look for two consecutive days of favorable movement in the spread and enter on the following day's open.* When exiting a spread position, the reverse occurs: *Look for two consecutive days of unfavorable price movement and exit on the following day's open.* While these two rules are quite simple, they can keep you from hanging onto a deteriorating position.

Let's say you are trading the intercrop July–November soybean spread. In recent years, the big money (as much as $10,000 on a single spread position) has been made on the so-called bear, or "back," spread—that is, selling the old-crop July and buying the new-crop November. Let's say you are monitoring the spread, looking for a spot to start selling July and buying November. At first, the spread may look as if the July contract shows the strength. July may indeed be trading above November by a few cents. But then the spread might go to even money and the November may even achieve a premium over July. This is the sign you have a winner. Begin spreading the two contracts. If you are right, you'll know almost immediately, since the trend will likely continue. Assuming you do indeed achieve profits, however, you then have to turn around and look for weakness in November in terms of July. Should November start to lose its premium—run. You'd be surprised how well this simple rule works in practice.

The Two-unit Method

The two-unit method is a conservative trading program for spreads that is designed to combine maximum safety with ample opportunity for profit. When employed as a money-management tool with the limited-risk spread, it is the most conservative means of participating in substantial market moves when they occur, without incurring large risks. To apply the method, you must always trade spreads in multiples of two. One spread is always liquidated at a realistic, predetermined profit level. The other spread is held for the longer term, hoping for the bigger move. Since even the most well-thought-out spread position is subject to revisions once it is initiated, this method will ensure you a modest profit on one spread and a chance for a larger profit on the second. Remember, a major news development, in the form of a crop disease, weather damage, political instability, wars, and other unforeseen events, can wreak havoc with any spreading program. On the other hand, just such an unforeseen event can result in windfall profits for the spread trader already in position to benefit from such a development. The second spread, using the two-unit method, will occasionally bring you enormous profits when inverted markets (nearby selling at a premium to the distant months) occur.

How to Analyze a Good Spread Trade

We have mentioned some of the requirements for putting on a bull and bear spread, but how does one recognize the existence of a potential good spreading opportunity in the first place? A variety of methods are outlined below, but the spread trader must always remember that an absolute rise or fall in price will not help him unless such price moves are accompanied by a broadening or narrowing in the initial price relationship. Keep this major qualification in mind as you read the following guidelines for analyzing a spread trade:

1. *Spread Charts*. An important first step in initiating a spread should be the analysis of a current chart of the spread relationship. As in outright positions, charts are critical timing aids that provide a historical view of the price action. Spread charts differ from normal price charts in that they show the relationship between the two contract months. Thus the spread itself, as measured in points, is charted, not the absolute price level. For example, let's assume you wish to follow the price relationship of July and September wheat. For intracommodity spreads, the spread difference plotted is always the price of the nearer month (July) minus the more distant month (September). Thus, by subtracting the one from the other, you will have a value which can then be plotted on a graph. When July is at 286¾ and September is at 292, the spread will be 5¼ September over—a normal market spread. But if bullish influences begin to push the July contract up faster than the September contract, the spread will narrow and July might even go to a premium. Let's say the July contract rises by 9 cents to 295¾, but the September rises only by, say, 5 cents to 297. The spread will now be 1¼ cents September over. Continuing the rise, the July now goes up by 9½ cents to 305¼ and the September rises by 5¼ to 302¼. We now have a premium spread with July selling 3 cents over September—an 8¼-cent improvement over the point of initiation. Given this price action, the relationship between the contract methods should be easy to chart. First you list the price data, and then you plot the chart as follows:

	WHEAT	
July	*September*	*Spread*
286¾	292	−5¼
295¾	297	−1¼
305¼	302¼	3

Such an extreme move is highly unlikely between two adjacent months of wheat, but this does illustrate how a spread is charted. Assume for a

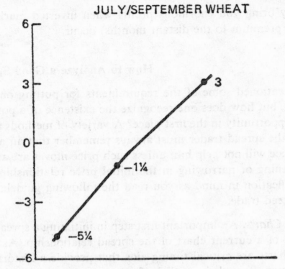

Figure 1. The July/September wheat spread went from 5¼ cents July under to 3 cents July over.

moment that the spread returns to normal and the spread difference falls below the zero line, with September selling at a premium to July. In light of the recent movement, you might then want to initiate a long July / short September wheat spread in the hopes that July will again gain ground at the expense of September. It is unlikely that July and September would ever sell for more than the carrying charge, which is 10 cents September over, so if you put on the spread at 5 cents September over or better, your risk is clearly limited. Spread charts help you identify the potential risk areas and clearly reveal the past patterns of spread relationships.

2. *Seasonal patterns.* Very often a spread will exhibit a very definite seasonality, narrowing or broadening at a particular time with a great degree of consistency over many years. These spreads are known as seasonal spreads and offer some of the best opportunities for consistent profits in commodity futures trading. To take advantage of seasonal spreads, you have to go back and analyze five to eight years of price data and see how many times the spread behaved in a predictable pattern. Moreover, you have to take into account the present supply-and-demand situation in the market to see whether past market action applies in the current year. So-called "analogous studies" are performed by many market analysts in order to identify the primary motivating factors which may or may not justify the spread seasonality. For seasonals to be reliable, it is important to identify the significant variables that are the primary motivating forces for change. In commodities, these variables often center around crop-production and harvest considerations, inventories, domestic consumption, and

export demand. A list of the most consistently reliable spreads follows. Among them are seasonal spreads which should be initiated and liquidated within a one- or two-week period, such as May/June corn. Although such a spread contradicts the rule which states that you should trade only in nondelivery months, this seasonal spread is an exception. Seasonal spreads, like seasonal outright position trades, do not work every year like clockwork. They may be late in occurring, they may not occur at all. But the patterns are such that they occur with sufficient frequency to warrant listing. Accordingly, the following list of seasonal trades (with the long month stated first, the short month second) are given with the initiation periods indicated in chronological order.

Seasonal Spreads

SPREAD	INITIATE	LIQUIDATE
JUL/MAY corn	January	April
DEC/MAY corn	January or February	March or April
JUL/MAY oats	January	April
MAY/SEPT corn	February or March	May
OCT/SEPT soybean oil	February or March	July
MAY/DEC corn	March or April	May
JUL/SEPT corn	March or April	June
JAN/JUL soybeans	March or April	July
NOV soybeans / DEC wheat	March or April	July
DEC/SEPT Chicago wheat	April or May	July or August
JUL/AUG soybeans	April or May	July
MAY/JUL corn	May	May
DEC/SEPT corn	May	September
MARCH/SEPT Kansas City wheat	May	August
AUG/DEC soybean oil	June or July	August
Chicago DEC wheat / Kansas City DEC wheat	June	November
DEC wheat / DEC corn	June or July	October or November

SPREAD	INITIATE	LIQUIDATE
MARCH/MAY Chicago wheat	July or August	December
DEC/MARCH Chicago wheat	August or September	December
DEC/MARCH Kansas City wheat	September or October	December
JUL/MARCH soybeans	September	March
DEC/MARCH corn	October	December
SEPT/MAY corn	October or November	February or March
AUG/JUL soybeans	October or November	March or April
SEPT/JUL corn	November or December	February or March

3. *Historical analysis.* Before you trade a spread, you should investigate what that spread has done in the past six to eight years. It is not necessary to go back further than that, since the futures markets have changed drastically in the past ten years. Six to eight years, therefore, should provide you with a variety of markets from which to judge the spread's performance. Historical charts, of course, are ideal for this purpose. If charts are unavailable, look for historical data that can provide a clue to the spread's behavior. The point is, you want some evidence of a spread moving in a certain direction in the past. While the work involved in gathering such data may be considerable, not to have some indication of the spread's past performance is risky at best and can prove disastrous if unforeseen circumstances are not taken into account.

4. *Isolation of similar periods.* Don't compare dissimilar periods when looking for an indication of spread performance. As a rule, spreads react to similar supply-and-demand forces in a similar manner. Thus, in a period of sharply rising prices, look to previous bull markets for an indication of possible price action—and vice versa. There was a period in the early seventies when inverted markets were the rule. Later, more normally structured markets prevailed, but a few tight-supply markets—coffee and cocoa, among them—remained inverted. Knowing the factors that bring on imbalances in the market, and knowing how specific commodities react to these imbalances, can provide you with valuable clues for trading a certain spread.

Money Spreads

Money spreads are intercommodity spreads in which the contract sizes differ. For example, when you spread cattle against hogs, you have one contract consisting of 40,000 pounds of live cattle, and another consisting of 30,000 pounds of live hogs. As a result of the differences in the contract sizes, a move of comparable points will not generate equal dollar amounts. Thus, to equate the price differentials between commodities of differing contract sizes, the trader has to translate the price movements into dollars and cents.

Let's look at a hypothetical money spread between December live cattle and December live hogs. If you anticipated that cattle would gain ground over hogs during December, you might have put on an intercommodity spread by buying December cattle and selling December hogs. Let's say you purchased cattle at 43.27 cents per pound and sold hogs at 36 cents per pound, and that you could have liquidated the spread when cattle were selling for 45.70 and hogs were selling for 38.10 cents. You would have netted a profit of 2.43 cents on the cattle and lost 2.10 cents on the hogs. The arithmetic of this money spread would appear as follows:

> *Established spread:*
>
> BOUGHT one DEC cattle at 43.27
> ($.4327 × 40,000) = $17,308
> SOLD one DEC hogs at 36.00
> ($.3600 × 30,000) =   10,800
> Dollar Value Differential $ 6,508
>
> *Liquidated spread:*
>
> SOLD one DEC cattle 45.70
> ($.4570 × 40,000) = $18,280
> BOUGHT one DEC hogs at 38.10
> ($.3810 × 30,000) =   11,430
> Dollar Value Differential $ 6,850

The 2.43-cent gain on the long cattle represented a profit of $972; the 2.10-cent loss on the hogs represented a loss of $630. Before commissions, therefore, the spread trader earned $342, or a net profit, after deducting commission costs of $100, of $242. You should note that in intercommodity spreads full commissions must be paid.

Spread Rules

There are only about thirty-five commodities you can trade, but there are several hundred different spread positions. As a result of the many combinations of contract months and related commodities, you will be faced with many possible choices. In this chapter we have outlined the basic principles on which spread trading is based. Spreads can be very profitable on a consistent basis. Just remember that you have a trade-off when you undertake a spread position: You are willing to give up some potential gain in exchange for safety. Given the considerable risks that outright position traders must face daily in the markets, the spread trader gladly gives up his opportunity to make an overnight killing in return for more modest gains and survival. This is not to say that spreads are without risk. If you spread the wrong way or are careless in the manner in which you put on a spread, you may very well end up with a loss. The following spread rules are given to make you a better spread trader. Read them over carefully and make sure you understand them before attempting to trade a spread position.

RULE NUMBER 1. *Always be specific in your spread orders.* When the two months of the spread are very close in price, extra care should be taken to specify clearly which month is the premium month in the order. For example, if you want to put on an intermarket spread between Minneapolis and Chicago July wheat, you might say: "Buy Minneapolis July wheat / sell Chicago July wheat, Chicago five cents over." This will tell the broker not the absolute price level to put on the spread, but, more important, the spread difference at which you want to put on the spread. Thus, the order may come back filled at long Minneapolis July wheat at $2.85 per bushel and short Chicago July wheat at $2.90 per bushel. Should this spread improve in your favor while you hold the position, you will earn a profit. Let's say you expect the Chicago wheat contract to sell at a lower price than the Minneapolis contract. You may then put in an order that says: "Liquidate the spread at Chicago three cents under." In this instance, Chicago will have gone from selling 5 cents over Minneapolis wheat to 3 cents under, resulting in an 8-cent, or $400, profit exclusive of commissions. What you should not do in putting on a spread is to say: "Buy Minneapolis July wheat, sell Chicago July wheat." Indicate the spread difference you want and you will make out much better. Use a limit order, not a market order. When you place a market order, you're instructing your broker to buy or sell each leg of the spread at whatever price can be obtained at that time in the market. More often than not, the intraday price swings will not result in the spread you want. It is, therefore, better to pick the spread difference you want by using a limit order.

RULE NUMBER 2. *Do not liquidate spreads one leg at a time.* This is another common and costly error which has caused many a good spread trade to end in a loss. When you initiate a spread, especially an interdelivery spread, you put both legs on at the same time. However, some traders have a tendency to "play the market" when it comes to getting out of the spread. For example, let's say you put on a spread and you have a decline in prices. Rather than liquidating both sides of the spread, you might then want to take profits on the short leg and leave the long leg on in anticipation of an improvement in prices. You are then net one long position. However, if prices continue to fall, you will incur a larger loss on the long position that you already have and will be without the protection of the short leg of your spread. Don't do it. Keep your spread trading separate from your net outright position trading. Otherwise you will turn profitable spreads into losses.

RULE NUMBER 3. *Do not use spreads to protect an outright position which has gone sour.* Traders who are incapable of taking losses have a tendency to engage in the dangerous practice of spreading a loss in hopes of some miracle taking place. For example, you are long a commodity and the market moves against you. The correct action would be to take the loss and exit the trade. But you are the hopeful type and you decide to watch the market. It declines further and you have a larger loss. Now, to avoid a margin call or worse, you call your broker and tell him to sell short another contract month of the same commodity, resulting in a spread. You reason that if prices continue to fall, the short side will make up the loss on the initial long position—which it will. But what about the locked-in loss you now have? Sooner or later, this paper loss will have to be realized.

The one exception to this rule occurs when the market locks limit against you. That is, it moves the limit on the opening and trading ceases for the day. When this happens, you must go to the next-most-distant month and take as many opposite positions as are necessary to offset the damage to your initial position. For example, you are short January orange juice, a sudden freeze occurs, and the market moves limit up. Chances are, you won't be able to get out of your short position in the January contract for five or six days. In the meantime, however, you are in deep trouble because the market is locking limit against you every day. What do you do? The best strategy is to go to the next contract month—March, in the case of orange juice—and purchase two or more contracts for every contract you are short in January. If you can't buy into March, go to the next contract month: May. And so on. The strategy here is not to make a profit, but only to minimize the damage in an intolerable situation. Since the nearby month will rise faster than the distant months in a situation like this, it is necessary to compensate for the loss on the short position by taking additional long positions. Again, this is strictly a defensive strategy. If you are short and the market moves against you, *and you have an opportunity to get out by buying back your contract, do so.* Spread a losing position only when you are faced with a string of limit moves against your position. Otherwise, take your loss and get out. In most cases, spreading to put off a loss usually results in further loss.

RULE NUMBER 4. *Spread only liquid months.* Liquidity refers to the number of participants in a commodity and can be determined by referring to the open interest in each month. A lack of open interest is a sure sign that you won't be able to get in and out of a commodity contract without a price dislocation away from the present prevailing price. As a result, what looks good on paper may result in real problems. For instance, you see that your spread has widened to the point where you have a profit and you give your broker an order to liquidate at a given limit. He calls you back, after communicating with the floor, and says that there aren't any buyers or sellers at the price you want. Will you take less? Well, the difference might just be your profit. Liquidity is a problem especially in spreads involving distant back months. Remember, a lack of liquidity can significantly increase your loss when getting out of a spread that has gone awry. Of course, a spread may be sufficiently attractive despite the liquidity of one or both of its contracts. But you should be mindful of the extra risks involved.

RULE NUMBER 5. *Do not trade spreads in markets you are unfamiliar with.* This rule is only common sense. If you want to trade an intermarket seasonal spread between corn and wheat, for instance, you will want to know that July is traditionally the month for seasonal lows in wheat, while corn is seasonally strong in July. This is the kind of fundamental information you must know before you trade spreads.

RULE NUMBER 6. *Do not overtrade spreads because of lower margins or risks.* If the margin for an outright position is $2,500 and the margin for an interdelivery spread in that commodity is $500, don't trade five spreads rather than one outright position. You will only be defeating the limited-risk aspect of the spread and jeopardizing a greater amount of your equity. In addition, the commission costs will be five times as high as a single outright commission.

RULE NUMBER 7. *Don't ignore spread seasonality.* Seasonal patterns are among the most consistent of all patterns in the futures markets. These patterns reflect "normal" crop production and harvest conditions. Failure to take them into account usually leads to losses.

RULE NUMBER 8. *When spreading contracts of different specifications, always think in terms of a "money spread."* Since point differences between varying commodities are not apt to be identical, you should keep track of spread changes in terms of their dollar-and-cents price movement. This is true not only in domestic markets where you might be spreading cattle against hogs or hogs against pork bellies, but also in international markets when you arbitrage New York cocoa against London cocoa or New York copper against London copper.

RULE NUMBER 9. *Do not automatically assume that a spread trade is necessarily a low-risk trade.* Sometimes a spread may entail greater risks than an outright position. This is especially true in nonstorable commodities such as eggs, live cattle, live hogs, or broilers. In these commodities, in which the fundamentals can change quite rapidly, you could theoretically be long a month that goes down in price and short a month that rises. The net result would be that you would lose on both legs of the spread. There are low-risk spreads. But not all spreads are low-risk.

RULE NUMBER 10. *Avoid spreads involving soon-to-expire contracts,* for the same reason you shouldn't trade the delivery month in an outright position—the chance that you might be given a delivery notice. Since there are a few notable exceptions to this rule, such as the May/July corn seasonal spread, which is both initiated and liquidated during the delivery month, the rule could be modified somewhat to mean you should not carry a spread beyond the first notice day. But, as a rule, delivery months mean problems. In addition to the prospect of getting a delivery notice, you have to contend with markets that are highly volatile due to the absence of trading limits.

RULE NUMBER 11. *Concentrate on trading the bear spreads.* The reason for this rule is simple. Statistical studies have shown that the bear spreads are much more consistent than the lower-risk bull spreads. That is, spreads tend to go up at different times, but on a seasonal basis they tend to move back down much more consistently. The definition of a bear spread for most commodities is long the back, or deferred, month and short the nearby month. One such spread has worked consistently over the past fourteen years, the May–February pork belly spread. Specifically, this bear pork belly spread has returned profits 100 percent of the time in the past fourteen years when the nearby February contract is sold short during the month of October and the more distant May contract is purchased. For whatever reason, the February contract has a strong tendency to "go off the boards" weak in terms of the May contract.[1] There are many, many other examples of bear spreads that have shown consistent seasonal patterns over the past twelve to fifteen years. Most of them occur in the grains and the meats. Given the bearish nature of the market in recent years, of course, the likelihood of these spreads proving profitable isn't surprising. What *is* surprising, however, is the tendency for the bear spreads to work even during those periods of time when the market has been rising.

RULE NUMBER 12. *Insist on spread commissions.* As long as you follow the previous rules and place and liquidate your spreads both legs at the same time, you are entitled to spread commissions. Typically, your brokerage house may charge you the full commission on each leg—one for the long and one for the short—but most will then credit your account with an adjustment. What should you be paying? With commission rates negotiable these days, it is hard to say. But let's say you are used to paying $18 per contract on a round-trip basis. The spread commission shouldn't be twice this amount, but, rather, five or six dollars lower—say, about $30 per spread. When placing the trade order, make sure you instruct the order taker or broker that you are placing a spread. He or she will then know that you are entitled to the spread commission. One other thing: remember, to receive the spread commission, you have to treat the position like a spread. That is, you'll want to both place and liquidate the position with both legs at the same time. Don't lift just one leg and expect your brokerage house to treat it as a spread—even if you are out of both legs on the same day. Some brokerage houses will attempt to charge you full commission for both legs; it is up to you to see that you receive the spread commis-

---

[1] For additional information on seasonal spreads, see my recent book *Real-Time-Proven Commodity Spreads,* available from Windsor Books, Inc., P.O. Box 280, Brightwaters, N.Y. 11718.

sion. Commission costs, over a period of time, can be significant. Don't pay more than is necessary.

RULE NUMBER 13. *Monitor your spread position daily.* Although spread trading has been likened to "watching paint dry"—boring, yet predictable —there are risks involved. For this reason, you'll want to monitor at least the closing prices daily. Recently, a $10,000 profit in the volatile November–July intercrop spread became a $5,000 loss in about ten days' time. So it is not as if spreads are risk-free. It only makes sense to follow your position and make sure there are no sudden reversals which might leave you in a vulnerable position.

4

Hedging Strategies

HOW TO HEDGE

We introduced hedging in Chapter 1 as the act of taking equal and opposite positions in the cash and futures markets, with the hope that the net
result will prevent a loss due to price fluctuations. It is a risk-reducing
strategy used by those who produce and process raw commodities. As we
have seen, there are essentially two kinds of hedges: the buying hedge and
the selling hedge. The selling hedge is a marketing tool used by a producer
or owner of a commodity to establish a price for his crop prior to bringing
in the cash commodity. The buying hedge is used as a purchasing tool by a
user of a commodity who wants to fix the price of commodities needed at a
later date or the price of products to be sold at a later date. In every
instance when a hedge is placed, the purpose is the same: risk reduction.

The fundamental reason that hedging cash positions with futures positions is an effective means of protection is that cash and futures prices have
a tendency to move in concert with each other and maintain essentially
predictable relationships in situations of fairly normal supply and demand.
Thus, the risks of change in the difference between the cash price and the
futures price are much less than the risks of change in the price of either
the cash or the futures. As a result, a loss in the cash position will be offset
by an equal gain in the futures position—or vice versa. It is this relation-

ship between cash prices and futures prices that makes the principles of hedging reliable.

The Basis

The difference between the cash price at any location and the futures price in any futures exchange is known as the *basis*. Basis, or the amount of difference between cash and futures prices, is the main consideration of hedgers, who largely ignore the price level of the commodity. For it is the change in the basis, rather than the absolute price level, that will determine a hedger's ultimate success. Basis is generally much more stable and predictable than the price level. For the commodity owner, basis may signal when and where to hedge, and knowledge of basis behavior over time marks most successful hedging programs. For the user of a commodity, basis knowledge will help him to know when and where an advantageous purchase can be made. Basis will differ from area to area; generally, when a hedger refers to basis, he means "his basis," or the basis for his local area. The concept of basis is at the heart of every hedging program. It is an important concept that every hedger must understand.

A basis may be said to be either "weak" or "strong." When you have a "weak" basis, you will have a wide difference between futures and cash; when you have a "strong" basis, only a narrow difference exists between futures and cash. Whether the commodity you wish to hedge has a weak or a strong basis will be dependent upon a number of factors. Included among these factors are the following:

1. The overall supply and demand of the commodity
2. The overall supply and demand of substitute commodities and comparable prices
3. Geographical disparities in supply and demand
4. Transportation considerations
5. Available storage space

The Selling Hedge

In a selling hedge, the hedger owns the cash commodity or financial instrument. Thus, his first transaction in the futures market is to sell futures and become hedged. Any downward movement in the market, therefore, will result in a profit in futures and a corresponding, if not comparable, decline in the underlying cash asset, whether it be an agricultural commodity, a financial instrument, or foreign currency.

For example, a portfolio manager might have recently purchased securities valued at $4 million. Assume the stock portfolio has a *beta* (a stock market measure that tells the volatility of a certain stock in terms of major indices) comparable to the Standard & Poor's 500, the leading market average. The manager might feel justified in hedging against the portfolio by *selling* S&P 500 futures. To achieve a comparable protection in the short hedge, the portfolio manager would have to sell a sufficient number of contracts to cover the value of the cash portfolio. At a price of 170, the September S&P contract has a value of $85,000 (five hundred times the index price). Thus, he will sell forty-seven contracts to make the hedge equal in value to the cash position. By placing the hedge, he protects the portfolio value *regardless* of the subsequent movement in the market. Let's assume that, over the period he holds the short hedge, the market declines to 165. The loss in the cash market will be offset by a corresponding gain on the short futures position as follows:

The Selling Hedge—S&P 500

CASH	FUTURES
July 1:	
Owns stock valued at $4 million	Sells 47 contracts of September S&P 500 futures at a price of 170 (value: $3,995,000)
September 15:	
Owns stock valued at $3.80 million	Buys 47 contracts of September S&P 500 futures at a price of 165 (value: $3,877,500)
loss: $120,000	*gain:* $117,500

NET RESULT: −$2,500

In this instance, the basis remained the same throughout the time the hedge was held. But consider what would happen if, say, the futures declined at a slower rate than the stock portfolio. If the cash stock declined in value faster than the futures fell, the result would be a greater loss. Fortunately, the hedger has a means to cope with this situation. When the *beta* is greater than one, the hedger will know to increase his stock index futures position to cope with the greater volatility of the instrument being hedged. Let's assume that instead of selling forty-seven contracts, the short hedger sold fifty-five contracts to cope with the heightened volatility of his stock portfolio in terms of the S&P average. The result would be as follows:

The Selling Hedge—S&P 500

CASH	FUTURES
July 1:	
Owns stock valued at $4 million	Sells 55 contracts of September S&P 500 futures at a price of 170 (value: $4,675,000)
September 15:	
Owns stock valued at $3.80 million	Buys 55 contracts of September S&P 500 futures at a price of 165 (value: $4,537,500)
loss: $120,000	*gain:* $137,500

NET RESULT: +$17,500

By increasing his commitment slightly, the hedger increased his downside protection sufficient to gain a profit in a declining market.

Whenever you hedge using futures contracts, both cash and futures prices will do one of three things: they will rise, fall, or stay where they are. The relationship between the cash and futures as each rises or falls will determine the profitability of the hedge. In a selling hedge, you will profit when one of the following conditions occurs:

1. Futures fall while cash stays the same
2. Futures stay the same while cash rises
3. Futures fall while cash rises
4. Both rise, but cash rises faster
5. Both fall, but futures fall faster
6. Cash goes from below futures to above them

The Buying Hedge

Price fluctuations affect buyers of commodities as well as sellers. To minimize risk, therefore, buyers—who may be elevator operators, processors, cattle raisers, feedlot operators, manufacturers, and exporters—take the opposite role of the sellers by placing buying hedges. By definition, the buying hedge consists of a long futures position and a short cash position. For example, a flour miller, who requires wheat in his milling operations, will place a buying hedge to establish his cost objective. The hedge will protect him against the possibility of an increase in the price of wheat. Let's assume that the flour miller decides on September 1 that he needs 5,000 bushels of wheat at a price of $3.15, and his local basis is 10 cents under Chicago. Assuming the basis is expected to stay the same, he will then look for $3.25 Chicago wheat to meet his price objective. If he needs the wheat in December, he will then instruct his broker to buy December

Chicago wheat at $3.25. If we further assume that wheat rises 20 cents in both the local cash market and in the futures market by December 1, the transaction will appear as follows:

The Buying Hedge—Wheat

CASH	FUTURES
September 1:	
Short equivalent of 5,000 bushels of wheat at $3.15 in milling operations	Buys 5,000 bushels of December wheat at $3.25
December 1:	
Buys 5,000 bushels of cash wheat at $3.35	Sells 5,000 bushels of December wheat at $3.45
loss: $1,000	*gain:* $1,000

NET RESULT: $0.00

In the above example, the hedge served a very valuable function. It saved the flour-milling operator $1,000 that he would have lost had he remained naked and not hedged his need for wheat. By using the hedge, the initial requirement for $3.15 wheat was assured, as the hedger was compensated in the futures market for the subsequent higher cost of cash wheat.

Now let's consider a similar example in which there is a change in the basis from 10 cents under Chicago to 25 cents under Chicago. In this example, we will assume that both cash and futures decline in price, but that cash falls faster, resulting in the basis change. In addition to establishing a favorable price objective, the hedger will profit as a result of the change in basis. The transactions might appear as follows:

The Buying Hedge (Basis Change)—Wheat

CASH	FUTURES
September 1:	
Short equivalent of 5,000 bushels of wheat at $3.15 in milling operations	Buys 5,000 bushels of December wheat at $3.25
December 1:	
Buys 5,000 bushels of cash wheat at $2.90	Sells 5,000 bushels of December wheat at $3.15
gain: $1,250	*loss:* $500

NET RESULT: +$750

A change in the basis resulted in a $750 profit in the above example. As a rule, a basis change in a buying hedge will prove profitable when the following conditions prevail:

1. Futures rise while cash stays the same
2. Futures stay the same while cash falls
3. Futures rise while cash falls
4. Both rise, but futures rise faster
5. Both fall, but cash falls faster
6. Cash goes from above futures to below them

As you can see, familiarity with basis changes can help you reap profits in addition to protecting your cash position. Even a small change in a basis can more than offset commission costs. Perhaps these illustrations serve to show the importance of understanding the basis, and how basis changes can result in enhanced profits for the knowledgeable hedger.

How to Predict a Basis Change

We know that the basis is the difference between a local cash price and the price of the nearby futures month. In addition, we know that the basis can and will change over time and that hedgers can make or lose money from a fluctuation in the basis. Given this information, it should appear valuable to know what the basis will be at some time in the future. Although it is impossible to predict the basis exactly, the so-called *basis risk* is much lower than the risk associated with a change in price level. Because the basis can be predicted with far greater accuracy than can the level of prices, hedgers are far safer in taking their chances on an unfavorable change in the basis than on an unfavorable price level change.

To understand a change in the basis, it is necessary to understand the meaning of futures prices. The futures price for any given commodity at any moment in time reflects a genuine "consensus" judgment of that commodity's worth formed by every hedger and speculator participating in the market. Accordingly, as sentiment turns bullish, additional buying will push prices higher; and, conversely, bearish sentiment will tend to have the opposite effect on prices, causing them to decline. Moreover, it is important to recognize that a sudden change in this "consensus" judgment can occur at any moment. But what about the relationship between different futures months? Why does March corn trade at one level and July corn at another? Is there rhyme or reason behind these price differences in the same commodity traded a few months apart? There is indeed. And the reason behind the pricing structure is also the reason why basis changes are apt to be much more predictable than price level changes. As you may remember from our discussion of carrying charges, the normal pricing structure of a commodity is such that each successive commodity month will sell at a slightly higher price than the nearer month. The higher prices reflect the expenses of storage, insurance, interest on the invested capital, and the like. Because these carrying charges are readily predictable, each month in a market trading at full carrying charges will fully reflect this built-in cost. Thus, if the total cost of storing corn were, say, 4 cents a month, March would be 8 cents under May, May would be 8 cents under July—and so on. For example, the 4-cent-a-month carrying charges would be reflected in a stair-stepped fashion as follows:

September $3.09

July $3.01

May $2.95

March $2.85

This is a theoretical price structure. Futures often trade at less than full carrying charges, due to various supply-and-demand forces, but rarely at more than full carrying charges. When they get out of line, traders, sensing an opportunity, will buy or sell the errant month and bring it promptly into equilibrium with the others. As a result, a consistent and predictable pricing structure exists. In normal markets, the distant months will sell at a premium to the nearby months. This structure is likely to persist throughout a given crop year.

There are, of course, exceptions to this rule. In our discussion of spreads, we mentioned that there is such a thing as an inverted market in which distant months sell at a discount to nearby months. In an inverted market, which often reflects a short supply situation causing traders to bid up the price of the nearby months, the pricing structure will stair-step downward. Thus, a series of hypothetical futures prices might decline as follows:

January $106.60

March $106.30

September $105.40

November $104.60

Since the cash price reflects the current supply-and-demand situation in the commodity—which, in the case of an inverted market, is often bullish —cash commodities will frequently be selling at or near the nearby futures and well above the distant futures.

There is a third price configuration that can affect the basis change, and that is one that covers two crop years. You may well have a normal market in both the old crop and the new crop, but for all practical purposes, the new crop year is frequently priced according to a whole new set of supply-and-demand statistics. For example, if the old crop corn, with a well-balanced supply and demand, ends in September, and a bumper new crop is expected to be harvested for delivery in December, the December price may be below September as follows:

September $3.07

July $3.02   March $3.02

May $3.00   December $2.88

A variation of one of these three pricing structures will prevail in every commodity you trade. It is important to recognize that a relationship between futures months does exist and that carrying charges are the key to the price relationships in most instances. The cost of storage, insurance, and transportation is reflected in every futures price. Futures prices are quotes for delivering a designated commodity to a specific place at a specific time. The same commodity, it stands to reason, delivered to a different place at a different time will have a different price. As a result, the number of price possibilities (even for the same commodity) is practically unlimited. Saying that prices differ from one location to another is the same as saying that the basis differs from one location to another. In Chicago you will have one corn price, in Kansas City another, in Omaha yet another, and in Duluth yet another—all on the same day. In each of these commodities, there is obviously a different basis. The differences will reflect transportation, storage costs, local supply-and-demand conditions, and other considerations. A knowledge of the basis helps you keep these price relationships clearly in mind. Your local basis—the difference between your local cash price and the nearest futures—will provide the key to your hedging strategy. Do you expect your basis to narrow or widen over time? Why do you expect the basis to change? How does the basis traditionally move at this time of the crop year in your local area? These are the questions you must ask yourself in order to hedge successfully.

To calculate your local basis is simplicity itself. Subtract your local cash price from the *nearest* futures price and you will have the basis. For example, if it is January and your commodity is corn, you subtract your local cash price from the price of March corn, the nearest futures month. If the local cash price is $1.92 on a given day in January and March corn is at $2.25, the March basis is "33 cents under." When you reach the delivery month of the nearby future, you switch to the next month to calculate the basis. For example, after March you will calculate the basis by subtracting your local cash price from May corn. As the year proceeds, you continue to use different months to calculate the basis. As a rule, in normal markets, the cash price will be below the futures price of the nearby month due to the existence of carrying charges. When you get into inverted markets, however, where considerable pressure is exerted upon the cash commodity, cash prices will soar and go to a premium over futures. When this occurs, you will quote your basis as so many cents over a given month. For example, if cash corn is $3.09 a bushel and the nearby September contract is at $2.56 a bushel, your basis will be "53 cents over."

Now let's look at the components of a basis price in order to see exactly what the basis tells us. The first component, if we are dealing in a Chicago-traded commodity, will be the difference between the Chicago cash price and the local cash price. The difference in these two prices will be, more often than not, the cost of transportation. If you could imagine a situation in which all transportation were free or in which the cost of transportation were not related to distance, then the cost of a commodity would be practically the same in every location. But this is not the case. Therefore, if you are in the corn-growing region of Kansas, your cash price will be below the cash price of the city of Chicago, where the corn must be shipped in. Accordingly, if the cost of shipping is, say, 50 cents a bushel, Chicago cash will trade at a 50-cent premium to your local cash corn in Kansas.

Price difference due to location can change, of course. A location that may enjoy an advantage at one point in time may be at a disadvantage at another point in time. For example, if you are a grain grower in Iowa, you may be at a disadvantage compared to a grower in Illinois, nearer to the Chicago markets. But should a sudden short supply develop closer to Iowa —say in Nebraska or in the Far West—your proximity to those areas will make your grain cheaper than grain that must be shipped from Illinois or Missouri. Thus, today's disadvantages can turn into tomorrow's advantage as far as transportation costs are concerned.

The other component of a basis price is the difference between the nearby Chicago futures and the cash Chicago commodity. This difference is due to a number of factors: storage costs (including interest and insurance), handling costs (the expenses of loading and unloading), and sellers' profit margins. Let's say Chicago cash is 4 cents under Chicago futures. The total basis will be the sum of the differences—comprising the costs of transportation and storage, handling, etc.—or, in our example, 54 cents. Thus, if the local cash is $1.50 and transportation is 50 cents, Chicago cash will be $2.00. Add to this the cost of storage—4 cents—and you will have the nearby futures price: $2.04 a bushel.

Now, to go a step further, let's consider what happens when the market moves. Will the nearby futures, Chicago cash, and local cash move in concert with one another? Not necessarily. The three prices may move in similar directions, but not necessarily at the same rate. Depending on a multitude of market variables, the basis may widen or narrow in response to market forces.

Using our illustration above, we will begin with the following three corn prices:

Chicago nearby futures	$2.04
Chicago cash	$2.00
Local cash	$1.50

In this example, the basis is 54 cents under. If sudden demand enters the market, futures may rise to $2.10 and cash may rise to, say, $2.08. Now, instead of Chicago cash being 4 cents under, it is only 2 cents under. The basis has narrowed. If, in addition, the local cash price out in Kansas raises a corresponding 8 cents—to $1.58 a bushel—the Kansas-based farmer's basis narrows to 52 cents under from 54 cents under.

Conversely, a weakening in the demand for corn may cause the cash price in both Chicago and Kansas to fall at a faster rate than the futures, resulting in a widening of the basis. For example, if Chicago cash falls 10 cents while Chicago futures falls only 2 cents, the basis will widen from 54 cents under to 62 cents under. In this example, the respective prices will appear as follows:

	First Day	Second Day
Chicago nearby futures	$2.04	$2.02
Chicago cash	$2.00	$1.90
Local cash	$1.50	$1.40

Again, there are many possible variations. For instance, futures may stay the same while the cash prices fluctuate. Or the futures may fluctuate while the cash remains stationary. In addition, cash does not always follow futures. Nor, for that matter, does local cash follow Chicago cash. Higher transportation costs or a heightening or lowering of the demand for the cash commodity in that specific area of the country may account for fluctuations in the local cash price—and corresponding changes in the basis.

There is one predictable feature of the basis, and that is its tendency to narrow—by the amount of the reduced storage cost—as the delivery month is approached. This tendency of the basis to narrow over time as the delivery month is approached is known as *convergence*. For example, if storage costs are, say, 7 cents per month, you can expect the basis to narrow by this amount each month. If, therefore, on October 1, the local basis is 30 cents under with December futures at $2.30 and local cash at $2.00, expect the basis to narrow by 7 cents each month. Assuming all other factors remain the same and December futures stay at $2.30, the local cash should go to $2.07 by November 1 and to $2.14 by December 1. The 16-cent difference that still exists by December 1 will reflect transportation costs. The basis pattern for distant delivery months is similar to that for the nearby delivery month. That is, the basis tends to narrow—by the amount of the reduction in carrying costs—as the delivery month is approached. This tendency is illustrated in Figure 2.

Figure 2 illustrates an important principle: *On the day of delivery the nearby futures ceases to exist and becomes the cash commodity.* That is, for a Chicago commodity, the Chicago cash price will be identical to the expiring futures contract on the day of delivery. The prices for the cash commodity in, say, Atlanta or Dallas or Denver, of course, will all be different due to different transportation costs. Cash and futures must converge as the delivery date approaches, because the forces of the marketplace would direct them together were they to stay apart. For example, if the cash remained below the expiring futures, traders would simply short the futures (driving down prices), buy the cash commodity, and deliver the

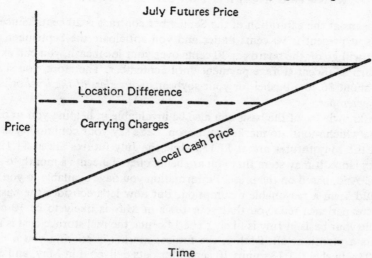

July Futures Price

Price

Location Difference

Carrying Charges

Local Cash Price

Time

Figure 2. The principle of convergence governs cash and futures prices.

cash against the futures and profit from the difference. Conversely, if cash were to be trading above futures near the expiration date, it would pay to buy the futures (driving up prices) and take delivery at the lower prices. In short, if the two prices are out of line, they won't remain so for long.

This tendency for cash and futures prices to converge as the delivery date approaches provides hedgers with what amounts to a payment for storage. As we indicated earlier, a change in the basis can result in additional profits to those that are earned as a result of simply having one's cash position hedged. This is a perfectly legitimate strategy, and one with which every hedger should be familiar.

The amount of the approximate payment for storage can be determined simply by comparing the current local cash price with the futures price minus the probable basis at the time of delivery. As you can see, to calculate this payment it is necessary for you to have some idea of what the basis will be at the delivery date. Fortunately, unlike general price levels, the basis tends to remain similar year after year. Thus, if you have four-dollar corn, the basis might be identical to the basis in a year when you have, say, two-dollar corn. Remember, the basis is the difference between the cash and the futures. It has nothing to do with price level.

Let's assume you are a soybean farmer who wants to hedge his crop still in the field. Since you are currently long cash soybeans, you want to lock in a price by putting on a selling hedge and giving delivery next September. If the local cash market is quoting $6.00 a bushel, and the September futures in Chicago is $6.90 a bushel, your present basis is 90 cents. Let's assume you know, from many years of experience, that the local basis for soybeans at the expiration of the September contract is 20 cents. Since the basis at present is 90 cents under and you anticipate the September contract will go off the boards at 20 cents over your local cash, you can expect to earn a 70-cent storage payment until September. Therefore, you should net about $6.70 a bushel for your soybeans *regardless of the level of prices in September.*

A knowledge of the basis can also be invaluable in helping you to determine which month to market your crop. Let's say your commodity is oats and the May futures are at $1.13, while the July futures are at $1.19. At first glance, it may seem that you are being offered 3 cents a month to store oats. And, based on the present information you have available to you, this would seem a reasonable assumption. But now let's consider the basis. If past experience tells you that your basis in May is likely to be 10 cents, while your basis in July is likely to be 14 cents, the real storage cost is not 3 cents a month at all. Rather, the futures market is offering you a net of $1.03 a bushel ($1.13 minus 10 cents) for oats delivered in May, and $1.05 a bushel ($1.19 minus 14 cents) for oats delivered in July. Chances are you would not want to store oats for a payment of only a penny a month.

As a hedger, you will find many opportunities in which you can speculate on a change in the basis. Since it involves so much less risk than a change in the *level* of commodity prices, a basis change offers one of the safest methods of participating in the futures markets. Unfortunately, this opportunity is available only to hedgers and not to speculators, who must assume much greater risks. To speculate on the basis, you must compare the present basis with the usual basis for a given time of year and attempt to make a prediction as to the direction in which the basis will move. For example, if you are a producer and are anticipating a selling hedge, look for a wide basis that is likely to narrow over time. The inevitable narrowing in the basis will mean extra dollars in the bank to you.

Likewise, as a commodity *buyer* who uses the futures market to hedge against *rising* prices, you can benefit from a knowledge of the basis. The buyer, unlike the seller, will want the basis to widen while he is hedged. For example, if you are a candy manufacturer who uses a great quantity of sugar in your manufacturing operations, you will want to put on buying hedges to protect yourself against a price rise. Let's say you have a need for sugar next May. You can take delivery now of cash sugar and store it at your own expense, or you could buy a May futures contract and expect to pay the built-in storage cost that is reflected in its selling price. To put on this hedge, first calculate today's basis for sugar and compare it with the usual basis next May. For example, May futures may be at 8.50 cents per pound, while cash sugar is at 8.43 cents per pound. Thus, the present basis is 0.07 cents per pound. If the usual basis is higher—let's say it is 0.18 cents per pound—you can expect the basis to widen over time. As a buyer of futures, you stand to earn a profit from placing your hedge when the basis is narrow and lifting the hedge when it widens. Your profit on the hedge will be equal to the difference in the two basis prices. In this example, if the basis widens, as expected, to 18 points, you will make an 11-point profit.

When to Lift a Hedge

A hedge can be lifted at *any* time simply by offsetting your position. The short hedger buys back the contract he previously sold; the long hedger sells the contract he previously bought. For example, let's assume that at the harvest you placed your grain in storage and simultaneously sold futures contracts to protect against a decline in price. But now you suspect that prices are about to rise and you don't want to lock out a potential profit on your grain. You can simply buy back those futures contracts you previously sold short and you are completely unhedged and capable of benefiting from any price rise. Since you are now unhedged, however, and still long the grain you have in storage, you are also vulnerable to a price decline if your market judgment proves wrong.

Another opportunity to lift a hedge might be provided by an unexpected favorable movement in the basis. For example, you are short-hedged and the basis narrows earlier than you had anticipated. You now have a profit on the change in basis and wish to take that profit before it moves against you. Lifting the hedge and selling your crop sooner than planned, to take advantage of the narrow basis, could result in a higher price for your crop and a savings of storage costs. What might be a clue that it is time to take such action? Any sudden and unexpected movement in the basis, such as a significant increase in the local cash price relative to futures, or a larger decline in the futures price than in the local cash price. In either instance, the basis will narrow, resulting in an opportunity for you to lift your hedge and sell your cash commodity. There is no rule that you have to hold your hedge into the delivery month—unless, of course, you plan to deliver your cash commodity against the futures contract and therefore wish to hold it until maturity.

What should you do if the basis is unfavorable—and the hedge doesn't develop according to plan? One alternative to consider is moving the hedge forward into another delivery month in the hope it can eventually be lifted at a higher net price. This can be accomplished by simply buying the existing contract and simultaneously selling a more distant contract. This practice is known as *switching*. A short hedger might, for instance, buy in January and simultaneously sell March.

Keeping Track of Basis Information

Since basis is such a key determinant in whether you put on a hedge, lift a hedge, select one delivery month over another, or hedge at all, it pays to keep records of basis changes. Some hedgers keep track of the basis every trading day. Others prefer to track the basis weekly. If you use the latter method, select one day of the week and use settlement prices on the futures. To calculate the basis, you subtract futures from cash and arrive at a positive or negative figure. Always use the nearby month until the delivery month arrives. Then switch into the new nearby month. It is best to track the basis for those months when you normally market your crop. Thus, if you are involved in marketing year round, keep basis records for the entire year; if you market only between January and April, track those months. A hypothetical set of records might appear as follows:

Commodity: Lumber

DATE	LOCAL CASH PRICE	MARCH FUTURES	BASIS
Jan. 2	221.40	231.90	−10.50
Jan. 9	231.40	241.10	− 9.70
Jan. 16	233.10	242.30	− 9.20
Jan. 23	241.90	253.40	−11.50
Jan. 30	246.30	258.90	−12.60
Feb. 6	243.50	257.10	−13.60
Feb. 13	239.50	251.70	−12.20
Feb. 20	240.50	250.50	−10.00
Feb. 27	252.60	262.80	−10.20

Local cash prices can normally be obtained from a local elevator operator, newspaper, or radio broadcast. Futures prices are readily available from commodity brokers and *The Wall Street Journal* and other major newspapers as well as many local newspapers. To construct a history of prices, you may have to do some back-checking; your commodity broker, a local elevator operator, major newspapers, or a commodity data bank can provide the kind of information that will be necessary to establish basis records for your area.

Many hedgers also keep basis charts to graphically portray the relationship of cash to futures prices on the same chart. The difference between them is the basis. This method has the advantage of actually showing the dollars-and-cents value of the cash and futures as well as the basis. A sample basis chart is shown in Figure 3 below:

Hedging a Currency Transaction

Every commodity traded on a futures exchange has hedging possibilities. But unless you are involved in the cash commodity, in one form or another, the opportunities to hedge are strictly limited. All of us, however, use money, and many of us frequently buy and sell things that can be purchased with foreign currencies. As a result, we can be vulnerable to currency fluctuations. If you own, for instance, an asset in a foreign coun-

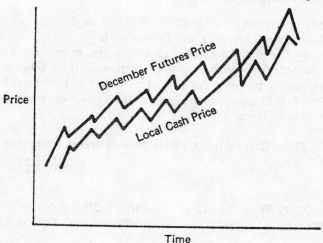

Figure 3. The basis chart.

try that you paid for in a foreign currency, that asset may become more or less valuable, according to currency fluctuations, while you own it. Not long ago, many Americans, encouraged by the high interest rates available in Mexico, put their money into Mexican pesos. A sharp devaluation in the peso, however, not only wiped out whatever high interest was being paid on those accounts, but contributed to a loss of much of the principal because the devaluation was so steep. This need not have happened—if the owners of those pesos knew how to hedge their currency holdings.

Hedging a currency is the same as hedging any physical commodity. To become fully hedged, you must take a position in the futures market opposite your position in the cash market. Let's consider an example of an American citizen who purchases a house in Switzerland. Let's assume the American signs a contract on March 1 saying he will purchase the house for 250,000 Swiss francs payable on December 1. He knows the balance due on the house the following December, but not the cost of money at that time—that is, what the exchange rate will be nine months from the day he signs the contract. To protect himself against a rise in the value of the Swiss franc, therefore, the American home buyer can place a long currency hedge. Being short the desired commodity (Swiss francs), the American hedges his vulnerable position by buying currency futures.

Why should the American take such protective action? Simply to try to guard against an unforeseen rise in the price of the commodity he intends to purchase: Swiss francs. His intention, as every hedger's, is to shift the risk of being short a commodity (Swiss francs) from himself to someone else. Of course, by hedging his currency transaction, he gives up something: the opportunity to profit from a windfall profit if the price of Swiss francs falls between March 1 and December 1.

Assuming the price of Swiss francs does rise during the nine-month period, the hedge can provide good protection. In the following example, the Swiss franc is quoted in dollars and cents carried to the one-hundredth place. Thus 0.4113 quoted as the value of the Swiss franc means each franc is worth 41¹³/₁₀₀ cents.

The Currency Hedge—Swiss Francs

CASH	FUTURES
March 1:	
Short 250,000 SF at 0.4113 = $102,825	Buys 2 SF December futures contracts at 0.4223 = $105,575
December 1:	
Buys 250,000 SF at 0.5559 = $138,975	Sells 2 SF December futures contracts at 0.5623 = $140,575
loss: $36,150	*gain:* $35,000

NET RESULT: −$1,150

In this example the sharp rise in the price of Swiss francs would have resulted in an added $36,150 expense to the purchaser of the house, due to fluctuations in the currency exchange rates. Since the cash market rose a little faster than the futures market, the loss in the cash market wasn't entirely offset by the rise in futures. However, most of the loss was offset, and the hedger preserved the purchasing power of his investment in a highly inflationary period.

In summary, the steps to take in placing a currency hedge are similar to any buying hedge. First, purchase a futures contract that will cover the exposure in the cash market. As with any commodity futures contract, this will require the posting of margin and the payment of normal round-turn commissions. Second, when you must purchase your foreign currency in the cash market, close out your futures position. The gain or loss experienced in the futures market will be offset by the currency's movement in the cash market.

The Interest-rate Market Hedge

The introduction of interest-rate futures trading in recent years has been met with enthusiasm by speculators and hedgers alike. The speculators have been drawn to the markets by the tremendous leverage—as little as $1,500 can control a Treasury bill with a one-million-dollar face value—and banks, portfolio managers, and corporations are finding the markets highly suitable for protection against fluctuations in interest rates. The speculator or hedger in the interest-rate futures market behaves like any other commodity trader—with one exception. Rather than be a buyer in anticipation of higher prices, the trader who is bullish on mortgage interest rates would sell short the futures, while the bearish interest trader would purchase futures contracts. This is the exact opposite of normal commodity futures market practice. The reason for this is that interest rates move in a direction opposite to the value of the underlying certificates. Like the prices of corporate bonds and Treasury bills, the price of Ginnie Mae futures contracts declines as interest rates rise—and vice versa. A trader who is bearish on interest rates, therefore, will buy Ginnie Mae futures and make his profit as the price of the contract rises.

For hedging purposes, the interest-rate futures markets are particularly valuable to savings-and-loan associations, small banks, and members of the seasonal construction industry. Because interests on home mortgages have fluctuated considerably in recent years, lenders and borrowers alike have been exposed to substantial risks in conducting their normal business. Huge sums of money are involved in the home-building industry. And the variation in interest rates can spell the difference between profit and loss for builders and developers (borrowers) and banks, savings-and-loan institutions, and other mortgage investors (lenders). By transferring the money-market risks to speculators through hedging on the futures markets, borrowers and lenders can calculate the known cost of money on their operating margins.

As with any hedge, there are parties, depending upon their market exposure, on both sides of the transaction. A financial manager, for instance, who anticipates having funds to lend or invest in the short-term money markets at some known time in the future would want to hedge against falling interest rates. Unhedged, his risk would be that the rates may drop by the time such funds are available. To protect himself, therefore, the financial manager will go long interest-rate futures. Then, if rates go down between the purchase date and the delivery date, the contract will appreciate in value.

Conversely, borrowers in the money markets would use interest-rate futures to protect themselves against increases in short-term rates with a "short" or "sell" hedge. The short hedge in the futures market is used to offset increased borrowing costs. The financial manager simply sells an interest-rate contract for futures delivery. If the interest rates rise between the contract sale date and its delivery date, the value of the futures contract will drop and the hedger can make a gain by buying back, for a lower price, the contract he sold previously at a higher price. With the gain from his futures contract, the borrower is thus able to offset the increase in his cash borrowing cost.

Before you begin a hedging program involving interest-rate futures, it is important that you explore a number of questions. These questions concern the size, length, and duration of the market exposure and one's estimate of the direction money markets will take in the next six months to a year. At best, these may be reasoned guesses, but you should try to answer them before committing yourself in the market. The most important questions are as follows:

1. What is the organization's exposure?
2. Are there seasonal or cyclical factors in a company's interest-rate exposure?
3. What is the company's hedgeable base?
4. How much risk should be taken?
5. What is the firm's basis?
6. What is the outlook for short-term interest rates?

There are many potential users of the interest-rate futures market—from import/export companies to corporate treasurers and finance companies. Because the movement of interest rates is more or less parallel for a variety of money-market instruments such as certificates of deposit, prime commercial paper, bankers' acceptances notes, and federal funds, the would-be hedger who participates in any of these money-market instruments has a visible hedging instrument in the Treasury bill.

Let's look at an example of a hedger who might use the interest-rate futures market to offset his exposed risk. A money-fund manager might make a commitment on March 1 to provide $1 million in funds to a mortgage pool on December 1. Since he commits the funds at the current rate of interest, his risk is that the market price might fall between now and December 1. To offset this risk, he will enter the futures market and sell ten Ginnie Mae contracts (each contract has a face value of $100,000). Assuming a fall in the market price, and a corresponding rise in interest rates, the transactions would appear as follows:

The Interest-Rate Hedge—Ginnie Maes

CASH	FUTURES
March 1:	
Makes commitment for $1 million mortgage pool, based on current Ginnie Maes' cash price of 99–24 (current yield 7.989%)	Sells 10 December Ginnie Mae contracts at prevailing market price of 99–00 (current yield 8.092%)
December 1:	
Sells $1 million of Ginnie Maes to investors at market price of 92–24 (current yield 8.992%)	Buys back 10 December Ginnie Mae contracts at prevailing market price of 92–00 (current yield of 9.105%)
loss: $70,000	*gain:* $70,000

NET RESULT: $0.00

To fully understand these calculations, it is necessary to know that Ginnie Maes are quoted in thirty-seconds. Thus, 99–24 means 99²⁴/32. A 1/32 move in the market represents $31.25, the minimum fluctuation. A full point, or 32/32, therefore, is equal to $1,000 per contract ($31.25 × 32 = $1,000). Since the market moved from 99–00 to 92–00, the move represented $7,000 per contract, or $70,000 for ten contracts. As a result of placing the hedge, the money manager saved his firm a potential loss of $70,000, which would have been sustained in the cash market had the offsetting hedge not been placed.

Hedging Rules

We know that hedging is a means of offsetting risks that occur as a normal process of doing business in the cash markets. Whether your commodity is hogs or commercial notes, you will have a need to protect yourself from these day-to-day business risks associated with either holding commodities or being short commodities for futures delivery. In an uncertain economic world, therefore, the futures market provides the businessman with a degree of certainty he could not readily find elsewhere. It is this economic function which is so valuable. Unsophisticated in the role of hedging, a number of businesses and corporations lose thousands, tens of thousands, and even millions annually.

Hedging, like speculating in the volatile futures market, is an art that requires experience and sound knowledge of the important variables involved. Although the principle of hedging—which is to take the position in futures opposite to your position in the cash market—is simple, applying this principle in practice can be difficult. For this reason, the hedger must know his commodity, his exposure, his basis, and the dynamics of the market in which he operates. Having the correct information is a necessary first step to a successful hedge; knowing how to apply it is a second. The following rules should help you to become a better hedger.

RULE NUMBER 1. *Always keep track of your local basis.* You can track the basis daily or weekly by keeping the price information in a notebook, as explained earlier in the chapter, or by keeping basis charts.

While a change in basis can be crucial to your overall hedging strategy, the basis is normally much more predictable than the level of prices. For this reason, you should not avoid placing a hedge simply because you don't have adequate basis information. Assuming you have a legitimate hedging situation in your commodity, you are much better off hedging than not hedging, regardless of your knowledge of the basis.

The basis is affected by a number of factors, including the size of the crop and the availability of storage space. In years of large crops and short storages, the basis is likely to be wider—particularly during the harvest months—than during years of small crops and ample storage.

A knowledge of your basis can help you "localize" a given futures price.

That is, it can tell you the price the futures market is offering you for your commodity delivered in your local area. This price will be the futures prices *minus the basis*. For example, if during April the futures market is offering you 43.00 cents per pound for June cattle, you may want to translate this into a local price two months hence. If you know that the normal basis in your area during June is about 0.70 cents, you can quickly calculate that the futures market is offering you approximately 42.30 cents per pound for your cattle to be delivered locally in June.

Most importantly, the basis can tell you when to buy and sell a commodity. The basis is a key marketing device that can be of value to every hedger.

RULE NUMBER 2. *Never attempt to hedge by taking the same side in futures that you already have in cash.* By definition, a hedge involves taking a position in futures *opposite* the one you have in cash. But sometimes a hedger will want to speculate on a price rise in his commodity by taking a long position on the same commodity he holds in cash. This is known as a "Texas hedge." It is named after Texas ranchers who, already owning cattle on their ranches, purchased cattle futures in anticipation of a price rise. This practice is fine *if* the market rises. But it isn't hedging. If the market moves against you when you are on the same side in both cash and futures, you lose on both accounts. Few successful businesses can be operated on this principle. Hedgers shouldn't try to speculate on the price level of their commodity. The purpose of the futures market is to transfer the risk from hedger to speculator. For the hedger, assuming more risk than is already inherent in the producing and processing of volatile commodities amounts to inviting trouble.

RULE NUMBER 3. *Discuss your hedging strategy with your commodity broker and your banker.* A knowledgeable commodity broker can provide you with vital information concerning effective hedging strategy. He has access to basis charts, a multitude of cash price information around the country, wire service reports, reports from the floor of various commodity exchanges, a research department, and much more. Unfortunately, many brokers are not oriented to hedgers and their needs, so you may have to look for a while before you find someone with sufficient expertise to advise you. Brokers in the Midwest, who work closely with the trade, are apt to be more knowledgeable about hedging practices. The banking community is also more sophisticated about hedging in the Midwest, and chances are your banker will insist that you hedge your crop. Outside the Midwest, however, bankers are not as familiar with the benefits of hedging, and you may have to impress it upon your banker that your hedging is a benefit to *him*. As a rule, in circles where the strategy is understood, creditors are 100 percent behind hedging, because it means *their* investments are safer.

RULE NUMBER 4. *If you have an active marketing program, use a perpetual hedge.* A perpetual hedge is one which is continuous over time. Thus, instead of placing all your short futures positions in one month, spread your sales "across the board." You can then begin a program of switching. You can continue to switch as long as you are able to replace a nearby short contract with a more distant short sale. By staggering your hedges, you limit the possible adverse effects of an unusual market situation existing in the future.

RULE NUMBER 5. *Always try to hedge your full exposure.* If you are holding 50,000 bushels of soybeans, don't settle for hedging 10,000 bushels with the hope of waiting around to see what the market does with your other 40,000 bushels. A hedging program is either sound or unsound. A decline in the price of soybeans, in this instance, will not be adequately offset by a partial hedge. Some hedgers fail to measure their risk before contemplating a hedge. This is a mistake. Know your risk, select a price you will settle for in the market, and hedge accordingly. This is the path to sound business profits. A few years ago, a number of cattle producers had an adequate price in the futures market, but they refused to hedge, because they felt the market was headed higher. It wasn't. They ended up unloading their cattle at a loss. Be sensible and settle for a reasonable business profit in your hedging operations.

5

How to Use Market Orders

Most novice traders think that you simply call your broker when you want to purchase or sell a commodity, wait around for a few days, weeks, or months for the market to move in a favorable direction, and call the broker again when it is time to liquidate. But, as with so many popular impressions, nothing could be less true. Timing is absolutely vital when you enter or exit a market. And good timing means entering and exiting trades with pinpoint accuracy. To simply jump aboard a commodity because you anticipate a price move is often reckless and costly. Markets do have certain behavioral patterns, and the trader who wishes to maximize his profits will attempt to trade with these patterns and not tempt fate by going against them. One way to achieve success in commodity trading is to have a sound knowledge of market orders. By using orders effectively, you can fine-tune your trading activities and minimize many of the costly errors that traders make daily.

To gain perspective on the problem of placing orders, let's look at a typical trader who uses the most common type of order, known as a *market order*. A market order is an order to buy or sell without regard to a specific price. When you buy or sell at the market, therefore, you are willing to take whatever price you can to get in or out of the market. For example, you instruct your broker to buy one contract of September lumber at the market. He, in turn, relays this message to the floor of the Chicago Mercantile Exchange, and you are soon long one lumber contract. But the problem with market orders rests with *where* you get filled. More often than not, market orders for purchase are filled near the highs of the day, while market orders for sales are filled near the lows. Why is this? There may be a variety of reasons. A number of buy orders, each of them contributing to higher prices, may precede your order to buy. Floor traders, mindful of bullish sentiment, may be buying earlier in the trading session, and selling their contracts to you on a modest run-up in prices. If you buy early in the day, near the opening, you may be a victim of the morning "bulge," when bullish traders are most apt to bid up prices on the opening. Regardless of the reason, a market order, which must be executed at the best possible price at the time the order reaches the exchange floor, can result in higher purchase prices and lower sale prices. To avoid all this, you may wish to use a variety of other orders which specify when, how, and at what price a commodity is to be bought or sold.

Types of Orders

A commodity broker can take almost any order that the floor can be made to understand. One popular order is known as a *stop-loss order*. The purpose of the stop-loss is, as the words suggest, to limit losses. Stops are particularly useful in trend trading when a speculator places the stop away from the market in hopes that it will not be hit. The purpose of the stop-loss order is to limit losses to a predetermined amount. Once "hit," of course, a stop-loss order becomes a market order, and the trader is taken out of the market at the prevailing price. According to Chicago Board of Trade Rule 40, the definition of a stop-loss order, or stop order, is as follows:

> An order to buy or sell when the market reaches a specified point. A stop order to buy becomes a market order when the commodity sells (or is bid) at or above the stop prices. A stop order to sell becomes a market order when the commodity sells (or is offered) at or below the stop price.

For purposes of illustration, let's assume you are long September corn at $2.42 per bushel. You think prices will rise, but if they don't you want to be out of the market at a small loss. So you place a stop-loss order with your broker to *sell* one contract of September corn at, say, $2.38—4 cents below the market. Should the market then reverse and trade at $2.38, your stop-loss order will automatically become a market order, and you will be out of the market. This does not, of course, guarantee you the price of $2.38. Rather, that is the price at which the market order will be triggered. Should prices rally after hitting $2.38, you may be out at a smaller loss

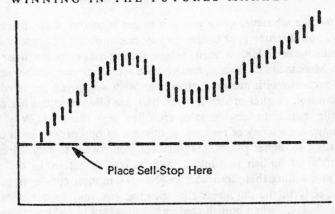

Figure 4.   The sell-stop order is placed below the prevailing market price.

than 4 cents; should prices continue to move sharply downward, you may sustain a bigger loss. Since prices are volatile, no one price can be guaranteed.

Unlike buyers, short sellers will place their stop-loss orders *above* the

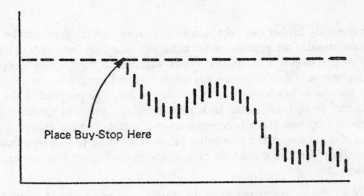

Figure 5.   The buy-stop order is placed above the prevailing market price.

prevailing market price. Had the same corn trader who had bought at $2.42 sold short instead at that price, he might have put the stop-loss at, say, $2.46—4 cents above the market. Being short, his stop-loss order would be to *buy* or liquidate his short position at $2.46. Thus, traders who are long will place their stops *below* the market, and traders who are short will place their stops *above* the market. The stop-loss order used by the purchaser of a commodity is known as a *stop-sell* or *sell-stop*. Conversely, the stop-loss order used by the short seller is known as a *stop-buy* or *buy-stop*. Figures 4 and 5 illustrate the placing of the sell-stop and buy-stop, respectively.

When you place a stop-loss order, you must decide how far away from the prevailing market price to set the stop. Your dilemma is that a stop placed too close to the market will almost certainly be hit, resulting in a number of small losses; on the other hand, a stop placed too far away from the market will only occasionally be hit, but the losses will be much greater. You have to work out your own compromise based on the number and kind of losses you are willing to sustain.

Some traders place their stops according to how much money they are willing to lose on a given position. For example, if you are a lumber trader and you are willing to give up, say, $130 exclusive of commissions, you would place your stop 100 points away from the market.

Others place stops according to daily limits. As a rule, one and a half daily limits is considered a good place for a stop-loss below a long position, and two daily limits is considered a good place for a stop-loss above a short position. The live-cattle trader, therefore, would be willing to give up 225 points (150 points is the daily limit), or $900, on a long position, and 300 points, or $1,200, on a short position. The reason for this difference is that markets tend to be more volatile at tops, where short selling is desirable, than at bottoms, where one is more likely to be a buyer. To compensate for this difference in volatility, it is necessary to risk a little more at a market top than at a market bottom.

There are a number of developments that may make you want to move your stops closer to the market. For instance, a lessening in volatility would be one. You also might want to move your stops closer if you can identify what are known as *support* and *resistance* zones, which are fully explained in Chapter 8.

Professional traders and those close to the market often keep what are known as *mental stops.* These stops exist only in their heads and are not written down. The reason why some traders shy away from placing stop-loss orders is that many floor traders have a tendency to "gun" for stops. That is, they estimate that many stop-loss orders exist just below the market, and they try to run the market down to "take out" or activate the stops, and then run the price back up again. In the markets that are quite volatile, like the pork belly market, the price might be bid "limit-up" or offered "limit-down" several times during the day. For traders with *close stops,* those resting near the market, some commodities are virtually impossible to trade successfully. However, if you do decide to rely on a system of mental stops to trade the market, you must have iron discipline. If you refuse to take your losses when they are small, they will surely grow larger, to your subsequent regret.

Stop orders have three general purposes. They are as follows:

1. *To limit losses when the market moves against your established position.* You use a buy-stop above the market when you are short, and a sell-stop below the market when you are long. Should your stop be hit, the stop order will immediately become a market order and your position will automatically be liquidated at a small, and predetermined, loss. To prevent small losses from becoming large losses, it is absolutely necessary to take losses quickly when they develop. A stop-loss order can help you do this.

2. *To protect profits on a previously established position.* Once you earn profits in the market, stops can help you keep them. You simply move your stops along with the trend in prices, always keeping the stop an established number of points away from the market. This is known as placing a *trailing stop.* For instance, you are short July pork bellies at 55 cents with a protective stop at 56½ cents—1½ cents above the market. Prices then move downward in your favor to, say, 54 cents. So you move the stop to 55½ cents. Next, the market moves down another cent to 53 cents, and you lower the stop to 54½ cents. When the market reaches 50 cents, your stop will be at 51½. The market may then rally and touch off your stop at 51½ cents, and that will be the price at which you liquidate your position. Thus, the stop will help you stay with the market as long as it is trading in your direction. As you can see, this encourages you to let your profits ride, while quickly minimizing losses.

3. *To initiate new positions.* A buy-stop or sell-stop need not to be a stop-loss order. Traders use stops to initiate positions when the market hits certain levels. For instance, a chart trader might spot a potential "breakout" point on his charts and place a buy-stop when the market reaches the breakout level. In this fashion, the stop serves to get a trader into a market once a trend has been confirmed.

A complex variation of the limit order is known as the *combination order.* A combination order, as the name implies, combines two limit orders, with the cancellation of one contingent upon the execution of the other. For example, "Sell May soybeans at $2.27 open stop or sell May soybeans at $2.31 O.C.O." is a typical combination order. Translated, this order means: sell one contract of May soybeans at $2.27, with the provision that the order is to be kept open indefinitely until filled or canceled with a stop-loss provision. Alternatively, if the price $2.31 is reached first, the May soybeans should be sold at that level. The letters "O.C.O." signify that the filling of one order cancels the other. Typically, such a combination order will be used when the market is in a trading range and chances are the market may go one way or another before finally asserting itself. In either instance, the trader wishes to get aboard the move either at the higher, more advantageous level, or, barring that, when it breaks out to the down side, at the lower price. Chartists and other technicians use combination orders to guarantee their participation in the markets at price levels they deem vital.

Another limit order popular with traders who follow charts is known as the *fill or kill order.* This is an order that must be filled immediately or canceled. A trader using such an order might bid a price just under the market in hopes of getting the price he wants. Unfilled at this price, however, the same trader prefers to stand aside and await another opportunity. Timing is everything in the futures markets, and traders who use fill or kill orders recognize this. If they can't get the price they want at the time they want it, they prefer to wait for another opportunity.

When you trade spreads, you will also probably want to use limit orders —with one important difference. In a spread, you aren't so much concerned with the price levels of the two commodities you are spreading as with the relationship between them. As a result, you may instruct your broker to buy March oats and sell September oats, March eight cents under. This will indicate the spread you want between them but not their price levels. If the order comes back filled with March at 153 and September at 161, or March at 159 and September at 167, you will be equally satisfied because the spread difference in both instances is identical.

When you want to limit the broker to a given price or better (lower in the case of a buy order, higher in the case of a sell order), you should use a *limit only stop order.* This prevents a limit order from becoming a market order, as is the case with many stops. When you use this order, however, you must weigh the relative benefits of prompt execution within the current market price range against holding the broker to execution at a limit price. Because you are insisting on a specific price, you are much more likely to miss the market when you use a limit-only stop order. In addition, you may qualify your order further by indicating the time of day when you want the order executed. Many traders prefer to do their buying or selling "at the open" or "at the close." Such transactions need not be the first or last of the session but must be within the opening and closing range of transactions as defined by the rules and regulations of the exchange. Brokerage houses accept such orders on the condition that they will do their best to fulfill the terms of the order, but they will not be held liable for failure to do so. When you use a highly specialized order, and the order is not filled, you have little recourse except to chase the market by putting in a market order (meaning you will take any price you can get), or simply put in another limit-only stop and hope for the best. The fact that a market trades at the price you desire, moreover, is no guarantee that you will be filled. You probably aren't the only trader with an order in at a given price, and there may well be hundreds before you at the same price.

Where should you place your limit orders? As a rule, you should try to avoid round numbers whenever possible. For example, if you want, say, a price of 538.00 on a contract of silver, put in your order just a little higher or lower—at, say, 538.10 or 537.90. This will give you an edge on other traders who are apt to use the round number. If you trade grains, tack on a quarter to your price. If you want wheat at 294, put in your order for 294¼. This is especially important where stop-loss orders are concerned, because it means if your stop is just a little above or below the crowd when the floor trade comes "gunning" for the stops, you will be missed. You

don't have to trade commodities long before you will recognize the uncanny ability of most markets to sweep down and take out your stops—
and your money—and reverse right back up to the level where you previously purchased. The reverse, of course, is true when you have a short
position. Using such a defensive strategy with your stops can go a long
way toward earning you profits over the long run.

The Intraday Trailing Stop Order

The intraday trailing stop order is a method of entering the market that
helps you to achieve the following:

1. Obtain the best entry price for a new position
2. Take a position only when the market is moving in your direction
3. Use the closest possible protective stop

It can be used either to buy or to sell, but it *is not* an exchange order.
This means your broker must execute it by watching the market. He cannot give the order to the floor. It requires that he or you monitor the price
range of the commodity you want to buy or sell at frequent intervals
during the day. The rules to buy and sell are as follows:

1. To purchase a commodity: buy on stop on a rally (rising prices) at X
number of points above the intraday low. (The intraday low is defined as
the lowest price encountered so far in the trading day, starting with the
prior day's close.)
2. To sell a commodity: sell on stop on a reaction (falling prices) at X
number of points below the intraday high. (The intraday high is defined as
the highest price encountered so far in the trading day, starting with the
prior day's close.)

In using these rules, it is important to move the stop in accordance with
the movement of the market. For example, if the market moves lower to a
new intraday low, lower your buy-stop; if the market moves higher, to a
new intraday high, raise your sell-stop.

Let's assume you want to be a short seller using Rule 2. First, you must
decide how many points off the intraday high you will be a seller. Let's say
you want the market to move 3 cents down before you feel a trend has
been established. Without this move, you suspect the market is still in a
trading range and you aren't interested in entering at a price that doesn't
exhibit signs of weakness. Next, you have to watch the market to establish
the intraday high. Let's say the market opens at $2.33 and rises a penny to
$2.34 by 10 A.M. This is now your intraday high. As long as prices don't
go above this point, you will know to place your sell-stop at $2.31—3 cents
below the intraday high. If, however, by 11 A.M. the market has again
risen to, say, $2.35, a penny higher, you must now revise your sell-stop
upward by one penny—to $2.32. And so on. The point is that the sell-stop

is flexible. If a market gains momentum off the intraday high, the short seller will very likely end the day at a profit. And the same is true for the buyer who uses Rule 1 to purchase a commodity. Traders who have used the intraday trailing stop order to enter a market have had good results with the method. It does take a little work on the part of the person entering the order, but it is worth it in good fills. Moreover, it is especially valuable on the occasions when you don't get filled as well. Consider the market above if prices had *failed* to fall. A short seller on the open might have ended the day with prices limit up against him. With the intraday trailing stop order, it would be impossible to sell short in a market that didn't react X points off the high of the day.

Another advantage of this method is that it enables you to use close protective stops. Because the trend is moving in a direction favorable to you at the time you initiate your position, your stops can be placed only a few points above or below the market. For example, if cattle rallies to 47.60 or higher, you might place an order to sell-on-stop 50 points below the intraday high, and protect with a buy-stop 75 points above the entry point. In this instance, you are using two stop orders—one to initiate the position, and one as a protective stop in case the market doesn't go your way. If 47.60 is the intraday high when the market falls 50 points to 47.10, you will be short one cattle contract. At the same time, you will enter an order to liquidate or buy back your short position at 47.85 in case the market goes against you. Again, the important point is that the order is not executed until the market has turned and gained some momentum in your direction. This momentum at the outset of the trade can clearly spell the difference between success and failure. Figures 6 and 7 illustrate the use of the intraday trailing stop order.

In Figure 6, the market declined on the open, establishing an intraday low. This enabled the trader to place his first buy-stop. But after a modest rally, the market again declined, making a second intraday low. Because this second low had broken the previous low, the buy-stop was also lowered. The market soon after rose, and the second buy-stop was triggered and a long position assumed. Had the market risen but failed to trigger the second buy-stop, a third buy-stop would have been indicated *if another intraday low had been established*. Always take the lowest price of the day and place the stop X points away from it.

In Figure 7, the market rose on the open, establishing an intraday high. A sell-stop was then created, while the broker or trader continued to monitor the market. But later in the trading a second intraday high was established, and the sell-stop lifted. This second stop was then triggered as prices fell, and the trader was short in the market.

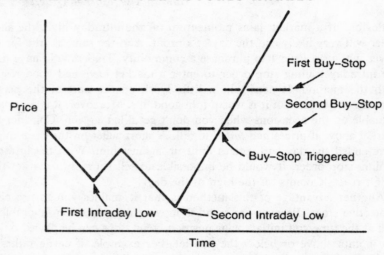

Figure 6.   Use a buy-stop to purchase a commodity on a rally from the intraday low.

Fading the Violation of the Intraday High and Low

One very effective rule for entering the market is to fade the violation of the intraday high or low. A trader who "fades" a market goes the opposite way; thus, a trader who fades a break in a market will buy it, and the trader who fades a rally sells. Before we go farther, however, we have to define our terms. What constitutes the intraday high or low? Our arbitrary definition is the *high or low after one hour of trading.* Although this is clearly arbitrary, it does seem to work in a number of markets, especially those which are highly volatile and unpredictable, such as the stock index markets.

To utilize this rule, you wait for one hour of trading to occur. Then you take note of the intraday high and low. For example, let's say the September Standard & Poor's 500 has an intraday high of 187.90 and an intraday low of 187.55 after one hour of trading. The rule: you wait for either the high or the low to be violated, and you either a) *sell if the high is violated first,* or b) *buy if the low is violated first.* You don't necessarily buy or sell immediately upon the violation of the intraday high or low. Rather, it is preferable to wait for some predetermined—or, ideally, flexible—penetration. Let's say you are looking for a penetration of .35 points. In the illustration above, you would be *buying* at 187.20—*if* the intraday low is violated first.

It might help to understand why this seemingly perverse strategy works so well. After all, most traders will be selling as the market breaks. It only makes sense. At first, the sell-stops will be triggered, driving down prices.

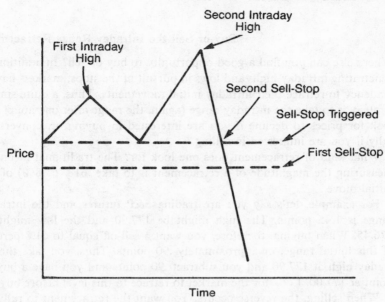

Figure 7.   *Use a sell-stop to sell a commodity on a reaction from the intraday high.*

Then, once the trend becomes "known" and lower prices appear to be a "sure-thing," a number of short sellers will jump on the bandwagon. Unfortunately for them, however, they will often be too late. The break in the market, in reality, is nothing more than a running of the stops. Typically, when the stops are hit, a flurry of sell orders will hit the pit, driving prices down. But the move is only temporary. Often, in time, the selling will dry up and the real buying will begin.

The same thing occurs at the top, of course. The intraday high is established, and then the market is taken higher. This serves to panic the nervous short sellers, who, as a group, become buyers and bid up the market. They usually have little trouble finding sellers, however. This is another illustration of the running of the stops: what has been called "market engineering." Because mob psychology is such a predictable thing, this is easy money for the floor and other knowledgeable traders who engage in the practice of so-called *highballing* and *lowballing* the market—bidding it higher or offering it lower—in hopes of triggering the stops. To make money using this strategy, you simply join the professionals and "fade" the move.

Buy or Sell the Intraday Range Retracement

Where else can you find a good opportunity to buy or sell? In addition to penetrating intraday highs and lows in pursuit of the stops, markets have a tendency to retrace their intraday initial movements. Thus, a quite simple strategy is to take the intraday range (again, the range after one hour) and look for prices to decline if you are interested in buying or, conversely, rally if you are interested in selling.

What kind of retracement does one look for? The traditional means of measuring the magnitude of a retracement is to take .618 (61.8%) of the initial move.

For example, let's say you are trading S&P futures and the intraday range is 1.45 points. The high might be 177.90 and the low might be 176.45. When buying, therefore, you want a sell-off equal to 61.8 percent of this initial range, or approximately .90 points. Thus, you take the intraday high at 177.90 and you subtract .90 points and you have a buying point at 177.00. Look for the market to retrace to this level before buying.

When selling, the reverse occurs. You want the retracement to rally by .90 points before putting on the short sale. Thus, if, as in our example, the intraday low is 176.45, you want to add .90 points and begin selling at 177.35. You'd be surprised how often the market will trade to precisely the .618 retracement point before reversing and going the other way.

Here again, there is a reason why this rule works. Buying and selling tends to get overdone during the day, and the inevitable pullbacks occur. For instance, take a case where the stops are run and the market breaks. Panic selling drives the market lower. For the lucky short sellers who sold at the top, however, the profits can only be realized if they turn around and buy. The buying causes the market to rally and even feeds on itself as buyers have to bid up prices in order to find a seller. In time, this buying dries up and the market is free to fall. For this reason, you should try to avoid joining in the panic once it occurs—that is, unless you are fading the move. Instead, in the example above, patiently wait for the retracement rally to begin, and then sell. The same, of course, is true when you want to buy and the market is bid up on you. Wait for the pullback.

This retracement rule can also be used to tell when you are on the wrong side of the market. Let's take a case where you are selling the retracement rally. The idea is to sell as close to the last top as possible. So if the retracement occurs and you sell, you want prices to move lower. When they don't move lower—that is, when the retracement no longer seems like a retracement but instead like a genuine rally—you have to admit defeat quickly and exit the market (albeit with a loss). You can't hesitate when this strategy fails. More than likely, the market is staging a rally and you must run as quickly as possible.

Market Order Rules

We have discussed some of the possible uses of market orders in establishing and exiting a position. The following rules should help you to avoid the common pitfalls of many traders who don't understand the value of using the right orders when trading the market.

RULE NUMBER 1. *Limit the losses on every position you take by placing appropriate stop-loss orders.* In following this rule, you will place two orders every time you enter a trade—one to initiate the trade, and one as a protective stop. In this manner, your potential loss will be strictly limited, within a certain trading range, and your profits will be free to increase if the market moves in your direction. Some traders also enter a third order when they trade, an order to exit the market at a specified profit. In many circumstances, this is a good practice. But in a runaway bull or bear market, it could limit profits.

There are two basic kinds of stop order—*regular stop orders* and *stop limit orders.* The regular stop order becomes a market order when a particular price above or below the market is reached. The stop limit order is a two-price order, with the first price (essentially an ordinary stop order) actuating the order, and the second limiting the fill price to a specified amount. For example, a buy stop 692 limit 693 for soybeans means the order cannot be actuated until the prices trade up to 692 and cannot be filled above 693.

RULE NUMBER 2. *Use limit orders whenever possible.* Limit orders are better than market orders—except when you absolutely must get in or out of a market at any cost—because they let you decide the exact point where you will enter or exit the market. Often, if you miss a market because an order cannot be filled at the limit you specify, you are better off not chasing it with a market order. Opportunities abound in the futures market, and you will do better if you carefully select your trades and price orders. In addition, the skillful selection of price orders will give you a psychological boost from knowing that you are in command of your trading plan and not simply the recipient of lucky breaks. Successful commodity speculation is a business—not a crapshoot. Pick your spots carefully and you are much more likely to end up a winner.

RULE NUMBER 3. *Don't place an order before you consult a commodity price chart.* So many commodity traders use charts that it is foolish not to consult one before you trade. The very fact that so many people follow charts often results in a sort of self-fulfilling prophecy. Hundreds of chartists buying a price breakout will cause prices to rise; similarly, the breaking of a support level will cause chartists to rush to the short side of the market. Price charts contain much valuable information. By looking at a chart, you can easily see where the previous tops and bottoms occurred, well-known chart configurations (to be explained in Chapter 8), trendlines, support and resistance zones, dramatic movements in volume and open interest, the crossing of moving average lines, and much more. You should place your orders away from the crowd. Too many traders on one side of the market (although buying and selling are always equal by definition) will only result in not getting filled at the right price. Therefore, if you anticipate a substantial rise in prices, but also feel that the buying power at a certain point in the market will be overwhelming, place your order to buy before the market runs away from you. Since markets tend to fall twice as fast as they rise, you should also be prepared to sell before the crowd gets wind that a top has been created. If you are late in predicting a top, you often miss the down move entirely. Charts can help you forecast many of the important turning points in a market.

RULE NUMBER 4. *Always use the intraday trailing stop order when entering a market.* There should be no exceptions to this rule. If a market is already gapping the limit when you decide to buy or sell, it is too late to get aboard safely. Over a year's time, this single rule could save you thousands of dollars. It is a sound basis for a trading program, offering, as it does, momentum in a favorable direction and the ability to use a close protective stop. The only drawback to the rule is that it requires close monitoring of the market on the day you execute your initial buy or sell order.

RULE NUMBER 5. *Fade the breakout of the intraday range.* After one hour of trading, anticipate a run on the stops, either above or beneath the market, and fade the move. Specifically, if the market breaks under the intraday low, look to buy; and if the market breaks above the intraday high, look to sell. This rule is also helpful in pinpointing the direction the market will take on the day. That is, a move down typically means prices will trend higher, and a move up will often mean lower prices ahead. In using this rule, you must be careful to exit quickly when you are wrong. For example, if the market breaks lower and you buy futures contracts, make sure to then sell them if prices can't rise. After all, sometimes the market opens lower and trades down all day. The key to whether the strategy will be successful is how it trades after the violation of the intraday high or low. If the market rebounds, you'll know you made an intelligent trade. If it doesn't rebound, and you have losses, run.

RULE NUMBER 6. *Buy and sell on the .618 retracement of the intraday range.* Once the intraday range has been established, look for the market to retrace the day's range by 61.8 percent. This rule, known as the "Golden Rule," is one of the most predictable and understandable rules in futures trading. Support and resistance levels should—and often do—exist at this retracement level.

RULE NUMBER 7. *Use MOC orders.* Whether you are a day trader or simply want to get out of the market on a given day, the "market on close" order is a good one to use. First, with a market on close order you will know the position is liquidated for sure. If you try using a limit order, the market may not trade at your limit and you may or may not be filled. This results in all sorts of problems such as margin calls and so on. Second, you always want to trade in as liquid a market as possible. At the close, the floor is "evening up"—that is, the sellers are buying, and vice versa—and there will be an abundance of buyers and sellers. This means you probably won't have to pay more than a tick to get out. Third, statistically speaking, the close tends to be near one end of the range and the open at the other. Thus, over time, you should do well by initiating your position in the first couple of hours of trading and liquidating near the end of trading. Although there are many exceptions to this rule, the close is an excellent time to exit the market. Lastly, when you exit the market at the close, you go home "flat." As a result, you don't have to worry about overnight political or weather-related developments, since you no longer have a position. You can then come back in the morning with a fresh outlook to really earn profits again.

6

Moving Averages

THE TREND-FOLLOWING APPROACH

Commodity traders are forever looking for a system that will help them make money consistently in the futures market. They want a method that is easy to understand and use and effective in minimizing losses and maximizing profits. Moreover, they want a technique that works as well in Treasury bills as it does in pork bellies. They want it to work in bull markets and bear markets, during periods of high volatility and low volatility. In short, they want a sure thing.

Unfortunately, there is no one system that works all the time under every type of condition in the futures market. But there are methods that work better than others, and even some that show a profit over a long period of time. Quite a few of them are trend-following methods. A trend follower, by definition, doesn't attempt to forecast the market. He simply follows a trend that has already developed. To follow the trend, he generally relies on some sort of mechanical device that tells him when the market has turned. Once this signal is given, he takes his position and waits for another reversal signal. Once the system has been developed, and the trader knows how to "read" the reversal signals, his job is simply to do what the market tells him. This is not always easy, however. Quite often, the market tells him one thing and then changes its mind. This results in losses for the trader. At other times, the system will earn profits month after month, and then suddenly go into a period when it only produces losses. At times, the trader will grow impatient with the system and attempt to forecast the market by picking tops and bottoms, a strategy that rarely leads to success. Trend followers tend to make bad forecasters. Faced with a string of losses, trend followers often give up their attempts to trade altogether and exit the market losers. Often, if they are honest, they will admit that their discipline failed them—not their method.

How to Spot a Trending Market

A market trend is best ascertained by looking at prices. Do prices tend to rise over time? Or do they tend to fall? Or move sideways? One way to know for sure is to draw a *trend line* on a commodity price chart. A trend line is a line drawn along the tops or bottoms of daily prices in the direction of the prevailing trend. Trend lines—which can denote both uptrends and downtrends, depending on how they are constructed—serve as reliable guideposts for a trader. For as long as a trend line remains intact, you can feel secure that you are on the right side of the market. Trend lines are also important as points of reference for placing stop orders to enter or exit the market.

In a *rising market,* the trend line is constructed by drawing a straight line connecting three or more *lows* (see Figure 8). In a *falling market,* the trend line is constructed by drawing a straight line connecting three or more highs (see Figure 9).

The difference in construction is significant. Once violated, a trend line serves as a warning signal that a trend has reached its conclusion. Unless the trend line has been constructed properly, it will be impossible to tell whether this violation has indeed occurred. For example, a downtrend line constructed by connecting daily low prices won't be violated when a trend reversal pushes prices lower. Thus, it is important to connect the high prices in a downtrend and the low prices in an uptrend. A violation of each signals a trend reversal.

There are other mistakes you can make in identifying trends. If, for example, you construct your trend line based upon just two or three weeks of trading activities, you are likely to find your trend line broken repeatedly. In this instance, a genuine trend reversal may not have occurred, however. Drawing in the trend line may simply have been premature. You must then construct a new line, using the new data you have available to you. When trend lines are repeatedly broken, the chart will tend to look like a fan with a series of trend lines, all originating at the same point, spreading out upon the chart. Since there is no surefire way of knowing when this fanning effect represents a less steep trend or an actual change in trend, you have to make the best approximation of the true trend that you can. In general, however, you can judge a trend line as reliable if it has been accurate for a long time; others, especially those with steep slopes, may be valid for only five or six days. Always consider the slope of the trend line. Those above 45 degrees are apt to be too steep to hold for long.

By way of illustration, two general statements are appropriate when discussing trend lines: the first is that *a commodity unable to decline will advance* (note, in Figure 8, how the progressive lows trade at higher and higher prices as you move from price A to price B to price C); and the second is that *a commodity unable to advance will decline* (note, in Figure 9, how the progressive highs trade at lower and lower prices as you move from price A to price B to price C). The result is the creation of an *uptrend line* and a *downtrend line,* respectively. In either instance, the trend line will indicate the general tendency of a commodity to sell at progressively higher or lower prices.

Not every commodity trends well. A commodity will often be up three or four days and then down for three or four days. For the trend trader, these choppy markets are a disaster. When you think a long position is called for, the market suddenly reverses itself; so you take a short position, and the market rises. *Whipsawing* is the term applied to the action of a market that constantly goes against you as you switch from one side to the other. It is a frustrating situation that trend traders attempt to avoid by staying with markets that are known for their trending qualities. While all markets frequently change character, some are known for their tendency to stay in a trend for long periods of time. Studies have revealed that the following commodities tend to trend best:

Cattle	Hogs
Soybeans	Copper
Wheat	Cocoa
Sugar	Cotton
Pork Bellies	Soybean Oil

Now that we know the basic characteristics of a trending market and some of the commodities that are most likely to trend well, we want to know how to spot a trend in its infancy—before it has time to develop and move away from a top or bottom. Chartists are quick to point to broken trend lines as a clue to a trend change. An uptrend line will be broken by prices moving lower, and a downtrend line will be broken by prices moving higher. This method of forecasting price movements is fine for some traders, but true trend followers, who contend that money can be made more consistently by establishing some tested criteria for measuring the trend, prefer a more precise trend-determining rule—one that won't require so much subjective judgment. Normally, they rely on a *moving average.*

A moving average is defined as "the quotient of any sum divided by the number of its terms." It "moves" in the sense that the results of the most recent trading sessions are incorporated into the average, and those of the

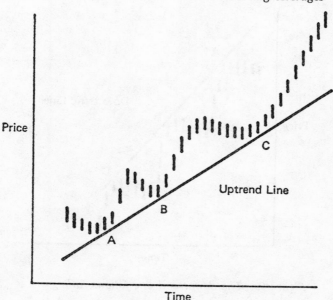

Figure 8.   The uptrend line follows rising prices.

most distant sessions dropped. The number of days in an average is purely arbitrary; there are five-day averages and twenty-day averages, as well as ten-day averages. The difference is primarily a question of "lag." That is, the length of time necessary for the moving average prices to respond to a current change in prices. This is a matter of sensitivity. For example, moving averages calculated on a five-day basis are apt to be more sensitive than ten-day averages, but this very sensitivity tends to cause a trader to get whipsawed in the market by reversing positions on simple minor reactions. On the other hand, the twenty-day average tends to cause the trader to hold on too long, as the built-in "lag" period requires more time before a move can be said to have reversed itself. To benefit from the disadvantages of both long and short averages, many trend followers use a combination of two averages to establish buy and sell points, such as a five-day and a twenty-day average or a three-day and a ten-day average. How the averages are used together will be explained in a moment, but first let's look at the construction of a simple moving average.

The Simple Ten-day Moving Average

The construction of a ten-day moving average is relatively easy to accomplish. All that is required is a list of past prices of the commodity, simple mathematical ability, and time to do some calculations.

There are numerous ways to calculate a moving average, but the two

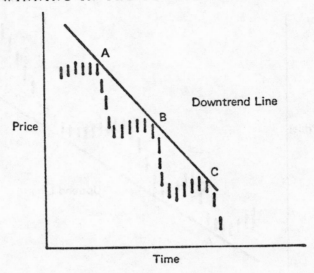

Figure 9.   The downtrend line follows falling prices.

most prominent methods involve the use of either (1) closing or settlement prices, or (2) an average of the high, low, and close. Either method is acceptable. For our illustration, we will use the second method.

The first step is to gather together the high, low, and closing prices of a series of *consecutive* trading sessions. To begin, you should consider going back as far as six or seven weeks in order to get a representative sample of prices. This also gives the average some time to develop. The first two weeks or ten trading days will be without a moving average because ten trading days are required before a determination of an average can be made. As each day passes, an average of the high, low, and close may be calculated by adding the three figures and dividing by three. In column form, then, these initial data may appear as follows:

DAY	(a) HIGH	(b) LOW	(c) CLOSE	(d) AVERAGE
1	11.00	10.70	10.85	10.85
2	10.99	10.89	10.97	10.95
3	11.39	10.95	11.33	11.22
4	11.16	11.05	11.05	11.09

The figures that appear in column (d) are the sum of the high, low, and close—(a), (b), and (c)—divided by three.

The next step is to continue taking such a daily average for the next few days until a total of ten averages (days one to ten) have been calculated. You are now ready to determine the first point of the ten-day moving average. As we've already indicated, the ten-day moving average consists of the average price of the last ten trading sessions. Thus, add the ten figures (on day ten) in column (d), divide by ten, and the resultant figure is the moving average on day ten. For example:

DAY	AVERAGE OF HIGH, LOW, AND CLOSE	TEN-DAY AVERAGE
1	10.85	
2	10.95	
3	11.22	
4	11.09	
5	11.20	
6	11.40	
7	11.52	
8	11.92	
9	11.77	
10	11.67	11.36

Only after ten full trading days can the first figure of the ten-day moving average be calculated. It is for this reason that several weeks of previous prices should be considered when beginning to construct a moving average.

The following day, *day eleven*, a new price will be entered into the column listing the average of the high, low, and closing prices. To incorporate this figure into the average, the figure for *day one* must be dropped from the ten prices considered for the day. Hence, on *day eleven* the ten-day moving average will be an average of days two–eleven inclusive. Assume that the average for the high, low, and close is 11.81 on day *eleven*. The figure of 10.85 (day one's average) will be dropped from the list and 11.81 added. Thus, the moving average price will be 11.46. On *day twelve* the average of the high, low, and close will be added to the list and the average for *day two* will be dropped. And so on. The moving average will, therefore, always comprise an average taken from just ten individual figures.

When plotted on a price chart (assuming the averages are plotted on top of the future prices), the ten-day average will form a line above or below the level of prices. If prices are rapidly rising, the average, due to its inherent lag, will be below the current price; if prices are failing, the lag will keep the moving average line above the current price. If you use two averages, the shorter average, being more sensitive, will jump up and down with almost every change in price, while the longer average will be more smooth and slower to change its direction.

How to Use Two Averages Together

The relationship of a short and long moving average together can be used to generate buy and sell signals. A buy or sell signal is normally indicated when one average crosses the other. Because the shorter-term average is more sensitive than the longer-term average, it will respond more quickly to price changes. The rules for using a short and long average are as follows:

1. When the shorter-term average crosses the longer-term average in an *upward direction,* a buy signal is generated.

2. When the shorter-term average crosses the longer-term average in a *downward direction,* a sell signal is generated.

More sophisticated trading systems incorporate another feature into the simple buy and sell rules explained above. Usually, these systems call for a specific degree of penetration to occur before a genuine buy or sell signal is issued. Because all moving average systems are inherently late, other traders attempt to overcome this disadvantage by taking the ratio or the difference between the two averages as a signal to reverse positions. For example, let's say the three-day average is well below the ten-day average line. This is a sign of rapidly falling prices. But a movement of the three-day line up toward the ten-day line will signal a slowing in the rate of the decline. This slowing in price movement can be used as a signal to reverse a position in the market and go long—before the three-day line penetrates the ten-day and prices actually move upward.

How to Use a Simple Moving Average with Price

When a moving average is plotted on the same scale as prices, the buy or sell signal is generally given when the average penetrates prices by a specific amount. The amount of penetration is relatively arbitrary, although too much penetration will mean missing markets, and too little penetration will generally result in whipsaws as the signals quickly reverse themselves. To understand how a five-day simple moving average is used with prices and how penetration is recorded, consider the following actual example of a five-day moving average of December 1977 copper prices. Here closing prices are used to construct the average, and column 3 indicates net change of prices from the current date, once the average commences, to the closing price six days back. The column marked "Penetration of Average" indicates the magnitude and direction of the closing price minus the five-day moving average. The general rule for using this method states: *When the closing price falls below the moving average by a specific amount (penetration), a sell signal is issued; conversely, when the closing price rises above the moving average by a specific amount (penetration), a buy signal is issued.* In the following example, a penetration of 100 points or more, as the specific amount required, would have resulted in a sell signal on October 28, 1977. Had the degree of penetration been greater than 118 points, however, no signal would have been issued.

Computation of Five-Day Moving Average of December 1977 Copper (Closing Prices)

(1) DATE	(2) CLOSING PRICE	(3) 5-DAY NET CHANGE (A)	(4) 5-DAY TOTAL (B)	(5) 5-DAY AVERAGE (C)	(6) PENETRATION OF AVERAGE
10/24	56.90				
10/25	56.80				
10/26	55.70				
10/27	54.90				
10/28	54.60		278.90	55.78	−1.18
10/31	55.00	−1.90	277.00	55.40	− .40
11/ 1	54.70	−2.10	274.90	54.98	− .28
11/ 2	55.00	− .70	274.20	54.84	+ .16
11/ 3	54.70	− .20	274.00	54.80	− .10

(a) Difference (+ or −) between latest close and sixth close counting back.

(b) Sum of five latest closes.

(c) Column 4 divided by the number 5. These figures in sequence make up the moving average.

Drawbacks of the Simple Moving Average

The simple moving average, which assigns equal weight to each of the base observations, has a couple of drawbacks. First, the simple average doesn't allow for the most recent prices to have greater impact upon the average than the older, more distant prices. It would seem logical that more recent observations should by their very nature be more important and should receive more weight in the average. Secondly, as a simple average moves through time, its point-to-point fluctuations are strictly dependent upon two numbers: the one being added and the one being dropped. As a result, fluctuations in the simple moving average are dependent solely upon two numbers, and one of these is older and of questionable relevance. To compensate for this problem, traders rely on several methods of assigning weights to moving averages.

Weighted Moving Average

DAY NO.	WEIGHT	$\times$	PRICE	$=$	WEIGHTED PRICE
1	1	$\times$	10	$=$	10
2	2	$\times$	12	$=$	24
3	3	$\times$	13	$=$	39

DAY NO.	WEIGHT	×	PRICE	=	WEIGHTED PRICE
4	4	×	15	=	60
5	5	×	18	=	90
6	6	×	22	=	132
7	7	×	28	=	196
8	8	×	32	=	256
9	9	×	37	=	333
10	10	×	40	=	400
	55		227		1,540

The Weighted Moving Average

One method that assigns greater weight to more recent observations is known as the *weighted moving average*. By increasing the importance of more recent observations and decreasing the importance of more distant observations, the weighted average helps to make the average more representative of general price direction and hence more accurate. To establish this average, you have to assign weights to each of the days under observation. For example, if you are constructing a ten-day average, you might want to assign day one a weight of 1 and day two a value of 2—and so on. In this manner, day ten will receive ten times the importance of day one. In a ten-day average, after assigning weights to each of the ten most recent days, the weighted average is finally calculated by dividing the sum of the weighted prices by the sum of the weights. A representative weighted moving average is calculated in the accompanying chart.

In the calculations the weighted average is 28—1,540 divided by 55. A simple ten-day average in this case would have been equal to 22.70—227 divided by 10. On day eleven, the weights would all have to be moved up one price. The 40 price will now have a weight of 9, and the new price on day eleven will be assigned a weight of 10.

The Exponential Moving Average

Like the weighted moving average, the *exponential moving average* assigns greater weight to more recent observations. The proportional weight assigned to the most recent observations is frequently called a "smoothing constant." This exponential smoothing constant is determined by simply dividing the number "2" by one more than the number of terms in the simple moving average you wish to duplicate. For example, if you wish to duplicate a ten-day moving average, you divide 2 by 11. The result—0.18 —is the smoothing constant. The exponential moving average is based upon a system that assigns a fixed weight (the smoothing constant, which in this case is 18 percent) to the current price, and all the remaining weight (in this case 82 percent) to the previous value of the moving average itself.

After arbitrarily establishing the moving average as equal to the first day's price, the moving average is updated by multiplying the newest price by 0.18 and adding that to the product derived from multiplying the previous exponential moving average by 0.82. Using the same prices we used for the weighted average in the previous illustration, the calculations for a ten-day exponential moving average would appear as follows:

Exponential Moving Average

DAY NO.	PRICE	METHOD OF CALCULATION	EXPONENTIAL MOVING AVERAGE
1	10	(to start)	10.00
2	12	(.18 × 12.00 + .82 × 10.00)	10.36
3	13	(.18 × 13.00 + .82 × 10.36)	10.84
4	15	(.18 × 15.00 + .82 × 10.84)	11.58
5	18	(.18 × 18.00 + .82 × 11.58)	12.74
6	22	(.18 × 22.00 + .82 × 12.74)	14.41
7	28	(.18 × 28.00 + .82 × 14.41)	16.85
8	32	(.18 × 32.00 + .82 × 16.85)	19.58
9	37	(.18 × 37.00 + .82 × 19.58)	22.72
10	40	(.18 × 40.00 + .82 × 22.72)	25.83

As you can see, the ten-day exponential moving average is 25.83. This is above the simple ten-day moving average of 22.70 but below the weighted moving average of 28 in the previous illustration. The value is greater than the simple moving average because proportionately greater weight has been assigned to the more recent, and in this case higher, prices.

The Donchian Five- and Twenty-day Moving Average Method

Traded continuously under actual market conditions since January 1, 1961, by its founder, Richard D. Donchian, a vice president of Shearson, American Express, this method is a conservative trend-following system that proves that you can make money in commodity futures over the long run. A relatively easy-to-understand method that uses a five- and twenty-day simple moving average, the Donchian method relies on a penetration system for determining when to buy and sell. Initially calculated by hand, the system is now completely computerized. More important, despite periods when losses were incurred, the Donchian five- and twenty-day moving average method has a twenty-six-year history of continuous profits. During that time, the method has been most successful trading, in the order of profitability, the following nine commodities:

Soybeans	Wheat
Copper	Cocoa
Silver	Hogs
Soybean Meal	Cattle
Cotton	

When Donchian created the five- and twenty-day moving average method, he wanted to avoid many of the mistakes of the average speculator: taking profits too early, overstaying a market, poor money-management practices, and lack of discipline. To do this, he realized that he would have to rely on a purely mechanical system whose buy and sell signals would be clear and not subject to individual interpretation. Moreover, he decided that he would act on every signal generated by his system—that is, he would take a long or short position each time a signal was given. If he was long in the market when a sell signal was given, he would automatically liquidate his position and sell short. If he was short, the reverse would occur.

Because the method is almost entirely automatic, indecision and errors of judgment aren't a problem. In addition, the Donchian method fully complies with the market dictum to cut losses and let profits ride. It also offers adequate diversifications—as many as twenty-six commodities can be traded with it. There are drawbacks to the method, however, foremost among which is the number of losses that must be incurred as a result of a lag in the signals. Another has to do with margin. If you are going to trade this method correctly, and trade even one contract of each commodity followed, you are going to need $40,000 in margin to begin. This will cover the margin on fourteen commodities. If you wish to include cocoa in your trading, the margin is $50,000. And $70,000 is required to trade all twenty-six commodities followed. Yet, despite these drawbacks, the results of the Donchian method are impressive. Based on past performance, you can expect a net gain of 20 to 40 percent on your investment per year.

Buy and sell signals, using the Donchian method, are generated when prices penetrate the averages. But before a signal is considered valid, the penetration must be of sufficient magnitude. In addition, it must exceed the previous penetration of the line that occurred in the same direction. This principle—the requirement that a penetration of the moving average exceed one or more previous penetrations—is a feature of the five- and twenty-day Donchian method, which distinguishes it from other moving average methods.

To apply the following rules, the extent of penetration of the moving average is broken down into units as follows:

COMMODITY PRICE	UNIT VALUE
less than 4.00	.01
4.00–15.00	.03 or nearest fraction
15.00–40.00	.05 or nearest fraction

40.00–100	.10 or nearest fraction
100–400	.20 or nearest fraction
over 400	.40 or nearest fraction

The first general rule is as follows: *No closing price penetration of the moving averages counts as a penetration at all unless it amounts to at least one full unit.* For example, if your commodity is sugar trading at 9.00 cents per pound, a .02 penetration would be disregarded, but a .03 penetration would count.

The basic rules of the system are as follows:

Basic Rule A: Act on all closes which cross the twenty-day moving average by an amount exceeding by one full unit the maximum penetration in the same direction on any one day on the preceding occasion (no matter how long ago) when the close was on the same side of the moving average. For example, if the last time the twenty-day average was penetrated, gold prices reached $5.00 an ounce over the twenty-day average line, then prices must exceed this level for the signal to be considered valid.

Basic Rule B: Act on all closes which cross the twenty-day moving average and close one full unit beyond (above or below in the direction of the crossing) the previous twenty-five closes.

Basic Rule C: Within the first twenty days after the first day of a crossing which leads to an action signal, reverse on any close which crosses the twenty-day moving average and closes one full unit beyond (above or below) the previous fifteen daily closes.

Basic Rule D: Sensitive five-day moving average rules for closing out positions and for reinstating positions in the directions of the basic twenty-day moving average trend are as follows:

1. Close out positions when the commodity closes below the five-day moving average for long positions, or above the five-day moving average for short positions, by at least one full unit more than the greater of (a) the previous penetration on the same side of the five-day moving average, or (b) the maximum point of any previous penetration within the preceding twenty-five trading sessions.

2. After positions have been closed out by Rule D, reinstate positions in the direction of the basic trend when the conditions in the above paragraph have been fulfilled.

Supplementary general rules for entering the market using the Donchian trend-following method are as follows:

1. Action on all signals is deferred for one day except on Thursday and Friday. For example, if a basic buy signal is given for wheat at the close on Tuesday, action is taken at the opening on Thursday morning.

2. For signals given at the close on Friday, action is taken at the opening on Monday.

3. For signals given at the close on Thursday (or the next-to-last trading day of the week), action is taken at the Friday close.

4. When there is a holiday in the middle of the week or a long weekend, signals given at the close of the sessions prior to the holiday are treated as follows: (1) for sell signals, use weekend rules; (2) for buy signals, defer actions for one day, as is done on regular consecutive trading sessions.

The Donchian five- and twenty-day moving average method is not infallible, by any means. Most certainly its success rests on its considerable diversification. The commodities that are in a pronounced trend, and are not giving new signals, are frequently so profitable that the losses on the other, nontrending commodities, are more than compensated for. Should you wish to use the method on just one or two commodities, rather than the fourteen, fifteen, or twenty-six used in the Shearson, American Express trading account, be forewarned that your risks are increased to an inordinate degree. There is nothing magical about the five- and twenty-day average designation. Indeed, studies by Dunn & Hargitt, a leading statistical firm, have revealed that each commodity tends to have its own pair of moving averages that works best in generating buy and sell signals. But you can't knock success. For additional information on the method, you should contact Richard D. Donchian at Shearson's offices in Greenwich, Connecticut.

Disadvantages of Trend-following Methods

There are two major problems related to any trend-following method. The first is that whipsaw losses are inevitable. A commodity moving within a trading range will provide the trend follower with seemingly endless losses until a major trend is initiated. Should this occur when a trader first enters a market, he may not have sufficient resources to ride out this difficult period until the market starts trending and profits develop. Obviously, this can be a serious disadvantage. Secondly, a trend follower must act on all signals if he is going to follow this system. Since all purchases must be made on the way up after a bottom, and all sales made on the way down after a top, it is obvious that if you were clairvoyant and could recognize tops and bottoms, you could buy and sell at much more favorable points than the trend-following action points. But no trend-following method anticipates the market. As a result, purchases and sales made on trend-following action points never look smart. This disadvantage is not as great as it seems, however, because few, if any, trading systems are capable of consistently picking tops and bottoms anyway. Rather, the trend-following method serves to get the trader into the market near the bottom, and subsequently gets him out following the creation of a top—or vice versa. Furthermore, because optimum rules established for a trend-following method during one period of time may result in a poor performance during another period, it is hard to generalize about what constitutes a good average.

Advantages of Trend-following Methods

A trend-following technique is, by definition, objective. As a result, most of the subjective trading decisions so many speculators face can be dispensed with. With a trend-following method, you don't have to decide between entering the market now or later. The entry points, and the exit points, are clearly indicated by the trading plan. Moreover, emotions, which are invariably harmful influences in the market, do not play a role in a trend follower's success or failure. Indeed, all the elements must be clearly defined before a trend-following method can be put into practice. This helps to minimize uncertainties. Most important, the trend follower can be confident that when a genuine trending market develops, his system will get him into the market and keep him on the right side of the market until it exhausts itself.

Trend-following Rules

If you are to trade successfully on the basis of moving averages, you must take several factors into account. This does not mean, however, that to do so is difficult or time-consuming. It isn't. But you should have a good grasp of your trading plan before you begin, and you should give your trading approach a reasonable time to prove itself before you abandon it in favor of another method. In addition, if you decide you want to be a trend follower, don't start second-guessing the market and become a forecaster. You will probably only take the worst of each method and end up with losses. Rest assured that the trend-following method will make you money *if* the market you are trading begins to trend. If you find yourself in a trading market, however, where prices are confined to a narrow range, the trend-following method will almost certainly result in losses. For as soon as prices begin to rise—and you go long following a buy signal—the market will surely reverse itself. Remember this: The most important ingredient for success as a trend follower is the nature of the market you are trading when you are trading it. Even good trending markets go into trading ranges. Expect them and you won't be disillusioned when your trend-following method stops working for you.

We have mentioned some of the advantages of using averages that are weighted in favor of the commodity's most recent price behavior. The weighted and exponential moving averages are among these, but these averages are often more complicated to calculate than the simple moving average which assigns equal weight to each base observation.

The type of average notwithstanding, their chief value rests on a very simple premise—namely, that no commodity can ever stage an uptrend without the price rising above a moving average; and, conversely, no commodity can ever form a downtrend without first showing evidence of more selling than buying by the prices falling below a moving average. To refine your trend-following system, you may want to look for a certain relationship between moving averages as well as between one or more averages and the price. All systems based on moving averages share certain similarities. Among these similarities are the length of time used in computing the average and the degree of penetration required. Please note that too little penetration of the average by the price results in whipsaws and excessive trades, while too much penetration has the effect of cutting down profits on successful signals.

Most trend followers will find the following rules helpful.

RULE NUMBER 1. *Never try to outguess an average.* Some traders grow impatient when trading with moving averages and see tops and bottoms when the market may have only paused to rest for a moment. If you fail to stay with a winning trend when you have one, you will probably fail in your overall trading efforts. The average will keep you on the right side of the market until a reversal is clearly indicated. Don't attempt to pick tops and bottoms when using averages. The average will tell you soon enough. Once you miss a market, as you most certainly will if you are prone to wait around to see whether a given signal is valid or not, you will be demoralized and will then probably have to chase the market. To avoid all this, simply establish your rules before going into a trade, and stay with them. You will most certainly have a number of losses for the reasons we have already mentioned, but if you get your share of trending markets, you will have substantial profits as well, and letting your profits ride is the name of the game where winning commodity trading is concerned.

You should feel comfortable with the averages you use when going into any trading plan. Two averages are recommended. Some traders use three, and some use only one. But a relatively short-term average, which is highly sensitive to price changes, and a relatively long-term average, which will reveal a longer, smoother trend, are perhaps the best combination. What two averages should you use? The three- and ten-day average is popular, as is the five- and twenty-day average used in the Donchian method. Traders who use three averages often use a four-, nine-, and eighteen-day average. The four-day average is often used as an alerting indicator, the nine-day average actually signals the reversals, while the eighteen-day indicator follows the main trend. Once you decide on a given method, don't start shifting around in mid-trade, however. If you feel that a given set of averages isn't doing the job for you, take your loss or losses and then experiment with other averages or other trading techniques. Patience will often be rewarded when trading with moving averages.

RULE NUMBER 2. *Keep trading to a minimum.* The fewer the number of trades you make in a year the more money you will probably make. If you can limit yourself to four or five good trades a year (some of which may persist for many months), you will find you are coming out ahead. If you make too many trades, you will lose through commissions and slippage. Thus, you take larger risks when you trade frequently. Strict trend traders tend to stay in the market at all times. For example, they will stay long when prices stay above a ten-day average, and automatically go short when prices fall below the ten-day average. In a trending market, they may stay long or short nine or ten months at a time. To stay with a market, according to the rules of a trend-following method, requires discipline. Your broker will be constantly calling to tell you to take profits, suggesting other trades, and trying to get you interested in some other action. Don't listen to him. Brokers hate any trade method that doesn't stimulate a lot of trading—and commissions. And if you have ever tried to be an in-and-out trader, buying and selling a dozen times a week, you will know the feeling of satisfaction that will come from being able to say you rode orange juice or coffee or sugar or whatever to the top—and then reversed positions and got in on the downtrend. Most traders never do this. The impulse to overtrade is too strong. Keep your trading to a minimum. You will be well rewarded for it.

RULE NUMBER 3. *Use the Donchian Four-week Trading Rules.* This is a trend-following rule that has worked well for Richard D. Donchian. Unlike his five- and twenty-day system, it does not use moving averages. The rules are as follows:

1. Whenever the price exceeds the highs of the four preceding full calendar weeks' ranges, buy and cover short positions.
2. Whenever the price falls below the low of the four preceding calendar weeks' ranges, liquidate long positions and sell short.
3. Close out positions at the close of the last of the month prior to the delivery month.

This method has had the best results with December wheat, January soybean oil, May copper, August pork bellies, May potatoes, and June cattle. A similar set of rules, but with a two-week rather than a four-week comparison, has proved exceptionally valuable in the copper market. If you doubt the value of the two- or four-week rule, take a commodity price chart and test the method yourself. It is one of the best, and simplest, trend-following methods yet developed.

RULE NUMBER 4. *For best results, trade a commodity mix of at least six to eight commodities.* If you limit your trend trading to just one or two commodities, you will do either very well or very badly. This is because you need trending commodities to make money with a trend-following system. Such a portfolio should include the following: cattle, hogs, copper, soybean oil, sugar, corn, and wheat. Although it is not always possible, you should try to trade equal margin in each commodity. That is, if you select seven commodities to trade and have $14,000, you would trade $2,000 in each commodity. A rule that will conserve your capital and also protect you against margin calls is to have double margin in your account when trading. At six-month intervals you should take down 50 percent of your profits and let the rest constitute equity. For example, if you begin with $14,000 in trading capital and over six months' time the account grows to $20,000, you should take half of your $6,000 profits and let $17,000 remain in the account. With this additional capital you can increase your positions by taking on additional futures contracts. But it is best to take on new positions after you have had a slight drop in equity. The reason for this is that market success goes in cycles. If you reinvest at the top of a cycle, you will be hurt worse than if you reinvest as you are coming off a temporary setback.

RULE NUMBER 5. *Use moving averages to establish "buying" and "selling" prices.* A moving average can readily be used to determine buying and selling levels when plotted against the daily prices on a regular bar chart. In order to calculate these figures, you have to establish a daily price range. This is easy. Simply subtract the low of the day from the high of the day. This might appear as follows:

		PRICE RANGE
HIGH	LOW	FOR DAY
16.34	16.26	.08

Using a ten-day average (this can also be done with other averages), a ten-day average price range is then calculated as soon as ten consecutive prices are recorded. This ten-day average price range figure is then *added* to the ten-day moving average to establish a "buying price," and, conversely, *subtracted* from the ten-day moving average to establish a "selling price."

For example, a trader gathers together a series of prices from which he makes a list of the average daily price ranges. His next step is to calculate his buying and selling points. Assume that the ten-day moving average is 12.49 and that the futures price is somewhat higher—at, say, 12.75.

How do we establish a buying price? If we assume the average daily range is .12, we can add this to the ten-day moving average figure and reach a price of 12.61. This is our buying price. The calculations are as follows:

12.49	Ten-day moving average
+ .12	Ten-day average price range
12.61	Buying price

The trader would not be a buyer unless the market dipped down and reached this price. This buying price figure is good for only one trading day. The new buying price must be calculated at the end of each trading day for the next morning's open. The most common method of getting this order filled is to place a buy-stop limit order with your broker prior to the opening each morning.

As long as the ten-day moving average lies below the market price (as it will in a rising market), prices will have to move down or "react" before a purchase can be made. Not to wait for this reaction to occur is to invite losses by buying on strength, rather than price weakness.

The rule for buyers can be stated as follows: *Buy only when market price and "buying price" meet.* The corollary of this rule is to stay either (1) on the sidelines or (2) in a previously initiated position until this condition comes about.

In bear markets, the ten-day moving average can be used to establish "selling prices." These prices, like buying prices, have two key functions: (1) to initiate a new position and/or (2) to close out a losing position previously entered into. Thus, in our illustration indicated above, a selling price could serve as a protective stop in the event that the market sustained a significant reaction. For example, let's assume that the market touched off a buy order at 12.61 and continued lower. Where would you take your loss and, perhaps, reverse yourself and go short? The ten-day moving average can be of use in this instance by pinpointing the spot where the indicators would tip in favor of the short side. As we've indicated, this price would be arrived at by *subtracting* the ten-day average range from the ten-day moving average, thus:

$$
\begin{array}{rl}
12.49 & \text{Ten-day moving average} \\
-.12 & \text{Ten-day average price range} \\
\hline
12.37 & \text{Selling price}
\end{array}
$$

The rule for sellers can be stated as follows: *Sell only when market price and "selling price" meet.*

If prices continue to trade within the 24-point range between 12.61 (the buying price) and 12.37 (the selling price), you will hold on to your long position in hopes that prices are simply experiencing a minor reaction and will shortly reassert themselves in an upward direction. Once 12.37 is hit, however (note here that this "selling price" is good for one day only, tomorrow's being subject to a completely new, updated calculation), you will be quick to take your loss and, if you so desire, take the other side and immediately go short.

Assume that prices do indeed trade at 12.37 and fall still lower. By taking a loss on the long position, reversing yourself and going short, you are now prepared to make a profit if prices continue to fall. Again, each new day will present a new set of figures, continually changing the ten-day moving average and the respective buying and selling prices. By keeping a close watch on your calculations, you can guarantee that most of the time you'll be on the correct side of the market by using this "buying price" and "selling price" moving average method.

RULE NUMBER 6. *Stay with trending markets.* No matter how good our trend-following method, you aren't going to make money with it unless you are in a trending market. Concentrate on those markets which have a history of trending well, such as wheat, cattle, copper, pork bellies, and sugar. A good trending market is characterized by good commercial support, sufficient volume to keep prices moving in a single direction over a period of time, and consistency. Orange juice, potatoes, and eggs are bad for trend followers, because they are inconsistent markets. While you are waiting for a move to occur in these markets, you will get whipsawed to death. When you do catch a move, however, these markets can be exceptionally profitable. Silver is another commodity that doesn't trend well. Consult a price chart before you select a market to trade, and see if its history is characterized by long trends. If there is a lot of choppy up-and-down movement, chances are you will be better off in another commodity.

RULE NUMBER 7. *Expect modest profits.* If you are going to trade a diversified portfolio of commodities with a trend-following method, you should give up the idea of making a big killing. As in any type of investment or speculation, gain is commensurate with risk in the commodity world, and trend followers gladly give up their opportunity to make a fortune overnight in hopes of an annual gain of 20 to 60 percent on their invested funds. This is not to say that profits are limited. They are not. But the number of losses you will have over time will tend to lessen the profit potential. Of course, if you do hit a series of runaway markets, such as occurred during the early seventies, your short-term profits can be enormous. But, as a rule, in a diversified portfolio you will have a number of small whipsaw losses and a lesser number of large gains. Trend followers, as a group, tend to be content with these results. If you want better results, you are going to have to take more aggressive steps—and sustain much greater risk.

7

The Trading Plan

HOW TO PUT YOUR MARKET STRATEGIES INTO ACTION

Knowing a lot of market techniques isn't very helpful unless you also know how to put your strategies into action. Too many traders approach the market with the notion that they will figure out what to do after they watch prices for a while; or, even worse, they will take a position and then decide if it is the correct course of action. Chances are, if you trade in this manner, you will lose money. Commodity futures speculation is a business. Those who don't treat it like a business are much more likely to be careless in their trading. The vast majority of first-time speculators are very careless. They enter the market at vulnerable points, they place their stops either too close or too far away from the market, and they often don't have definite goals—in short, they lack the discipline necessary to win.

A sign of careless trading is the absence of a trading plan. The trading plan is your blueprint for success in the market. It can tell you where you are and where you are going. And it can also tell you when it is time to change your plan.

The average small speculator has a market life of approximately eight to ten months. This is usually the time it takes a trader to decide that futures trading is not for him. The odds against a trader's making net profit in any given year are about four to one. The records of one brokerage house showed that the percentage of traders concluding the year with net profits ranged from a low of 14 percent to a high of 42 percent, with an average of 28 percent. This is not exactly promising. Nevertheless, some traders consistently make fortunes trading commodity futures contracts.

You have to remember that commodity trading is the truest form of speculation. While low margins provide the opportunity to establish large positions on small margin capital invested, a relatively small adverse price fluctuation can create large losses relative to the capital employed. Commodity trading is the fast track. There are few faster ways to turn a relatively small amount of money into a great deal of money in a short period of time. But the risks are commensurate with the potential gain. You must decide if you have the temperament to endure high risk day after day.

You also have to understand the competition involved as well. For you to make money trading commodities, someone else has to lose it. Each trader is trying to be just a little faster, a little smarter, than every other. Do you have this ability to be just a little quicker, a little more astute, than your fellows? Commodities trading will certainly give you an opportunity to put your talents to the test.

The fear-greed syndrome is one that every futures trader ultimately has to come to terms with. On the one hand, you can't be so fearful to act that you put off taking a position until it is clearly too late; the majority are invariably wrong when the big money is being made, especially at market turns. On the other hand, you can't ever lose sight of your own vulnerability, or you may overcommit on the mistaken notion that you have beaten a market.

Who makes money trading futures? The minority—the professionals who take losses in stride, yet who have courage in their market actions and respect for price behavior. They know that they can't always understand market behavior, yet they are quick to take a chance when they sense an incipient market trend. Many futures markets are dominated by large speculators and hedgers. Because these large traders have a history of being on the right side of the market, small traders with the instinct for winning soon learn to find out what the market powers are doing and tag along. A study conducted some years ago revealed that large speculators tended to show a profit 80 to 85 percent of the time. This consistency of the profit-making capacity of the large speculator should make the small trader pay heed to their market actions.

Area of Specialization

Before you embark on a trading program, you should select one area of specialization. One way to do this is to limit yourself to one type of commodity: the grains, the metals, or the meats. A meat trader, for instance, should concentrate just on cattle, pork bellies, and hogs. Or a trader specializing in world commodities might limit his trading efforts to the cocoa, sugar, and coffee markets. When you limit yourself to a commodity group, you will be able to use the same general body of knowledge in your analysis of each commodity. In addition, this group approach should provide you with ample opportunities for trades, since generally at least one commodity in a group will be moving even if the others are inactive. You need not be overwhelmed by the amount of knowledge and analysis required to trade a given commodity group, because there are usually one or two limited issues on which the price turns in a particular situation. As a rule, since supply factors are more readily known than are demand factors, it is best to concentrate on knowing the potential demand changes and their impact. The principle is to challenge the markets where they are weakest.

You can also specialize by limiting yourself to a specific kind of trading. You may want to concentrate on spreads, for instance, or you may want to limit your participation in the market to day trading. After some experimentation, many traders adopt a style of trading that suits them best. You have to decide on your own style. Do you feel comfortable with position trading that requires staying with a commodity for weeks or months at a time? Or do you want to be an overnight trader who takes profits more frequently?

What about your method of trade selection? Here again, it is best to stay with one or two reliable market tools. If you get a trend follower, it is best not to get involved with market forecasting. On the other hand, don't feel obligated to stay with a trading method that isn't working satisfactorily. Successful market forecasters often rely on several indicators to help them make trade selections. When three or four indicators all point to the same selection, they feel more confident in making a trade. You may want to sort out in advance your reliance on your broker and commission house advice. Brokers can be useful; but, depending on their own temperaments and skill, they can also be counterproductive in advising against potentially profitable trades. There is no easy method to decide when you should follow someone else's advice. But where brokers are concerned, you should always be mindful of the built-in conflict of interest that exists. Your broker wants you to make money in the market because it will generate more commissions for him; this is a plus. But he may simply want to see you trade, win or lose, for the same reason. Cynicism is rampant in the commodity market, because so few traders make money. As a rule, a broker knows that a given client will generate an amount equal to his initial equity in commissions over a year's time—if he trades frequently enough. So be prepared for a lot of advice concerning in-and-out trading. The broker doesn't get paid according to how much you make or lose in the market. So his real interest lies in seeing that you generate commissions.

You must also remember that commission house advice is often provided with the same goal in mind. To encourage speculative activity, commission house research departments are continually turning out recommendations. Perhaps the customers themselves are partially to blame for this, since they want advice given to them. And commission houses may have a bias toward telling customers what they want to hear. As a rule, commission houses usually concern themselves with price changes; the whole area of capital and risk management is left to the customer. Since risk management is vital to success in the market, you must still do a lot of managing for your own account. This is not to say that commission house advice is bad. Much of it is first-rate. But a weekly market letter can only tell you so much about a market. A large part of the decision-making process that will affect the success of your account remains in your hands.

Some traders rely on market advisory letters published by independent analysts for their market advice. These letters, which are strictly limited in their circulation and which very often offer specific buy, sell, and stop-loss advice, vary greatly in the quality of their advice. If you find one you like, you may want to stay with that service. This kind of specialization can also lead to success.

Record Keeping

Accurate record keeping is a must for the futures trader. Your broker will provide you with computerized statements of your trading activity, but it is absolutely necessary that you keep your own records as well. The reason for this is that you want to know what open positions you have at all times. Your records will tell you where you are in the market. You can also use them to place stop-loss orders and to alert you when a contract is reaching maturity.

Since most traders may be long or short more than just one or two commodities at a time, a good record-keeping system will keep track of the positions that are outstanding and those that have been liquidated for a profit or a loss. The records are also invaluable at tax time and in checking out statements you receive from your broker. When you receive a verbal confirmation over the phone from your broker, enter that trade in your records. When the confirmation slip arrives a day or two later, compare them to see whether what your broker told you over the phone is identical with the information written on the slip. Do the same at the end of the month, when you receive your monthly profit-and-loss statement.

There are a number of ways to keep records, but the important point is to list all the relevant information. This should include the following: the date, whether you bought or sold, the position size, commodity, and price. Later, when you offset your trade, you will want to calculate your profit or loss, including your commission cost. In the hypothetical records that follow, we use the letter "B" or "S" to indicate bought or sold. The profit/ loss and commission columns are filled in when a trade is liquidated.

Commodity Transaction Record

DATE	BOUGHT /SOLD	QUANTITY	COMMODITY	PRICE	COM.	PROFIT/ LOSS
8/18	S	10	Jul Coffee	177.10		
9/ 6	S	6	Nov OJ	104.60		
10/24	B	6	Nov OJ	76.30	$330	+$ 25,140
10/26	B	10	Jul Coffee	131.10	$450	+$149,550
1/19	S	3	May NY Sil	597.70		
1/19	B	3	May NY Sil	604.30	$ 90	−$ 1,080
2/ 7	B	10	Apr Hogs	44.80		
2/17	S	10	Apr Hogs	40.50	$475	−$ 13,375
3/20	B	7	Aug Soy Oil	21.13		
3/20	S	7	Aug Soy Oil	21.38	$224	+$ 826

In the five completed trades above, the speculator made a total net profit of $161,061. This includes the deduction of all commissions and two losses sustained in a day trade of May New York silver and a loss in April hogs. You should note that the transactions are recorded in chronological order. Thus, a short position in ten July coffee contracts was initiated on August 18 and liquidated on October 26. In the meantime, the trader shorted six contracts of November orange juice and closed that position out on October 24. To arrive at the commission cost, you simply take the overnight round-turn (assuming, of course, that the position is held overnight) and multiply it by the number of contracts. For example, the overnight commission on coffee is $45. Ten coffee contracts, therefore, will have a commission of $450. When you calculate the net profit or loss, you must *add* the cost of the commission to a loss and *subtract* the cost of the commission from a profit. In the transactions above, both the silver and the soybean oil were initiated and liquidated within the same trading session. This is known as a day trade. Day-trade commissions are generally about half the cost of overnight commissions. The respective profit-and-loss results are calculated by multiplying the number of points difference between the buying and selling points by the value of one point. The result is then multiplied by the number of contracts. Lastly, the commission is added or subtracted to arrive at the net profit or loss. For example, let's examine the loss that was experienced in April hogs. Anticipating higher prices, the trader went long April hogs at 44.80 cents per pound on February 7. Ten days later, on February 17, the price of hogs had fallen to 40.50 cents per pound and the trader offset his position by buying back his ten contracts. The price difference between where the hogs were purchased and where they were sold is 4.30 cents or 430 points (44.80 − 40.50 = 4.30). Since each point movement in hogs is equal to $3.00, the 430-point movement has a value of $1,290 (430 × 3 = 1,290). This is the loss on each contract.

Since there are ten contracts involved in this trade, the total loss prior to commissions is $12,900. When you add the commission costs of $475 ($47.50 × 10 = $475), the total net loss comes to $13,375.

You should note that every position was completely offset by the close of trading on March 20. That is, the ten coffee contracts sold short were subsequently offset by the purchase of ten coffee contracts in the same contract month. The six November orange juice contracts sold short were offset by the purchase of six November orange juice contracts. And so on. Unless the quantities purchased and sold match, the trader will remain long or short a commodity. It is, therefore, important to take note of your initial position when you are liquidating your contracts.

By looking at the record, you can see at a glance exactly what commodity positions you hold at what prices, the date you initiated a position, and the size of your commitment. By comparing your entry price with the daily newspaper settlement price, you will know exactly where you stand. If you are in a loss position, this will tell you how much margin you still have left and whether or not you are approaching the maintenance margin figure. Of course, your brokerage house has a computer that keeps track of this information, but it helps to be able to anticipate these things rather than receiving a surprise margin call and perhaps having your position automatically liquidated by the brokerage house. On the profit side, your records can tell you what your present equity figure is and perhaps provide a clue as to where your stop-loss orders should be placed. As soon as a transaction is closed out, you will enter the closing data and compute your profit or loss. All these figures are the net figures, after adding or subtracting the commission. You may want to add a column which will be a cumulative total of your gains or losses. This will be the real bottom-line figure, the result of all your closed trades to date.

Creating the Trading Plan

The trading plan has more to do with how you go about trading the commodities you select than the actual selection process. Its prime concern will be proper money management. Of course, no money-management program can make profits for a speculator who insists on making bad trades; conversely, excellent trade selection and timing cannot guarantee profits for the trader with poor money-management techniques. The two are vital to one another.

The first part of your trading plan will concern the amount of funds you have available for trading. These funds should be strictly risk capital. You shouldn't have to rely on them for living expenses, nor should their disappearance in the market lead to bankruptcy or insolvency in one form or another. You should establish your initial trading capital with the notion that you could lose all these funds and more if you aren't careful. With this idea firmly in mind, you want to establish a point beyond which you will risk no more funds in the market. Let's say your initial risk capital is $20,000. You may be willing to risk 25 percent of this amount to gain, say, $25,000, which is not unreasonable in futures trading. So you are willing to risk $5,000 in hopes of gaining $25,000. Should you lose the $5,000, you must then leave the market and tell yourself that you have failed to reach your goal. It is best to write this kind of information in your trading plan before you begin trading.

Please note that the 25-percent rule is purely arbitrary. Some traders would be willing to lose more and others to lose less. You have to determine where your stop-loss point is in terms of your overall capital.

Secondly, you have to decide what portion of your available risk funds you are willing to lose on any one trade. Of the $5,000 you will be risking, you may wish to commit no more than 10 percent, or $500, to each trade. This figure will help you to determine where you must exit the market at all costs. Remember to include the cost of commissions when you calculate this figure. For example, let's say you are a sugar trader. Sugar is the only market you are interested in, and you are willing to risk $5,000 over a period of time in order to make $25,000 or more. Moreover, since you are willing to risk 10 percent of your capital on each trade, you know you have at least ten trades, with losses limited to $500 each, to achieve your goal. You need not lose $500 on each trade, of course. You may indeed limit yourself to $200. But $500 is as high as you will go, regardless of what the market does. If you assume a commission cost of $75 for sugar, you have $425 in adverse market action available to you before you must exit the market on each trade. Each point movement in sugar is valued at $11.20. So by dividing this number into $425, you realize that the market can move approximately 38 points against you before you must liquidate your position. This is a reasonable assumption under normal conditions. But in volatile markets, sugar can move a whole cent or 100 points in a single trading session. If you get such a move against you, it will cost $1,195 including commissions. And, of course, if you get a string of limit moves it could cost you a lot more.

At this point, you have to evaluate the market in terms of its potential for an adverse limit move. If there is a genuine likelihood of an adverse limit move, perhaps you shouldn't be in the sugar market at all. Given your risk commitment, you may want to settle for a less volatile market.

Next, you may want to determine how many positions you are willing to carry at once. With only $5,000 in trading capital available to you, you will be severely limited in the number of positions you are able to carry. At $2,000 margin per sugar contract, your $5,000 will limit you to just two contracts. But let's say equity isn't a problem. You may want to limit yourself to the number of contracts held in one commodity and the number of contracts held overall. Again, write down your decision before you trade. This can help you acquire discipline at a time when other traders are plunging carelessly. You may want to limit yourself to just three commodities, or to no more than six positions each. If your commodities are sugar, copper, and cocoa, and the margin requirements are $2,000, $750, and $1,500 respectively, your total commitment for six positions each will be $25,500. Now, if you are willing to lose 25 percent of your equity, your self-imposed potential loss will be $6,375. These kinds of guidelines are sensible. Too often, traders don't have any idea of what they are risking to reach a profit. Risk has to be analyzed in terms of what it means to you. Since you will be wrong from time to time in the market, you certainly don't want to risk all your funds on one trade. But are you willing to risk them on seven or eight trades?

You must also decide how aggressive you are going to be. For instance, are you going to pyramid? Pyramiding, you will recall, is a money-management technique in which you use paper profits from your previously initiated positions to finance additional positions. The drawback to pyramiding is that it raises your average purchase price, or, in the case of short sellers, lowers the average sell price. As a result, even a modest adverse movement against such a position can result in serious losses.

Stops, either mental or actual, should always be used when you trade commodity futures. You should incorporate the placement of your stops into your trading plan. One method is to place stops according to a percentage of equity discussed above. Another is to determine how much of an adverse move you are willing to sit through. A limit and a half is often a good rule.

You might also adopt the method of writing down your reasons for making a trade. This will force you to pay close attention to the market and to use discipline. As a rule, traders tend to act too quickly when trying to make a trade, and too slowly when trying to protect their money. A written trading plan can help slow down the process of selecting a trade, and speed up the process of exiting the market when things go wrong. Both can be beneficial to overall trading results.

The following hypothetical trading plan gives you an idea of some of the considerations a trader might commit to paper before taking his chances in the market. As you can see, the market is already trending when he enters, and he has definite plans to abandon his position in case of a price reversal.

Trading Plan

Trade:	Long May potatoes
Size of Position:	8 on scale up (4-2-2)
Date:	Oct. 17-20
Initiate Trade:	7.85 or better
Price Objective:	13.10
Profit Objective:	$20,000 +

Margin:	$750 per contract, or 8 for $6,000
Place Stop Orders:	7.50; thereafter below trend line
Risk:	$1,800–$2,350
Reasons for Trade:	Tight supplies. Seasonal bias toward higher prices in spring. Already in uptrend. Breakout from previous resistance. Three-day average above ten-day average.

Most of the information in the trading plan above is self-explanatory. The "4–2–2" designation on position size indicates that the trader wishes to acquire four contracts initially, followed by two contracts at a higher level, and an additional two at a still higher level. His price order at $7.85 or better suggests he will use a limit order to initiate the trade; his stop orders are relatively indefinite at this point, since he plans to use trailing stops as the market rises. Most significantly, the potential loss is only about one tenth the size of the potential gain. Should the market indeed reach his price objective, the risk involved in this trade will have been well worth the effort. You should note that the trader is planning to acquire the entire position within a four-day period. Too many traders tend to delay action until the bull market is proved correct, and then take a position only after half the move has occurred. The trading plan helps you to enter the market when the time is right. If a position cannot be obtained at the right time and price, the trading plan will also help you to stand aside.

Paper Trading

Many analysts suggest that a novice trader attempt to trade commodities on paper before he takes a plunge in the market. Paper trading is simply selecting a trade and writing it down but without actually committing funds to the market. This technique has one serious deficiency: it doesn't work. When you don't have real money riding on your trading decisions, it is quite easy to ignore minor reversals in the market. But when you actually hold a position, the fear-and-greed syndrome begins to operate and you are tempted to take quick profits, let losses accumulate, and make a host of other mistakes. For this reason it is better to learn to play the market through actual participation.

General Trading Rules

There are almost as many market strategies for playing the commodities market as there are speculators. So it is best to adopt your own style, one you feel comfortable with when you trade. Many traders attempt to take the best from a variety of trading techniques and use them together. Others follow the advice of professional market-letter writers. Still others— those who follow the contrary-opinion approach—go counter to the prevailing majority opinion as expressed by the leading market letters. You may want to base your trading decisions solely upon technical analysis. Or you may want to take the fundamental approach or wed fundamental analysis with technical analysis. Regardless of which approach you use, you will want to use a trading plan—one that you develop yourself and with which you feel comfortable. The guidelines that follow are only some of the more obvious factors to take into account when you develop your trading plan.

RULE NUMBER 1. *Establish profit objectives.* Never enter into a commodity trade unless the profit potential is several times the possible risk. Stops can help you limit risk. A knowledge of trend lines, support and resistance zones, chart patterns, and general price behavior can also provide valuable clues pointing to strong and weak areas within a market. As a rule, risk is proportionate to potential gain. You will often have to take sizable risks to make sizable profits. Conservative gains, of course, can also be obtained by taking conservative risks. To keep the risk/reward factor in balance, it is necessary to understand what you are trying to accomplish when you enter a trade. A day trader, for instance, who may make six or seven round-turns within a single trading session has significantly different goals from the position trader, who may stay with a market for six or seven months. The point is to know what kind of profits you are looking for when you enter a trade. Of course, you will never know exactly what to expect. Often, the market itself will let you know when it has run its course, and you will have to do the sensible thing and liquidate your position when this occurs. In other markets you will realize you did the wrong thing right at the start and that you will have to take quick, appropriate action. Profit objectives are important because they give you a realistic goal to shoot for. If the objectives are not reached, you should have a contingency plan to exit the market. If, on the other hand, the goals are reached, you should use trailing stops or some other method to get out of the market with your profit intact.

What should your goals be? Ideally you should look for a percentage of your total trading capital over a year's time. For example, you may want 50 percent of your capital per year in profits. To gain this profit, you may be willing to risk 20 percent of your capital. On individual trades it is much more difficult to set percentage limits, because there are so many factors involved. Nevertheless, you should try to set both an objective (in terms of overall profit and commodity price) and a risk point on every trade.

RULE NUMBER 2. *Decide on the maximum capital commitment to be made at any one time.* Your exposure should be limited on each and every trade to a predetermined amount of money. Again, mental or actual stops generally will prevent you from letting a loss get out of hand. The best method is to set a percentage of your total trading capital, then translate this percentage into a dollar amount. A bad habit to get into when you trade futures is to keep writing checks to your broker. Start out the year with the total amount of money you wish to commit to the market, and let that be the last check you write. Should your equity shrink below a reasonable level, you should take this as a sign that you are making too many mistakes in the market and that you should stop trading for a while.

RULE NUMBER 3. *Write down the size of the price move you are looking for.* The price objective should be clearly translated into a specific market goal. You can then put in an order to liquidate your position when the objective has been reached. The price move should be in keeping with the amount of risk, and should take into consideration commissions and possible bad fills.

RULE NUMBER 4. *Select a contingency plan for increasing or decreasing your position.* Most traders like to add to a position once the market shows signs of moving in their direction. If you plan to take on additional contracts, do so in a reasonable manner. Pyramid profits from a large base with smaller increments. When exiting a profitable trade, it is a good idea to sell into strength and buy into weakness. For example, let's say you have acquired a ten-contract position in a bull market. Rather than simply selling all ten contracts at once, you may begin to sell a couple of contracts on each rally until you have liquidated the entire position. By selling into strength, you will avoid the rush to liquidate once a market peaks. Conversely, the reverse is true when you are exiting a bear market. You will then want to buy or offset your short position on weakness.

Pyramiding is the fastest way to make profits in the futures market. It can also be very risky. If you are going to pyramid, do it right. Put your base on at the beginning of a big move, and add as fast as your funds permit. This will keep your average price at a manageable level and enable you to derive the maximum benefit from the market move. When pyramiding, you must move fast or not at all. Write down the price levels at which you plan to pyramid, and then follow through on your plan. Once the market fails to behave as you anticipated, however, you must be prepared to liquidate in a hurry, regardless of losses. Your trading plans should pinpoint all potential trouble areas.

8

Chart Trading Techniques

THE TECHNICAL APPROACH
TO MARKET ANALYSIS

Having familiarized yourself with the basic functioning of the futures market, you may be ready to formulate an approach to outguess it. Commodity forecasting techniques fall into three general categories: the fundamental, the psychological, and the technical. Fundamental analysis tends to paint the price-forecasting picture in broad strokes. It deals with underlying supply and demand. A fundamentalist will want to know the size of last year's crop, whether there is any carryover, the potential of this year's crop, whether demand for the commodity in question has risen or fallen, the impact of government programs on supply and demand—and so on. The trader who looks at the psychological pulse of the market is often a contrary-opinion trader, who attempts to understand what the majority is thinking—and then takes a position opposite to the majority in the market. Contrary-opinion theory holds that the majority is always wrong at the key reversal points in the market. By taking a position opposite to the majority, the contrary-opinion trader hopes to find himself on the right side of the market. The technical trader maintains that the only thing that counts when you trade commodities is price action. Price action, according to the technician, reflects the supply-and-demand equation far better than any fundamental analysis. For this reason, the true technical trader will ignore fundamental news and other information, such as crop reports and the like, in favor of price action and the technical indicators that reflect the action of market participants.

By far the most valuable trading tool of the technician is the price chart. Practically every technical trader uses one or both of the two popular forms of charting: bar charting and point-and-figure charting. The *daily vertical line chart*, or *bar chart*, is constructed by plotting a small horizontal "tick" mark to indicate the close. The top of the line corresponds with the high price of the day, and the bottom of the line corresponds with the low price of the day. The range of the day's trading is thus reflected by the length of the vertical bar. Bar charts can also be constructed that measure weekly or monthly prices as well. On a bar chart, the horizontal axis measures time, and the vertical axis measures price.

Unlike the bar chart, the point-and-figure chart disregards time and concentrates on measuring price reversals. Small *X*'s and *O*'s are used to trace price moves until a trend changes by registering a new higher or lower price. When a market moves a preestablished amount, the point-and-figure chartist will switch from using the "X" designation to the "O" designation, constantly alternating with each trend change.

The horizontal axis of point-and-figure charts is a measure of the number of price-movement reversals. As long as prices continue to advance, the X's will continue to move higher vertically. As soon as there is a reversal of prices, however, the previous vertical column is abandoned and a new, adjacent column is started. This new column follows prices as they continue in the reverse direction.

How to Construct Price Charts

Whether you intend to keep your own charts or purchase them from a professional charting service, you will want to know how a chart is constructed and what each indicator means. Different traders rely on different indicators, but most chartists follow price action, open interest, and volume. To begin, you need some graph paper and pencils. Next, you must have access to an accurate source of data. If you want to go back in time, copies of *The Wall Street Journal* (available through your local library) should provide you with the necessary information to construct a couple of months of price action. You will want to record high, low, and closing prices for each day a commodity contract trades, as well as total open interest and volume. In *The Wall Street Journal,* open interest generally runs a day behind prices and volume, so you should take note of this in collecting your data. A typical entry might appear as follows:

COMMODITY	DATE	HIGH	LOW	CLOSE	VOLUME	OPEN INTEREST
March copper	12/27	61.40	61.00	61.40	2,141	48,260

This gives you all the information you need for one day's entry on a bar chart. You simply draw a straight vertical line connecting 61.40 to 61.00 on the graph, with a slight horizontal tick on the high at 61.40 for the close. Price information for each succeeding day is plotted toward the right, across the horizontal time axis. Volume is generally recorded on the bottom of the chart as a vertical line corresponding to a separate volume scale. Open interest, which also appears at the bottom of the chart, is generally just a dot corresponding to an open interest scale. As each new entry occurs, the dots are connected to form a smooth line. Since volume and open interest are generally plotted in the same general area, the volume scale can be plotted on one side of the chart, with the open interest scale plotted on the other side.

It is important to keep up your charting every day if it is going to be of value to you in the market. Since the statistics are available from your broker, you can call him at the close of trading and fill in your chart each afternoon.

Point-and-figure charts are constructed somewhat differently from bar charts, since these charts ignore volume, open interest, and time. On a point-and-figure chart, therefore, the horizontal axis has neither vertical bars to measure volume, as do bar charts, nor any reference to time. Price-reversal signals are designated by the movement of X's and O's. The vertical axis measures price. The horizontal axis measures movements in the market, but not in a strict chronological sense. Rather, as market reversals occur, the chartist will fill in X's and O's, causing the chart to move to the right.

In constructing a point-and-figure chart, you use X's when prices are rising and O's when prices are falling. As long as the price is rising, you continue to add X's. Likewise, as long as the price is falling, you continue to add O's. The decision to start a new column of X's or O's is based on a price change of a predetermined amount in the opposite direction. You must decide what the value of a box will be as well as what kind of a reversal you desire. A popular change or reversal is three boxes. Therefore, if you use a scale of one cent per box for soybeans, then a reversal amount would be three cents. Assigning these values must be somewhat arbitrary. All published charts will reveal the value of a box and the number of boxes required to call for a reversal. Point-and-figure charts can be made more or less sensitive by altering the value of the boxes. The larger the price increments, the less sensitive the chart will be, and vice versa. These values can often be arrived at only by trial and error. If you make the mistake of constructing a chart that is too sensitive to minor fluctuations, you will have the problem of constantly being whipsawed, of taking a position on one side of the market only to incur a loss when the market reverses. On the other hand, if you use increments that are too large, you'll have the problem of missing out on the beginning of price movements. Fortunately, there are some guidelines. As a rule, the price increment should represent approximately one tenth to one fifth of a limit move. Price reversals can generally be measured by a three- to five-unit move.

For example, let's say you are an orange juice trader and you want to use 30 points as your basic increment, with three spaces, or 90 points, signifying a price reversal. Since each 5/100-minimum "tick" in orange juice represents $7.50 per contract, the 30-point increment would represent six times this amount, or $45. The 90-point reversal would represent $135 per contract. Since 300 points represents a limit move in orange juice, a price movement of this magnitude would be represented by ten X's or O's on the chart.

Using these values, how might a point-and-figure chart be constructed in the orange juice market? For each 30-point rise, the chartist will add one X on top of the previous column of X's. The chartist will move over one column and start plotting O's *only* when the market falls by at least 90 points from its previous high. If the market continues to rise with reactions no greater than 90 points, more X's will be added in the original X column. Once a downtrend begins and the chartist adds an O for each fall of 30 points, no X's will be added in a new column *unless* the market rallies by 30 points or more.

When plotting X's, wait for the price to fill the whole box before adding an X; in other words, round the price down. When plotting O's, wait for the price to drop to fill the whole box before adding an O; in other words, round the number up.

How to Interpret Chart Patterns

The proper interpretation of chart patterns is one key to success in futures trading. There are many chart patterns that traders rely upon to help them in their forecasting activities. Some patterns are more reliable than others, and some are subject to a variety of interpretations. The major disadvantage of chart trading is that a trader may see a pattern where none exists. A major advantage is that so many traders use charts that a given signal may encourage chartists to enter or exit the market and bring about the predicted price move. Regardless of the validity of certain chart patterns, price movements do influence trading activities. As a result, every trader should be familiar with the most common patterns.

The patterns that follow are applicable to both bar and point-and-figure charts. Regardless of the charting method you use, you should try to identify them whenever possible and let them guide your trading behavior. As a technical analyst, your concern is not why a commodity is rising or falling, but what today's price action means in terms of tomorrow's price behavior. To make such an analysis you have to be familiar with these typical chart patterns and what they mean.

Trend lines. The chartist looks for certain formations, the most significant of which is the trend line. The definition and construction of a trend line were discussed in Chapter 6. Whether you are a trend follower or a market forecaster, however, the existence of trend lines will play an important role in your trading behavior. As a rule, in the long run you will always want to be trading on the side of the major trend. Day traders and short-term traders do follow the minor trend, which is usually the opposite of the major trend. But before you decide to go against a trend, you should know clearly what the major trend is and have a plan to take advantage of it.

Trend lines are drawn in on a chart on the basis of price patterns. Rising markets will have an uptrend line connecting three or more lows, whereas falling markets will have a downtrend line connecting three or more highs. When a trend line is broken, the violation of the line signals a price reversal. Longs should liquidate and go short when an uptrend is broken. Conversely, shorts should cover and go long when a downtrend line is broken. The problem with this rule rests with the trend line itself. Some trend lines are too steep and are easily broken by minor price reactions or rallies, even though a given trend is still intact. When a market breaks a trend line but continues on an upward or downward path, a new trend line must be drawn. The longer a trend line is intact, however, the more valid it should be considered.

In Figures 10 and 11, the violation of an uptrend line and that of a downtrend line are shown respectively. Note that the breaking of the trend line is the signal that the trend has reversed and that the trader should likewise reverse his position.

When rising or falling, prices tend to stay within a narrow band known as a *channel*. The channel, or *channel line,* is identified as a line parallel to the trend line. As counterpoint to the trend line, the channel line in a bull market will connect the progressive *highs,* and in a bear market the progressive *lows*. As long as prices stay within the confines of a channel, a trader can rest assured that the market is behaving with some degree of predictability. Major trend traders will *buy on price reactions to the trend line in a rising market and sell on price rallies to the trend line in a falling market.* These simple rules are illustrated in Figures 12 and 13.

There will be times when prices move out of the channel. This occurrence often denotes a change in the character of the market. For example, when extreme pressure is brought to bear upon a bull market, prices may begin to rise at a much quicker rate and move right out of the top of the channel. In such a runaway market, the slope of the trend line will become quite steep. However, very steep trend lines cannot be maintained for very long. As a result, traders who go long a commodity once it moves up sharply from a trend line are taking extreme risks. Such markets often fall even faster than they rise. To be on the wrong side of such markets is to invite disaster.

Support and resistance. Support and resistance zones manifest themselves quite clearly on a price chart. By definition, a support level exists at

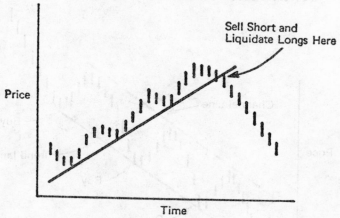

Figure 10. The breaking of an uptrend line signals the point to liquidate long positions and sell short.

the price at which a considerable increase in demand will generate additional buying; conversely, a resistance level exists where increased supply will generate additional selling. Support zones are characterized by bargain hunters purchasing contracts, thus forming a "support" for a commodity;

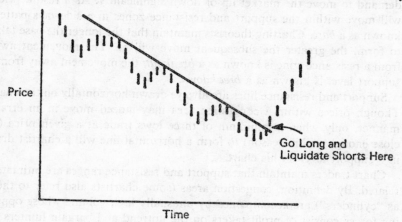

Figure 11. The breaking of a downtrend line signals the point to liquidate short positions and go long.

resistance zones are characterized by profit takers selling on rallies, creating a "resistance" beyond which prices have a hard time rising. Significant moves away from support and resistance levels are generally preceded by a great deal of uncertainty in the market when a genuine battle exists between buyers and sellers. This so-called period of *consolidation* or *conges-*

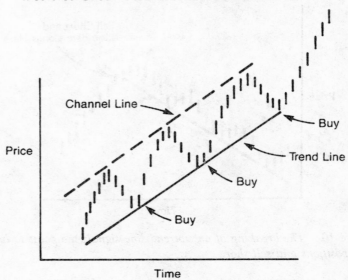

Figure 12. In an uptrend, trend traders buy on reactions to the trend line.

tion merely reflects the inability of the aggregate forces of supply and demand to move the market up or down significantly. As a result, prices will move within the support and resistance zones in a sideways pattern known as a *base.* Charting theorists maintain that the longer the base takes to form, the greater the subsequent move will be. The movement away from a resistance zone is known as a *breakout;* the movement away from a support level is known as a *breakdown.*

Support and resistance lines are always drawn horizontally on the chart. Though prices within a congestion area may indeed move in an erratic manner, only when a minimum of three lows trade at a given price (or close enough within reason) to form a horizontal line will a chartist draw in a support level on his chart.

Chart traders maintain that support and resistance ranges are intimately related. By definition, congestion areas (some chartists also refer to them as "cylinders") are accompanied by unusually high volume whose opposing forces consist of profit takers on the uptrend and bargain hunters on the downtrend. These two forces manifest themselves on the price chart as resistance levels and support levels respectively. Figure 14 illustrates this phenomenon.

Like trend lines, support and resistance areas are fairly easy to spot. They may be of either short or long duration and are noted for their propensity to form near historical bottoms and tops.

Another characteristic of support and resistance levels is that one may, upon penetration, become the other. For example, in Figure 15 the initial resistance encountered at A and B becomes a potential support when

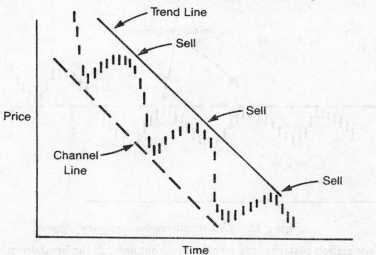

Figure 13.   In a downtrend, trend traders sell on rallies to the trend line.

tested at C. Likewise, in Figure 16, the reverse occurs as the initial support at D and E becomes a potential resistance when tested at point F.

Support and resistance levels are important because they tell you where prices are likely to break. The best way to trade markets that are forming

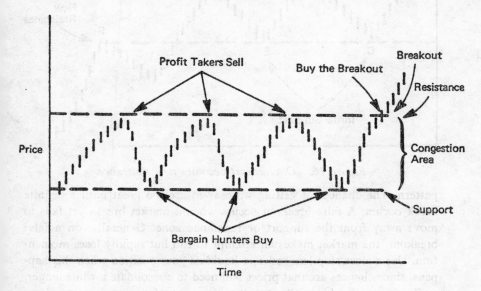

Figure 14.   Support and resistance levels are created by a preponderance of buyers over sellers and sellers over buyers respectively.

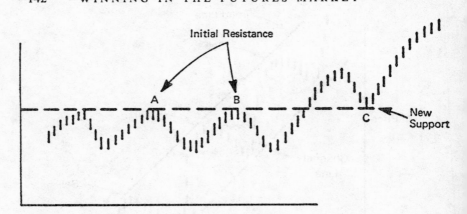

Figure 15.   Old resistance becomes new support.

congestion patterns is to buy the breakout and sell the breakdown. Place a buy-stop just above a resistance in a market you think will break out. Place a sell-stop just below a support in a market you think will break down. Don't purchase or sell short a commodity that remains in a consolidation

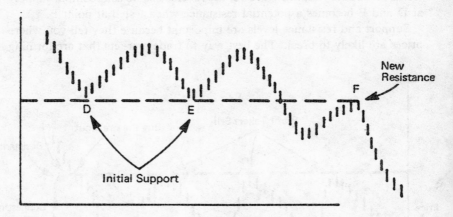

Figure 16.   Old support becomes new resistance.

pattern. The chances of getting whipsawed are too great until a definite break occurs. A false breakout occurs when a market breaks yet fails to move away from the support or resistance zone. Generally, on a false breakout, the market makes an attempt to run but rapidly loses momentum. Use a close stop-loss order to liquidate your position when this happens, since chances are that prices will need to consolidate a while longer.

Head and shoulders. Chart patterns consist of two major groupings: those that signal a price continuation (continuation patterns) and those that signal price reversals (reversal patterns). The head-and-shoulders for-

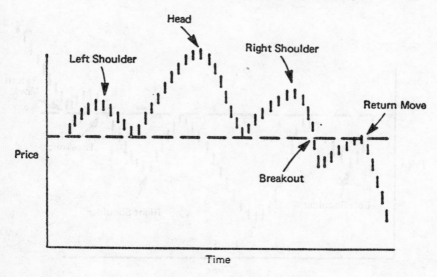

Figure 17. Head-and-shoulders top.

mation is perhaps the most significant of all top-and-bottom reversal patterns. Not only is it a reliable chart configuration, but the ensuing move is generally of sufficient magnitude to warrant continued observation. The one drawback in using the formation is that it is difficult to predict in its early stages. There are normal head-and-shoulders patterns—consisting of a left shoulder, a head, and a right shoulder (see Figure 17, above)—and so-called inverted head-and-shoulders patterns. They are both reversal patterns. However, the normal head-and-shoulders pattern signals a downward price move, while the inverted head-and-shoulders pattern signals an upward move. These two formations are also known as a head-and-shoulders top and a head-and-shoulders bottom, respectively. Figures 17 and 18 illustrate the two patterns. In the illustrations, you will see a line drawn connecting the bases of the two shoulders. This line, which need not be horizontal, frequently has a slope to it and is known as the *neckline*. A general rule states that a subsequent move away from the neckline generally carries at least as far as the tip of the head is away from the neckline. Quite frequently the move is far greater. Following the *breakout* from the neckline, the head-and-shoulders pattern often forms a price pattern known as the *return move*. This is a brief pause when prices retreat back to the neckline prior to resuming their initial direction. The return move is found in only some of the head-and-shoulders patterns, however, and is not considered an integral part of the chart pattern.

Double tops and bottoms. A thorny problem is presented by this chart pattern, because in the normal course of price action and reaction a multitude of tops and bottoms seem to present themselves. Not always, unfortunately, are chart patterns what they seem. Therefore, you must not be too

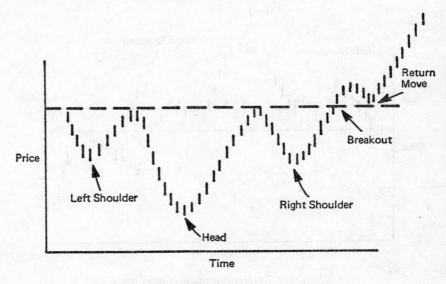

Price

Left Shoulder

Head

Right Shoulder

Breakout

Return Move

Time

Figure 18.   Head-and-shoulders bottom.

hasty in calling a double top or bottom. Like head-and-shoulders patterns, double tops and bottoms are reversal patterns. Like any significant reversal pattern, they take time to develop and frequently don't have perfect symmetry. In fact, the most reliable patterns frequently show weakness (in the case of a top) and strength (in the case of a bottom) on the second half of the formation.

Among the key indicators to spotting a valid double top or bottom is volume activity. Any unusual volume—either excessively high or unusually low—should be noted when trying to determine whether a chart pattern is an incipient double top or bottom. One peak might have abnormally high volume; the next, abnormally low volume.

Because markets don't give up and change direction without going through the throes of development, you should not expect a top or bottom to be formed easily. A market nearing a top, for example, will often change direction, react, change direction again, react again, and take one final lunge at the top before plummeting.

Double tops are also known as "M" formations, because they resemble the letter M, while the double bottom resembles the M turned upside down, or a W. Because prices tend to zigzag, these reversal patterns may appear quite frequently. However, most would-be double tops and bottoms often turn into simple continuation patterns. To avoid taking the wrong position when you suspect that a double top or bottom is forming, you must wait until a greater portion of the pattern is worked out and prices begin to move in the opposite direction. Unfortunately, by the time this occurs, you have often missed a significant portion of the move.

In analyzing a top or bottom reversal pattern, you should always be aware of the dynamics taking place in the market. At a top, the first peak represents the area where profit taking puts an end to the upward momentum of the price. When prices react off the top, bargain hunters, still bullish on the commodity, rush in and buy, pushing prices up once again. More profit taking enters the market and prices again retreat. If the same pattern repeats itself, you may have a *triple top.* If prices react below the previous low, however, anxious longs may rush into the market to sell out their positions, and the market decline will be under way. The exact opposite occurs where a bottom is concerned. While there are additional variations on this theme, the basic double top and bottom appear in Figures 19 and 20.

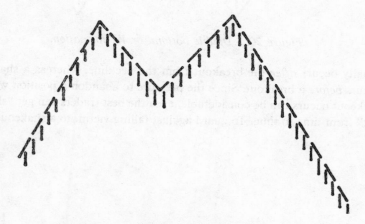

Figure 19.   Double top, or M, formation.

Lines and saucers. A true line, or saucer, formation is among the most favorable of the chart patterns. Usually a long time in the making, lines and saucers frequently serve as a prelude to dramatic market moves. Moreover, the magnitude of the ultimate move is often related to the amount of time required to form the line, or saucer, base pattern. The key to trading this pattern is to wait until the breakout occurs.

The curve of the saucer points to the direction prices will take once it breaks out. Many saucer formations form a platform prior to the breakout on increased volume. A saucer bottom appears in Figure 21.

Shakeouts. A shakeout is a false move that occurs just prior to a significant breakout in the opposite direction. Shakeouts have a tendency to occur when traders least expect them. Moreover, they have an uncanny persuasive quality, causing even the most skilled technical analysts to abandon their positions prematurely.

A shakeout is similar to the return move indicated in the head-and-shoulders pattern. The difference between the two is that the return move

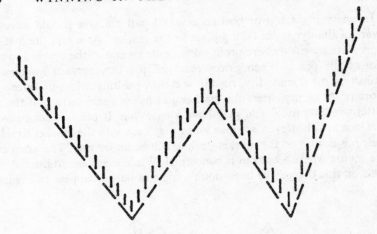

Figure 20.   Double bottom, or W, formation.

usually occurs *after* the breakout from the neckline, whereas a shakeout occurs *before* a breakout. Since the pressure to abandon a position when a shakeout occurs can be considerable, even the best traders can get "shaken out" from time to time. To guard against falling victim to a shakeout, you

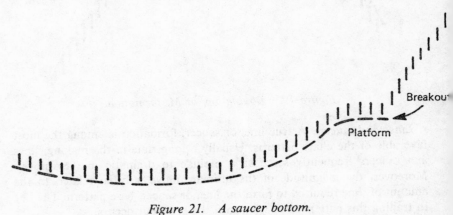

Figure 21.   A saucer bottom.

must either be convinced that the move is genuine or have the courage and money to hold on despite the reaction of the market. This latter suggestion is given advisedly, mindful of the fact that occasionally what seems to be a shakeout won't be a shakeout at all—but a genuine move.

Broadening formations. Broadening formations occur as a commodity begins to experience greater and greater volatility, usually just prior to a breakout, causing each successive high to be higher and each successive low to be lower, until the market ultimately makes up its mind and asserts itself in one direction or another. In general, the formation is characterized by a series of waves. Until at least three of these waves are completed, however, the formation is usually not considered developed, making an analysis of its ultimate direction difficult. Figures 22 and 23 show two examples of broadening formations.

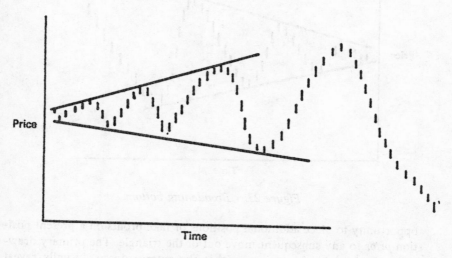

Figure 22.   Broadening top.

Triangles. These patterns are relatively easy to spot on a chart. Essentially, there are three types: symmetrical, ascending, and descending triangles. The symmetrical triangle, as the name implies, is shaped equally on all sides. As prices near the right apex of the triangle, volatility decreases substantially. This "tightening" in volatility is followed by a sharp breakout signifying the direction prices will take. Price movements out of a symmetrical triangle are frequently quite large; often there are self-fulfilling aspects to this chart formation, resulting in chartists entering the market *because* the market is slanted to move.

Ascending and descending triangles, as their respective names imply, portend price movements in the general direction that predominates within each triangle. Thus, if the lows are becoming progressively higher within the triangle, it is an ascending triangle and prices can be expected to break to the upside; conversely, a succession of progressively lower highs would indicate a descending triangle, from which prices could be expected to break lower. The descending triangle formation is particularly useful when the market has had a good rally and prices appear overvalued; the ascending triangle formation, on the other hand, works better at low levels when prices are building a base from which they will rise.

Triangles are considered to be continuation patterns; they give prices a chance to consolidate and gather strength before continuing in their original direction. As with any consolidation phase, triangles offer the trader an

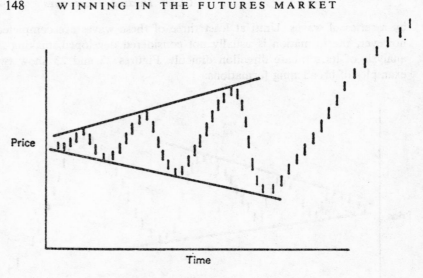

Price

Time

Figure 23.   Broadening bottom.

opportunity to place additional positions or take profits on a present position *prior* to any subsequent move out of the triangle. The primary drawback of triangular formations is that the pattern doesn't usually reveal itself until near completion. But this, unfortunately, is a drawback with many chart formations.

Figures 24, 25, and 26 illustrate the symmetrical, ascending and descending triangles.

In addition to the triangles indicated above, there are several variations on the triangular theme. One is the inverted triangle, a broadening formation with the apex pointing to the left. Another variation is the coil, which also culminates in an apex, followed by a move in the direction of the breakout. These are generally continuation patterns.

Other continuation patterns. A wide variety of chart patterns have been recognized and given names according to their predominant shapes. You should always keep in mind that continuation patterns have been known to slip into reversal patterns without warning, however. The following formations include the most frequently occurring chart patterns that you are likely to encounter.

1. *Boxes and rectangles.* The most significant factor to remember about these chart patterns is that their breakouts are apt to be valid. Boxes and rectangles are among the more reliable continuation patterns. Figures 27 and 28 illustrate the two patterns.

2. *Flags.* There are two types of flags: *up flags* and *down flags*. The two most notable characteristics of a flag are the "pole" from which it flies and the slant of the flag. The flagpole is usually formed on heavy volume,

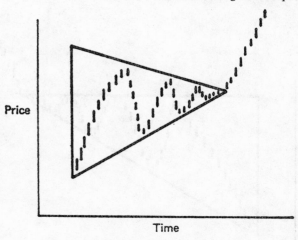

Figure 24.   The symmetrical triangle.

whether prices are rising or falling. The slant of the flag runs *counter* to the direction of the price trend. Therefore, an up flag will slant downward, and a down flag will slant upward. When quickly and tightly formed, flags are noted for their reliability as continuation patterns. An up flag and a down flag appear in Figures 29 and 30.

3. *Wedges.* Wedges are similar to triangular chart patterns except that they slant either upward or downward. Like flags, they also come in two varieties: *falling wedges* and *rising wedges.* The falling wedge slants downward and signals an upturn in prices; the rising wedge slants upward and signals a downturn in prices. Like most other continuation patterns, wedges are formed on relatively light volume, with trading activity picking up on the breakout.

4. *Pennants.* The pennant is identical to a symmetrical triangle except that it has a "pole" attached to it. There are both *up pennants* and *down pennants,* their only difference being the direction that prices take on the breakout from the apex. Since a pennant is a continuation pattern, prices entering the formation from above will usually break to the downside; and prices entering from below will usually break to the upside. The "pole" is almost always formed on significantly heavy volume.

5. *Diamonds.* Of all the continuation patterns, diamonds (characterized by a seesawing in prices) are the most likely to give the trader reason to pause. Just as prices seem to break one way, they will suddenly reverse and swing the other way. Uncertainty in the market is responsible for the diamond's formation, with first buyers and then sellers predominating. Nevertheless, the diamond is generally considered a valid continuation pattern. It is most often found following a big swing. Figure 31 illustrates the diamond formation.

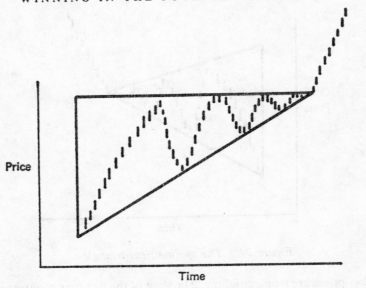

Figure 25. The ascending triangle.

Gaps. A gap is created when a commodity opens at a price higher than the high for the previous day or lower than the low for the previous day. If, during the course of the day's trading activities, the gap remains *unfilled* (meaning the commodity will not trade at a price that would fill the

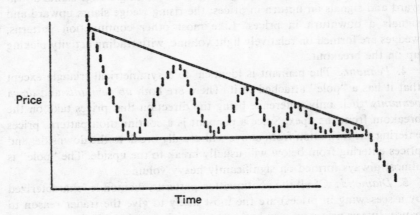

Figure 26. The descending triangle.

gap), a space will appear on the bar chart. For those on the right side of the market, gaps can be among the most promising signs, as they usually occur when limit moves are being made; for those who might have the market

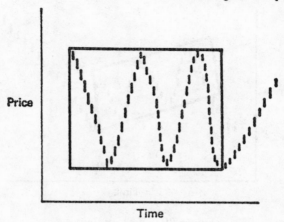

Figure 27. The box.

move against them when a gap occurs, however, the gap is more often a sign of disaster.

As a rule, gaps tend to be filled soon after they are created. For this reason, many chartists prefer to wait for the gap to be filled before they

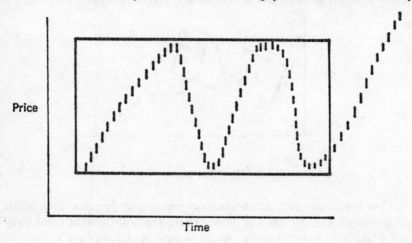

Figure 28. The rectangle.

enter the gapping market. There are, of course, times when the gap remains unfilled. When this occurs, it is often better to let the market run.

There are four major types of gaps, each of them uniquely indicative of a particular stage of a bull or a bear market. In order of their likely occurrence, they are as follows:

1. *The common gap.* The common gap is often caused by a momentary flourish of interest in a commodity caused, for instance, by a crop report.

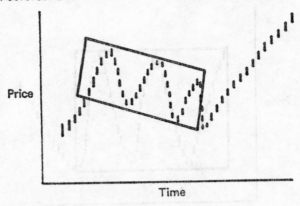

Figure 29.   The up flag.

It rarely signifies any great change in the nature of the market and is, for that reason, quite likely to be filled. In thin markets, which are not known for significant trading volume, common gaps are apt to occur frequently, as almost any order of significance will have to be filled away from the market in order to draw out the necessary buyers or sellers.

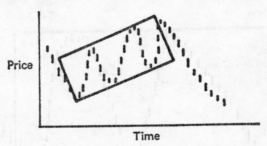

Figure 30.   The down flag.

2. *The breakaway gap.* The breakaway gap frequently reflects the initial enthusiasm of a major market move. There are both *upward* breakaway gaps, which are characterized by heavy volume, and *downward* breakaway gaps, in which volume is less important. Breakaway gaps usually develop on market-changing rumors or news. Because of the suddenness of the underlying motives prompting a breakaway gap to occur, traders are hard put to predict them in advance and, more often than not, are caught by surprise and have to run after a market—which, in turn, adds even more fuel to the fire.

3. *The runaway gap.* Also called the "measuring gap," the runaway gap is the culmination of trader expectations not being fulfilled. After a breakaway gap occurs in a market, traders generally look for a place to "get

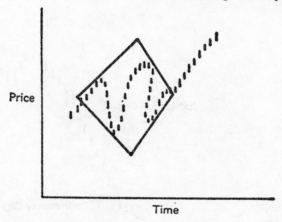

Figure 31.   The diamond.

aboard" a move. Being cautious, however, they often await a reestablish-
ment of some stability in prices first. When a market fails to stabilize,
however, and prices continue to move in the direction of the initial move, a
sort of panic sets in and traders become willing to pay almost anything to
get in on what seems an excellent opportunity. This, of course, causes
prices to move even faster—resulting in the runaway gap. Look for this
gap to occur about halfway through a major bull or bear market.

   4. *The exhaustion gap.* The exhaustion gap represents a major reversal
in the market. Since a market that experiences a gap of this kind is almost
always overbought or oversold, time usually brings a correction to pass.
Try to avoid markets in which the final stages of a major move are under
way. A market in the exhaustion-gap stage is almost always too volatile to
trade with reason.

   Reversal days. Reversal days signal a reverse in the direction of the
market. Since markets do not give up one direction easily, reversal days
are characterized by a frenzy of buying and selling, resulting in extremely
high volume. They are also characterized by unique price chart patterns.
The most common reversal-day patterns are the following:

   1. *Top reversal days.* This pattern is characterized by prices rising into
new high ground and then plummeting to close lower than the previous
day's close. Although a new top is made on a top reversal day, a loss is
experienced on the day.

   2. *Bottom reversal days.* This is the reverse of the above pattern. Prices
fall into new low ground and then gather strength to close higher than the
previous day's close for a gain on the day.

   3. *Key reversal days.* While this pattern may be similar to either of the
above, its singular characteristic is that it is a *genuine* top or bottom; too

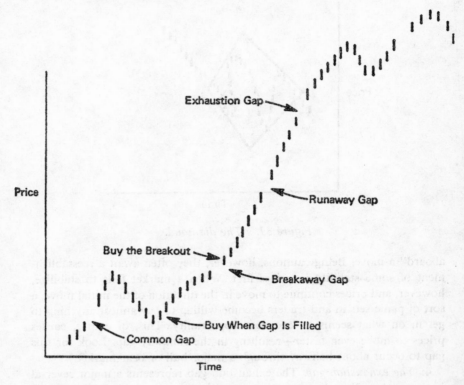

Figure 32.   Gaps.

often, prices following a top or bottom reversal day change direction only for a few trading sessions and then revert to their former course.

4. *Two-day reversals.* A variation of the above patterns, two-day reversals manifest themselves by closing first on a new high and then, the second day, closing on the low of the day. Bottom two-day reversals consist of patterns in which the commodity first closes on a new low and then on the high of the day during the following trading session.

The measured move. The measured move is a fairly large price swing that is halted at its midpoint for a corrective phase prior to resuming its original direction. It refers to the total price trend that a commodity may be on and applies to both bull and bear markets. Although it is difficult to see in its initial stages, the measured move is frequently easily identifiable once the market reaches its corrective phase. The pattern has three separate components: a first leg, a corrective phase, and a second leg. The two legs are approximately equal in length. During the first leg, prices generally hold to a trend channel. When the corrective phase is reached, prices may break the trend line as the market temporarily goes against the major trend. Lastly, the second leg will again adhere to the original trend line's slope and equal the length of the first leg.

The measured move is valuable because it can often provide a clue as to how far a market will run. If the market you are following, for instance,

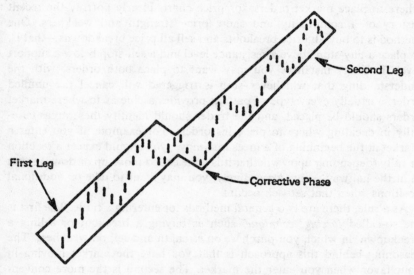

Figure 33. The measured move up.

makes a steady 300-point rise before beginning a sideways movement, you can expect the market to rise another 300 points prior to reaching its top. The same pattern applies to bear markets as well. Figures 33 and 34 illustrate the measured move up and the measured move down respectively.

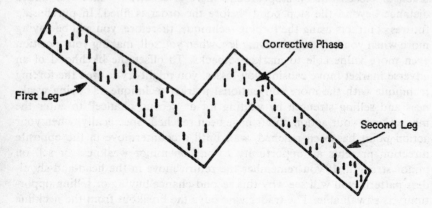

Figure 34. The measured move down.

How to Use Charts for Placing Orders

The most valuable function of the price chart is its ability to tell the trader where to place market orders, for price charts clearly portray the recent history of a commodity and show price strength and weakness. One method is to buy all price breakouts and sell all price breakdowns—that is, to place a buy-stop above a resistance level and a sell-stop below a support level. In many instances you may want to place both orders, with the understanding that whichever stop is triggered will cancel the unfilled order. Virtually every type of pattern provides a clue as to where market orders should be placed, and the trader should identify these areas carefully in deciding where to place his orders. For example, if you enter a market at the beginning of a measured move, you should expect a reaction or rally (depending upon whether it is a measured move up or down) to set in at the halfway point. Accordingly, you may want to take on additional positions when that setback occurs.

As a rule, there are two general methods for entering a trade. The first is the so-called *forcing technique,* such as buying a breakout or selling a breakdown, in which you purchase on strength and sell on weakness. The reasoning behind this approach is that you have the market moving in your favor when you enter the market. The second is the more conventional technique of buying weakness and selling strength. Here the reasoning is that when you buy on a reaction, the market has already declined and probably isn't about to decline further; and, conversely, when you sell on strength, the market has already risen and probably isn't about to rise further. In either situation, you are less vulnerable to an adverse move. Whichever method you use, you should realize that when positions are taken or closed out on stop orders, there is usually a "skid," or added distance beyond the stop point, before the order is filled. In purchasing futures contracts using the forcing technique, therefore, you will be paying more when you buy and receiving less when you sell, making your position even more vulnerable to market setbacks. To offset the likelihood of an adverse market move causing you losses, you might try to wed the forcing technique with the more conventional market technique of buying weakness and selling strength by waiting for a "second chance" to enter the market once your action points have been reached. Specifically, when your action point has been reached, wait until a countermove in the opposite direction presents an opportunity to buy on minor weakness or sell on minor strength. If you remember the return move in the head-and-shoulders pattern, you will see why this second-chance buying or selling opportunity is so valuable. The trader who buys the breakout from the neckline or sells the breakdown from the neckline in the head-and-shoulders pattern will probably be stopped out as the market temporarily moves against him. But the trader who awaits the second-chance buying or selling opportunity will be in the market at precisely the right moment. Unfortunately, it is not always possible to determine in advance which method is best. Some head-and-shoulder patterns, for instance, don't have a return move following a breakout. But for those who wish to wait for a countermove in the market to occur, here are some suggestions. Second-chance buying or selling points can be predetermined by taking action on: (1) the opening the day after the first close in the opposite direction; (2) the first countermove of X distance from the signal point; or (3) the first countermove of X distance from any point reached after the action point is triggered.

To use this method, you first have to establish the initial action point. This would be the point at which you would buy or sell if you used the forcing technique. Secondly, if you are going to use the second or third suggested method, you have to establish the number of points in the countermove before you actually take your position. In Figures 35 and 36, you can see a breakout from a symmetrical triangle. In the first illustration, the forcing technique is used to buy the breakout. In the second illustration, the market is purchased only after a countermove occurs.

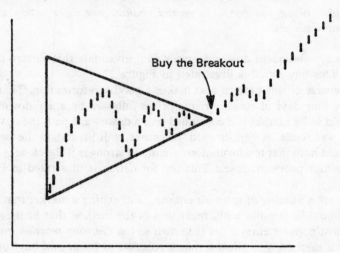

Figure 35. The forcing technique calls for buying the breakout.

Charts are particularly useful in pinpointing market tops and bottoms— if you know what to look for. One of the best market bottom indicators on a bar chart is presented when prices make a steady market decline of at least four days in duration followed by an upside gap. To ensure that this is a valid buy signal, the closing price after the gap must be higher than the four previous closing prices. Moreover, within two days a higher high and a higher close above the high and close of the day when the gap was made must occur for this pattern to be considered legitimate. This is the buy

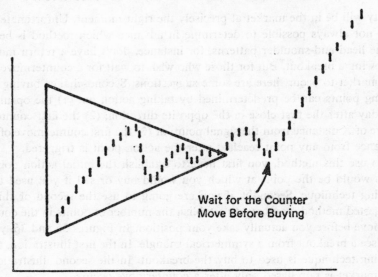

Wait for the Counter
Move Before Buying

Figure 36. When you try for a second chance, you defer action until a countermove occurs.

signal. Any subsequent downside gap would invalidate this pattern immediately. This buy signal is illustrated in Figure 37.

The reverse of this pattern also makes a good top formation. That is, if you have four days of steadily rising prices followed by a gap downward, you would sell a market if it continued on its downward path the day after the gap was made. A gap upward, of course, will invalidate the pattern. You should note that top formations are much stronger if the close is lower than the four previous closes. This top formation is illustrated in Figure 38.

There are a number of rules for entering and exiting a market that every trader should be familiar with, regardless of the method that he uses. One of the most popular entry rules is known as the *four-day reaction method*. Using this method, you allow a minor reaction to occur and buy (or sell) on the four-day down (or up). This method generally enables you to buy on weakness or sell on strength just as prices are about to move in your favor. The buy signal is illustrated in Figure 39.

Another popular entry method is known as the *40 percent rule*. This method of entry calls for purchases on a correction of 40 percent from the difference between the low and the high of the current rally. For instance, if corn prices rise, say, 5 cents, you should look to be a buyer on a reaction of 2 cents, or 40 percent of the original move. The 40 percent rule is illustrated in Figure 40.

The *thrust day method* calls for buying on the first sign of strength following a reaction in a market that is in an uptrend. To give this method

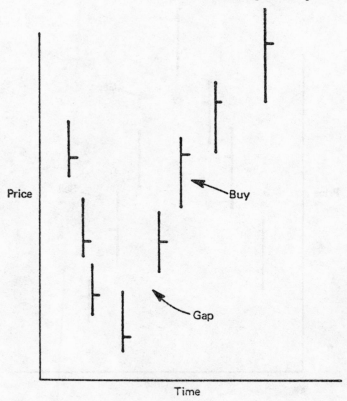

Figure 37. Buy a market bottom once it gaps up after a decline and continues higher.

added validity, the day before the thrust day should have a high lower than the previous day's high, and a low lower than the previous day's low, as in Figure 41.

In looking for a thrust day, you should ignore all so-called *inside days*. An inside day is one in which the high is below the previous day, and the low is higher than the previous day. In a downtrend, the reverse of this pattern indicates a selling point.

In a gapping market, a common practice is to wait for the gap to be filled before entering a buy or a sell order. In a rising market, for instance, the gap will be created as buyers rush in and bid up prices following some dramatic news event such as a bullish crop report. The sudden rise, however, generally results in considerable profit taking, bringing the market down to a more reasonable level before prices again move up. The rule is to buy when prices reach the level where the initial gap (often a breakaway gap) occurred. In markets in which a gap occurs on the charts but no

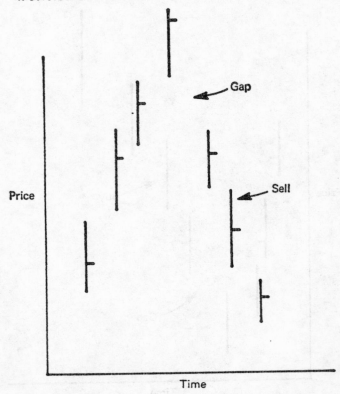

Figure 38. Sell a market top once it gaps down after a market rise and continues lower.

reaction occurs, it is best to stand aside unless you got in on the breakout. Such markets are frequently too volatile to trade with caution. Figure 42 illustrates where you should buy a market that forms a gap in the early stages of a bull market. In declining markets, the reverse strategy also applies.

In placing stop-loss orders to exit a trade, your primary concern is that a market has turned against you before you decide to liquidate your position. When you have a market that turns against you, the rule is that you should act quickly. Don't wait around to watch the market once it goes against you. Get out and take a loss if necessary. One chart method is to place your stop the minimum fluctuation below the low of the day preceding the thrust day, as in Figure 43.

Another method used to exit a market is to keep a sell-stop on the close below the low of the last six days. This gives the market time to swing but still keeps the stop reasonably close. Like a trailing stop, this six-day method will call for raising the stop in a bull market.

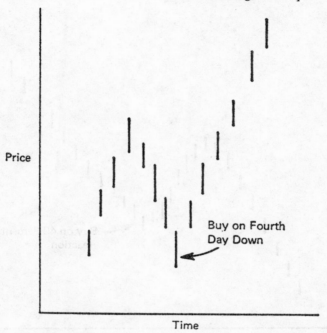

Figure 39. The four-day reaction method calls for a purchase on the fourth day down following a rally.

Some conservative traders don't wait for prices to move against them, but, rather, take profits when they have reached a predetermined goal. One popular rule is to take profits when they reach 25 percent of the initial margin. For example, using this method, a wheat trader who deposited $1,500 per contract in initial margin would take profits each time his position grew by 25 percent, or $375. Translated into cents per bushel, this would mean a sell-stop would be placed 7½ cents above the entry point. In a steadily rising market, the speculator using this method would make a number of trades before the top was ultimately reached. This method, of course, can be used in conjunction with other methods, should the 25-percent goal not be reached.

Swing Charts

Swing charts measure price movement in terms of predetermined price swings. Like point-and-figure charts, swing charts do not measure time, nor are they concerned with volume or open interest. To construct this chart, you simply draw a vertical line in the direction of the first price move. Let's say you consider 50 points to be your minimum price swing. You draw a vertical line for each 50-point move until the market changes

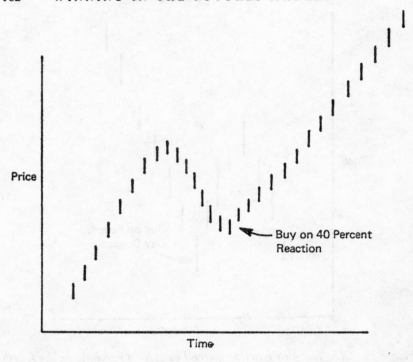

Figure 40.   The 40 percent rule calls for a purchase on a 40 percent reaction from a rally top.

direction. You then draw a small horizontal line to the right and a vertical line in the reverse direction to record a swing of 50 points or more in the opposite direction. You will continue to switch directions as long as price reversals are greater than 50 points. A typical swing chart appears in Figure 44.

. Buy and sell signals are generated by a swing chart when the previous high and low prices are penetrated by a predetermined amount. The swing chart is essentially a trend-following method. You either sell weakness and go with the downtrend, or buy strength and go with the uptrend, when you use a swing chart. As you can see from Figure 44, this method doesn't catch tops or bottoms, but it does keep you on the right side of the market for the major part of most moves.

When you construct a swing chart, you must decide the amount of minimum swing to be charted and the amount and type of penetration, if any, required to signal a price change. Some chartists also require a price reversal to stay above a previous high, or below a previous low, for a day or two before a reversal signal is issued.

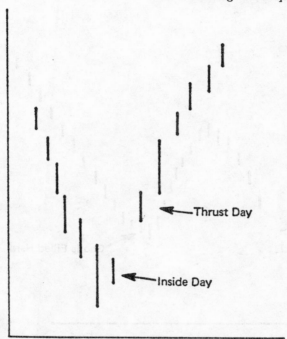

Thrust Day

Inside Day

Figure 41.   The thrust day method calls for buying on strength following a reaction.

Three-dimensional Charting

Developed by William Ohama, a broker and analyst with E. F. Hutton in Los Angeles, three-dimensional charting is a technique for pinpointing market reversals. In 1969, Ohama discovered that price divergences occurred just prior to major reversals in the market. These price divergences would develop between different contract months of the same commodity (3-D patterns) or between different contract months of related commodities (4-D patterns). The reasons for the price divergences between contract months is related to hedging activity. Hedgers, who are the major market forces, are frequently quite secretive about their trading activities. Because of this secrecy, it is often difficult to find out what they are doing in the market. But through 3-D analysis it is possible to discover their hidden footprints.

Most charting methods are limited to portraying time and price. But the Ohama 3-D technique adds a third variable to the traditional techniques of market analysis by looking at the interrelationship of contract months. By doing so, it attempts to discover the *quality* of participation in a market as a key indicator of future price direction.

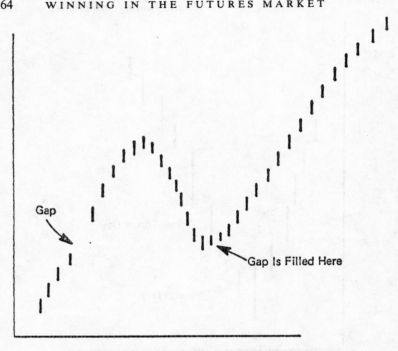

Figure 42.   Buy when the gap is filled.

Large traders, especially large hedgers, have a unique ability to place and offset their positions at important reversal points in the market. That many hedgers have an uncanny ability to do their buying and selling at key reversal points in the market should come as no surprise. After all, they produce and process the commodities, they have the resources to research the market thoroughly, and, most important, they often have enough buying and selling power to influence those markets in which they operate. Given the hedgers' propensity to be on the right side of the market at the right time, it behooves us to try to make some sense out of their trading behavior. Fortunately, the Ohama 3-D technique provides the basic clues to what the hedgers are doing in the market.

The key to understanding the meaning of hedging behavior is an accurate analysis of price divergence. Price divergence occurs when one contract month moves in one direction while another moves in the opposite direction. This is significant because related contracts almost always move in tandem with one another due to the nature of carrying charges and the built-in cost of holding commodities from month to month—that is, one month may rise or fall a little faster than another contract month. But, as a rule, if the September contract rises, so also will the November contract and all the rest of the contract months. Moreover, related commodities also tend to parallel one another in their price movements. If soybeans are

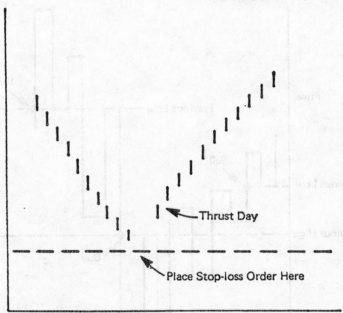

Figure 43. Place a stop-loss order below the low preceding a thrust day.

down, chances are, soybean oil and soybean meal will also be down. And so on. But when extensive and important hedging enters or exits a market, those contracts that are experiencing considerable pressure due to hedging buying and selling will tend to behave differently from the contract months in which no extensive hedging is taking place. As a result, a price divergence may be created. It is this very price divergence that often points to an important market reversal.

The rules for spotting 3-D price divergences at tops and bottoms are simple and easy to understand. They are as follows:

1. A top reversal is imminent when a commodity begins to make new intermediate and major highs in most contract months, and when one or more contract months fail to enter new high ground, creating a price divergence. Sell only the contract months that are not making new highs.

2. A bottom reversal is imminent when a commodity begins to make new intermediate and major lows in most contract months, and when one or more contract months fail to register new lows, creating a price divergence. Buy only the contract months that are not making new lows.

On a day when a *change in trend* is noted by the daily highs (in the case of a top reversal) or the daily lows (in the case of a bottom reversal), followed by a close in the direction of the reversal by the weak or strong month, a 3-D pattern has been established. The order to take a long or

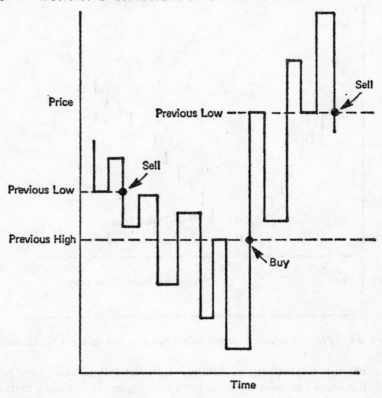

Figure 44. A swing chart changes direction only when the market exceeds the predetermined minimum swing in the opposite direction.

short position, depending upon whether a top or bottom configuration is signaled, should be placed the following trading day.

To perform a complete 3-D analysis of a commodity or related commodities, you must follow every contract month traded from the day each contract month commences trading to the day it goes off the boards. In addition to the charts, you should keep numerical tables listing the intraday highs, lows, and closes for each contract. For easier trend spotting, you can list the numerical tables in two different colors—one color to signal a rise in prices from the previous day, and another color to signal a decline in prices.

You should look for a variety of configurations in your chart and numerical table patterns. Sometimes alternating months will show the price divergence; at other times, the spot and distant months will go in one direction and the middle months in another. Moreover, the divergence can occur between old-crop and new-crop contracts, or even between cash prices and future prices. Often the first contracts of a new crop year reveal price divergences. Key contract months to look at are as follows: February pork bellies, November soybeans, December soybean meal, July wheat, December corn, March sugar, December cotton, and January orange juice.

In cash premium markets, most of the tops occur when the spot contract doesn't make new highs. This situation is best taken advantage of by putting on a bear spread: selling the nearby month and buying the distant month. The most conclusive patterns occur when one contract month trades up the limit while another, simultaneously, trades down the limit. In the past, this particular configuration has appeared in cattle, hogs, eggs, and wheat, among other markets.

Four-dimensional Patterns

When you make comparisons of commodities in interrelated markets, you add a fourth dimension to the chart analysis. Such comparisons might be between lumber and plywood, wheat and corn, wheat and oats, corn and oats, soybeans and soybean oil or meal, silver and gold, Swiss francs and Deutschemarks, Ginnie Maes and T-bills—or a number of other related commodities.

The soybean complex is perhaps the best group of related commodities in which 4-D patterns occur. When soybean meal makes a new high and soybean oil fails to follow meal's lead, the 4-D analysis calls for shorting the oil; conversely, when the meal makes a new low and soybean oil doesn't follow suit, the oil is considered a good buy. In the past, the concept has also proved itself sensitive to nearly all the major and minor swings of international currencies. The Swiss franc and Deutschemark markets have been particularly good candidates for 4-D analysis. And in the interest-rate futures market, price divergences, pinpointing key reversals, can often be found between different months of T-bills and Ginnie Mae contracts.

To spot divergences, you have to continually ask yourself questions as you compare your charts. Has one contract refused to break a low that another contract has fallen through? Has one contract held its gains better than the rest of the group? Has one commodity contract shown a tendency to rally more or have a wider daily range?

As we have said, when you compare different months of different commodities, you add another variable to the analysis. This *four-dimensional* analysis, despite the added complexity involved, is accomplished in much the same manner as is the 3-D analysis, except that you have to compare seven or eight contract months of two or three commodities.

How to Detect Basic Point-and-figure
Buy and Sell Signals

Point-and-figure charts, like bar charts, form support and resistance lines, head-and-shoulders formations, triangles, and many of the other chart patterns we have already discussed. In addition, point-and-figure charts form *specific* buy and sell signals that every knowledgeable trader should be aware of. The simplest buy and sell patterns are generated by a resistance or support being formed that is subsequently penetrated. For example, in the *simple buy signal pattern,* the commodity forms a resistance or top that is later broken. The buy signal is issued when the previous high is exceeded for the first time, as follows:

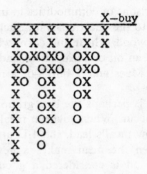

Figure 45.

The *simple sell signal pattern* is characterized by falling prices that reverse and rally and then fall again prior to penetrating a previous support. The sell signal is issued when the support is penetrated for the first time, as follows:

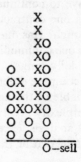

Figure 46.

The Angular Theory of Price Trends

Every commodity tends to have its own personality in terms of price angles, the slope at which prices tend to rise or fall. But there are two key angles that chartists use to help determine the subsequent trend of prices.

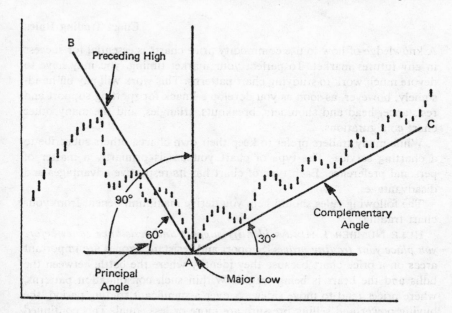

Figure 47. The sum of the principal angle and the complementary angle will always equal 90 degrees. The principal angle is established by drawing a straight line from a major low to a preceding high. The complementary angle is established by calculating the difference between the principal angle and a 90-degree angle.

The first angle, which is the key to determining the subsequent upward trend, is known as the *principal angle*. This angle is created on a price chart by drawing in a straight line between the most recent major low and the preceding high. By measuring the slope of this angle and subtracting it from 90 degrees, you establish the slope of the second angle, known as the *complementary angle*. It is this angle that determines the slope of an upward trend line following the establishment of a major low. In Figure 47, line AB, drawn from a major low to a preceding high, establishes the principal angle. By taking the difference of the principal angle and a 90-degree angle, the complementary angle—established by line AC—is created. The theory holds that the subsequent trend of prices will rise in a trajectory that is consonant with the complementary angle.

A knowledge of the angular theory is one of the most valuable tools a chartist can have. As a rule, the larger the angle employed, the shorter its time of applicability; the smaller the angle, the greater its time of applicability. Many commodities have angles that persist for many months. But the relevant angles for each contract month of every commodity are usually different.

Chart Trading Rules

A knowledge of how to use commodity price charts is essential for success in any futures market. To perfect your market timing, you may have to devote much work to studying chart patterns. This work will pay off handsomely, however, as soon as you develop a knack for spotting support and resistance, head and shoulders, breakouts, triangles, and the many other chart configurations.

While many traders prefer to keep their own charts, others subscribe to a charting service. The type of chart you use is primarily a matter of personal preference. Each type of chart has its respective advantages and disadvantages.

The following rules should help you derive maximum benefit from your chart trading.

RULE NUMBER 1. *Always identify support and resistance zones before you place your trading orders.* Support and resistance zones are important areas on a price chart because they identify where the battle between the bulls and the bears is being waged. Within such consolidation patterns, where prices tend to move sideways over a significant trading period, the buying power and selling pressure are more or less equal. This continued churning of prices within a small area is comparable to tightening the string on a bow. A certain amount of tension is built up, which inevitably expends itself once either the bulls or the bears gain control.

As a rule, a breakout from a support or resistance zone will carry a distance equal to the horizontal distance covered in the consolidation phase. Using this method, point-and-figure chartists measure the number of boxes a chart pattern covers horizontally prior to the breakout. They then attempt to predict how far the move will carry horizontally by counting an equal number of boxes up or down. This practice is known as "taking the count."

A more conventional rule is to place buy- and sell-stops above and below the resistance and support zones respectively. The triggering of either order will generally result in profits unless a false breakout occurs.

Support and resistance lines can also be used to establish objectives. The satisfaction of seeing a market carry right to the line you have drawn on the chart will provide you with the confidence to place your market orders and trade aggressively. Moreover, when a market doesn't behave as you suspect (as when a trend line is broken), you can use this knowledge to rethink your strategy and perhaps reverse yourself. As long as you remain flexible and unwedded to any fixed notion of how prices must act, you will be in a good position to profit from any sudden price move. Simply identify the key market levels and wait for prices to move. For example, you identify a resistance near a previous market top and draw in the resistance line. Next, you watch prices. If they can't break the resistance, where, by definition, selling previously entered the market, you go with the sellers as a double top is formed. Should the resistance or previous top be broken, however, you would do the reverse and buy the commodity as prices enter into new high ground.

RULE NUMBER 2. *Always buy the strongest contract months and sell the weakest contract months.* The Ohama 3-D technique can help you identify which contracts are strong and which are weak. Strong contracts will rise faster than other contracts, and weak contracts will fall faster. Many traders make the mistake of trading a contract simply because it is the one they are following. In most instances, the nearby contract will also be the most volatile. And this will be the contract that will rise fastest in a bull market and fall fastest in a bear market. For instance, in a recent bull market in soybeans, the nearby contract rose 13½ cents on the same day that the most distant month rose only 2 cents. Obviously, a speculator bullish on soybeans would do better trading the nearby month.

RULE NUMBER 3. *Look for the gap between cash prices and the nearby futures prices to narrow as the nearby reaches maturity.* Because the nearby futures price becomes the cash price upon expiration, the two must narrow over time. If cash is above the nearby, one of several things must happen as the delivery date approaches. The cash must decline or the futures must rise—or a combination of both must occur. The reverse is true when the cash prices are below the nearby futures prices. Many traders plot cash prices on their charts along with futures prices to establish this important relationship. Remember, upon expiration, the nearby futures and the cash prices are always identical.

RULE NUMBER 4. *Learn to count cycles or waves as prices rise or fall.* A stock market technician named Ralph Elliott established a theory in 1939 which states that price trends are governed by cycles. According to the theory, prices tend to move in a predetermined number of waves consistent with the Fibonacci series of numbers. (Leonardo Fibonacci was a thirteenth-century Italian mathematician who discovered the series in which each succeeding number is the sum of the two numbers immediately preceding: 1-1-2-3-5-8-13-21 . . .) Elliott used this idea to predict the movement of stock prices. He felt that prices tended to move in a five-wave sequence in line with the direction of the main trend, and in a three-wave sequence during corrective moves against the main trend. In keeping with the Fibonacci series, Elliott maintained that prices did not necessarily have to have five waves. They might, for instance, consist of three waves, composed of two waves down and one wave up. An eight-wave trend, therefore, would have five waves with the major trend and three waves against it. Because price waves are virtually impossible to see except on a price chart, it is important that chartists keep alert for them when they occur.

RULE NUMBER 5. *To predict price trends, use speed resistance lines.* Speed resistance lines are trend lines which are drawn on a chart once a bottom and an intermediate top have been established. There are two basic types: the one-third speed resistance line and the two-thirds speed resistance line. The two-thirds speed resistance line is calculated by taking a bottom or the beginning of a price move and the most recent top, and calculating two thirds of the total move. For instance, if a move has carried 500 points, the two-thirds figure will be 333 points. You then add this figure to the beginning price. You then plot this point directly below the recent high and connect it, with a straight line, to the initial price. This is the two-thirds speed resistance line. According to the theory of speed resistance lines, any reaction in price should hold at this line. If this price is broken, however, the theory states that prices should react down to the one-third speed resistance line. The one-third speed resistance line is calculated in a similar fashion, except that you add only one third of the total price to the initial price. If the two-thirds line is broken, the one-third line should hold. If the one-third line also fails, a new trend has clearly been established and the trader should reverse himself. Speed resistance lines are also applicable in declining markets.

RULE NUMBER 6. *Look for evidence of price strength or weakness in price swings.* The trend-following principle of price swings is simple and easy to understand. A commodity able to rise above a previous high is considered to have strength. A commodity that falls below a previous low is considered to be weak. When a price trend fails to exceed a previous high or low, depending on the direction of the market, it is said to be a *failure swing.* At the point of failure, when it attempts to exceed the previous high or low but does not, the market is ripe to be purchased or sold. In a *nonfailure swing,* a market will exceed the previous high or low, but then react in the opposite direction. Close stops must be employed in such markets to avoid losses.

RULE NUMBER 7. *Pay attention to price divergence.* Three- and four-dimensional charts provide some of the best market reversal signals. Based on price divergence between contract months of the same and related futures contracts, the Ohama technique pinpoints where the hedgers are entering and exiting the market. It illustrates what markets and contract months are particularly susceptible to a market reversal at a particular moment. More important, it generates the buy or sell signal before the reversal is under way.

RULE NUMBER 8. *If you do not keep your own charts, subscribe to a chart service.* Charts are so important that every futures trader should have them. Whether you keep your own or subscribe to a professional chart service is largely a matter of personal preference. But in deciding upon a service, there are some important features that you should look for. The charts must be accurate and they must arrive at your office or home within a reasonable period after the last entry was recorded. They should be easy to read and lend themselves to updating after each day's close. You can purchase charts which use the point-and-figure technique or the bar chart method. Some services also feature such items as open interest and volume, moving averages, and cash prices. One of the most comprehensive charts on the market is published by the Professional Chart Service, in Pasadena, California. It features, in addition to prices, moving averages, volume, and open interest, such items as *Commitments of Traders* reports issued by the CFTC, key dates applicable to the commodity, contract specifications, the bullish consensus percentages, an interpretation of each day's news, and more. The ultimate charting service is the "Videcom" graphic display quotation service available from Comtrend, Inc., in Stamford, Connecticut. The Videcom system not only displays a chart pattern on a video monitor as it occurs, but it will also print out a chart in any format you choose, such as a swing or bar chart. It records spreads as well as individual contract months, and it provides you with statistical information about most commodity contracts from 1961 to the present. The drawback with Videcom is price. The machine leases for $1,400 a month. The following is a list of the more conventional charting services:

The Professional Chart Service
  61 South Lake Ave.
  Pasadena, Calif. 91101

Commodity Trend Service
  Cove Plaza
  1224 U.S. Hwy. 1
  North Palm Beach, Fla. 33408

Commodity Price Charts
  219 Parkade
  Cedar Falls, Iowa 50613

ADP Comtrend
  1345 Washington Blvd.
  Stamford, Conn. 06902

Financial Futures
  200 W. Monroe St.
  Chicago, Ill. 60606

Spread Scope
  Golden State Commodity
    Publications
  Box 832
  San Fernando, Calif. 91341

Commodity Research Bureau, Inc.
  75 Montgomery St.
  Jersey City, N.J. 07302

Graphix Commodity Charts
  Suite 1432
  30 West Washington St.
  Chicago, Ill. 60602

Quotron Futures Charts
  P.O. Box 1424
  Racine, Wis. 53401

Commodity Perspective
  30 South Wacker Dr.
  Chicago, Ill. 60606

Dunn & Hargitt
  22 North Second St.
  P.O. Box 1100
  Lafayette, Ind. 47902

RULE NUMBER 9. *Watch volume and open interest for price clues.* The interaction of price, volume, and open interest is crucial in analyzing a bar chart. The term *volume* refers simply to the purchases and sales of a commodity during a specific period of time (usually on a daily basis). It may be reported as the number of contracts traded or, as in the case of grains, the number of bushels. The term *open interest* has a somewhat different meaning. Open interest refers to the purchase or sale commitments that remain unliquidated. Thus, when open interest is high, a great many traders are holding on to their positions or entering into new positions; when these same traders decide to offset their positions—by taking profits or losses—the open interest is reduced.

By carefully studying the movement of the two figures, differences in the *character* of the buying or selling can be ascertained. For example, if a great deal of buying is observed in a market and the open interest is likewise rising at a rapid rate, you can assume that new buyers have entered the market. This is the result of *old* buyers holding onto their unliquidated positions and *new* buyers finding new sellers from whom to purchase their contracts. Conversely, the opposite could also occur. If a great deal of buying is accompanied by a fall in the open interest, you can assume that the buying is largely a result of previous unliquidated shorts offsetting their positions. The two could have significantly different meanings in terms of price direction.

Likewise, volume and price statistics are interrelated. In general, the relationship of volume and price can be summarized as follows:

1. When a major price advance is under way, volume tends to increase on rallies and to decrease on reactions.

2. During a major price decline, volume tends to increase on down moves and decrease on rallies.

3. Volume expands sharply as bottoms and tops are approached.

When volume and open interest are combined, buying and selling rules can be formulated, since a knowledge of what both indicators are doing provides a clear picture of an overbought or oversold market. Chartists try to interpret the meaning of rising and falling open interest and volume. When you attempt to interpret chart patterns, keep the following four rules in mind:

1. When volume is high and open interest is up on rising prices, the market is strong and should be bought.

2. When open interest is falling and volume and prices rising, the market is weak and should be sold.

3. When prices are down and open interest and volume are high, the market is weak and should be sold.

4. When prices are down and volume and open interest are also down, the market is strong and should be bought.

Other significant volume and open interest generalizations pertain to climactic moves such as major tops and bottoms and breakouts from support and resistance zones. For example, so-called *blowoff* tops occur when volume increases sharply along with prices and open interest drops precipitously. Frequently, this takes place during a single trading session, followed by dramatic moves to the downside.

Likewise, major bottoms are characterized by climactic selling. After a long decline, prices plummet on heavy volume and a sharp drop in open interest, as long and short alike jump to the sidelines in fear of the erratic movements such markets are likely to demonstrate.

The validity of moves out of support and resistance levels is often confirmed by checking volume statistics. Almost without exception, breakouts to either the upside or the downside will be accompanied by significantly increased volume. Moreover, the magnitude of the move is likely to be proportional to the increase in open interest during the consolidation phase. Thus, the churning of prices near a support or resistance level is indicative of accumulation or distribution of futures contracts, respectively, by buyers and sellers. Each time a futures price reaches a given level within a congestion area, buyers will buy up the supply offered, thus bidding up prices and creating a valid support; conversely, selling may enter a market at another stage, creating a resistance.

Prior to a breakout, a market slowly gains strength until the majority of the buyers are holding onto contracts and new buyers have no alternative but to bid up prices in order to purchase additional contracts. When this happens with sufficient magnitude, a breakout occurs; then still more buyers are attracted into the market, and both prices and volume begin to soar.

Open interest can also provide a valuable clue as to what the hedgers are doing in the market. Since hedgers are the dominant force on the short side of the market, an increase in open interest is apt to signify that they are placing short positions; conversely, a decrease in open interest would probably signify that the hedgers are lifting their short positions in anticipation of higher prices.

The rule for following hedging activity can be stated as follows: *When the open interest drops sharply, look for the market to rise; when the open interest rises sharply, look for the market to fall.* The reasoning behind these statements is that hedgers, being long the cash commodity, are mainly on the short side in futures. As a result, they want to place their short hedges at the top of the market (increasing open interest) and lift their short hedges at market bottoms (decreasing open interest).

9

Commodity Funds
and Managed Accounts

LETTING SOMEONE ELSE
MAKE THE DECISIONS

You have two alternatives if you want to trade commodity futures but don't want to make the trading decisions yourself: you can join a commodity fund, or you can enter a managed-account program. A third way, perhaps, is to give your commodity broker discretion to trade your account, but this is practically the same thing as a managed-account program. Whichever method you choose will have an important bearing on the overall health of your equity at some point in the future, so you should know what to look for when you shop for a fund or a manager. Let's begin with a brief description of what's available for the potential futures speculator who wants someone else to handle the decisions.

The Offshore Commodity Fund

The offshore commodity fund notion is an idea that originated in Great Britain in response to the British prohibition of mutual funds trading commodities. To get around the ruling, funds specializing in commodity trading had to locate "offshore," generally in such exotic spots as Bermuda, the Bahamas, or the Channel or the Cayman islands. Oriented toward

Britain, the funds concentrate mainly on London commodities. But this should not be a drawback to an American investor, since many of the London commodities are also traded in New York. A more significant feature is that these offshore funds are denominated in British currency and, being unregistered funds, are difficult to locate with ease. Thus, the potential investor has to seek out an offshore fund on his own. A definite plus is that these funds are generally situated in places that are tax havens. Presumably, what arrangements you make between an offshore fund and your own offshore banking connections is a confidential matter. The precautions you should observe in investing in any fund or management program should likewise be followed when selecting an offshore fund. The fact that a fund is situated out of the country should make you even more cautious, since you won't have U.S. law or regulatory authorities to fall back on should your account be mishandled.

The Domestic Commodity Fund

A commodity fund may be defined as a business which is similar to an investment trust, syndicate, or similar form of operation that solicits, accepts, or receives from others, funds for the purpose of trading in any commodity for future delivery, subject to the rules of any contract market.

Most commodity funds are not mutual funds in the traditional sense that funds devoted to security trading are, but are, rather, limited partnerships consisting of a number of limited partners and a general partner who raises the money, hires the management personnel, and oversees the operation of the fund. Commodity funds may range in size from several thousand dollars to $10 million, though the majority of funds are capitalized at $1 million or under. Compared with a stock mutual fund, the average commodity fund is quite small. But you must realize the differences between investment in securities and speculation in commodities. Whereas the huge security funds are devoted to fulfilling the needs of the large corporate, labor, and insurance institutions, the commodity fund is solely the vehicle of the small trader. So the orientation of a commodity fund is different from its cousin in the securities markets as well.

The key advantage of any pooled-money approach is professional money management and diversification—certainly worthy objectives for any intelligent investment or speculation. But the number of hidden and not-so-hidden fees associated with the fund approach to commodity trading can outweigh any advantage to be gained from a pooling of monies. Quite often the cost of grouping investors is high. As a result, the fees, costs, and charges that go with a fund must not be overlooked. You must remember that trading decisions result from research, statistical compilations, and counsel from advisers—all of whom must be paid. In addition, a prospectus, literature, and follow-up salesmen must be paid for. In the final analysis, a commodity fund is only as good as the people who do the trading.

And if you don't have a good trader at the helm, all the computers, proprietary trading systems, professional advice, contacts, and high fees will have been for nothing.

In recent years, commodity funds using highly sophisticated computer trading programs have become very popular. During the runaway bull markets of the mid-seventies, many of these funds showed impressive results—mostly from standard trend-following methods.

Managed-account Programs

A managed account is similar to a commodity fund, except that your funds are not pooled. Each account is segregated from every other, and a single trader or group of traders is in charge of all trading activities regarding that account. You may have a managed account with a single commodity trading adviser or be part of a program consisting of a large firm handling hundreds of accounts at the same time. As with a commodity fund, a managed account can be excellent or poor. Your account may be handled skillfully and profitably, or it may be churned mercilessly for commissions in a manner that skirts the edge of the law. The fees associated with managed-account trading can vary widely. As with a commodity fund, a managed-account program usually—but not always—carries the provision that your liability is limited to the amount of money you contribute.

A managed-account program can be very valuable to a futures speculator who lacks the time or skills to trade his own account. But the key to his success will be the selection of his trading manager or adviser. All commodity advisers who give market recommendations or trade commodity accounts for others are required to be registered with the National Futures Association, a self-regulatory body of the futures industry. But this registration alone does not necessarily qualify him as a competent adviser. You must determine his qualifications yourself. Remember, a good trading adviser or manager can spell the difference between success or failure—*if* he knows what he is doing and is not charging excessively for his services.

How do you decide if an adviser is qualified to handle your funds? You might start by seeing whether he has a following. Since success in futures trading is difficult to achieve, an adviser who has built up a favorable market record probably won't have much difficulty finding clients. Chances are, he won't advertise in the newspaper. Moreover, like any successful professional, you probably won't find him using the high-pressure tactics employed by so many firms that require a new influx of capital to replace disgruntled former clients.

Incidentally, firms that employ salesmen to solicit new accounts to place under management must often charge more for their services, since the higher overhead—sales fees, advertising costs, and other promotional expenses—must be paid for by someone.

The operators of any managed-account program will probably be able to offer you a copy of past performance. But a word of caution: past performances are easily doctored to suggest better-than-average results. Just as nearly every futures trader has had some degree of success at one time or another, an account manager or management firm can easily stress past victories while minimizing the failures. Thus, a profit-and-loss statement showing a series of profits and few, if any, losses may not reflect the true state of affairs.

When evaluating a management program or a commodity fund, special attention has to be paid to the fee structure. In our discussion of fees applying to limited-partnership programs, we will mention the prominent fees that partnerships and managers charge.

Another consideration is, Who trades the account? For it is the responsibility of the trader to see that the account is handled in a responsible manner. In larger firms the account trader or manager is apt to be someone in Chicago or New York who is close to the markets. But physical proximity to the markets—even if the man in charge is a floor trader—is of little advantage if the account is being churned for commissions or otherwise mishandled.

Unless you monitor the progress of the account yourself or, otherwise, have implicit trust in your adviser, you will probably not even be aware of the negative effects of overtrading. But too many small profits, coupled with the inevitable losses, will soon manifest themselves in the form of decreased equity.

Despite the abuses that any managed-account program is subject to, a choice handful of trading advisers have superior records and maintain trading results that are far superior to the average futures speculator, who, after all, tends to end up losing his margin money.

How do you find such advisers? It isn't easy, but some firms specialize in referring potential clients to managers who have solid track records. By using a continuous monitoring system that is designed to select managers on the basis of ongoing performance, one New York firm attempts to match client with adviser on the basis of a comprehensive questionnaire that it sends free of charge to anyone requesting it.

The firm charges no fee to the client but is compensated by the adviser when a client is placed. Significantly, the relationship does not end when a client is matched with an adviser. Rather, a monitoring program is then begun. Should a loss be reported in the account, you are notified immediately, and the adviser responsible for the loss is also notified. This third-party watchdog is beneficial to all participants, since it allows adjustments to be made and encourages the trading manager to exercise due diligence.

As a rule, you can expect to deposit a minimum of $25,000 with a trading adviser if you want individual attention paid to your account. There are advisers who will take less, but you are unlikely to receive the kind of specialized work on your account, which you are paying for, unless you deposit this amount.

One way to participate in a managed-account program with less money is to join a syndicate. Syndicates tend to have a limited life—say, twenty-four months—and once fully subscribed, they are closed to additional investors. Each member of the syndicate shares exactly in proportion to his percentage representation. You can generally join a syndicate for several thousand dollars and by paying a modest, 2 or 3 percent, sales charge. Your ultimate success or failure, of course, rests in the hands of the trading adviser.

Should you decide to enter a management program, pay special attention to the account card you will be asked to sign. This spells out the contractual agreements between you and the adviser and gives the adviser power of attorney to trade your account.

A management firm will usually take your funds and then deposit them with a brokerage house. Some small firms, however, prefer that you deposit the funds with the brokerage firm and then give them power of attorney to trade the account. In either instance, be certain that your funds are segregated from the funds of others. This will ensure that you pay only for your own losses and enjoy the benefit of all your profits.

In addition to having your funds segregated, be certain that you understand who is responsible for margin calls and equity deficits. Although some account managers, confident of their expertise, will assume liability for all losses beyond the deposited equity, others clearly state that the responsibility rests with the client. The typical account card, drawn up by lawyers, clearly states such caveats as: "Only risk capital should be used for commodity trading"; "Substantial losses can and do occur in commodity trading"; and "Client is responsible for any and all losses that might occur in client's account."

The rules for selecting an account manager or management firm should be the same as for selecting any professional. Identify your needs, but only what you need, and, above all, use proper caution.

Discretionary Accounts

Discretionary accounts are those in which you give your broker written permission to trade your account for you. Some brokerage houses insist that discretionary accounts have a minimum capital requirement; others only allow their senior staff brokerage people to handle such accounts. Still others don't allow discretionary accounts on an individual basis at all. Usually, in this latter situation, the house has a managed-account program or fund that it is aggressively promoting, and it doesn't want any competition from its own salespeople. As a rule, the fees associated with a discretionary account are only commissions. But the trader must realize that the broker handling a discretionary account is often involved in a powerful conflict of interest. He profits if your account is heavily traded; you profit only if your equity increases. Extensive trading is often detrimental to profits.

There is no reasonable way to say whether discretionary accounts are good or bad. Obviously, there are excellent brokers who make fortunes for their customers. On the other hand, there are plenty of brokers who benefit only themselves by churning their client accounts. The best rule is to know your broker before you ever think about giving him discretion with your account.

Track Records

Much is made of track records in the commodity business. Advisory letters advertise their track records, mutual funds publicize them, and brokers are quick to tell you of their trading successes. But the emphasis is misplaced, because many track records are misleading and some are fraudulent. The fine print following any claim to a market victory will usually state that past performance should in no way be taken as an indication of future success. But still, everyone loves a winner. So you can expect to see continued emphasis on how well a fund, managed-account program, or broker did in the past.

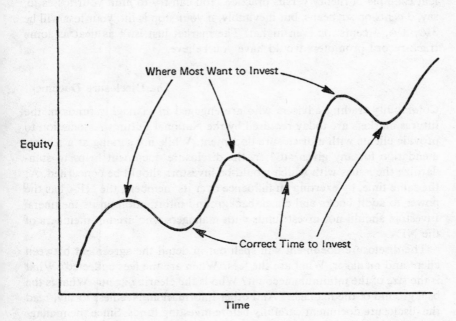

Figure 48.   Most people want to invest when equity is at a peak. The correct time to invest, however, is when a manager has run into a series of setbacks.

To understand problems that might arise when you rely on track records, look at Figure 48. You will notice that the typical trader or manager tends to make profits in a cyclical pattern. He may run into a series of successes in the market and his equity will rise, but there will then be a falling off and his profits will decline. Well, the problem is that most investors want to join a manager right when his success is at an all-time peak. They will inevitably have to ride into the next trough with that manager and see their equity decline. Of course, this doesn't always happen. But it happens frequently enough to create a pattern. Be aware of the existence of this pattern, and remember that most managers can tell you where they are in terms of their trading cycles.

There are other problems related to track records. The first involves the difference between a paper trading record and an actual trading record. The two are never the same, the paper trading record being invariably better. So when you are told a certain manager made so much in profits, check to see if they are based simply on recommendations, which may or may not have been filled, or whether he actually held contracts that earned him so much after commissions. Every experienced commodity trader will tell you that what looks easy on paper is difficult to achieve in practice. You only have to notice the difference between where the market is when you put in an order and what price you receive when the order comes back filled, to see the wisdom of this statement. Stop orders are another excellent example of theory versus practice. You can try to limit your losses to, say, 3 cents on soybeans, but inevitably, if your stop is hit, your loss will be 3½, 3¾, 4 cents, or even higher. The market just isn't as neat as some track-record promoters would have you believe.

The Disclosure Document

Commodity trading advisers who are engaged in managing funds in the futures markets are today required by the National Futures Association to provide clients with a disclosure document. While not serving as a recommendation for any given adviser, the disclosure document helps to standardize the issues with which would-be investors should be concerned. At the same time, by exerting an influence over its members, the NFA has the power to audit books and check background information on its members. Investors should not invest funds with managers who are not members of the NFA.

The disclosure document will spell out in detail the agreement between client and manager. What are the fees? When are the fees collected? What is the size of the minimum account? Who is the clearing agent? What is the background of the manager? And other information. Needless to say, read the disclosure document carefully before investing funds. Since the managers are required to spell out commission costs and the like, the disclosure document can be very, very revealing about the ultimate profitability of a managed account. In addition, the document must reveal whether an individual manager is engaged in any litigation regarding his past market activities.

The disclosure document will have a number of places where you must place your signature if you agree to open an account with the manager. All commodity accounts, including those you manage yourself, must be accompanied by a signed "Risk Disclosure" statement. This statement simply says that you acknowledge the high risk associated with futures trading and that you are willing to undergo the risk in your account. In addition, the disclosure statement will have a "Fee Payment Authorization" form. This form instructs the clearing firm to pay out directly to the manager. Typically, the incentive fee will be paid out on a quarterly basis with a sliding scale of payments to the manager for outstanding performance—say, 50 percent appreciation. In this instance, the form might call for an additional payment of 15 percent of net appreciation *above* the 50 percent appreciation in assets.

Lastly, the disclosure statement will reveal the past performance of the manager. Pay close attention to the manager's record. Top managers will show a steady progression in their trading equity. And despite occasional losing periods, the best managers will show a healthy bottom line.

With a few possible exceptions, the manager is prohibited by law from directly receiving the funds to be placed under management. Rather, these funds must be deposited with a brokerage firm, and the manager is provided with discretionary authority to trade the account.

Three Proven Commodity Futures Trading Managers

Each month, *Futures Magazine,* the leading journal of the commodities and options industry, publishes a monthly review of about one hundred leading public funds. The results tend to range from average to awful, depending on the type of market and the particular fund. The typical fund averaged just 4 percent growth in equity during 1984, and the leading fund obtained results in the 50 percent growth range. The funds have some drawbacks that the potential client should be aware of, namely high fees and commissions. When you factor in lackluster trading ability on the part of the managers, the would-be investor can see that he would be better off finding a perhaps less well-known, but more performance-minded, manager.

Three managers who have demonstrated outstanding success in the markets and who are known to be excellent traders are Ginger Heller, of Aarith II Commodities, Inc., in Greenwich, Connecticut; Barry Haigh, of Haigh & Co., Inc., in Chicago; and Tom Willis, of Willis-Jenkins, in Chicago. Each offers a different type of trading program.

In brief, the following describe the approach and trading philosophy of each of these three proven managers:

1. *Aarith II Commodities, Inc., Two Sound View Drive, Greenwich, Connecticut 06830—(203) 869-2500.* Aarith II is a long-term technical approach to the futures market based on a proprietary trading system developed by the company's president, Ginger Heller. Before the system was traded, it was tested extensively on back data by MJK Associates, in Santa Clara, California. For 1984, its first year of actual market experience, Aarith II averaged over 60 percent net gain in its trading accounts. The system trades an average of six futures contracts—Japanese yen, platinum, corn, Treasury bonds, gold, and silver—on which twenty-eight specific variables have been identified and computer-tested. At times, depending upon market conditions, the system may trade as many as twelve commodities. Each commodity has its individual variables that enable the managers to pinpoint exactly when and where to enter the market and place stops in their daily trading activities. Aarith II charges a monthly management fee of one half of one percent as well as a quarterly incentive fee. The commissions are determined by the individual client's agreement with his clearing firm. Aarith II limits its accounts to individuals willing to deposit $75,000 in capital, the major portion of which is deposited in Treasury bills.

2. *Haigh & Co., Inc., 30 South Wacker Drive, Chicago, Illinois 60606—(312) 454-3295.* The accounts of Haigh & Co. are managed by one of the top S&P floor traders in the country, Barry Haigh. During the first fifteen months of his company's existence, Haigh's accounts have averaged a 30 percent return. He primarily trades the S&P contract and other futures on the Chicago Mercantile Exchange, where he is a member. Haigh has demonstrated phenomenal trading ability over the past five years, increasing his net trading capital by some 200 to 300 percent annually. Using a proprietary trading system that he has developed, he day-trades the volatile S&P futures contract and takes longer-term positions in other commodities and options. His commission fees are among the lowest of any adviser. He is compensated solely on an incentive basis equal to 30 percent of the profits.

3. *Willis-Jenkins, Inc., 141 West Jackson Boulevard, Chicago, Illinois 60604—(312) 922-3666.* Willis and Jenkins are both professional floor traders who have turned in excellent results in managing accounts. Not one of their clients ever lost money. And in the three-year period between June 1982 and June 1985 the net equity of the accounts managed by Willis-Jenkins increased from $19.7 million to over $34.6 million, a growth of almost 76 percent. Willis and Jenkins trade a group of commodities for relatively short-term moves. On the basis of their success, they have been appointed trading managers for the Collins Futures Fund II.

Limited Partnerships

Since most commodity funds are limited partnerships, you should be familiar with how this type of pooling operation works. Basically, such a fund is organized by a general partner, often a former broker who has specialized in handling commodity futures accounts. The general partner is responsible for keeping the books and, sometimes, trading the account. Many general partners, however, hire an advisory service to supervise the trading activities. The limited partners invest in the fund and participate in the profits or losses according to the size of their initial contribution. The limited partners enjoy limited liability and are not responsible for any managerial duties regarding the fund.

Often sold in units with a minimum contribution requirement, a limited partnership operates like a closed-end mutual fund: that is, once the initial offering expires, no new investors are allowed in. For example, a fund capitalized at $2.5 million might have five thousand units available at $500 each. The minimum contribution might be $2,000, or a total of four units. Once trading commences, the fund's value will be quoted in its value per unit.

Since funds organized on a limited-partnership basis differ significantly, you should read the prospectus or Articles of Limited Partnership carefully before you purchase units in a fund. This document will indicate the terms of your legal agreement. It is especially important that you fully understand the costs associated with any fund you join.

There are four types of fees that funds charge. Typically, a fund will charge one or more of these fees, but rarely all of them. The first is a *sales fee*. This is usually a percentage of the total initial contribution. A partnership that charges a 5 percent sales fee, for instance, will deduct $500 for every $10,000 it collects. The drawback with this type of fee arrangement is that it lowers the equity available for trading right at the outset. A second type of fee is the *management fee*. This is a small percentage of total equity taken on a monthly, quarterly, or semiannual basis. Another fee, known as an *incentive fee*, compensates the general partner on the basis of his performance in the market. Thus, with an incentive fee, the general partner will benefit in direct proportion to his success in the market. A typical incentive fee is 20 percent of the net profits quarterly. A fourth fee, which is often hidden, is the cost of doing business, or *commissions*. Most investors don't realize it, but many limited partnerships charge excessively high commissions.

Since the best-performing funds are rarely offered to the public, the success of a fund is usually in direct proportion to its obscurity. Well-known, heavily promoted funds are apt to have the highest fee structure and the poorest performance records. But this should not dissuade you from joining a fund—if you can find the right one. Some limited partnerships are very profitable to all the partners in the fund. But you probably will never hear of these funds in advertisements or elsewhere, nor is it likely that you will be asked to join such a fund. The reason is that these unpublicized funds are often organized for a small group of speculators who are personally known to the broker or analyst trading the account. They usually consist of from six to a dozen limited partners who have complete confidence in the general partner. And, because they are set up to make money for all the partners in the fund, rather than merely enrich the general partner, these funds are often quite successful.

Your Own Fund

If you cannot find a suitable fund to join, you may want to set up one of these small limited partnerships yourself. Assuming you have a good manager and an interested group of investors, the mechanics of setting up a limited partnership are relatively simple. This is especially true if the partnership is to consist of ten partners or less, as no registration with the SEC or other regulatory bodies is required. You have only to draw up the partnership agreement (a suitable format can be found in any law library), collect the trading capital, and open an account in the name of the fund. The trading manager will do the rest. While you aren't permitted to advertise an unregistered fund, you can attract potential limited partners by word of mouth. Your tax problems will not increase as a result of participating in a fund, since so-called *conduit* taxation applies to limited partnerships. This means that profits are taxed only once—just as when you trade futures on an individual basis—and that the partnership is not taxed as a business. In addition, commodity pooling operations are generally considered as "syndicates," allowing for interpretation under a body of law known as "syndicate law"—as opposed to the more complicated and regulated corporation law.

In addition to spelling out the fee structure, the Articles of Limited Partnership will contain the conditions under which collected monies may be *impounded* or the fund *dissolved*. The impoundment condition refers to the period after the partnership begins collecting money and before it actually starts trading. This impoundment period gives the manager or general partner sufficient time to raise the necessary capital to fulfill the minimum objectives of the fund. In the event the objectives are not reached by the date stated in the partnership agreement or offering circular, the money is returned, usually without interest, and the offering becomes void. As for dissolution, most funds have provisions for terminating their activities when the general partner dies, retires, or is bankrupt, or whenever the general partner wants to liquidate the fund. A fund may also be dissolved when a limited partner or group of limited partners, owning in excess of 50 percent of the units of the fund, decide that dissolution is necessary. In addition, some funds have provisions for dissolution when equity falls to a certain percentage of initial net asset value.

To follow the progress of any partnership you join, you will be issued monthly or quarterly statements. While most limited partnerships do not provide for regular periodic cash distributions, any limited partnership can usually redeem for cash any or all of its units at the end of any quarter.

Disadvantages of Buying a Fund

Many futures traders prefer to make their own trading decisions, something that is virtually impossible with a fund. Others derive pleasure from the daily tally of winnings and losses; this sense of participation is also difficult to achieve with a fund. While the pooled-money concept has its advantages, the disadvantages can weigh heavily in a would-be investor's mind. Before you take the fund approach, you should take into account some of the following drawbacks.

First, you have to consider the fee structure of a fund. You aren't going to make money if the limited partnership is charging inflated commissions, high management fees, and incentive fees. Obviously, management has to be compensated. But excessively high fees are a sure sign that you are going to lose by going into a commodity fund.

Second, you have to consider the possibility of entering the fund just prior to a losing streak. Few managers, no matter how skillful their trading abilities, can avoid losses all the time. So if you join a fund just prior to a decline in equity, you may be sitting on a loss for a period of time.

Third, and most important, a fund, by virtue of its commitment to diversification, cannot give you the superior profit potential that the enormous leverage of commodity futures offers. As a rule, profits in a good commodity fund will average between 25 and 50 percent annually—well below the 100 percent plus that good speculators can make. So you must be willing to give up some profit potential in return for a more conservative approach when you join a fund. A fund cannot plunge into a runaway bull or bear market the way an individual trader can. Indeed, some have written provisions stating that they will commit no more than 15 to 20 percent of the fund's assets to a single commodity. Due to these limitations, funds are often in one or two excellent markets while the rest of their trading capital is tied up in nonproductive markets. This lack of flexibility is a real drawback for anyone who wants to profit from the enormous leverage associated with trading commodity futures contracts.

Since funds are most appropriate for the small trader who cannot afford the services of a commodity trading adviser, it is ironic that another facet of the fund concept discriminates against the small trader. And this is in the area of eligibility requirements. Some funds may be sold only to residents of a given state, and other funds may be sold only to individuals with a net worth that meets certain eligibility requirements. Generally, such requirements are mandated by state regulatory authorities. Unfortunately, these requirements tend to deny access to the futures markets to those who are most in need of the professional guidance and supervision that the funds provide: small speculators.

Advantages of Buying a Fund

Diversification and professional management are the two key advantages associated with owning a commodity fund. As we have just mentioned, diversification is not for everyone, nor is it desirable at all times. But over a period of time, there is something to be said for diversifying, especially if you are a small trader. With a fund, you get a degree of diversification you couldn't possibly accomplish with less than $25,000 in margin money. Generally, a small account in a brokerage house is handled by a broker who is primarily a salesman—not a commodity analyst. Fund capital, on the other hand, receives full-time professional supervision. With the advent of computerized advisory services, fund managers have access to trading information that is not generally available to the trading public. Good management is the key to a fund's success. Since the majority of winners in the commodity markets are full-time professionals, this factor can be especially important.

Another advantage a fund offers—and this is true of only some funds—is the opportunity to earn interest on margin money through its placement in U.S. Treasury bills. But even funds that do deposit their margin money in Treasury bills sometimes fail to pass the interest along to the client. As a result, prior to joining a fund or a managed-account program, you should inquire whether margin monies are deposited in Treasury bills and whether the interest is passed along to the client.

The prospect of no margin calls or limited risk, as we've mentioned, is not as beneficial as it seems, but this should nevertheless be included among the advantages of fund ownership. When a speculator joins a fund, his liability is strictly limited; his losses cannot exceed the cost of his initial contribution. Typically, adverse limit moves and unforeseen market setbacks are disastrous to a small individual trader. With a fund, however, this need not be the case, since such an occurrence will affect only a small portion of the portfolio, and the effect upon a single limited partner's equity will be marginal. Should the entire fund begin to lose money at an accelerated rate, the limited-partnership agreement will probably have a provision stating that the fund will be liquidated when assets shrink to 50 percent, or some other percentage, of their initial size. Because of this provision, it is highly unlikely that the fund will ever have a margin call. As a result, it is easy to insure you, the limited partner, against ever having a margin call as well.

Can a Fund "Beat the Market"?

What are the chances that participation in a fund devoted to trading commodity futures contracts will increase in value over time?

While there is no way to guarantee anything in the commodities markets, there are funds that make money consistently. Unfortunately, past success is no guarantee of future performance, but a solid track record over time is a sign that management is doing something right. Since the best funds keep a low profile, you would do well to ask around among friends for a fund that they have profited from. Eager salespeople promoting a fund with optimistic predictions are a sure sign that the fund should be avoided—not only because of the unwarranted claims but because you will have to pay the salesperson's commission. Any reluctance to talk about fees associated with the fund, or any attempt to minimize the impact of a loaded fee structure, is another sign that you are about to be parted from your money permanently. The typical response to questions about high fees is, "What do you care as long as we make you money?" Well, the point is, at best, that they will be using your money to make money for themselves. At worst, they might only make a little and you will lose a lot. To be safe, before investing in any fund, consider the following points:

RULE NUMBER 1. *Read a fund's prospectus, offering circular, or Articles of Limited Partnership carefully.* Several years ago, one would-be general partner revealed in his offering circular that he had indeed been barred from the New York Stock Exchange because of fraud charges. Most investors in his fund probably missed this small piece of information—because they didn't bother to read the prospectus.

RULE NUMBER 2. *Don't ignore a partnership simply because it is small.* Several years ago, a couple of brokers in California took their five wealthiest clients and created a fund which is now worth several million dollars more than when it was originally organized. As a rule, small, unregistered partnerships keep a low profile. So you may have to look awhile to find such a profitable fund. Needless to say, successful managers can ask for—and receive—large initial contributions. And they can also be quite selective about whom they decide to take into a fund.

RULE NUMBER 3. *Pay attention to the fee structure.* There is virtually no way you can overcome a loaded fee structure. Understand the fees and make sure you have them in writing.

RULE NUMBER 4. *Try to determine management's goals.* Depending upon a fund's size, you can expect a general description of what trading techniques the fund manager expects to employ. Some funds, for example, won't allow pyramiding. Others spell out the percentage of total assets which might be placed in any specific position, or whether or not a fund plans to take spread positions. Other questions you may want answered include: Does the fund specialize in foreign currency futures, grains, or metals? Is the fund traded aggressively or conservatively? Who is responsible for trading the fund? Is he a floor trader? A clearinghouse member? Is it likely he can achieve what he sets out to do in terms of the growth of the fund's equity? The answers to these questions can provide you with valuable clues as to whether the fund is suitable to your needs.

RULE NUMBER 5. *Are you temperamentally suited for the fund approach?* Do you want to pay the added expense of letting someone trade for you? Are you willing to forget about the market on a day-to-day basis? Many commodity traders, addicted to the action of the marketplace, are not temperamentally suited to let others call the shots for them. Ironically, these traders are the ones who could often best profit from turning their trading affairs over to someone else.

10

Contrary-opinion Trading

THE PSYCHOLOGICAL APPROACH

Contrary-opinion theory is perhaps the best antidote to market madness yet devised. It is a thinking man's trading tool, and one of the most profitable approaches to the futures markets you will find anywhere. Yet it is deceptively simple, for a contrary-opinion theorist would explain his attitude to the market by saying, "Establish positions opposite to the prevailing majority opinion, and you will make money." Paradoxically, the contrary-opinion trader will insist that the more convinced the majority of traders are that the market is headed one way, the more certain the market is to reverse direction and head the other. Neither a fundamental nor a technical approach to the commodity markets, contrary-opinion theory is based on the psychological notion that mass behavior is invariably wrong when it becomes too one-sided. "When everybody thinks alike," said Humphrey B. Neill, the father of the contrary-opinion theory, "everybody is likely to be wrong." Because the crowd—whether in politics or economics—tends to be wrong when mass sentiment becomes overwhelmingly one-sided, Neill suggested that one take the contrary viewpoint in order to see things as they really are. Essentially, he advises to go against human nature. Applied to market behavior, which is well known for its ability to react to human emotions, contrary-opinion theory would advocate selling when things are good and buying when the skies become cloudy. Indeed, the contrary-opinion trader would tell you that success in the marketplace can be assured for the speculator who fully comprehends this notion.

But does such a simple idea really work?

Let's look at a typical bull market and explore the motivations of its participants. In its early stages, buyers will be attracted by the *possibility* of a price rise. Should the market actually begin to rise, still other traders, who were formerly on the sidelines, will now become buyers, convinced that the market is headed still higher. Pretty soon, assuming all the new buying continues to push prices higher, the profits being made in the market will gain greater attention and the fundamentalists will begin to look very bullish. This creates still new buying and the market will predictably rise still further. Sooner or later, a genuine buying frenzy will have developed and the news and general market sentiment will have become overwhelmingly one-sided. New buyers—many of whom have perhaps never traded commodities before—will now be entering the market. Indeed, the majority of all traders—85 to 90 percent or more—will now anticipate still higher prices. About this time, the very last buyer will have entered the market, awaiting his profits, and the market will be ripe for a reversal.

At this stage, all the buyers, who anticipate still higher prices, will have done their buying. They are already in the market awaiting another price rise. Who, then, is left to push prices higher? No one. That's right, there is no one left to bid higher for the commodity. As a result, prices *must* decline. As soon as buyers abandon a market, sellers—profit takers and new short sellers—rush in. Since just a little profit taking causes a market decline, the former buyers, who are sitting on vulnerable paper profits, will soon create a stampede to be first to exit the market. Since no new buyers are available to support the price decline, the market must fall fast, resulting in sizable losses to those who bought at the top and sizable profits to the minority with the foresight to sell when the crowd was still buying.

And at the bottom? Here the reverse situation will apply. Bearish sentiment will be so prevalent that no "thinking" speculator will want to buy. Indeed the majority will expect prices to continue to fall, and sell short at the bottom. But once again, the majority will be wrong. For at this juncture, the market will stage a sharp rally.

Knowing that the crowd is generally wrong at the major turning points in the market, the contrary-opinion trader will take the unpopular position of going short in a bull market and going long in a bear market. Because market sentiment is overwhelmingly one-sided at the time such contrary trades are placed, they rarely look smart in the beginning. But given the propensity of contrary-opinion theory to be correct 100 percent of the time, such traders frequently reap handsome rewards.

The Bullish Consensus Percentages

The major problem with the contrary-opinion theory lies in determining a quantitative measure of the psychological profile of the market. After all, how do you tell when the majority of traders are anticipating higher or lower prices? The task is not easy. For it is obviously impossible to conduct a poll among traders to determine whether the market is overbought or oversold.

When James Sibbet, the founder of *Market Vane,* a commodity advisory service that bases its recommendations on contrary-opinion theory, decided to apply contrary opinion to the commodity futures markets in 1964, he devised a method whereby he could quantify the bullish or bearish sentiment in a market at a given time. Sibbet reasoned that since the majority of all traders lose money when they begin trading commodities, they soon turn to professional sources, namely brokers and market-letter writers, for advice. If one could only "measure" the sentiment among the respective advisory services and brokers influencing traders' activities, Sibbet reasoned, one could have a pretty good idea of the psychological state of the market. With this reasoning in mind, Sibbet set about reading all the major market letters from around the country weekly in order to gain an insight into what the market was thinking. To further refine his method, he placed a weight upon each rating according to the potential influence of the market-letter writer or brokerage house. Thus, Merrill Lynch's weekly opinions on the sugar market were given greater weight than, say, the opinion of the sugar analyst at a small, regional brokerage house, because it is obvious that a Merrill Lynch, with offices throughout the world, would have greater market impact than a small commodity house with just five or six offices.

Today, *Market Vane,* a weekly market advisory letter (Hadady Publications, 61 South Lake Avenue, Pasadena, Calif. 91101), publishes the *Bullish Consensus Percentages* each Tuesday afternoon after analyzing more than sixty-five market letters. The higher the percentage figure, the more bullish market sentiment is said to be. Thus, a 90 percent bullish consensus would indicate considerable bullish sentiment; a 10 percent bullish consensus would indicate little bullish sentiment. Remember, the contrary-opinion trader takes a position *opposite to the prevailing market sentiment.* Accordingly, when the bullish consensus is high, the contrarian would look to sell a commodity; when the bullish consensus is low, the contrarian would look to buy a commodity.

A number of advisory services publish a weekly market-sentiment index. If you don't wish to subscribe to *Market Vane,* you may use the results of one of these other services or, if you wish, you may devise your own method of attempting to measure the degree of bullishness in a market.

The primary point to remember is that reversals generally occur when market sentiment is overwhelmingly one-sided.

How to Use the Bullish Consensus

There are two ways to use the bullish consensus: as a contrarian trend tool and as a trend-following method. When you place a contrarian trade, you always go opposite to the prevailing market sentiment. When you use the consensus as a trend-following tool, however, you trade with the trend, in a noncontrarian manner. Whether you should trade with the trend or against it is determined by the bullish consensus. Specifically, you place a contrarian trade whenever the consensus exceeds 80 percent or is less than 30 percent. Between these extremes, you should use the consensus for noncontrarian, or trend-following, trades. In short, when the consensus is at its extremes, you trade against the trend; when the consensus is mixed, in the mid-range area, you trade with the trend. You should note that we have never said that the majority is always wrong in the marketplace. Rather, the majority is always wrong at the *major reversal points* in the market.

In using the bullish consensus percentages, you must be willing to wait until the market becomes so one-sided that a price reversal is inevitable. This can take time. Even the best markets have only four or five contrarian trade possibilities per year. But these trades are worth waiting for. Often, a lag period of a week or more may follow an extreme reading of the consen--sus before the market begins to move. In part, a lag exists because traders are reluctant to buy bottoms or sell tops. And those few contrarian-minded traders who do have the presence of mind to sell into a rising market or buy into a declining one often lack the power to reverse market momentum single-handedly. Contrary opinion can give you a good indication that a market reversal is at hand, but you may want to rely on other technical indicators to time your trade for maximum profitability.

General Consensus Rules

The two general rules for using the bullish consensus are as follows:

1. An overbought or an oversold condition begins to occur when the consensus exceeds 80 percent or is less than 30 percent respectively, and the open interest is either stable (changing less than 3 percent per week) or decreasing. A contrarian position can normally be taken when a bullish extreme greater than 90 percent or less than 20 percent is reached.

2. When the consensus is in the 60 to 80 percent area and a large decrease occurs (10 percent or more in two weeks' time), a sell signal is issued. When the consensus is in the 30 to 50 percent area and a large increase occurs (10 percent or more in two weeks' time), a buy signal is issued.

The Best Markets for Contrary-opinion Trading

A number of factors make some markets better for the contrary-opinion trader than others. In general, the greater the percentage of speculators operating in a market and the larger the open interest, the better the market is for the contrarian trader. This is because speculators, especially small speculators, behave differently in the market than do hedgers. More likely to be thinly margined, the small speculators are more vulnerable to market reversals and must rapidly exit a market that shows signs of changing direction. This is in contrast to hedgers, who may maintain a position regardless of its profitability. Moreover, the aggregate action of many speculators tends to enhance the momentum of market reversals, resulting in substantial profits for the astute contrarian trader.

Thin markets are bad choices for contrary-opinion traders. A thin market is more easily manipulated by large trading interests and less responsive to the emotionalism that affects the crowd of speculators who make contrary-opinion trading so profitable. As a rule, you should avoid markets that don't have at least eight thousand open contracts. A brief, but by no means comprehensive, list of the markets you should *avoid* in contrarian trading would include: oats, iced broilers, coffee, orange juice, eggs, and ninety-day commercial paper loans.

A large open interest in a commodity you consider as a contrarian trade possibility signifies a better profit potential and lower risk. There are certain trends in the open interest statistics that you should watch for. For instance, if the number of open contracts is increasing steadily, do not take a contrarian position, regardless of the bullish consensus reading. The consensus is likely to remain high until the number of contracts stabilizes. And prices are also likely to continue in an uptrend so long as the open interest is increasing. A decreasing open interest, on the other hand, near a bottom should also be viewed as suspect. Only a small contrarian move is likely to occur following such a decline in the open interest.

Once the bullish consensus reaches an extreme, signifying one-sided sentiment in the market, the strongest signal you could have that a market is ripe for a reversal is a news event favorable to the consensus that fails to move the market. For example, let's say the bullish consensus reaches 90 percent and a strongly bullish news report is issued. If this news cannot make the market rise further, you should take your position contrary to the consensus as quickly as possible. More than likely, the first contrary news event will result in a large price move favoring your contrary position. At market bottoms, of course, the opposite set of circumstances will prevail.

Why Contrary Opinion Works So Well

The roots of contrary opinion go back to the ancient Chinese philosophers. The Chinese philosophy known as Taoism (pronounced Dowism), which was founded by a man named Lao-tzu over twenty-five hundred years ago, contained many elements that hint at the psychological cause of events. According to contrarians, in the years since Lao-tzu's time, men have merely complicated matters by trying to reduce everything to numbers—an attempt, in Lao-tzu's words, "to catch running water in a bucket."

Translated into English, the Tao means "The Way"—the way of the universe, which cannot be easily described in words. Yet it is the vital missing factor that stock and commodity analysts need in order to trade successfully. How does ancient Chinese philosophy relate to the futures market? By illuminating the missing vital signs that cannot be reduced to numbers. It is the ability to see an event before it is definitely known that it is the key to success. For example, do you exit a trade before or after it is obvious that you are on the wrong side? Obviously, the trader who can sense impending trouble and can act on that notion has a better chance at success.

Nowhere is this intuitive ability to act on what is known as "soft data" more valuable than in the futures market. After all, once the reality of an event is known, it is too late to profit from it. This is where the old adage "buy the rumor, sell the news" comes from. The person who "buys the rumor" is operating on soft data. And it is contrary opinion that enables one to take such a stance. Once the information is freely available to everyone, it becomes quite useless. At that point, in Humphrey Neill's words, everyone is "thinking alike."

Learning to think intuitively about the market can be worth a fortune. To develop the necessary insight to use the soft data, you need to become familiar with the particular market situation, but at the same time you do not want to become overly dependent on the "facts." By definition, the futures market provides price information about the future. Often, therefore, the futures market will move first, providing the clue that the underlying cash market will likewise soon rise. By the time the cash catches the futures, however, the move has already taken place. So, to profit in this situation, you need all the signals you can find that will suggest or imply that conditions are about to change. Thus, it is the intuitive, far-thinking trader, who can foresee events, who will profit tremendously if he can only harness the information that is available to him.

In the world of Taoism, this ability to use both analytical and intuitive skills, relying on both right and left hemispheres of the brain to process and analyze information, is the key to understanding. But first you have to bring your thoughts to bear on the facts of the situation—and only then, significantly, you have to let go. This is the incubation stage, where you are letting your thoughts go where they may. You'd be surprised how often this technique will enable you to find a solution before it is available to others.

Let's consider an example in which the "soft data" provided a glimpse of the developing situation. Several years ago, when the gold market was going to break over $100 an ounce in a week's time, it began to react quite strangely. Prices bounced around a previous bottom and refused to go higher. Then prices slipped a couple of dollars. Still no support. Suddenly, someone must have sensed that the market was about to break, because hundreds of sell orders entered the pit. At first, the buyers, sensing they were seizing an opportunity, were happy to purchase gold futures contracts at a "bargain" price. After all, there was no news at the time. But then prices broke. Again, an attempted rally failed. Prices broke lower. And then the bottom fell out. What happened? Oil prices were lowered and the event was later interpreted as bearish for gold. The point is, only those traders with the ability to act on incomplete information were able to capitalize on the event. By the time the news was out, the fortunes were already won—or lost.

As you can see, it helps to be ahead of the crowd. The thousands of traders who comprise the worldwide network of the Wall Street community today react like any other large group when threatened with financial stress: they panic. It is precisely this mob psychology that caused one market pundit to write that the well-known *Wall Street Journal* column "Heard on the Street" should be renamed "Herd on the Street." Any one-sided viewpoint is certain to result in a market-moving retreat once the facts become known. Thus, it is the wise trader who tries to ferret out the truly valuable information—and acts on the knowledge—before it becomes widely known. This is the edge that will enable him to profit from contrary-opinion trading.

"Who's in Trouble?"

One sure way to anticipate a reverse in the market before it is generally known is by sizing up the situation in terms of the underlying psychological factors. The psychological factors are those elements of fear and greed that drive a market. The real winners are often those best able to either see and/or manipulate the emotions of the crowd. As you can understand, when it comes to the large financial commitments involved in the futures markets, the large market forces have a decided advantage at playing this game to their own advantage.

One way the large market manipulators succeed is to instill fear in the ranks of smaller investors. Fear has a strange effect on people. When it comes to losing, fear often gives way to panic quite suddenly. Knowing this, the large traders frequently attempt to manipulate prices. They know the crowd will react if prices can be changed by only a modest amount.

Consider the following scenario: A market opens higher and begins to gain strength. Why? No good reason. This may simply be the path of least resistance on this given day. As the move gets underway, there will certainly be a group of winners all congratulating themselves on a wise trade. These are the early buyers who may have purchased contracts a day earlier, or even a week or a month earlier. At the same time, of course, there will be a corresponding group (but not necessarily the same in number) of traders who will be losing money, because they sold short and the market rose. Thus, buying will beget more buying. The next wave of buyers will buy because they sense the market is headed higher. Lastly, the market will be pushed even higher by buying created by the hapless short sellers, who must now exit their positions at a loss. The concerted action of these different groups will push the market higher—at least temporarily. But, to the seasoned trader, the rally contains the seeds of its own destruction. After all, the buyers entered the market to earn profits, not to lose money. And the short sellers who purchased contracts in an effort to prevent additional losses wanted to limit their losses. But why would sellers sell in such a situation?

Differences of opinion make the market. And the sellers represent the other side of the equation. We all know that with all this buying going on —new buyers, old buyers, short sellers covering, and so on—there have to be a number of sellers willing to take the other side of the trade. And, since there is a seller for every buyer, it stands to reason that a relatively small group of sellers are fading the more determined group of buyers, who, after all, in their boundless enthusiasm, had gained the upper hand shortly after the open. But this temporary rise in prices may indeed be short-lived. Why? Because, given the leverage involved in futures trading, only a modest drop in prices will result in wholesale selling among the larger group of buyers, who will all try to take profits at the same time. Massive selling, of course, will drive prices lower. Indeed, if prices fall far enough, the selling will feed on itself, and more and more selling will enter the market, causing prices to break even further. This, in a nutshell, is contrary opinion in action.

There is another consideration as well. Public traders, for whatever reason, favor the long side of the market. This means that they like to buy but not to sell. At times, public traders number as much as 70 percent to 80 percent—if not more—of the long positions. Also, as a rule, there are many public traders compared to the few floor traders, who number no more than several hundred even in the largest trading pits. What's more, brokerage houses tend to bunch orders together to save time, money, and energy in the executions. As a result, one brokerage house may come into the pit with an order to buy two hundred or three hundred contracts—and chances are one or two locals in the pit will take the other side of the entire order. So you have an unbalanced situation: the many on the one side and the few on the other.

Now consider for a moment what happens when the market turns. First, you have the stops being hit on the initial rally. This will cause an initial burst of buying. In hopes of getting a rally going (to *sell* into, of course, not to buy), a well-financed local might indeed bid on a couple of contracts *above* the market. This, having the impact of immediately raising the bid *and,* significantly, the offer, will get the ball rolling. If stop orders exist at the price at which the market is bid—a technique known as "highballing" —a flurry of new buy orders will hit the pit. And prices will rise. This is especially effective when the stops are bunched together. Then the order fillers will have to trip over themselves in order to draw out sellers by bidding up the price. The result? You guessed it. The buying will feed on itself and the market will rally. The sign of an imminent reversal will be the market going "dead" at the top. Sensing the reversal, sellers will soon push prices lower and, often within minutes, there will be a sharp price break. Knowing how to trade these fast rallies and breaks is the key to capitalizing on contrary-opinion theory. Almost without exception, when the crowd is predominantly one-sided about the market, the likelihood is that a sharp reversal will occur.

The Balanced Approach

Contrary opinion provides a balanced approach to the market. Fundamental and technical analysis, on the one hand, concerns itself with numbers: counting bushels of grain and numbers of livestock on feed, measuring rallies and declines. The psychological approach, on the other hand, is much more subtle, more intuitive, more uncertain, and, finally, balanced. Whereas the traditional methods of technical and fundamental analysis can be measured and served up in some sort of totally rational package, measuring the psychological factors underlying a market is interpretive in nature, and therefore difficult to grasp. Significantly, it is the balanced approach that works. Whereas the more traditional methods of sizing up a market look to the past for an indication of the future, the psychological approach looks to the future to interpret the future. This is an important difference.

How does one prepare himself to be an effective contrarian? By allowing the answers to emerge over time. There are four stages: preparation, incubation, illumination, and verification. You must avoid acquiring either too little or too much information. You need to be knowledgeable about a situation, but you don't want to suffer from information overload. Information is ineffective when it exists in either extreme. Once you enmesh yourself in a trading situation, you will become sensitive to subtle movements in the market—you'll be able, in short, to "read" the market.

Trading is an art, not a science. To truly master the market, therefore, you must retain a flexible approach and be willing to change direction at a moment's notice. Above all, you must remember that detailed knowledge is *not* more valuable than a comprehensive fluid approach that embraces change rather than rigidity. Only amid an environment of wonder and respect can you correctly judge events. "When men do not have a sense of awe," said Lao-tzu, "there will be disaster."

To effectively size up a market, you have to watch for the ever-present signals that opinions are about to change. Paradoxically, the early indicators of a change typically occur outside the area that will be most affected. Contrarian thinking can help you identify a possible market-reversal situation in its early stages of change long before it is widely known. By seizing the moment, long before the news is widely accepted, you can become a winning contrarian. What better way to trade than to buy early, when the crowd is selling, and to be out the door and long gone when the panic selling begins? Contrary-opinion trading will give you the added edge no matter what other indicators you rely on.

Contrary-opinion Rules

As we have noted, contrary-opinion theory was originally developed by a business writer named Humphrey B. Neill, who revealed how its principles applied to a number of economic events ranging from the notorious tulipomania craze in Holland to the 1929 stock market crash. In each event, Neill pointed out that economic and social disasters tended to be magnified by the pressures of mass opinion. Because people tend to follow the herd instinct and rely on emotion, rather than reason, during critical times, their judgment is frequently wrong. In order to arrive at the correct approach to a market situation, therefore, Neill suggested that a man acting alone has the best chance to assess a situation if he successfully avoids the mass hysteria associated with such emotional endeavors as trading the stock market or predicting economic events.

Since the development of the bullish-consensus percentages, in 1964, contrary-opinion theory has accurately predicted many of the major reversals that have occurred in the futures markets, resulting in tremendous profits for contrarian traders. In addition, the consensus has provided the basis for many more noncontrarian trades based upon following a rise or fall in the precentages within a certain range. The following rules can help you become a better trader if you keep in mind Neill's original adage: "When everybody thinks alike, everybody is likely to be wrong."

RULE NUMBER 1. *Only place contrarian trades when market sentiment is at an extreme.* Unless a market is close to unanimity on either side, it will do you little good to take a contrary-opinion trade, because the crowd is not wrong at every juncture in the market but only at the key reversal points. Therefore, be patient and wait until market sentiment is overwhelmingly one-sided, and then go against the crowd.

Because the market has a bullish bias, when a commodity achieves 90 percent bullishness in the consensus it is considered ripe as a short-sale candidate, and when it achieves 20 percent or less in its bullishness (more than 80 percent bearish) it is a good prospect for a rally.

Paradoxically, even the most bullish commodities tend to develop bearish supply-and-demand statistics overnight—and vice versa—once a reversal occurs. This is because fundamentals lag behind technical and psychological indicators.

RULE NUMBER 2. *Always take a market position contrary to a crowd of speculators—not hedgers.* Speculators behave differently in the market from hedgers. They are more likely to be quick to enter or exit a position and much more volatile in their behavior. They are also much more likely to be wrong. Gripped by emotional influences, speculators tend to be most enthusiastic about a market when they should be cautious, and most cautious when they should be enthusiastic. Eager buyers at market tops and equally eager sellers at market bottoms, they provide the huge profits for the minority of traders who understand market psychology and have the courage to act contrary to mass market sentiment. Among the best speculator-dominated markets are the meats—cattle, pork bellies, and hogs—which enjoy considerable speculative activity and are best known for making sudden reversals contrary to popular sentiment.

RULE NUMBER 3. *For a confirming signal that a market is about to reverse when the consensus is at an extreme, look for bullish news at a market top that fails to move the market higher, and bearish news at a market bottom that fails to move the market lower.* This is perhaps the strongest evidence you can have concerning a market reversal. When news that can be interpreted as bullish or bearish fails to carry its respective impact, it means that the market has already digested that particular news item and that the market's interpretation is fully reflected in the present price level. As a result, the news can be said to have been discounted by the market already and is awaiting still more dramatic events to cause it to continue on its present path. When no fresh news is forthcoming, the market often stages a sharp reversal within several days.

Typically, a commodity may be soaring to life-of-contract highs on highly bullish fundamentals, such as a new Soviet grain deal, when volume begins to dry up in the very midst of a bull market. Chances are, the market is already overbought and ripe for a turnaround. With no bulls left to buy, the market has but one direction to take as the nervous bulls begin to sell out their positions: downward. This is especially true of speculator-dominated markets, where the margins are razor thin and the crowd is quick to be pushed into a panic selling once the market tide shows signs of turning. At market bottoms, the sign that a commodity is about to stage a rally is bearish news that doesn't result in lower prices. When this occurs, the market is already oversold, with few new bears available to push prices lower.

RULE NUMBER 4. *In closing out a contrarian trade, rely on technical analysis.* Contrary-opinion theory provides the necessary information for spotting incipient market reversals, but it should not be relied upon for getting out of a market. This is because contrary opinion is not primarily a timing indicator, but, rather, a method of thinking about market changes and trader psychology. We have mentioned a number of technical indicators and trading techniques, from trailing stops to 3-D analysis, that can serve to pinpoint the exact time to enter or exit a position. These technically oriented techniques should be used in conjunction with contrary-opinion theory to achieve best results.

11

Gann Techniques for the Technical Trader

A METHOD FOR DETECTING MARKET REVERSALS

W. D. Gann was a legendary trader of the first half of the twentieth century whose theories and writings today are more popular than they were during his lifetime. Today you will find seminars devoted to Gann's work, charting services that specialize in Gann charting methods, and even brokerage houses that have capitalized on Gann's genius by borrowing his name. W. D. Gann, who has been dead for the past thirty years, serves as a sort of role model for today's traders. He was the consummate analyst, the market prognosticator whose predictions remain unchallenged after fifty years. Significantly, his theories, which some say are based on ancient geometry, seem to work extraordinarily well in today's markets.

Gann had the unique ability to deduce mathematical relationships within the stock and commodity markets. He used this ability to earn himself a fortune and to confound his critics. Once, when U.S. Steel was trading at a price of 50, he predicted that it would touch 58 but wouldn't break 59. The rise to 58 (but not 59), Gann said, would be followed by a break of at least 16¾ points. Right on target, U.S. Steel climbed to 58¾ and promptly broke 17½ points.

His most famous prediction occurred in the 1909 wheat market. At the beginning of September in 1909, he predicted that September wheat, with only a few weeks left prior to expiration, would trade at $1.20 a bushel. But as the remaining days in the soon-to-expire contract passed, September wheat prices gained little ground, and on the last day of trading it was still at only $1.08 per bushel. Gann was adamant. With just hours to go on the last trading day, Gann again asserted his belief that September wheat would trade at $1.20 per bushel by the close or, according to Gann, "it will prove that there is something wrong with my whole method of calculation." It clearly appeared that he was mistaken. "I do not care what the price is now," Gann is rumored to have said, "it must go there." Indeed, he was right. September wheat closed at exactly $1.20 per bushel that day.

Unfortunately, despite the volumes of work and many charts and calculations that Gann left behind, understanding precisely how he made his calculations is extremely difficult. So much of what Gann wrote was mired in mysticism and confusion that it is quite difficult to formulate trading rules out of his work. What can be inferred from his work, however, is a set of guidelines that pinpoint what to look for when a reversal is imminent. It is these precise market reversal points that pay dividends for whatever little understanding one can glean from Gann.

What Gann Believed

Above all else, Gann believed that the universe worked in a precise mathematical pattern that governed all things—even, or should we say especially, the markets. Not only were the cycles of economic events governed by mathematical rules, according to Gann, but they were knowable as well. The key to knowing the market was understanding these mathematical relationships.

Even amid the confusion that passes for intelligent Gann analysis, several clear-cut ideas emerge that are helpful to today's futures trader.

One, Gann believed in what has come to be known as *time and price*. Simply put, so much time must elapse before prices can reverse direction. Much is made of the notion of basing at support levels in the market. Point-and-figure charts analysts measure rallies based on the amount of sideways action preceding an upward move. Obviously, time is important in judging an imminent reversal. Even day traders, who are extremely limited in their time perspective, will tell you that time is vital in judging a trade. Fortunately, Gann left us some guidelines in measuring time.

Two, Gann believed that support and resistance would occur at precise levels determined by drawing so-called "Gann lines" from significant highs and lows, such as life-of-contract highs and lows. For the analysis to prove correct, however, the relationship of the chart had to be correct. That is, a move of X amount of time had to be offset by a move of Y amount of price volatility. Given the correct relationship of price to time, a line drawn at a 45 degree angle down from a significant high and up at a 45 degree angle from a significant low would meet at a place in time when a reversal in price was highly likely. Moreover, in addition to the 45 degree line, which Gann called a 1 × 1, there were other angles that would also serve to pinpoint reversal points.

The most popular type of chart used for Gann analysis is the daily chart, where the day's range is plotted, beginning with the first day the contract commenced trading. But advanced Gann students will also track the monthly and weekly ranges, and plot them on the monthly and weekly charts. These may extend backward in time to the beginning of the S&P Index, as compared to the beginning of S&P futures trading. Or, for commodities that have traded for years and years, like, say, cotton, the monthly or weekly chart might extend back to a depression low in the nineteen thirties or even into the nineteenth century. As you can see, maintaining the records for following Gann theory can be a formidable task.

Understanding the many ways in which Gann employed these notions of time and price is the primary challenge of the Gann analyst. Because the bulk of much of Gann's work is repetitious, not to mention enormously difficult to comprehend, we've concentrated on just a few of his more well-known pronouncements to see if we can't make some sense of it in the market. After all, if only one of these Gann techniques proves effective for you, you will stand to gain a substantial amount in trading profits.

Flexibility

First and foremost, Gann believed in being flexible in one's trading approach. Gann looked for certain things to happen within certain time periods or within certain price brackets. When the time period or price bracket was violated, he looked at the next one out in time to hold. In other words, Gann let the market tell him what it wanted to do. His approach to the market was simply one of tagging along with the trend.

Gann lines crisscrossing price charts from previous highs and lows frequently prove to be excellent points to buy or sell. On many occasions, you'll find that a declining market stopped exactly on a Gann line and rallied, or that the reverse occurred. Indeed, if you follow the markets closely, you'll find that this happens far too frequently for it to be mere happenstance.

The point is, regardless of the reason for the move to a Gann line, these lines are important support and resistance zones in the market. One rule is to *buy against all moves to a Gann line when prices are falling and sell against all moves to a Gann line when prices are rising.* On the other hand, you must be quick to liquidate your position once the line is violated. This is such a simple rule. Yet it can result in enormous profits.

Gann Charts

How do you know where the Gann lines are? The only way is to maintain either your own charts or published ones from a commercial source. There is even software available today that can create Gann charts for you.

One excellent charting service that maintains the charts in the format that Gann himself used, using X's and dots in lieu of horizontal lines representing the opening and closing prices, is the New York-based Conceptual Investments. Most of the charts are five or ten dollars each for a single contract month, and most contain key anniversary dates and are maintained in terms of market days with no spaces left for weekends or holidays—the format that Gann himself used. Conceptual's complete address is:

Conceptual Investments
Suite 706
90 West Street
New York, New York 10006
(212) 792-6300

Whether you purchase your Gann charts from a commercial source or make your own, you will want to have what is known as a "Gann Angle Finder," which is generally available for about $10. The Angle Finder is a plastic overlay that permits you to draw in the angles from primary tops and bottoms.

Plotting the Market Days

Once you have your daily Gann chart, you'll be ready to begin plotting the market days across the top and bottom. Remember, every vertical line on a daily Gann chart represents one trading session. Thus, to locate a trading session that occurs, let's say, thirty-four days later, you simply count across thirty-four lines. You'll see in a minute why "taking the count" in this fashion is important.

How many highs and lows should you select? There is no rule. Try to select at least four or five significant highs and lows and count forward every five or ten days. Day one will always be the day *following* the significant high or low. As a rule, to keep the chart understandable, you list market days from tops across the top of the chart and market days from bottoms along the bottom of the chart. As a result you will have five rows of numbers across the top of the chart and another five rows of numbers across the bottom.

What do you do with these numbers? Good question. The numbers measure market days from previous tops and bottoms. Thus you might have a significant top at point A and you might be able to use this point to forecast the *possibility* of a top *or* bottom at some significant time in the future.

We've mentioned thirty-four days. Thirty-four is a significant number, because it is one of the series of Fibonacci numbers that Gann analysts rely on: 1, 1, 2, 3, 5, 8, 13, 21, 34, 55, and so on. Notice how you add the last two numbers to get to the next number.

How do the Fibonacci numbers fit in with the market days? Ideally, you look for a confluence of Gann and Fibonacci numbers all occurring on the same day. Sometimes only one number will appear. At more significant highs and lows, you will have more than one number. The presence of two or more Gann or Fibonacci numbers suggests a possible reversal.

Market days from both tops and bottoms should be considered. At a recent low in the nearby S&P futures, the market-day reading along the top of the Gann chart showed that the low occurred precisely fifty-five market days from one top and exactly thirty-four market days from a more recent top—both Fibonacci numbers!

There are several sets of numbers you'll want to look for. It often helps even to list the numbers as a ready reference along the bottom of the chart. Gann maintained that many numbers are important, but we'll start with the so-called Gann numbers themselves. These numbers are derived by taking the 365 days in a year and dividing by 8, and then further dividing and multiplying. The key fourteen Gann numbers are as follows:

GANN NUMBERS

3.00	182.00
5.82	228.00
11.82	273.00
22.50	319.00
45.00	365.00
91.00	410.00
137.00	456.00

It is uncanny how accurate these numbers can be in calculating tops and bottoms. For example, when the life-of-contract high occurred, at a price of 198.00 in the September 1985 S&P 500 contract on Wednesday, July 17, 1985, the Gann analyst would have started his market-day count on the following day, July 18. Counting ahead exactly twenty-two market days, he would have projected the low to occur on Friday, August 16, 1985. Indeed, a low of 186.45 was made shortly before the close on Friday, August 16. The Gann number was right on the money! September S&P prices later traded under this low of 186.45, but first, prices rallied almost 4.00 points to above 190.20. From high to low, the market tumbled more than ten points, or $5,000 on a single contract, in just twenty-two market days. And this is just one obvious example that is readily evident to anyone who glances at a Gann chart.

There are many more examples of the Gann numbers pinpointing market tops and bottoms. Often, if the Gann number doesn't come up within the exact day, it will pinpoint the top or bottom within a day or two—even over a long period of time. For example, a top extending back over 137 market days pinpointed a recent market in the September 1985 S&P. However, the high on the following day exceeded the projected day high by just .15 points. So it was one day off. The subsequent decline, however, resulted in a move of 7.40 points ($3,700 per contract) in just ten market days.

The life-of-contract high in the September 1985 S&P contract fell precisely ninety market days from a significant previous high—just one day short of Gann's ninety-one-day forecast for the high to fall. Within two months' time, S&P prices had fallen some 17.00 points, or $8,500 per contract.

Gann also believed that the squares of numbers are significant. This is especially true when you get up to the square of 5 or 6 or above. So pay attention to the numbers 25, 36, 49, 64, 81, 100, 121, and 144. You'd be surprised how many tops and bottoms occur precisely 144 market days from a previous significant high or low. Again, you have to be flexible. A recent top in the September 1985 S&P 500 occurred at precisely 143 days from the previous high. In the sharp market break that followed, S&P futures tumbled 7.85 points in five market days—that's $3,925 per contract!

A bottom in September S&P futures recently occurred at exactly thirty-six market days from a previous top. And another bottom occurred precisely forty-nine market days from the life-of-contract high. This one would have netted you more than $5,000 per contract without any market adversity. From the life-of-contract high to another top occurred thirty-seven market days apart, just one more day than the square of six.

If you use no other Gann technique except counting market days, you'll find yourself well ahead of the game. First, to give yourself the confidence of using these numbers to pinpoint tops and bottoms, go back with a price chart and count forward and backward from significant highs and lows. You will find that the Gann numbers, the Fibonacci numbers, and the square of numbers "forecast" the new highs and lows again and again. Then decide for yourself if there is any merit in counting market days.

In the table below, you will find one market low and the life-of-contract high that actually occurred in the September 1985 S&P contract. By taking the counting and looking ahead in time, one could then arrive at a specific date when an anticipated major or minor top or bottom could be expected. The target date is listed along with the occurrence of the high or low, the actual date, and the price.

September 1985 S&P 500 Futures

Beginning Date	Market Days	Target Date	Occurrence
June 20, 1985 low at 188.55	23	July 24, 1985	low occurred at 191.60
June 20, 1985 low at 188.55	34	August 8, 1985	high occurred 1 day later, on August 9, 1985 (3rd anniversary of bull market low) at 189.50
June 20, 1985 low at 188.55	45	August 23, 1985	low occurred one market day later, on August 26, 1985, at 186.30
June 20, 1985 low at 188.55	55	September 9, 1985	high occurred at 189.40
July 17, 1985 life-of-contract high at 198.00	22	August 16, 1985	low occurred at 186.45
July 17, 1985 life-of-contract high at 198.00	34	September 4, 1985	low occurred 1 day later, on September 5, 1985, at 186.55
July 17, 1985 life-of-contract high at 198.00	45	September 19, 1985	low occurred 1 day earlier, on September 18, 1985, at 181.80

Major and Minor Seasonal Time Periods

Gann placed considerable emphasis on specific dates as the time when major or minor price reversals would occur in the market. His trading year commenced with March 21. This is the beginning of his trading year and the point from which he forecast into the future as the year moved in a circular fashion from this date. By dividing the year into 360 degrees, he could make each season represent a 90-degree quadrant. From here, he divided further, resulting in twelve key dates for each season, or forty-eight key dates for the year.

First, the four key seasonal dates are March 21, June 21, September 21, and December 21. The halfway points of the seasons, which would represent 45 degrees in the yearly circle, would be the following dates: May 5,

August 5, November 5, and February 4. The next tier of significant dates are listed below:

April 5	October 6
April 20	October 21
May 21	November 22
June 6	December 7
July 5	January 6
July 23	January 20
August 20	February 19
September 4	March 6

With half of the key forty-eight dates listed, you will have enough information to begin looking for tops and bottoms to occur on the dates shown.

Even a glance at a list of recent price behavior, and the dates on which short-term tops and bottoms occurred, will show you the significance of some of these dates. For example, during 1985, April 20 occurred over a weekend. On the following market day, April 22, the September S&P contract made a short-term low of 181.35. A short-term high occurred on Friday, June 7, in the S&P contract, one day after June 6 and only .25 points higher than the previous day's high. A significant low of 179.25 occurred in the March 1985 S&P contract on February 4, 1985. The market rallied almost four points up over the next five days! On May 20, just one day before the key seasonal day of May 21, the June S&P contract made a significant high. And on June 20, the September S&P contract made a significant low. An inference to be drawn is this: so many traders are watching Gann dates, that they are doing their buying and selling a day or two *prior* to the actual date, resulting in the actual high or low occurring a day or two earlier.

It shouldn't be necessary to belabor the point. Watch for market turns on these significant dates.

The Gann Rule That Can Make You a Fortune: the Halfway Point Rule

"You can make a fortune by following this one rule alone," Gann wrote in his well-known commodity trading course. Known as the "average" or "halfway point" rule, the rule is simplicity itself. You subtract the extreme lowest point from the extreme highest point of a price move and divide by two. You then take this 50 percent retracement of the previous rally or decline as a buying or selling opportunity, depending on whether prices are trending down from a top or rallying up off a bottom.

Moreover, when the market cannot hold and reverse at this 50 percent retracement point, you have another indication: namely, that the entire move will be retraced. When time and price meet, the prices should adhere to the 45-degree angle drawn up from a bottom. When the 45-degree line cannot hold, however, Gann considered the initial move, whether up or down, over. For this reason, he called the 45-degree line the "death angle."

Let's consider an example of how this 50 percent rule might work in practice.

In the final nine months of the September 1985 S&P contract, there was a significant low of 182.20 and a life-of-contract high of 198.00, a difference of 15.80 points. Fifty percent of this move amounts to 7.90 points. When *subtracted* from the life-of-contract high, which was made last, the 50 percent retracement point is 190.10. As prices traded down to the 190.10, the Gann trader could have placed buy orders at the 50 percent retracement point. The price of 190.10 was broken by exactly .30 points on a sharp one-day sell-off. The break was followed by a swift three-day rally that extended over 3.00 points upward. There the rally failed. On the subsequent break, the 50 percent retracement point was taken out and the market traded all the way back to the previous low.

As a rule, the wider the range and the longer the time period, the more significant the halfway point.

An Important Time Rule

Gann believed in counting the market days of rallies and declines and comparing them with one another in order to determine the trend. For instance, in a recent significant rally and decline in the S&P market that carried almost 16.00 points up prior to losing the entire move, there were several retracements that indicated the trend. Here's a listing of the respective moves together with the predominant trend:

DIRECTION OF PRICE MOVE	MARKET DAYS	TREND
UP	20	
DOWN	9	UP
UP	10	UP
DOWN	2	UP
UP	6	UP
DOWN	5	UP
UP	2	DOWN
DOWN	21	DOWN

The entire rally and decline, from bottom to top and back to bottom again, lasted only eighty-eight market days, just a day shy on either leg of the significant, 45-day cycle.

As long as the rallies were of greater duration than the declines, the trend was still considered up. Once the amount of time that the market spent going lower, however, was greater than the time spent on rallies, the trend had changed to down.

Important Time Intervals

In addition to the Gann and Fibonacci numbers, you'll want to pay attention to other significant time periods. Gann believed that market days were important, ignoring weekends and holidays. But he also placed an emphasis on following calendar days as well. To track the important time intervals, you begin by starting at major and minor market tops and bottoms and counting ahead in time. Frequently, the trend will change in one of the key time intervals listed below.

1. *Seven weeks, or forty-nine days.* Forty-nine, of course, is the square of seven and one of the important time intervals already mentioned. The June 6, 1985, high at 195.60 in September S&P futures was followed by a market bottom at 186.50 exactly forty-nine market days later! Not every move is so precise, but the general time frame is important. Look for a market reversal from the forty-ninth to the fifty-second day following a top or bottom.

2. *Forty-two to forty-five days.* The S&P market recently made a top-to-bottom cycle of forty-three days, falling within this significant market-day range. Forty-five is one eighth of the number of degrees in a circle.

3. *Ninety to ninety-eight days.* One quarter of a year. The life-of-contract high of the September 1985 S&P futures was made at exactly ninety days from a previous high. And a subsequent top was made at exactly ninety market days from a previous bottom. Here we had two key reversal days, both predicted from previous tops and bottoms, that occurred exactly ninety days forward in time.

4. *Seven weeks up or down, two to three weeks sideways.* The recent bull move in the S&P was marked by seven weeks advancing, two weeks consolidation, a one-week advance, and down. This pattern proved to be the sign of the market top.

5. *Two to three weeks down followed by failure swing up.* This is a highly significant pattern that often follows the creation of a market top. Following the failure swing, prices often break sharply.

6. *Monthly changes.* Reversals often occur on specific dates within a month. The important dates to watch for are listed below.

a. *6th or 7th.* On March 7, 1985, the June Treasury bond contract made a low. In September of the same year, S&P futures made a minor top in a declining market on the Monday following September 7, which fell over a weekend. On April 8, 1985 (April 7 fell over the weekend), the June S&P futures contract made a low at 179.70. Within four days it was trading almost 4.00 points higher. June S&P futures formed a minor top at 191.95 on June 7, 1985. A week later, the same contract was trading 6.75 points lower. The following dates are all significant Gann days: June 6, October 6, December 7, January 6, and March 6.

b. *9th to 10th.* June 1985 Treasury bonds made a significant high on March 11, 1985 (March 9 and 10 fell over a weekend) at 69-02. On Monday, September 9, 1985, September S&P futures were a minor top at 189.40. By Tuesday of the following week, September S&P futures traded as low as 180.40, a 9.00-point break in seven trading days!

c. *14th to 15th.* On Friday, March 15, 1985, June 1985 Deutschemark futures made a low of 29.63 cents per Deutschemark. Two weeks later, June Deutschemark futures were trading at 32.95 cents per Deutschemark, a change of $4,150 per contract. July 14 and December 14 are both important Gann dates.

d. *19th to 20th.* On Monday, November 19, 1984, December 1984 S&P futures made a low of 164.50. By Friday of the same week, December S&P futures were trading at 168.50, a $2,000 rise in the value of the contract. A low in U.S Treasury bond futures was made on March 19, 1985, in the June 1985 contract. March 1985 S&P futures made a top at 173.70 on Wednesday, December 19, 1984. The market then broke by almost five points in two days. May 20, 1985, marked a top in the June 1985 S&P contract at 191.00. The market had risen over ten points in two weeks' time. The March 1985 S&P contract made a high of 183.35 on Wednesday, February 20, 1985. The market then fell more than four points in two days. Other key Gann dates: April 20, August 20, January 20, and February 19.

e. *23rd to 24th.* On Tuesday, July 23, 1985, the September 1985 S&P contract made a high at 196.50, following the life-of-contract high at 197.90. Seven weeks later, September S&P futures traded as low as 180.30, a change in the value of one contract of $8,100. July 23 is an important Gann date.

f. *29th to 31st.* On Thursday, May 30, 1985, the June 1985 S&P contract made a low at 187.40. A weekend later, the market was over 4.00 points higher, a $2,000 gain. The March 1985 S&P contract made a top on Monday, December 31, 1984, at 170.90. Three days later, March S&P futures were trading at 166.00, a move of almost 5.00 points. June 1985 Treasury bonds made a low of 68-14 on Friday, March 29, 1985. November 30 is a key Gann date.

7. *Thirty calendar days, or multiple of thirty.* The low in the March 1985 S&P contract at 177.45 on January 28 was followed by a low of 180.45 on February 28.

8. *Anniversary dates.* Significant highs and lows often occur exactly one, two, or even three years apart. The August 9, 1982, low in S&P futures, which signaled the beginning of the bull market, was followed exactly one year later by another low prior to the resumption of the bull market.

9. *Monthly intervals.* Gann placed emphasis on several monthly intervals in terms of calendar dates. You take a significant high or low and look ahead three or four months, six or seven months, or ten or eleven months. Twelve months, of course, would be an anniversary date. Multiples of six months—18, 24, 30, 36, 42, 48 months, and so on—are also important time intervals. The life-of-contract high of 198.00 made on July 17, 1985, in the September 1985 S&P contract was followed by a low on August 16, 1985 (August 17 was a weekend), and yet another low the following month, on September 18, at 181.80.

Gann Angles

Above all else, the heart of Gann analysis rests with the angles. Starting with what he called the "square of 28," a geometric square that was twenty-eight squares, or spaces, across and twenty-eight squares, or spaces, high, Gann drew a 45-degree line. He maintained that this was the most important angle, the angle he called the "one-by-one" (1 × 1). In a rising market, prices will hold to the 45-degree, 1 × 1, line, rising off the line and then selling off again and gaining support back on the line. Accordingly, one of the simplest and easiest methods of detecting a bull market is determining whether it does indeed hold above the 45-degree line.

The rule for buying in a bull market using the 45-degree line is to make purchases on a retracement to the 1 × 1 line and place stop-loss orders below the line. Typically, if the line is ever violated, the rule is to begin selling, because it means the bull market is over.

The 1 × 1 line divides the square of 28 into two equal parts. As prices steadily rise along the line, price and time should come together. Thus, fourteen days across in time would match up with a price of 14, assuming one started at a price of zero. In fact, if a line were drawn downward from left to right at a 45-degree angle, the two lines would cross at the middle. This would be fourteen days across and fourteen price units high. In a bear market, of course, you would sell against rallies to this 1 × 1, or 45-degree, line, extending downward from a previous high.

One angle, however, is not sufficient to detect important support and resistance in the market. Gann's rule for using angles was this: if one angle is broken, the market will trade down (up) to the next-lowest (highest) angle. In reality, you will see that happening again and again in the market. The 1 × 1 line will be broken and the market will then trade to the next line, which is known, understandably enough, as the 2 × 1. The 2 × 1 line divides the space contained above and below the 1 × 1 in half, or into two equal parts. The 2 × 1 is an angle of 63¾ degrees.

Because the 2 × 1 rises at a more rapid rate than the 1 × 1 line, two units up for every unit across in time, the market is considered more bullish as long as it follows the 2 × 1 line. Once broken, the 2 × 1 line will give way to the 1 × 1. In fact, as bull markets occur and gain momentum, they will often hold the 2 × 1 line for a period of time, until the market trajectory is slowed. Then the 2 × 1 line will be broken, and one would look for the 1 × 1 line to hold. As the market turns from a bull to a bear, however, the 1 × 1 will no longer hold and, in time, the pace might accelerate still more. Then the 2 × 1 to the downside will (losing two units in price for every unit across in time) be the line that the market follows.

There are other angles. But the principle is the same. If one line can't hold, look for the market to trade to the next line. The five key Gann angles in order of importance are as follows:

1. 1 × 1: 45 degrees
2. 2 × 1: 63¾ degrees
3. 4 × 1: 75 degrees
4. 8 × 1: 82½ degrees
5. 16 × 1: 86¼ degrees

The angles are valuable not only as support and resistance lines, but as indicators of important reversal lines as well. The reversal point occurs where the *angles cross*.

For example, if you have a double bottom, you do the following. You draw the 1 × 1 up from the first bottom and then you draw both a 1 × 1 and a 2 × 1 up from the second bottom. Because the two 1 × 1 lines will be parallel, they will not meet. However, because the first 1 × 1 and the 2 × 1 drawn from the second bottom are drawn at different angles, they will eventually cross. Typically, *the point in time where the two angles cross will signify a change in trend.* It is not important that the two bottoms be at exactly the same price, but near the same price.

When you begin drawing in other angles as well, you will have more angles crossing. Pay careful attention to these points. The best signal of a major reversal in trend occurs where more than two angles cross. For instance, you may have a 1 × 1 line crossing a 2 × 1 line. But an 8 × 1 line, drawn from yet another top or bottom, that occurred perhaps a year ago, may also cross at the same point. This crossing of many angles suggests that a powerful reversal may be in order. If you track the Gann angles for a long period of time, you will find that this crossing of the angles is often uncannily accurate in predicting trend changes.

You should draw angles from any significant high or low in the market. For this reason, it helps to purchase Gann charts that track the entire history of the contract—even when it was thinly traded and the highest and lowest occur as mere dots on the chart. The most important highs and lows, of course, are the life-of-contract highs and lows that typically occur early or late in the contract's history.

Squaring Price and Time

The notion of squaring price with time is one of Gann's most important discoveries. It says essentially, when a market has moved up—or down—X dollars in X days, the price should hold the 1 × 1, 45-degree, line. When it cannot hold the line, the trend has changed. Put another way, an equal amount of points up or down balances an equal amount of time.

For instance, if you have a fourteen-cent gain in soybean prices over a fourteen-day period, then price and time are in balance and the next likely move is down.

The idea of squaring price and time also fits in with the generally accepted notion that markets take time before reversing. Only after this time has passed, can the reversal begin. This, by the way, is the reason for the age-old saying about trading with the trend. The only difficulty in modern markets is deciding what the trend is under volatile conditions.

Rules for Using Gann Analysis

Gann was such an undisputed master at understanding the markets that one could easily spend a lifetime learning all he had to say. To take such an immense body of work and summarize it in just a few pages is obviously impossible. Even the simplest and easiest-to-understand features of Gann analysis cannot be understood without a lot of study. It is those few brief, but significant, ideas that are summarized here for the student of Gann.

RULE NUMBER 1: *Use Gann charts and track market days.* The Gann charts are at the heart of Gann analysis, and the listing of the market days will help you pinpoint highs and lows in a visual manner. Starting with the day *following* a significant high or low as day 1, track the days in increments of five-, ten-, or twenty-day units to be able to visualize the market days from a high or low out to the future. Plot the market days from previous tops along the top of the chart, and the market days from previous bottoms along the bottom. It helps to have the key Gann days and Fibonacci days written right on the chart for easy referral. These numbers are listed below:

GANN NUMBERS		FIBONACCI NUMBERS	
3.00	182.00	1.00	34.00
5.82	228.00	2.00	55.00
11.82	273.00	3.00	89.00
22.50	319.00	5.00	144.00
45.00	365.00	8.00	233.00
91.00	410.00	13.00	377.00
137.00	456.00	21.00	610.00

RULE NUMBER 2: *Pay attention to anniversary dates and other time periods which are critical to Gann analysis.* Each time a significant high and low is made in the market, the Gann analyst will record the date, the price, and whether a high or low was made. In time, this collection of highs and lows will prove useful as you look ahead for dates thirty, sixty, ninety, and one hundred twenty days in the future. In addition, it will alert you when an important date is about to occur. When specific dates are used in conjunction with the number of market days from significant highs and lows, the possibility of a market reversal is often noted well in advance. Remember, time is vital in Gann analysis. The market cannot reverse until sufficient time has passed.

RULE NUMBER 3: *Time is the most important factor.* Record both market and calendar days of every rally and reaction. Then measure the number of days of the price reversal and compare it with the previous major trend. When the reversal exceeds in time the length of the previous trend, you can consider the trend reversed.

RULE NUMBER 4: *Watch for swing bottoms and tops.* When a market advances, it will continue to have higher bottoms and higher tops; when a market declines, it will continue to have lower bottoms and lower tops. When this configuration doesn't occur, you have a swing bottom or top, and a reverse in the market is likely. In an advancing market, look for a previous bottom to be taken out and a previous top to hold. This is the sign that the trend is changing.

RULE NUMBER 5: *Watch resistance levels.* When the 50 percent retracement level doesn't hold, it is a sign that the market is changing direction. Once you have a prolonged up move, look for the 50 percent pullback. If prices cannot hold the support, chances are the trend has changed to down. Conversely, in a declining market, look for rallies of 50 percent of the move to meet resistance. When the market trades higher than the 50 percent rally retracement, chances are, the trend has changed to up.

RULE NUMBER 6: *Buy new highs and sell new lows.* Although this rule is difficult to understand and hard to follow, it is quite profitable to follow. When markets rise and fall, they do so for a reason. By definition, a market that is advancing *must* make new highs. And declining markets *must* trade into new low ground. At the time, you may feel that you have missed the market. But, in fact, one of the safest places to buy a market is just above a previous high; and the reverse is true of declining markets. As a confirming signal, you should look for the market to continue to move in a favorable direction almost immediately. If it does, your profit is assured. If, on the other hand, the market reverses soon after you buy a new high or sell a new low, you will also know this immediately, since you will have losses. In this instance, double up and reverse. Chances are slim that a market will trade for long at a significant previous high or low.

RULE NUMBER 7: *Place orders to buy and sell at Gann lines.* Markets frequently trade precisely to a Gann line. For this reason, it pays to sell against all Gann lines above the market price and it pays to buy against all Gann lines below the market price. When the Gann line is penetrated, however, expect prices to trade to the next-highest or -lowest Gann line. If you are on the wrong side of the market, you should liquidate the position immediately to preserve your trading capital. The Gann lines are drawn from previous highs and lows using the angles discussed earlier in this chapter. Gann "angle finders" are available from commercial sources that publish Gann charts.

RULE NUMBER 8: *Pay attention to the Rule of 3.* Gann maintained that market patterns move in response to the number 3. He was the first to identify a three-day cycle that Taylor later used in the *Book Method.* Gann used a three-day charting technique that connected the high and low every third day. When the angle of the line connecting every third top changed from, say, up to down, he maintained that the trend had changed. This is just one way to use the Rule of 3, however. During the day, you will notice that when support and resistance are formed at an intraday low or high, prices tend to bounce off the support or resistance three times. Typically, if support or resistance is going to be broken, it will be penetrated on the third test of the low or the high. The Rule of 3 also applies to weekly highs and lows. When prices go down for three weeks, look for a reversal about midweek of the following, or fourth, week. The same applies to a market that rallies for three weeks; look for a top midpoint of the fourth week and an opportunity to sell. When a market reacts for three weeks, however, and continues lower in the fourth or fifth week, you have an opportunity to sell new lows. This is a sign of even weaker prices. And the reverse is true for a rallying market that continues to rally after three weeks up. In a recent three-week rally in S&P futures, the market moved up over twelve points in thirteen consecutive market days. It then sold off until the seven-teenth day and stopped at a Gann line and rallied over the previous high—the classic three-and-a-half-week pattern. It then made two more three-week patterns, until it reached the life-of-contract high. After that, all the tops and all the bottoms were lower than previous tops and bottoms and the market lost the entire gain made on the previous nine-week rally.

RULE NUMBER 9: *Be quick to take losses.* Gann, like all knowledgeable traders, knew that the secret of successful trading was dealing with losses, since the profits could take care of themselves. He stressed that you should never trade on fear or greed, but only reason. When wrong about the market, there is only one solution. Get out quickly! Not to do so only invites trouble. Gann stressed many paradoxes of the trade. For instance, he said that the longer the market rallies or declines, the stronger the rallies or declines will become. This, he said, was because in the latter stages of a bull or a bear market the mere fear that many traders have gives way to total despair. In other words, those who have sold futures contracts in hopes of the rally ending soon, only have to become forceful buyers as the market climbs higher and higher. The reverse, of course, is true on the downside. What's more, on a day-trading basis, this pattern also becomes evident. Typically, a market that is about to tumble will retreat only slowly, and perhaps rally a bit before the downturn begins. But, toward the end of the day, the bulls become panic-stricken and sell at any price just to be out of the market. This has the tendency to make prices break sharply. And by the way, it is also the reason why you can often safely sell more contracts at new lows. Once the sell-stops are hit, the bottom will fall out. Thus, when you are wrong, you have only one logical choice: Get out quickly. Take the loss.

12

Options on Futures

THE LIMITED-RISK APPROACH
TO THE FUTURES MARKET

Options on futures, the newest wrinkle in futures trading, offer some unique profit opportunities. With the introduction of options on futures, in the early 1980s, the futures trader found himself, for the very first time, a vehicle that limited risk while allowing for unlimited profit. For a one-time fee, known as the *premium,* the purchaser of an option on a futures contract buys the right—but, significantly, not the obligation—to buy or sell a specific futures contract. The premium represents the total risk involved. Thus, no matter how far prices rise or fall, the option buyer knows his risk at the outset. At the same time, the potential profit is unlimited—the same as if he had purchased or sold a futures contract.

The real advantage of dealing in options, as opposed to futures, is their inherent flexibility. Not only can you purchase options for their limited-risk features, but you can also sell them (known as *writing),* in which case you receive the premium income paid by the buyer. The writer, however, in return for the premium income, faces an *unlimited* liability—just like the futures trader. But his obligation can be dispensed with by buying back the option.

Like stock options, options on futures come in just two varieties: puts and calls. The call option provides the option holder the right to *purchase* the underlying futures contract at the agreed-upon price specified in the option contract, known as the *strike price*. The put option is the mirror image of the call, providing its holder the right to *sell* the underlying futures contract at the agreed-upon strike price.

There are options available on many, although not all, futures contracts, among them financial instruments, precious metals, currencies, livestock, and grain. A typical option is self-explanatory in terms of its features. For instance, if you were to purchase a December 300 wheat call for a premium of 7 1/4 cents per bushel, you would have the right to exercise the option and receive a long wheat futures contract at the striking price of $3.00 per bushel at any time prior to the expiration of the call, which would be in the month prior to the expiration of the futures. Your entire cost would be just $362 for the five-thousand-bushel contract. Thus, if December wheat futures were trading above a price of 307 1/2 cents per bushel, you would enjoy a net profit on the transaction exclusive of commission fees. A December 300 wheat put option, on the other hand, would provide you with the right to *sell* the underlying futures at the strike price of $3.00 per bushel at any time prior to the expiration of the option. In a declining market, the put option would prove profitable to its buyer.

The simplest and most elemental use of options on futures is to purchase a call option in anticipation of higher prices or purchase a put option in anticipation of declining prices. Options are more complex than futures contracts in the sense that they can be converted to futures contracts. That is, by *exercising* an option, one receives either a long or a short position at the option's strike price. The holder of a call option, therefore, who exercises, receives a long futures at the strike price; the holder of a put option receives a short futures at the strike price. For instance, let's say you purchase a December 185 S&P 500 call and December futures rise above the strike price of 185. Above 185, the 185 call will have what is known as *cash*, or *intrinsic*, value. This is the amount by which the call is said to be *in-the-money*, or the cash equivalent of the value between the difference of the strike price and the market price. By exercising the call, you will receive one December long futures contract at a price of 185. Thus, if the market price of December S&P futures is, let's say, 191, the difference of six points will constitute your paper profit, which you can realize by immediately selling the December S&P futures. For call options, the holder will only wish to exercise if the market price is *above* the strike price.

Now let's look at puts. If you are bearish on gold prices, you might purchase a December 340 gold put. This will give you the right—but not the obligation—to receive one short gold futures position at the strike price of $340 an ounce. Assuming gold futures prices fall below 340, therefore, you might exercise the put and you will receive a short futures position at the strike. Your profit will be determined by the difference between the strike price and the market price of December gold futures minus the premium cost of the put.

Let's say you paid $2.00 an ounce, or $200 per option on the 100-ounce contract, for the December 340 put. If prices fall to, let's say, $335 an ounce for December futures, you can exercise the put, receive the short futures position, and immediately cover (buy) the short position and realize a total of $300 exclusive of commissions. Here's how: The put premium's cost was initially $200. The amount realized by exercising was $500, or the difference between the short futures at the striking price of $340 and the market price of $335. The difference amounts to $300, commission costs aside.

What Determines Option Premiums

The cost of the option, known as the premium, is determined by several factors that every option buyer or seller should understand.

Option premiums, like futures prices, are established in an auction market on the floor of a futures exchange. Buyers "bid" for options, and sellers "offer," in the traditional open outcry manner that is used to trade futures contracts. Since options permit the buyers to either call away or sell the underlying futures, their pricing is reflective of the relationship of the option to the underlying futures instrument. First and foremost, therefore, the *relationship of the option to the underlying futures* will be a primary component of the premium price.

For understandable reasons, therefore, a call option whose strike price is below the market price of the underlying futures will have a greater value than a comparable call whose strike price is above the market price of the futures. The former option, in the nomenclature of the trade, is said to be *in the money,* whereas the latter is considered to be *out of the money.* If you have two December Treasury bond calls, one with a strike price of 68 and another with a strike price of 72, the call with the lower strike is going to be worth more money, since it permits the holder to purchase at a lower price. When you are talking about puts, however, the reverse is true. Higher-strike puts are more valuable, because they permit the holder to sell futures at a higher price.

As a matter of definition, lower-strike calls on the same underlying futures will *always* be more valuable than higher-strike calls regardless of whether the calls are in or out of the money. For puts, the higher-strike options will always command higher premiums.

There are two components to every option premium: the so-called *time value,* and the *cash,* or *intrinsic, value.* Time value refers to that portion of the premium price that accounts for its value apart from its current value if it were exercised immediately. Indeed, for many options that are trading out of the money, time value accounts for the entire premium value, since the option has no value apart from its potential value. This means it cannot be exercised at a profit in the market.

By definition, calls that have a strike price *above* the prevailing market price and puts that have a strike price *below* the prevailing market price of the futures have premiums made up of time value alone, since they are out of the money. With in-the-money options, however, you have options comprising both time and cash value. The cash-value component is determined by the difference between the strike price and the prevailing market price —that is, by how far the option is trading in the money. The time-value component will amount to the difference between the premium price and the cash value. Thus, with December cotton futures trading at 60 cents per pound in the market, the December 58 cotton call might be available for 2.10 cents per pound. Two cents of that premium would be attributable to its cash value; the remaining .10 cents of the call's value would be time value. By definition, all options cease to retain any time value at expiration. As a result, an option will be valued at expiration according to its cash value alone. The December 58 cotton call will have a value of two cents if it expires with December cotton at precisely 60, the December 400 gold call will be worth $50 if December gold is at $450 at expiration of the call, the November soybeans 450 call will be worth 25 cents if November soybeans are trading at $4.75 at expiration of the call, and so on. Call options that expire with the underlying futures at or below the strike will have no value; put options will cease to have value if they expire when the underlying futures price is at or above the strike price. As you can see, the relationship of the underlying futures price to the strike price will have an important bearing on the value of an option.

A second component of an option premium will be the value of the *time left to expiration.* All other considerations aside, time to expiration will reflect in an option premium by valuing those options with more time at a higher price than options with lesser time left to expiration. From the buyer's viewpoint, therefore, the higher premium cost will provide him with more staying power in the event prices don't move favorably in his direction right away. For the writer, the higher premium reflects the higher risk associated with writing the option, since the market may change considerably over a longer period of time.

Lastly, the *volatility* in the market will impact on put and call premiums alike. As volatility increases, the likelihood of both put and call premiums increasing rises as well. Ironically, even if underlying futures prices decline, the premiums of calls as well as puts are likely to increase when the decline is accompanied by an increase in volatility. The heightened volatility will aid buyers of options in the sense that the value of the options should increase in value; for the writers, the heightened volatility will translate into higher writing income to compensate them for the increased risks associated with selling options in a more volatile environment.

Some option traders also track interest rates, since a rise or fall in rates will impact on futures prices—indeed, on some, such as Treasury bond prices, more directly than others. Nevertheless, since we live in an interest-rate-sensitive market environment, fluctuating prices will impact on agricultural commodities, such as livestock and grain, and financial instruments and foreign currencies alike. Since fluctuating rates will impact on the underlying futures, it only stands to reason that the option premiums will reflect these changes as well.

Buying and Selling Options

While you can always exercise any option you purchase, there's an easier way to realize your gain. Instead of paying the commissions to receive the futures and subsequently liquidate the position, you can simply sell any option you own. Any gain or loss will be reflected in the option's premium.

For example, in the case of the put-option example above, any December 340 put will retain a cash value of at least $5.00 an ounce when the price falls to $335. This gain is reflected in the option's premium, because the option can be immediately exercised and a $5.00 gain realized. Remember, the put gives you the right to sell the underlying futures at the strike. In fact, the December 340 put will have a slightly higher price than $5.00, to reflect any so-called *time value* that may exist in the option. Hence, the December 340 put may indeed sell for $6.00, or $600 for the put, when the put is $5.00 in the money. The additional dollar in value will reflect the potential beyond the so-called intrinsic, or cash, value. Thus, options said to be *out of the money,* or of no cash value, will be priced solely according to their time value.

For instance, when December gold futures trade at, let us say, $345 an ounce, the December 340 puts will have no cash or intrinsic value. They will, however, have time value. Such an option might have a premium of $3.00 or $4.00, depending upon a host of factors such as market volatility, interest rates, time left to expiration, and so on. Such a price reflects potential value alone, however, since if expiration were to occur today, the option would have no value at all. Thus, on the last day of trading, options will be priced according to their cash value alone, since all time value at that point will have ceased to exist.

Therefore, the easiest method of realizing a profit on an option is to sell the option, rather than exercising and taking on the underlying futures contract. By exercising, your account will be credited with a long or short futures at the strike price on the underlying commodity, depending upon whether you purchased a call or a put. When this occurs, you will be responsible for another round-turn commission on the futures as well as having the obligation of fully margining the futures contract. The commission cost on the futures will be a relatively minor concern. But market volatility on the underlying futures may indeed wipe out your option profit if you aren't careful.

For instance, let's say you exercise your December 340 gold put when December gold prices are at $335 an ounce. As a result, you will be credited with a short futures at the strike price of 340. But what happens if prices rise? Your paper profit will vanish. At a price of 340, you will have broken even on the short futures position. But you will still have a loss, since you paid a $2.00 premium on the December 340 gold put. The net will be a loss of the put's premium cost.

One drawback of purchasing puts and calls, which is often cited by futures traders, is the cost of the option premiums. Once you pay a premium for the option, the cost must be recovered in a favorable movement in the option's price or you will sustain a loss. The premium, of course, will be paid to the seller, or writer, of the option. This is the amount he receives for taking the risk associated with writing the option—or providing you with the right to "call away" or "put" the underlying futures to him. His obligation to you is clearly stated in the option contract. He must provide you with a long futures at the stated strike price, in the case of a call, upon demand throughout the life of the option; if he writes a put, he must provide the buyer with a short futures at the strike. As a result, the buyer on either a put or a call requires a favorable move in the market to earn a profit; the seller, of course, who, in a sense, is betting against the buyer, simply needs a stationary market or an unfavorable move (to the buyer) to retain the full premium income.

Why Not Write Options?

One strategy that professionals frequently engage in is the writing of puts and calls. Unlike buying options, however, this strategy entails unlimited risk—comparable, in fact, to buying or selling a futures contract.

The risk is best understood in terms of the role of the option writer, or grantor. When you write (sell) an option, you agree to provide the buyer with either a long or a short futures contract, depending upon whether you write a call or a put, at the strike price. Since a market can move an unlimited amount away from the strike price, the risk is likewise unlimited. Moreover, since the option will only be exercised in the event that it is profitable to do so for the buyer of the option, the writer can count on sustaining a loss in the event that the market rises after writing a call or declines after writing a put. The specific amount of this loss, however, will be dependent on several factors such as the strike price and the amount of premium income received for writing the put or call.

When an individual purchases a call option, he pays a premium to the seller. In return for receiving the premium income, the seller agrees to allow the purchaser of the call to exercise the option and receive a long futures at the strike. Thus, the buyer of a call stands to gain a long futures position at the strike price and the seller is obligated to provide him with one in the event of exercise. The option may be exercised solely at the discretion of the buyer; the seller, on the other hand, has no choice in the matter; he must guarantee the performance of the contract.

When a call option is exercised, therefore, the buyer "calls away" the futures. His account is credited with a long futures. At the same time, the seller's account is credited with a *short futures at the strike price.* This is an important point to stress. Since an option will be exercised only when it is profitable to the buyer—he could, otherwise, simply walk away from the option, allowing it to expire—it will, by definition, be in the money and *unprofitable* to the seller. This is the risk that every writer must live with.

In the case of a put option, the roles are reversed. The put-option holder can exercise and receive a short futures position at the strike price; when the put is exercised, the put seller, or writer, is credited with a *long futures position*—again, one with paper losses. Unprofitable options are *never* exercised. With November soybean futures, for instance, trading at $5.00 a bushel, it would make no sense to exercise a call option to buy November bean futures at $5.50 per bushel—not when the same beans are available in the futures market for 50 cents less. Thus, only options that are profitable to the buyer will be exercised—the very same options that are unprofitable to the sellers.

If the sellers of put and call options on futures run such an unlimited risk, why write options at all? Good question. There are several good reasons. For one, assuming a stable market, the writers want to earn the premium income. Remember, whether the option is exercised or not, the premium is retained by the seller. For another, most options are never exercised. This suggests that most option buyers lose, whereas most option writers win. This is indeed the case. Yet the risks remain. When markets run in either direction, you can be sure that the option buyers are profiting and the option writers are losing. Moreover, the writers are limited in their maximum gain on an option to the premium cost—not a penny more. This gain in premium income, therefore, must be contrasted against the potential for unlimited loss. For many traders, writing options is too risky. The paradox is that the writers have the percentages in their favor, whereas the buyers are bucking the odds.

In-, At-, and Out-of-the-Money Options

Options are frequently referred to in terms of their relation to the strike price and the market price of the underlying futures contract. *In-the-money options* are those puts and calls which can be exercised immediately for a cash value. By definition, a call will be in the money when the strike price is below the market price of the futures; a put, on the other hand, is considered in the money when the strike price is above the underlying futures price. You can clearly see the benefit of exercising an option that will give you the right to purchase a futures below the prevailing market price or sell a futures above the prevailing market price.

Out-of-the-money options retain only so-called *time value*, or the value accruing to the option due to the time left prior to expiration. They cannot be exercised immediately for a profit. By definition, a call will be out of the money when the strike price is above the market price; a put's strike will be *below* the market price of the underlying futures to remain out of the money. At-the-money options, as the name suggests, are options whose strike prices are identical or nearly identical to the underlying futures.

Understanding the Nomenclature

Option nomenclature is easy to master once you understand that there are just two types of options—puts and calls—with standardized features. The call option provides the holder the right—but not the obligation—to purchase the underlying futures contract at the strike price. The put provides the holder the right—but not the obligation—to sell the underlying futures at the strike price.

Like the underlying futures, options are traded in designated contract months. The months will be identified in terms of the underlying futures. Thus, a December call will pertain to December futures, and a June call will pertain to a June futures contract. With the exception of the so-called *cash settlement* futures, such as stock index futures, options on futures expire during the month *prior* to the expiration of the underlying futures. This is an important fact to remember, since you may want to exercise your option and take on the underlying futures. Thus, November soybean options will expire during October; June live cattle options will expire during May, and so on. The options on cash settlement instruments, such as stock index futures, however, expire the same day as the futures, since there is no problem with delivery.

Options can also be categorized according to their strike prices. When a new option series is introduced, the exchanges try to offer a combination of in-, out-, and at-the-money options with the strike prices bracketing the current futures price. As the futures change in value, new-option strike prices are often introduced as well. To facilitate trading in the options, the strike prices are standardized according to some fixed price interval which will differ for different futures contracts. Options on gold futures, for example, are available at $10 intervals; options on U.S. Treasury bond futures have strikes that are two basis points apart; and options on soybean futures have strikes placed at 25-cent intervals.

The first-time option trader should note that option premiums are quoted in exactly the same terms as the underlying futures. Thus, gold options will be quoted in dollars and cents per ounce and soybean options in cents per bushel. An exception exists in U.S. Treasury bond options, where the price increments have been divided in half. Thus, whereas the underlying bond futures are quoted in thirty-seconds per basis point, the options on the futures are quoted in sixty-fourths per basis point. This is done to provide sufficient depth and liquidity in the Treasury bond options —which, by the way, are the most popular options on futures trading today.

With the minimum tick in the U.S. Treasury bond futures equal to $31.25, the minimum tick in the puts and calls on Treasury bond futures is half as much, or $15.62. Thus, with December Treasury bond futures trading at 75-19, or 75 19/32, the in-the-money December 76 put might be quoted at 1-11, or 1 11/64. In dollars and cents, this would translate into $1,171.82 for the right to sell December U.S. Treasury bond futures at a price of 76-00. With the December futures already trading at 75-19, the December 76 put is already 13/32 in the money. Thus, approximately $406 of the value of the December 76 put would be cash value, and the balance, of approximately $766, would amount to time value. Having paid 1 11/64 basis points for the put option, the buyer will need a comparable amount of movement down from 76-00 in order to break even on the option at expiration. As a result, December bond futures will have to trade at approximately 74-27 at expiration of the put for the put buyer to break even. Lower prices (of course meaning higher interest rates) will result in a profit for the put buyer.

The purchaser of a call option on gold futures would be quoted a price in dollars and cents per ounce of gold, the standard method of quoting gold futures contracts. Thus, if December gold futures were trading at about $329 an ounce, you might be quoted a price of $11 an ounce to buy a December 320 call. This would amount to $1,100 for the call on the 100-ounce futures contract. With December gold futures trading at $9.00 in the money, the $11 premium reflects $9.00 of cash value and $2.00 of time value.

Rules for Buying Options

We've seen how option buying is the simplest and easiest method of participating in the option-on-futures market. You select a put or a call to purchase, pay a premium, and await a favorable market development. But which option is the best to purchase? Do you purchase an option with a lot of time value? Or one that will expire in a month or two? Do you buy an option that is in or out of the money? Which are better investments: higher- or lower-strike puts? Higher- or lower-strike calls? Why? These are questions that will need answering if you are to become an intelligent option buyer.

First and foremost, the key advantages of option buying are limited risk and high leverage. Since option buying requires just a one-time premium payment, all option purchases are limited in risk to the cost of the premium. But, still, some are better investments than others.

For instance, since option premiums reflect both time and cash value, cheaper options will be at or out of the money and reflect time value alone.

For the option buyer, whose profit will be dependent on the return gained from the initial investment, the in-the-money options simply serve to cut down on leverage, since you are purchasing an option that already has a considerable cash value. Were the option to expire tomorrow, chances are you would receive a considerable portion of the investment back. But you don't buy options to receive back a smaller portion of your investment. Hardly. The idea is to take a modest amount of money and control an asset worth many, many times as much. Thus, using the leverage correctly, you need only a modest move in the underlying investment to generate a profit worth many times the cost of the initial investment. This is leverage in action. But when you purchase cash value in options—namely, options that are already in the money by an appreciable amount—you defeat the purpose of the high leverage. So forget about buying options that are deeply in the money.

What about out-of-the-money options? Here, the answer depends on how far the market price is away from the strike. After all, you have to be practical. If December gold futures are trading at the $330-per-ounce level in October and you have only one month prior to the expiration of the December call (in November), chances are the December 400 call is a bad investment. Why? Because, given the recent history of the gold market, it probably won't rise by $70 an ounce in four or five weeks—or, for that matter, four or five months! As a result, anyone who purchases a call that is so far out of the money and has so little time left to expiration is acting out of blind hope or sheer foolishness. Precisely because the December 400 call is so far out of the money, the premium will be low—perhaps just ten cents an ounce, or $10 on the $33,000 contract—but what are the chances of the call proving profitable at expiration? Almost zero. So you have to be practical. Concentrate on those options that are trading near or at the strike price and have a reasonable chance of proving profitable. With December gold futures trading at $330, you'd be looking at the December 340 or December 330 calls. Or, if you wish more time, you'd be considering the February calls.

Call buying is for the bullish investor, of course. You buy a call because you expect prices to rise. But because you must pay a premium for the call, you need more than a modest rise in the market; in fact, you require a rise sufficient to recover the initial cost of the call.

For example, let's say you pay $4.00 an ounce to buy a December 440 call when futures are at $440 per ounce. At expiration, your call will be worth whatever the difference is between the strike price and the market price of the December futures when the futures is above the strike price. Thus, at $450, the 440 call will have a $10 value; at $442, however, the call will only return $2.00; and at $440 or less, the call won't be worth a dime. Hence, to recover your initial cost of $4.00 per ounce for the call, you'll need a favorable move of at least $4.00 in the market. Strive to purchase calls, therefore, only in markets that have the potential to move more than the premium price.

The same, of course, pertains to put buying, only in reverse. The put buyer wants the market to move lower so that he can sell the futures at the strike price (or, more likely, simply sell the put prior to expiration for its cash value plus whatever time value remains). Again, similar rules apply. You don't want to buy a put that is either too far out of or in the money. And for the very same reasons. The put that is deeply out of the money will be relatively inexpensive, but the likelihood of its ever proving profitable is remote. On the other hand, you are in the option-buying game for the leverage. So you don't want to tie up your money in buying cash value. Concentrate on the puts that are near to the money, either slightly in or out of the money, and you'll get the best deal for your money.

Obviously, option buying requires both judgment and a bit of luck. No one can tell you for sure whether the market is about to run. But if you have an idea that a substantial move is coming, you can purchase either a put or a call, depending on your point of view, and profit accordingly if you are correct. What's more, if you are wrong, you'll know your costs at the outset. There will be no margin calls and no sleepless night's worry about the market being bid limit or asked limit against you. Clearly, this is a key advantage of option buying.

There are other, more sophisticated strategies that involve option buying.

Apart from merely speculating on the direction of the market, you can use a put or a call to protect a long or a short futures position—again, the insurance concept.

Think for a moment of the risk that every futures trader undertakes. If you purchase a futures contract, your risk is that the market may move lower. Not only do you stand to lose when the market retreats, as a holder of a long futures contract, but you face an unlimited—at least down to zero—risk. This could be many, many times your initial margin. Not a few hapless futures traders have learned the real risks of the market by being caught on the wrong side when it "locks limit." This means that you can't get out. And the market may break for several days consecutively. A real nightmare.

One option-buying strategy to protect a long futures position is to purchase a put with the strike at or near where you originally purchased the futures. Now if prices retreat, you are protected.

For example, let's say you purchase a three-month Eurodollar Deposit futures contract at a price of 90 and you simultaneously purchase a Eurodollar 90 put for a premium of .35, or $875. If Eurodollar futures soar, you simply abandon the put and earn your profit on the long futures. If, on the other hand, Eurodollar futures plummet, your loss on the futures is fully protected by the put. You simply exercise the put and the long futures position will prove a wash, commission costs and the put's premium cost aside. That is, you will have purchased one long Eurodollar futures at 90 and, by virtue of having exercised the put, you will have sold one futures at the strike of 90. Thus, you will have both purchased one contract and sold one contract at the same price. Your cost will be commissions plus the price of the put.

There are all sorts of variations on this strategy. To borrow the insurance analogy, you might have increased your "deductible" by purchasing an 89-strike put, for instance. The cost of the out-of-the-money put would be less, and you would have paid the one-point difference between where you initially purchased the long futures and where the exercising of the put would have taken you out of the market. This is just one strategy for protecting a futures position.

In addition, you have to look at the purchase of the put as a strategy designed to give you staying power. By owning the put, you can sit through a substantial decline without having to make any serious decisions. You know you are protected. You might, however, in the meantime be faced with margin calls on the losing futures position. But this consideration aside, you are indeed far more flexible. This is because you know your risk is limited to the cost of the put and not a penny more.

For short futures positions, calls serve a similar protective function. The short seller stands to lose if prices rally. Hence, a call at or above the selling point will serve as insurance against unlimited loss when you are a short seller. As with purchasing puts to protect the long position, the short seller has to ask himself if the premium cost warrants the lowered risk in using calls in this fashion.

Lastly, you want to buy options to add to a futures position—that is, purchase calls when you are a buyer of futures or purchase puts when you are a seller of futures. Depending on the particular option you select, you gain added leverage in your overall portfolio without taking on substantial additional risk. As with any option-buying situation, however, you'll want to be fairly certain you have a developing situation that is about to move the market substantially. You'll need the move to earn a fair return on your option investment.

Rules for Option Writing

Option buyers frequently complain that option premiums are too high. How can you make a profit when you have to recoup the cost of the premium? An ideal antidote to the problem of "high" premiums is to *earn* the premium income by writing options. The writer, after all, receives the premium that the buyer pays. And if the option premiums are indeed too high, it stands to reason that the writers will profit from the situation.

Before you think about writing, however, consider the risks. Unlike option buying, writing an option requires a commitment to make good on the bargain. Specifically, if the call buyer decides to exercise a call you have written, you have to give him a long futures (meaning you receive a short futures) at the strike price *regardless* of the price of the underlying futures. The reverse is, of course, true for the put writer. Is this a risk you are willing to undertake? Depending on the market and the type of option you write, you may indeed be attracted to the writing side of the option market.

There are several benefits to option writing, despite the risks. For one, most options remain unexercised at expiration. Why? Because the market didn't move above the strike, in the case of the call, or below the strike, in the case of the put. As a result, the writers simply bank the premiums received. For another, the writer has defensive strategies he can employ if the market starts to run and his short options threaten to go into the money (prove profitable to the buyer). The writer can, for instance, buy back his short options just as a short seller of futures can cover his position by buying back the short futures. Unfortunately, this can often only be accomplished at a loss. But better a small loss than a large one. Also, even if an option you have written threatens to prove profitable to the buyer (and unprofitable to you, the writer), you have a cushion of safety—namely, the premium you received for writing the option.

For example, let's say you write a November 550 soybean call for a premium of fifteen cents and bean prices move above the 550 strike. As the writer, you have a full fifteen cents protection (the premium income you received) before you will be in a loss position at expiration. Thus, as long as November beans remain below 565 at expiration, you will gain some profit on the transaction. If November beans are at 560 upon expiration of the 550 call, the buyer will receive ten cents back on his fifteen-cent investment and you, the writer, will pay back ten cents on the initial premium payment of fifteen cents. So you'll remain five cents per bushel ahead on the transaction even though your judgment on prices proved wrong!

This is the advantage of option writing. You receive premium income and the market has to move for the buyer to earn a larger amount than he paid. For the writer to profit, however, the market need only stay stationary or rise or decline a modest amount. In most instances, the odds favor the writer.

In order to earn the premium income, the writer wants the option to remain out of the money at expiration. In addition, he wishes to avoid having any option he has written exercised. Since only options that retain cash value, or are in the money, are in danger of exercise, the would-be option writer is wise to concentrate on writing at-the-money or out-of-the-money options. There is one drawback to this strategy, however. Options that are deeply out of the money—those which have the remotest possibility of being exercised—change hands for comparatively low premiums. As a result, the writer is taking in only a modest premium, while the opportunity always exists for one of these low-premium options to soar in value in a short period of time. For the writer, this would mean disaster.

While defensive writing strategies exist, most writers are better off selling only those options that are near the strike price. Not only will the writer of such options receive a relatively large time premium for undertaking the risk involved, but the liquidity of the at-the-money options will be far greater than in those options that are either deeply in or out of the money.

When you write or sell an option, you have only two alternatives when the market moves against your short position and in the favor of the buyer of the option. You can continue to hold the naked short option and sustain increasing paper losses, or you can buy back the option at the prevailing market price. Typically, the latter alternative is the only advisable strategy. Option writers, remember, must post margin to guarantee the performance of the contract. When the market moves against the writer, additional margin may be required and the writer's only alternative is to post the margin or have the position liquidated involuntarily. As a rule, you should monitor your option-writing positions carefully and never, never meet a margin call. After all, the most you can gain on an option-writing position is the initial premium. Why post an unlimited amount of margin in hopes of gaining a small, fixed amount? It doesn't make sense. Therefore, when you write an option, be careful to buy back any short option and exit the market at a small loss, rather than fight the market. Unlike the buyer, the writer doesn't have the luxury of time on his side. His risk is unlimited. He must treat his position, therefore, much like the futures trader and take small losses when his judgment is wrong.

Agricultural Options

After a ban of more than fifty years, options on futures were reintroduced during the early 1980s. At first, the options were limited to just a handful of selected futures contracts, including U.S. Treasury bonds, gold, sugar, and several of the new stock indexes. In more recent years, option contracts have been offered on a wide variety of futures, including currencies, financial and debt instruments, precious metals, and more recently, in late 1984, agricultural commodities such as the grains and meats. These so-called agricultural options were phased in over a period of time, with each futures exchange permitted just two option contracts. Today there are options available on corn, wheat, soybeans, live cattle, live hogs, and cotton, among the agricultural commodities.

The new agricultural options, which are also referred to as farm options, provide a new flexibility to the grower and user of agricultural products. For the first time, with the use of the new farm options, the grain farmer or livestock rancher can provide himself with a price floor or ceiling with the use of options.

Until the new options were introduced, the farmer or rancher could always hedge his products in the futures market. But this had its drawbacks. Specifically, the hedge, if misplaced, could result in the locking out of windfall profits. With options, the same farmer or rancher can avail himself of a specific price, but he is not locked into purchasing or selling at a fixed price. His premium cost is simply a sort of insurance payment.

Let's consider a specific example. Let's assume that you raise cattle and would, naturally, like to receive the highest price possible for your animals. With live cattle futures for December delivery trading at $60 per hundredweight, you have several alternatives.

First and foremost, you can remain unhedged and simply sell your cattle in the cash market in five or six months for whatever the market will pay. Unfortunately, this particular strategy is highly risky. You might, for instance, be able to make a profit at today's price of $60 per hundredweight. But at $50 per hundredweight, your profit margin may be wiped out. By doing nothing and remaining unhedged, you remain vulnerable to a price decline.

A second alternative is the futures hedge. Using this strategy, you can enter into the futures market and sell live cattle futures at the prevailing market price. This will lock in your selling price at $60 per hundredweight. Thus, if prices between now and the delivery date decline, what you will lose in the cash market, you will earn on the short futures hedge. The drawback with this approach, however, is that a *rise* in live cattle prices will be locked out by virtue of placing the hedge. The additional gain in the cash market will indeed be offset by a loss in the short futures hedge.

The third approach is to use options. Specifically, since you want to sell your cattle at today's price if prices decline, you would purchase a put option with a $60 strike price. The cost of the put option might be $3.00 per hundredweight, thus assuring that you receive a net price of $57 if you exercise the put. The benefit is that if prices do indeed rise, you can always walk away from the put and sell your cattle in the cash market at the prevailing rate. Thus, by purchasing the put, you have the opportunity to sell at the strike price of $60, but you also have the opportunity to participate in any subsequent price rise—an opportunity that was not available to the hedger who relied on the futures market alone. In this third example, the premium cost of $3.00 per hundredweight should be viewed as inexpensive price insurance.

There are many other examples of how the new agricultural options can be used as a complement or alternative to the traditional futures hedge. The key point is, however, the new options provide greater flexibility when used either in conjunction with or apart from the traditional futures hedge.

From the speculator's standpoint, the new agricultural options—indeed, like all the new options on futures—offer an opportunity to participate in the volatile futures market with strictly limited risk. This is a departure from futures trading in which the speculator, whether he buys or sells short, has unlimited risk on every trade he takes. Once the up-front premium cost is paid, the buyer of a put or a call can earn an infinite amount on his option. And his risk? His total risk is the premium cost.

Foreign Currency Options

Options on foreign currencies are currently traded on four exchanges in North America: the Chicago Mercantile Exchange, the Chicago Board Options Exchange, the Philadelphia Stock Exchange, and the Montreal Stock Exchange. The leading contracts are the Deutschemark, the Swiss franc, the British pound, the Japanese yen, the Canadian dollar, and the French franc. Not every contract is traded at every exchange, so you should check to make sure the particular contract in which you are interested is traded at the exchange you are considering. Only the Chicago Mercantile Exchange offers an option on a futures contract. The other exchanges offer options on the cash currency.

Since we are primarily interested in foreign currency options on futures, we will concentrate on the options traded at the Chicago Mercantile Exchange here.

The options are traded at the Index and Options Market, a division of the Chicago Mercantile Exchange. All quotes are in dollars and cents per unit of foreign currency. A Deutschemark 38 call, for example, would provide the buyer with the right to purchase one Deutschemark futures contract at the price of 38 cents on the standard 125,000 Deutschemark contract. Like the futures, the minimum tick in the Deutschemark options is .0001, or $12.50 per contract on the 125,000 Deutschemark contract. Thus, a call quoted at 2.82 would cost $3,525 to purchase (.0282 × 125,000 = $3,525).

In recent years, volatile exchange rates have made foreign-currency options one of the fastest-growing areas of the huge foreign exchange market. Once limited to the large multinationals, who need to hedge their currency transactions in the interbank market, today the foreign exchange markets serve a worldwide network of large and small firms engaged in foreign trade. As a result of widely fluctuating currency rates, the need for flexible foreign-currency-hedging vehicles has grown tremendously in recent years. Both the futures and the options-on-futures markets in foreign currencies have exploded in participation in just the past few years.

The gyrating dollar and the corresponding roller-coaster ride of foreign currencies have created a virtual minefield of potential trouble for firms engaged in foreign trade. For years, such firms relied on the huge interbank market, where they could obtain forward contracts to hedge their risk. Like a futures contract, a forward contract served to obligate a buyer or a seller to take delivery or give delivery of a foreign currency under the terms of the agreement. More recently, the interbank market has also created options that were "tailor-made" for the individual firm. Because the options were chiefly written by the big banks, however, the spreads were often more favorable to the banks than to the buyers. When they judged wrong, the banks, too, often found themselves in trouble by writing an option too cheaply.

Since the introduction of exchange-traded options, first in Philadelphia and now in Chicago, the firm wishing to cover all or part of its risk exposure has several alternatives for managing the risk.

The benefits of options are so apparent to their users that options use has become commonplace in many corporate hedging departments.

As with any hedge, the purpose of using currency options is to establish some sort of predetermined risk for firms engaged in foreign trade. A hypothetical example of a firm using options might be as follows: Assume that a U.S. firm doing business as a multinational in Europe writes a contract requiring payment in Deutschemarks. The firm's risk is that the price of Deutschemarks will decline in value at the time payment is received. One hedging strategy is to forward-contract to sell Deutschemarks at today's prevailing exchange rate; another is to sell short Deutschemark futures, again locking in today's price. The drawback to forward or futures hedging, however, is that it locks out the gain that would result from a positive move in Deutschemark currency. The option strategy is a third alternative. The firm becomes fully hedged by purchasing put options. This enables them to sell Deutschemarks at the agreed-upon strike price, *plus,* at the same time, it allows the firm to participate in any gain in Deutschemark values. If Deutschemarks have risen in value by the time payment is received, the firm stands to gain accordingly. The only cost resulting from this strategy would be that of the premium paid to purchase the put option.

The other side of the coin would be illustrated by an example of a firm obligated to pay bills in a foreign currency at some time in the future. This firm also has a foreign-currency exposure. A rise in value of the Deutschemark or other foreign currency would translate into higher costs; on the other hand, a decline in the value of the foreign currency would result in a windfall gain. Again, the traditional method of hedging involves forward contracting or purchasing futures contracts. This effectively sets the buying price for the currency. But, at the same time, it prevents the company from paying off its debts in new, lower-valued currency in the event of a decline in prices. The foreign-currency-option alternative allows the company to purchase calls to establish a ceiling price on its costs. At the same time, the firm stands to profit accordingly if the value of the currency declines. The cost is limited to the premium paid for the calls.

The two illustrations above are the most basic uses of foreign-currency put and call options. A U.S. multinational operating abroad, however, might decide to generate income on its foreign-currency holdings by writing options as well. For instance, let's say a firm engaged in foreign trade decides it is willing to acquire Deutschemarks at today's prevailing rates. To generate income, it might decide to *write* put options. By writing options, the firm agrees to buy Deutschemarks from the buyer of the put at today's rate, which is reflected in the strike price. For granting this privilege, the firm receives the premium income on the options. Its only commitment is to buy Deutschemarks.

If the value of the Deutschemark rises and the put remains unexercised, the firm gains the entire writing income—money that it can use to offset the higher cost of the Deutschemarks it needs to purchase. If the value of the Deutschemark declines and the put is exercised, the firm simply honors its commitment and purchases the Deutschemarks.

In reality, if the firm is using the options-on-futures market, there is a second step involved. First, it would receive a long futures contract. Then, if held to maturity, the contract would permit the firm to buy the Deutschemarks at the original strike, or purchase, price. In either case, the premium received is added income.

On the one hand, the writing income can be used to offset the cost of purchasing higher-valued Deutschemarks in the cash market; on the other, the writing income can be used to offset the loss resulting from having purchased the Deutschemarks at the higher price that resulted from exercise. And if the Deutschemark remains relatively stable during the life of the option, the rise or fall of the cost of purchasing the currency will be negligible and the premium income will simply be added to company profits.

Options on Financial Futures

Since the introduction of futures on Ginnie Maes and U.S. Treasury bonds and bills, in the mid-seventies, financial futures have been the fastest-growing segment of the futures industry. During the nineteen eighties, futures on stock indexes spurred the growth of this sector and, understandably, the options on these booming financial instruments burgeoned as well. Today, the popular options on U.S. Treasury bond futures traded at the Chicago Board of Trade change hands at the rate of thirty thousand contracts a day, with an open interest that is almost ten times as large. Indeed, the volume in the options on Treasury bond futures is larger than the volume on most futures contracts. The boom in options on financial futures has even spread abroad, where options on Eurodollar futures are traded in London.

Options on financial futures fall into two categories: those on financial futures such as Treasury bonds and notes and Eurodollars, and those on stock index futures such as the Standard & Poor's 500 and the New York Stock Exchange Composite Index. Each option provides the holder the right to either buy or sell a futures contract on the underlying futures at a specified price during the life of the contract. Like all options on futures, the options can be purchased or sold by themselves or in conjunction with a long or short futures contract to achieve a variety of investment goals.

Consider an investor who's bullish on the major stock averages but doesn't have a particular stock in mind. With the New York Stock Exchange Composite average trading at a price of 105, the investor might purchase a December 105 call for a premium of one point, or $500. In the event of a five-point rally in the average prior to expiration of the call, the investor would stand to earn back five points, or $2,500, on his $500 investment. Likewise, an investor who is bearish on the averages might purchase a December 105 put and profit if his judgment proves correct and the underlying average falls. The appeal of the options is the limited-risk aspect. The risk is known at the outset, and regardless of the subsequent movement of prices, the premium cost is the entire amount at risk.

The same investor, of course, might turn to writing puts and calls to achieve income. During periods of relatively stable prices, an investor who is mildly bullish or bearish might write out-of-the-money puts or calls—or even both, in a strategy known as a strangle, or combination. That latter strategy enables the writer to collect premium income on both the puts and the calls if prices remain stable. And if they do not remain stable, the additional writing income achieved by writing the option that remains out of the money at expiration will help offset the loss on the losing option.

Stock-index options, like the underlying futures on the major stock indexes, serve as a vital hedging tool for commercials engaged in managing investment portfolios or underwriting stock issues. The manager of a large portfolio is vulnerable to a stock market decline. By purchasing put options, selling short stock index futures, writing calls, or a variety of other tactics, the large portfolio manager can virtually tailor a hedge for his specific needs. This use of the options and futures markets provides him with an alternative to buying or selling stock—the options or futures contracts serving as a viable proxy.

For example, consider the case of an investment manager who anticipates lower stock prices, yet is reluctant to sell stock because of tax considerations, or, more important, because, longer term, he is bullish and wants to hold on to his stock.

He might purchase put options on a stock index futures contract. Should the decline indeed occur, the manager simply sells the puts at a profit and uses the gain to offset any temporary paper loss in his stock portfolio. In the event that his judgment proves wrong and the stock market soars higher, he abandons the puts and treats their purchase as inexpensive insurance against an eventuality that failed to occur.

Sophisticated stock managers will even write options against their investment portfolios during times of stable prices. The option premium income will add to the bottom line and improve the overall performance of the portfolio over time. In fact, many managers have an ongoing writing campaign to generate added income. As one option expires, another, more distant option is written. This will continue throughout the year as a regular writing program.

Options on Precious Metals

Gold options were first introduced in the original 1982 pilot program of options trading approved by the CFTC. Since that time, volume on gold options has quadrupled and options on silver futures have also been introduced at the Commodity Exchange, Inc. (COMEX), in New York, which is the world's largest precious-metals futures exchange. The New York-based exchange has more recently offered options on aluminum futures as well. Gold options are also available at the American Commodities Corporation, a subsidiary of the American Stock Exchange, and at the MidAmerica Commodity Exchange, which recently became affiliated with the Chicago Board of Trade.

Despite the relatively lackluster performance of the precious metals in recent months, the gold and silver options have won acceptance by the public and the floor traders alike. Precious-metal options offer the speculator an opportunity to participate in the overall performance of the highly leveraged underlying futures contract for the price of a single premium.

The hedgers use the options to protect their profit margins or fix the price of supplies for some time in the future. For example, a user of gold can hedge against the risk of higher gold prices in the future by purchasing calls. In the event of a price rise, the user will simply sell or exercise his call and realize a profit on the transaction. The profit can then be used to offset the higher cost of purchasing gold in the cash market.

For individuals who are uncomfortable with the unlimited-risk aspect of futures trading, gold and silver options offer an opportunity to begin trading those precious metals. More experienced futures traders will find that options greatly enhance the number of strategies available to them. Among those strategies is the writing of puts and calls on gold and silver futures contracts, a strategy that promises to provide income to the sophisticated trader who can handle the risks involved with this particular strategy. Other experienced traders may want to buy or write options-against-futures positions, or engage in a host of other sophisticated strategies designed to reap profit under varying market conditions, commensurate with market risk.

In short, precious-metals options provide a wide variety of opportunities for the novice and the seasoned trader alike. Finally, commercial users and producers of gold and silver products can find price insurance through the use of options. As with other options-on-futures contracts, gold and silver options offer a versatile approach to the market for a variety of users.

Option Spread Strategies

Options on futures, like the futures themselves, can be spread in various combinations to achieve profitability under a variety of market conditions.

A spread, as you may remember, is a strategy in which you buy one contract month and sell another, related contract month. Essentially, spreading option contracts works in the same manner as spreading the underlying futures, although you can spread option contracts of the same commodity and contract month against an option for the same commodity and contract month with a *different strike*. In the futures market, if you were to spread a July soybeans against a July soybeans by buying one and selling the other, you would simply offset one position with the other and you wouldn't hold a position. In the options-on-futures market, however, you can spread a long July soybean 500 call against a short July soybean 525 call and have a spread position.

There are many, many spread strategies using options against options— or options against futures, a strategy sometimes called "covered writing." Moreover, option spreading can be finely tuned to reflect varying market conditions. Thus, you might have bullish spreading strategies and bearish spreading strategies. What's more, you can have bullish or bearish strategies utilizing just calls or similar strategies utilizing puts. As if this weren't enough, you can have bullish or bearish strategies utilizing both puts and calls. Lastly, there are strategies designed to capitalize on neutral markets.

Entire books have been devoted to spreading strategies in puts and calls, so we can't cover every possible strategy in this chapter.[1] However, let's look at some of the popular spreading strategies.

One popular category of option spreading is known as the *calendar spread*, or *time spread*. This spread involves the sale of one option and the simultaneous purchase of another option of the same commodity and striking price but of a *different contract month*. For instance, you might write a nearby Eurodollar December 92 call and simultaneously purchase the more distant Eurodollar March 92 call. Because the nearer December call will expire before the more distant March call, the time value of the December call will tend to erode at a quicker rate. As a result, the option you sold will likely diminish in value faster than the option you purchased. The net result, assuming all other factors remain stable, will be a net gain on the spread.

Another popular category of spreads is known as the *vertical spread*, in which an option of one commodity and contract month is spread against another option of the same commodity and contract month but of a *different strike price*. Thus, instead of a Eurodollar December 92 call spread against a March 92 call, as in the *horizontal spread* or *calendar spread* above, the vertical spread might comprise a December 92 long call spread against a 93 short call. Thus, you are spreading the different strike prices. The typical vertical call spread—when the lower strike is purchased and

---

[1] Readers interested in option spread strategies in stocks should consult my prior book *Sure-Thing Options Trading* (Doubleday & Company, 1983; New American Library, 1984). Strategies for spreading the new agricultural options are discussed in my more recent book *Agricultural Options*, published by American Management Association, 1986.

the higher strike is sold—is known as a *bull spread.* Understandably, the bull spread makes money when the market rises. In fact, the maximum profit on such a spread will exist at the higher strike. At the higher strike, the long call purchased at the lower strike will be worth the difference between the lower strike and the higher strike. The short call, on the other hand, will have no value at its strike price. Thus, you will capture the entire premium-writing income on the short call sold at the higher strike and the difference between the strikes on the long call.

Like the purchase of a call option, the maximum risk on this spread will be the initial debit, or cost of the spread. That cost will be equal to the purchase price of the lower-strike call plus the writing income received on the higher-strike call. As already mentioned, the maximum profit will exist at the higher strike. Above that price, the higher-strike short call will lock out additional profits.

Let's look at an example of this bull vertical spread using calls.

Assume you are bullish on soybean prices but only anticipate a rise of 5 to 10 cents per bushel over the next few months. With January soybeans trading at $5.18 per bushel, you might purchase a January 500 call for a premium of 21½ cents and simultaneously write a January 525 call for a premium of 7½ cents. Your net cost, commissions aside, will be the difference between what you paid and what you received for writing the higher-strike call, or 14 cents. This is your total risk.

Assuming January soybeans do indeed rise in value, at expiration, with prices at $5.25 or above, the rise will result in 3½ cents in profit on the long January 500 call and the entire writing income of 7½ cents on the short January 525 call. The profit from both calls together will amount to 11 cents, or $550, on an investment of 7½ cents, or $375. This translates into a profit of more than 46 percent on the initial investment.

As you can see, this is a profitable strategy on only a modest rise in prices—from $5.18 per bushel to just $5.25 per bushel. Commission costs must be kept low, however, since a high commission rate will cut into the net profits. Fortunately, commission costs on options are being discounted to as low as just $5.00 a trade.

Another advantage of bull spreading in this fashion is to lower your net overall cost. By writing the higher-strike call against the long lower-strike call, you decrease the net cost of the strategy from 21½ cents (price of the long call) to just 14 cents (price of the bull spread), or about one third. As a result, you only need a modest movement in prices to generate a healthy percentage return.

Although we've mentioned just calls in these examples, vertical and horizontal spreads can be established using puts as well. The bullish or bearish aspects of the spreads may change as a result of using puts, but otherwise the principles should remain the same.

When both puts and calls are used in spread positions, you have what are known as *straddles* and *combinations,* which are also known as *stran-*

gles. The difference between a straddle and a strangle is subtle but important. In a straddle position you either buy or write both a put and a call at the *same strike;* in a strangle, or combination, you either buy or write a put and a call at *different strikes*—usually strikes that are on either side of the market price of the underlying futures.

For example, with December cotton trading at 60 cents, you would buy a December cotton straddle by purchasing the December 60 put and the December 60 call. Your cost would be the premium of both the put and the call. This, of course, would also constitute your total risk. To earn a profit on this straddle, however, the market would have to move at least as far as the cost of the two premiums together. Thus, if you paid five cents for each option, your total cost on the straddle would be twice as much, or ten cents. To achieve a profit at expiration, therefore, the price would have to be at least ten cents below the strike or ten cents above the strike. Typically, only one option will prove profitable in a straddle, although during the life of the two options both may be in the money at one time or another.

There are, of course, two sides to an option straddle: buyer and writer. When you pay ten cents for a straddle, the trader on the other side of the trade will be writing it and receiving the premium income. As a writer, this is his maximum gain. But as long as prices remain near the strike, the writer stands to earn a profit. If prices move fast, however, either up or down, the writer of a straddle could find himself in trouble.

The *strangle buyer* pays less for his position than the straddle buyer, since, typically, both options are out of the money. He buys an out-of-the-money call with the strike *above* the market price of the underlying futures and an out-of-the-money put with the strike *below* the market price of the underlying futures. Because out-of-the-money options have no cash value, they are cheaper to purchase than the option in an at-the-money straddle would be. One drawback, however, exists. For this strategy to prove profitable to the buyer, the market must move either up or down substantially. For the writer of the strangle, however, the premium is less than the straddle, but so is the risk. Since the buyer needs a bull or a bear market to earn himself a profit, the writer can only profit if steady prices exist to receive the full premium income.

During quiet times in the market, strangle writing can be quite profitable—even for months at a time. But, given the low premiums associated with strangle writing, the risks are abundant if a runaway bull or bear market occurs. Most strangle writers know this and willingly undertake the risk. But be cautioned that even the threat of higher interest rates or heightened volatility can cause put and call premiums alike to increase in value and threaten the profitability of a strangle-writing program.

To make sure you understand the difference between a straddle and a strangle, or combination, let's look at two different examples.

Let's say you anticipate a volatile interest-rate environment of the next six to eight months. While you think prices will be volatile, however, you have no idea whether they will rise or fall. So you decide to purchase a straddle on the June Treasury bond futures.

With June Treasury bond futures trading near 80-00, you decide to buy an at-the-money straddle by purchasing a June 80 call for a premium of 1-00 and simultaneously purchasing a June 80 put for a premium of 1-00. You have now paid two points, or $2,000, for the right to buy *or* sell one June Treasury bond futures at the strike price of 80. Since you are a buyer, your risk is known: it is limited to the premium. Your break-even point, however, at expiration will exist at 78-00 on the downside or 82-00 on the upside, since you must recover your premium cost in the market.

Let's assume that bond prices soar as interest rates plummet. The June futures rise to 88-00 by expiration of the call. The put, of course, will expire worthless; the call, however, will be worth at least eight points, or the difference between the strike price and the prevailing market price of the futures. The net gain on the straddle will be six points, or $6,000, exclusive of commissions.

In the same situation, the writer of the straddle would have to take defensive action lest he incur a substantial loss. He would probably buy back the short June 80 call for the prevailing price in the market as prices rise, perhaps sustaining a loss in the process. Whether he earns a profit or sustains a loss, however, will be determined by the size of the loss, if any, on the call. He will have the $1,000 writing income on the put to offset any losses on the call. Indeed, at expiration, his $2,000 in writing income will protect him all the way up to 82-00 on the call. Above that price, of course, he will sustain a net loss, since he will be paying out more to the holder of the call than he took in for writing the straddle.

The strangle, by comparison, involves less money paid out by the buyer and less money taken in by the seller. In the example above, the strangle buyer might have purchased the out-of-the-money June 82 call and the out-of-the-money 78 put. The premiums will be less than for the straddle, say 32/64, or $500 on each option. This will amount to $1,000 for the strangle. By paying less, the buyer achieves greater leverage *if* the market moves substantially. This is because the return will be compared to the invested funds.

Now, if bond prices soar to 88-00, the $8,000 gain on the call will be measured against a $1,000 investment as compared to a $2,000 investment in the case of the straddle.

The writer of the strangle, of course, has the opposing viewpoint. He is taking in less and has a thinner cushion of writing income to work with in the case of adversity. But the market *must* move for the strangle writer to lose money. If the market doesn't move, the strangle writer gets to keep the entire premium income.

Should you buy or write straddles and strangles? That depends on your judgment of the market. If you are in a potentially explosive situation, where prices could easily move in either direction, you want to stay away from the writing side. If, on the other hand, the market is about to enter the doldrums, the writers will get to keep their premiums with very little risk.

Typically, the size of the premiums will reflect recent market conditions. Thus, in explosive markets, buyers will have to pay larger premiums than at other times when the market is quieter. The risk, after all, will always be commensurate with the reward except under those few conditions when no one sees a change coming in the market. These few times, of course, will be characterized by opportunity for those who can anticipate the change.

Options-trading Rules

Options trading is the newest and least understood feature of the futures markets. Only in the past several years have the new options been introduced, and many traders, including many professional floor traders, are unfamiliar with their terms and features.

During 1984, the first agricultural options were introduced, and today there are options on such diverse commodities and financial futures as soybean, corn, wheat, live hogs, live cattle, cotton, sugar, Eurodollars, Standard & Poor's 500 stock index, British pounds, Swiss francs, Deutschemarks, silver, and gold, among others. We've covered only the most elemental features in this chapter. But by utilizing a variety of buy and write strategies, options trading can make your investment approach extremely versatile. What follows are commonsense rules that can make your option trading both safer and more profitable.

RULE NUMBER 1. *Only purchase puts and calls that have strike prices that are slightly in or out of the money.* When you purchase an option on a futures contract, you are paying for the time value of a highly leveraged contract with limited risk. Buying a put or a call that is deeply in the money only defeats the purpose of paying for the high leverage. The cash value of the option will needlessly tie up your available investment capital.

At the other extreme, although the option premiums are less on puts and calls that are deeply out of the money, the likelihood of their ever proving profitable is considerably less.

RULE NUMBER 2. *Always write options that are out of the money.* There is a good reason for this rule. When you write an option, you are selling time value. The purpose is to profit from the inevitable erosion in time value that occurs as maturity approaches. By writing an in-the-money option, however, you run the risk of having the put or call exercised against you. This cannot happen when an option is out of the money, since the buyer will have no incentive to exercise. Moreover, exercise involves having a long or short position deposited in your account which, by definition, will have paper losses. These losing positions will eventually have to be liquidated, of course, and additional commission costs will be incurred.

RULE NUMBER 3. *Commercial hedgers should purchase options as inexpensive price insurance.* Until the recent advent of options on futures, commercials had two choices: to hedge in the futures or forward markets and lock in a selling or purchase price, or to not hedge their crop or inventory and run the risk of market adversity. Now the new options on futures provide a third alternative. With options, the hedger can establish a floor or ceiling price, yet remain flexible to profit from any windfall gain.

For example, consider a jeweler who requires gold to manufacture his product. By purchasing call options, he can provide himself with the opportunity to obtain gold at a fixed price, yet, at the same time, allow himself an opportunity to purchase gold at lower prices in the event of a price break in the gold market. His only cost is the price of the call premiums. In effect, this amounts to buying insurance. His call position will protect him from paying higher prices should the gold market advance; yet, in the event of a gold-price decline, he'll be able to obtain his product at a lower cost.

The new options-on-futures market provides hedgers with a new alternative to the futures market. In years to come, more and more hedgers will be utilizing these new, versatile instruments.

RULE NUMBER 4. *Sell call options during periods of flat to slightly bearish markets and sell put options in neutral to mildly bullish markets.* Option writing can be a profitable undertaking when the market is trading sideways. You simply undertake a writing program to routinely sell calls when the market is unlikely to rise and to sell puts in markets that show a propensity to move higher. In such markets, the premiums should be sufficient to provide you with a cushion of income to protect you in the event that the options prove profitable to their buyers. A writing program, in which you write first one contract month and then "roll over" into the adjacent month, is the best method of obtaining writing income on a consistent basis. In general, assuming the market isn't widely volatile, most options will expire worthless and you will obtain the writing premium. This premium income should more than offset any losses resulting from a sudden market advance or decline that moves against you.

RULE NUMBER 5. *Only purchase options during times of price volatility.* Although option premiums tend to rise during periods of high price volatility, making options more expensive to purchase, the likelihood of an option proving profitable during a period of high volatility is greater than at times when the market is dormant.

Option premiums reflect the underlying market. For a seller to undertake the risk associated with option writing, he has to feel that he is being fairly compensated. Thus, he will want more when prices are volatile than at times of price stability. From the buyer's standpoint, the odds favor continued price volatility during periods when prices are sharply rising or declining, and continued price stability during periods of dormant volatility. Since the buyer requires a move in the price of the underlying futures to establish profitability in his option, the volatile price environment is preferable to a quiet market.

RULE NUMBER 6. *In a neutral price environment, write straddles.* The straddle writer is neither bullish nor bearish on the market, but instead expects prices to remain steady. So he writes both a put and a call with the same strike price. Typically, he selects a strike price that is close to the underlying futures price. As a result, neither the put nor the call will be far in the money. Unless the underlying price of the futures is trading exactly at the strike price at expiration (a highly unlikely event), either the put or the call will have some cash value at expiration.

The option writer's strategy, however, is to take in more from his writing activities than he pays out to the option buyer. By writing both a put and a call, the writer gains a greater cushion of safety than if he sold only the put or the call.

For example, let's say a straddle writer takes in 10 cents per bushel for writing a soybean straddle, with the put contributing 5 cents and the call contributing 5 cents. If the strike price of both the put and the call is 575, the writer has 10 cents of safety on either side of the strike before he will stand to lose money at expiration. Since only one option will prove profitable to the buyer, the other will, by definition, expire worthless. Thus, if soybean prices decline to, let's say, $5.68 per bushel at expiration of the options, the call will be worthless and the put will have 7 cents of profit to the put buyer. The writer's profit, therefore, will be the difference between what he took in for his writing activities and what he paid out to the buyer, or 3 cents per bushel. Of course, the closer the underlying futures price is to the strike at expiration, the greater the straddle writer's profit. At exactly $5.75 per bushel at expiration of the options, the writer will capture the entire 10 cents in writing income, the maximum profit on the straddle.

RULE NUMBER 7. *In a moderately bullish price environment, buy futures and write out-of-the-money calls; in a moderately bearish price environment, sell futures and write out-of-the-money puts.* This is a sophisticated strategy using futures and options together.

First, let's look at the bullish scenario. If, during a period of rising prices, you purchase futures and write a comparable number of out-of-the-money calls, you will profit on both legs as high as the strike price of the calls. For instance, with November soybean futures trading at $5.90 a bushel, you might purchase November soybean futures and write an out-of-the-money November 600 call for a premium of 8 cents, or $400. On any rise in November bean futures, the long futures will show a gain. At the same time, if November futures are trading at the strike price of $6.00 or lower at expiration of the calls, the entire writing premium will be realized as a gain by the call writer.

Thus, let's assume that at expiration of the call, the November soybean price is exactly $6.00 per bushel. The long November futures will show a gain of 10 cents per bushel, or $500, *and* the November 600 call will expire worthless. This will result in the writer's realizing another 8-cent gain, or $400. The total gain, therefore, between futures and options will be 18 cents, or $900, on only a 10-cent move in the market. The only risk is if soybean futures decline more than 8 cents. At $5.82 per bushel, the strategist who buys futures and writes calls will just break even. Below this price, the gain on the calls will be offset by greater losses in the futures market, assuming, of course, that he writes one call for every long futures in a one-to-one fashion.

If you are moderately bearish on futures price, the strategy works well by selling futures and writing puts. For instance, anticipating lower prices, you might sell soybean futures at $5.90 per bushel and simultaneously write a November 575 put for a premium of 3 cents. If November bean prices remain *above* $5.75 per bushel at expiration, the November 575 put will expire worthless. At the same time, if prices are *below* $5.90, the short futures will show a profit. Here again, the greatest profit on this strategy will result at the strike price of the option. There the seller of futures and writer of a put will receive a total of 18 cents in profit—the difference between the selling price of the futures and the prevailing market price of soybeans and the entire put premium. Above the strike price, the profit on the position, if any, will be less. The risk in this situation is if the market rises. Having taken in only 3 cents in writing income, the short seller has only a 3-cent cushion of profits to offset any loss on the futures position.

Buy-and-write or sell-and-write strategies can enhance your profit *if* you are expecting a modest rise or decline in the market and *if* the market doesn't move too far against the futures position. You must remember that in writing an out-of-the-money option, whether a put or a call, you are receiving only a fixed premium as payment. This payment must serve to offset any adversity experienced in the futures position.

RULE NUMBER 8. *Buy options to lock in profits on long-term futures positions.* If you are holding a long-term position in the futures market, you can use options to lock in a profit and still allow yourself to gain additional profits in the futures market. This strategy works as follows: Let's say you have purchased futures and prices have risen. As a result, you have a paper profit in the position. Rather than selling out the futures position and realizing the profit, you might wish to hold on to the position. Your risk, of course, is that futures might indeed decline. As an alternative to selling the futures, you might purchase a put. This will allow you to sell the underlying futures at the strike price regardless of the subsequent movement of the market. Moreover, should prices soar higher, you can always abandon the put and just let the profits accumulate on the long position—a position you might have prematurely sold had you not been able to hedge the position in the options market.

For short sellers, of course, the strategy works in reverse. Having accumulated profits on a short position, you purchase a call. This provides you with the right to buy the underlying futures at the strike. Hence, if prices move higher, you can always purchase the futures at the strike.

For example, let's say you sell December Treasury bonds at 72-00 and bond prices decline to the 70-00 price area. You now have a two-point gain on the short futures position. By purchasing a December 70 call, you maintain the right to purchase futures (cover your short position) at the strike. This serves to lock in the two-point gain in the futures—minus the call's premium, of course. At the same time, it allows you to continue to hold the short position in December Treasury bond futures. Thus, if prices rise to, let's say, 71-00 at expiration of the call, you would exercise or sell the call. This would result in an immediate one-point gain. The other point would be picked up in the futures market, where you could buy back the short futures at 71-00, gaining the one-point difference between when you initially sold and when you covered. Your only cost would be the cost of the call.

In this example, on the other hand, if prices continued to decline, you would abandon the call and simply cover the short futures position lower. Let's say prices declined to 65-00. Having originally sold December Treasury bond futures at 72-00, you would realize a seven-point gain, or $7,000, on the futures. The call's premium, of course, would be lost, as it served only as insurance in the case of higher prices.

By locking in profits on futures in this fashion, you have a heads-you-win and tails-you-win situation. Regardless of the subsequent movement of prices, you stand to gain. The only consideration is whether the option's premium price warrants the cost of the price insurance.

13

The LSS 3-day
Cycle Method

A DAY-TRADING APPROACH TO THE MARKETS

Given the volatility, pace, and high leverage of today's futures markets, it is surprising that more traders don't take this approach. Day trading, as the name suggests, is simply the completion of the round-turn, in-and-out buy and sell cycle within a single trading session.

The method is popular among traders for several reasons. First and foremost is the issue of safety. If you are not in the market overnight, nothing troublesome is going to happen to you on tomorrow's open. You'd be surprised how suddenly a seemingly profitable trade at yesterday's close can go sour on today's open. All you need is a little news overnight or an unexpected money-supply report. The damage to the unwary can be awesome. Second, day trading has reduced margin requirements. If you aren't holding a position overnight, chances are excellent you won't have a margin call. That is not to say, of course, that you can totally avoid losing trades. You can't. But the combination of no overnight jitters, no margin calls, and an overall relaxed method of rapid in-and-out trading can do wonders for the spirit.

In recent years, there has been a trend toward day trading among public speculators. To see how popular this form of trading has become, you only have to look at the volume and open interest statistics for the popular S&P

500 contract. On an average day, the volume will be twice the open interest—about sixty thousand contracts traded against about half that number held in open positions overnight. This represents a significant amount of in-and-out trading.

For years, professional floor traders relied on day trading—often, a specialized form of day trading known as *scalping,* in which small profits are taken over and over again throughout the day—for a very understandable reason: the professionals *know* the risks of holding onto a futures too long. Unlike the public trader, the floor trader, who is a member of an exchange, doesn't pay commissions. As a result, the floor traders do not have to worry about commission costs. Nevertheless, the real reason that the professionals concentrate on small, yet profitable, moves is due to the risk involved. For the trader who holds a position for a week or more, one mistake and he's finished. In contrast, the day trader can be wrong five or six times during the day and still emerge a winner.

Since today's discounted commissions are lower than ever before, the public speculator can now join in the fray with those specialized in-and-out traders down on the floor. It is still almost impossible to truly scalp from the outside, but day trading, in which you might take two or three trades during the day, is something else again. Down on the floor, a trader who just does two or three trades is considered a position trader—like someone who holds a position for three months on the outside. So it is truly a matter of perspective.

The Potential for Profits

Another reason why day trading has become popular is the genuine potential for profits. In today's volatile markets, where the value of a single contract may move up or down by a couple of thousand dollars during a single trading session, the potential for profits is considerable. When viewed in this fashion, the cost of a $20 commission suddenly becomes negligible. Large, aggressive floor traders in the volatile S&P pit can occasionally make six figures in a single trading session. So don't be put off when someone says, "What do you want to take 'small' profits for?" The answer is very simple. Because you want to be around to trade tomorrow. And, what's more, because you would like to grow rich in the process!

You hear so often that the serious money in futures is made on the so-called "big moves." What you don't hear about is the road to the big move —the days and even weeks in adversity when the really big traders have to finance their losing positions to the tune of millions of dollars. Clearly, the answer for the novice or small trader is to try day trading.

One rule if you are going to be successful at day trading is to select the right market. On this score, you want a market that both enjoys a wide participation and has sufficient volatility, to enable you to extract profits. A few years ago, you might have selected the gold market, which was second only to Treasury bonds in both participation and volatility. In those days, $15 and even $20 moves were common in the gold market. No more. Today, the gold market struggles to move $3.00 or $4.00 a day.

The selection of the market will be determined by economic conditions at the time you decide to trade. During inflationary periods and a weak dollar, expect gold and silver to prove volatile. But, at other times, you will have to look elsewhere. A glance at a recent newspaper shows that nearby Standard & Poor's 500 futures had a daily range of 1.70 points ($850 per contract) and nearby U.S. Treasury bonds had a daily range of 26/32 ($812 per contract). In contrast, during the same trading session, corn moved two and a quarter cents ($112 per contract) and oats even less, just a penny and a quarter ($62 per contract). Obviously, the S&P and bonds are better day-trading vehicles.

To find a good day-trading candidate, select only markets that have depth (liquidity) and volatility. Otherwise, you are going to be disappointed in your trading results. Recently, the stock index, interest rate, and currency futures have all offered worthwhile day-trading opportunities. One other word of advice: Try to stay with the leading futures of each group. That would mean the S&P, Treasury bond, and Deutschemark in the three respective groups listed above.

In recent years, the focus has shifted away from the agricultural commodities toward the newer financial futures. Given a resurgence in the agricultural sector, day traders may again find soybeans, among the grains, and pork bellies, among the meats, worthwhile day-trading vehicles.

Taylor's *Book Method*—The Genesis of a Trading System

During the nineteen fifties, a little-known grain trader at the Chicago Board of Trade published a manual known as the *Book Method.* The trader, George Douglas Taylor, maintained that the grain markets moved in a three-day cycle that could be tracked by measuring the rallies and declines. Taylor kept a record of grain prices and their respective rallies and declines in a notebook he carried with him—hence the title *Book Method.* What is remarkable today is how accurate this simple bookkeeping entry can be when applied to the markets of the eighties.

Although the grain markets of the fifties were far from turbulent, Taylor observed what he came to call "market engineering." He found a pattern in the market. By painstakingly recording the magnitude of market rallies and declines, which he kept in his notebook, Taylor found a three-day cycle that, despite occasional aberrations, repeated itself over and over again.

What's more, Taylor maintained that the natural rhythm of the market created a false move that served to fool traders into buying when they should be selling, and vice versa. The powers in the grain markets, Taylor maintained, frequently caused prices to decline in order to create a buying opportunity for themselves; within three days, after the market had rallied sufficiently to provide them with handsome profits, a short-term top was created in order to provide a selling opportunity. This was the market "engineering" at work. Although the pattern had remained hidden, with sufficient research and careful examination of prices, one could uncover these precise buying and selling opportunities. For anyone who has ever sought to utilize a trading system, this was powerful information.

Ironically, Taylor's method wasn't a day-trading technique at all—undoubtedly, given the ranges of those days, one would be hard put to pull day-trading profits out of the market—but a short-term trading system in which positions were held overnight. He gave a name to each trading day: the Buy Day, the Sell Day, and the Short Sale Day. Each day had its particular trading characteristic. For instance, the Buy Day was identified as the day in which prices either open at or retreat to a low prior to rising. The Sell Day, in turn, was characterized by prices trading at, below, or slightly above the previous day's high. And on the Short Sale Day the market took a final lunge upward, which was met by selling resistance, and prices broke. Then the cycle began all over again.

Although the notion of a three-day cycle, with the precise pattern described above, is highly simplistic, it has the elements of an idea that deserved attention. It meant that if indeed such a cycle did exist, and if one could successfully "read" the hidden intentions of the market at specific stages, then perhaps one could successfully trade from the winning side. Moreover, it posed several important questions. When is a rally not a rally, but, rather, a skillful attempt to lure buyers into a trap? Conversely, when is a price break simply a ruse to create selling to provide the powerful interests an opportunity to buy at low prices? Obviously, if one could indeed learn the hidden signals of the market, one's opportunity to profit would surely increase.

The *Book Method* Thirty Years Later

Over the years, the *Book Method*, which was self-published in notebook form, has become an underground classic of sorts among futures traders. Few copies are available, and those that can be found in trading libraries are dog-eared and well worn.

Unfortunately, Taylor's advice was exceedingly general. You should sell on the third day's rally at, through, or slightly below the previous day's high. You should buy on the following day, following a break in prices at, through, or slightly above the previous day's low. These, essentially, were his rules. Often, they were vague and hard to identify. Where do you buy? At a higher bottom (a very bullish sign, according to Taylor) or somewhere under the previous day's low? Do you always sell on the third day's rally?

Determining the cycle itself becomes problematic. While the three-day cycle is at the heart of the system, Taylor hedged and said that occasionally you will find a four- or five-day cycle. Well, how do you know when the longer cycle is occurring? And if you are selling on the third day's rally, what should you do with your short position while prices are rising? The answers to these and other questions remain inconclusive. At times, the cycle will change. And when the market breaks, you will have a series of so-called Buy Days in which lower lows are made daily. Which is the correct low to establish the Buy Day?

Despite these and other persistent questions about the *Book Method,* the basic pattern can be observed in a number of futures contracts—among them the metals, interest rates, and stock index futures, as well as the grains. What's more, the pattern seems even more identifiable among these newer financial futures than among the more traditional grain contracts. What's the pattern? How do you identify it? And, most important, how can you make money trading the three-day cycle as a day trader?

The Ideal Three-day Pattern

The ideal three-day pattern, which Taylor first identified, consists of the Buy Day, in which the low is established first and the market trades higher; the Sell Day, in which the Buy Day high is considered as a resistance point; and a third day, the Short Sale Day, in which the high of the Sell Day is challenged or taken out prior to a retreat in prices—at which point the cycle begins over again. The three-day pattern is illustrated in Figure 49 in which the horizontal ticks to the left and right respectively indicate the open and close. Note that the second day, or Sell Day, is an immediate day during which the market gains strength to challenge the high on the following day, the Short Sale Day—which, according to Taylor, is the day on which the market "engineering" works to fool the unwary that the market is indeed headed higher and create the ideal selling opportunity.

There is a paradox at work here that thoughtful traders should be mindful of when they place their orders:

1. The market is often taken down, in order to create selling, to provide a safe buying opportunity for the powerful market forces (see Figure 50).

2. The market is often taken up, in order to create buying, to provide a safe selling opportunity for the powerful market forces (see Figure 51).

The Order in Which the High and Low Occur

When identifying the three-day pattern, Taylor was careful to make a note on whether the high or the low occurred first during the trading day. He marked the low on Buy Days and the highs on Sell Days and Short Sale Days. If the low occurred first on the Buy Day, he would indicate this with

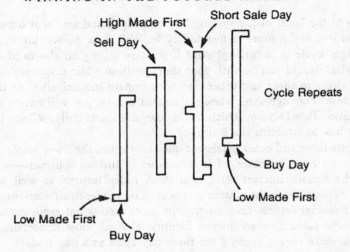

Figure 49.   The ideal three-day pattern.

an X (we've used an asterisk on our examples); if the low occurred last, he would place a check (we've used a double asterisk). On the Sell Days or Short Sale Days, he would place an X if the high occurred first and place a check if the high occurred last. The order in which each occurred was vital

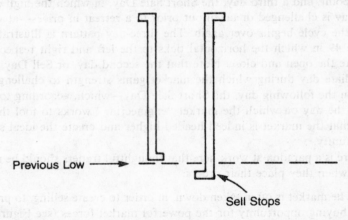

Figure 50.   A lower opening often signals a buying opportunity.

to the smooth functioning of his system, because when the high or low occurred out of sequence—that is, when the reverse was expected—he would often find that he could push the cycle ahead a day and the three-day pattern would again become evident.

In the table below, you will find price data on a recent contract of Standard & Poor's 500 futures. You should note which numbers are underlined and whether an asterisk or a double asterisk is indicated.

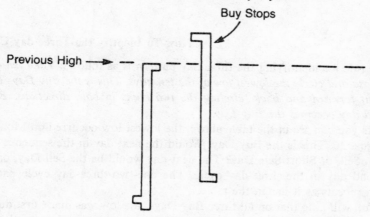

Figure 51.   A high opening often signals a selling opportunity.

Standard & Poor's 500

September 1985

Date	Open	High	Low	Close
Aug 19 - Mon.	186.80	**187.80	186.70	187.40
Aug 20 - Tues.	188.00	**189.50	187.80	189.35
Aug 21 - Wed.	189.50	190.30	*189.00	189.75
Aug 22 - Thurs.	190.00	**190.10	187.55	187.90
Aug 23 - Fri.	187.80	*187.90	186.85	187.40
Aug 26 - Mon.	186.80	188.15	*186.30	188.05
Aug 27 - Tues.	188.30	*188.65	187.80	188.35
Aug 28 - Wed.	188.25	**188.70	187.85	188.45
Aug 29 - Thurs.	188.45	188.80	*188.15	188.75
Aug 30 - Fri.	188.55	*188.90	187.55	187.90

Note that there are three Buy Days over this ten-day period. They are as follows: Wednesday, August 21; Monday, August 26; and Thursday, August 29. On each Buy Day, the low is underlined; on each Sell Day and Short Sale Day, the high is underlined. The asterisks in the Buy Days mean the *low was made first* during the trading session; the asterisks in the Sell Days and Short Sale Days mean the *high was made first* during the trading session. The double asterisk signifies that the underlined number was achieved last during the trading session.

How To Identify the Three-day Cycle

The rule for identifying the three-day pattern is as follows: *Take ten days of data and circle the lowest low of the ten days. This is the Buy Day. Then count forward and back, circling the two highs in both directions. Every third day becomes the Buy Day.*

As you can see in the table above, the lowest low occurred on Monday, August 26. This is the Buy Day. Would the next day in the sequence be a Buy, Sell, or Short Sale Day? The next day would be the Sell Day, or the second day in the three-day cycle. The one-two-three-day cycle pattern then repeats as it has in the table.

You will note that on all three Buy Days, the low was made first during the trading session. You can see that Wednesday, August 21, was the day to buy at the low made first. The third day, Friday, August 23, was the Short Sale Day with the high made first—the ideal three-day cycle. Although Friday's price was indeed lower then Wednesday's, the pattern persisted nevertheless. That is, you could have sold soon after the open on Friday, August 23, and made money, because the open was very close to the high of the day.

There are many more inferences to be drawn from the table of prices. For instance, while you could have purchased the low made first on Monday, August 26, three days later the reverse proved true. The high was made *after* the low, or last during the trading session. As a result, a short sale near the open on Wednesday, August 28, would not have been a good point to sell.

Before moving on to a more advanced concept, you should practice identifying the three-day pattern. First, you circle the lowest low of the past ten days and then count forward and back. Which is the Buy Day? The Sell Day? The Short Sale Day? Tomorrow's day is always identified by the previous day. Thus, if today is the Buy Day, expect the Sell Day to occur tomorrow. And so on.

Keeping the Book

Once you can identify the pattern, you can begin keeping the book. The book is at the heart of Taylor's system—and, as we shall see in the section on the worksheet, at the heart of the LSS 3-day Cycle Method as well. But before we can get to the LSS system, we should concentrate on what Taylor said.

Essentially, Taylor was a believer in measuring the rallies and declines. His was a percentage method in which he attempted to see how far a rally or decline tended to carry. Once it was measured, he could pinpoint changes in the market—and, more important, he could estimate how far a rally or decline was likely to carry.

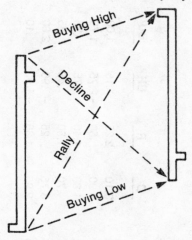

Figure 52. Taylor measured four key rally and decline figures as shown above.

Taylor made four key measurements—all of which have been incorporated into the LSS system as well. Illustrated in Figure 52, the measurements quantify the following:

1. *The Decline column (D)*—Difference between previous day's high and today's low

2. *The Rally column (R)*—Difference between previous day's low and today's high

3. *The Buying High column (BH)*—Difference between today's high and previous day's high

4. *The Buying Under column (BU)*—Difference between today's low and previous day's low

Actually, Taylor included a fifth measurement which was identical to the Buying High column. He gave it a different name because he used it on only one day during the cycle and not on the other two. In the interest of simplicity, this fifth column has been dropped. Moreover, since every measurement is taken every day, it would be redundant as well.

The best way to learn to keep the book is by example. In the following table we have listed the open, high, low, and close of seven trading days in the September 1985 S&P futures contract. From these prices, we have calculated the respective Decline, Rally, Buying High, and Buying Under column numbers. Make sure you understand how each number is calculated before moving on.

Consider the entries for Wednesday, July 24. On that day, the Short Sale Day, the market opened near its high and promptly sold off, completing the ideal three-day pattern and setting up an opportunity to go long on the

Standard & Poor's 500
September 1985

Date	Open	High	Low	Close	D	R	BH	BU
July 22—Mon.	196.20	196.35	**194.25	195.45	3.10	2.25	.15	1.00
July 23—Tues.	195.75	*196.50	193.25	193.55	4.90	.50	-2.75	1.70
July 24—Wed.	193.55	*193.75	191.60	191.90	1.80	1.40	- .75	- .35
July 25—Thurs.	192.30	193.00	*191.95	192.90	.70	1.50	.45	- .35
July 26—Fri.	192.80	*193.45	192.30	192.85	3.75	.25	- .90	2.60
July 29—Mon.	192.50	*192.55	189.70	189.75	2.95	1.35	-1.50	.10
July 30—Tues.	189.95	191.05	*189.60	190.50				

Note: *means that the highs and lows were made first during the trading session
**signifies a high or low being achieved last during the trading session

following day at the low made first. Looking to the right, you'll see that the entry in the Decline column was 4.90. This is the total range between the previous day's *high* and the just completed day's *low*. The rally entry on that day was just .50 points, the difference between the previous day's low and the next day's high. Looking at the Buying High entry, you'll see that a negative number appears. When this occurs, you know the day's high is *below* the previous day's high, since the formula is today's high minus yesterday's high equals the BH column entry. Lastly, the Buying Under column shows a positive number, because today's low was lower than the previous day's low. This column measures how far under the previous day's low the market traded. In this instance, the market traded precisely 1.70 points under the previous low.

Incidentally, on the day shown, you have the makings of an excellent buying opportunity on the following day. First, you'll notice you have the classic Short Sale Day pattern: high made first and then a break in the market with the close near the low. Second, you have the Buy Day occurring on the following day. The anticipated pattern, therefore, is for the market to rally—low made first and then up. Moreover, Taylor mentioned that the very strongest buying opportunity presented itself when you had the opportunity to buy a *higher low*. This means the low on the previous Short Sale Day holds and is never penetrated. Indeed, this is precisely what occurred. The low at 191.60 holds and the market rallies off the 191.95 point the following day and closes near the top end of the range. Over the next three days, the entire cycle repeats itself.

Before we move on, let's look at some more entries. Look at the entry in the BU column on Tuesday, July 30. The .10 entry means the market traded just .10 points under the previous day's low. Had it held a higher bottom, the number would have been negative, since you are taking today's low and subtracting yesterday's low.

How about the Buying High entry on Monday, July 29? Negative .90 points. This is the amount *under* the previous day's high where today's high occurred. A negative Buying High number means today's high is under yesterday's.

The LSS 3-day Cycle Method

So far, we've looked at the basics of Taylor's *Book Method:* finding the cycle, keeping the book, and so on. But, at this point, Taylor becomes somewhat vague. Where do you buy and sell? Taylor says, at the Buy Day low made first. This position is then liquidated on the following day, the Sell Day. Where? At, through, or slightly below the previous day's high. On the third day, the Short Sale Day, the *Book Method* calls for taking short sales on the high made first. Ideally, this will occur at, through, or slightly below the Sell Day high.

There are several problems with Taylor's instructions. First, how do you quantify the buying and selling points? Do you, for instance, take the entry in the previous day's Rally column and use that number to extrapolate a price at which to sell? Perhaps. Second, what exactly does at, through, or slightly below the previous day's high mean? Fifty points, a hundred points? Again, it is hard to say. While Taylor's theory appears sound, a more quantifiable approach is required. Lastly, the market doesn't announce whether a price is the high or low made first. During the trading day, when you are faced with a decision, you cannot tell whether what appears, say, as a low made first might not be, indeed, a high made first. So, there are clearly problems with Taylor's method.

In order to develop a system that would stand up to extensive computer analysis, it was necessary to develop rules that could be tested against the past. The rules couldn't be vague. They had to be specific. This has given rise to the LSS 3-day Cycle Method in its present form.

While the three-day cycle notion appears sound, the LSS system has refined the idea and incorporated a number of computer-proven ideas that Taylor never used.

For one, the LSS system is strictly a day-trading method. During Taylor's day, the grain markets rarely moved sufficiently to have a day-trading method that would work. Today, all that is changed. Soybeans can move 30 cents within a given trading session, and the stock index futures have no limits at all. Profits of three or four thousand dollars in a day's time are not uncommon on even a modest position for today's trader.

For another, the LSS system relies on a tier approach to putting on positions. Whereas Taylor tried to quantify trading days as better than others, the LSS system relies on letting the market decide the number of positions to take. There are three levels of trading. On any given day, you may take none or all three levels. The number of contracts taken at each level is the same. Although margin considerations and one's bankroll should determine the size of one's commitment in the market, the system was tested on a 3-3-3 contract basis. That is, during the day, you might have a maximum of three, six, or nine contracts. At day's end, of course, you will liquidate your entire position, win or lose. In this fashion, you will either profit or lose during the day. No positions are ever held overnight.

Developing a Consensus

Taylor had the right idea. There is a three-day cycle. It occurs on a regular basis. And it is identifiable. But the secret of market success isn't as easy as buying every third day—far from it. In reality, the market often gets out of "phase," and the cycle often becomes lost to the would-be three-day cycle trader. As a result, the low often doesn't hold on the Buy Day. Instead, the market breaks. And the buyer often has losses.

To cope with the unpredictability of the market, an element of flexibility had to be built into the system. To avoid confusion, the notion of Buy, Sell, and Short Sale days had to be dispensed with—at least, the names had to be changed, because one often gets confused when selling, for example, on the so-called Buy Day. This is where the LSS designation becomes important. The LSS really should read: L-S-SS, the letters standing for "long," "sell," "short sale." But the point is simple: *You can either buy or sell on any given day.* Don't let the name or letters confuse you.

The LSS system, which is based on computer-proven probabilities and percentages, is designed to react to market conditions as they unfold during the day. For instance, if computer studies indicate that the probabilities of a buying position on any given day are 75 percent in favor of its working as opposed to just 25 percent of its losing, you are better off buying. To establish the probabilities, the system relies on calculating averages, and averages of averages, and mixing them all together to come up with a trading recommendation—again, in response to actual market conditions. The market decides whether and when you buy and sell. As a result, the system is much more reliable than any forecasting method.

Computer studies have shown that 70 percent of all LSS winners are made by short selling. That's better than two to one in favor of a short-selling position working over a buying position. Actually, to an experienced futures trader, this shouldn't come as a surprise. As a rule, most public speculators are buyers—not sellers. Moreover, the vast majority of all futures traders end up with losses. This suggests that although there is indeed a buyer for every seller, there are many, many more buyers, in number, than sellers. That is, a relatively small pool of sellers routinely fades the buying public.

If you monitor price action over a period of time, you'll notice that price breaks tend to be considerably faster than price rallies. Again, this phenomenon suggests that the "herd" of buyers all panic and stampede for the exits at once. This is precisely what happens when the stops are run. First, the very thinly bankrolled traders run (and the knowledgeable few who are simply on the wrong side), then the stops are hit and, as the market breaks, larger and larger long-term traders begin to bail out of their positions. By the time the public funds are selling, you know the bottom has been reached. This familiar price action has been likened to rolling a large boulder up a mountain. It goes up very slowly. But once you push it off the cliff it breaks fast! The same thing is true in the market. And it explains why the short side of the market is so profitable.

The Trend Reaction Numbers

As part of the consensus, the system relies on the *trend-reaction buy number* and the *trend-reaction sell number*. These numbers are but one of four numbers that will be used to calculate the *buy* and *sell envelopes* that are so important to the LSS system. While the trend-reaction buy and sell numbers are often surprisingly close to the bottom and top of the day's range, respectively, they are *not* to be used as buying and selling points.

The formula for calculating the buy and sell numbers is as follows:

$$\frac{\text{High} + \text{low} + \text{close}}{3} = x$$

$$2x - \text{high} = \text{trend-reaction buy number}$$

$$2x - \text{low} = \text{trend-reaction sell number}$$

Assume the following:

$$\begin{aligned}
\text{S\&P futures high} &= 189.55 \\
\text{"} \quad \text{"} \quad \text{low} &= 187.75 \\
\text{"} \quad \text{"} \quad \text{close} &= 188.25
\end{aligned}$$

Using the numbers listed above, the trend-reaction buy and sell would be calculated as follows:

$$\frac{189.55 + 187.75 + 188.25}{3} = 188.50$$

$$2(188.50) - 189.55 = 187.45 = \text{trend-reaction buy number}$$

$$2(188.50) - 187.75 = 189.25 = \text{trend-reaction sell number}$$

Rephasing the Cycle

Taylor's rule for generating the cycle days is to take ten days of price data, take the lowest low, and call it the Buy Day, and then count forward and backward, circling the third low and the two intermediate highs. In this manner, the three-day cycle is determined. Unfortunately, this approach is too inflexible to take into account the many crosscurrents in the market. Even Taylor maintained that the three-day cycle was occasionally interrupted by a four- or five-day cycle. Moreover, where one begins the cycle count will determine what days are labeled Buy and what days are labeled Sell or Short Sale.

In designing the LSS system, therefore, there was a need to *rephase the cycle* when it got out of synch with the traditional 1-2-3 cycle pattern. What was required was a simple indicator that would tell when the market was changing trend. This indicator is known as the *trend momentum indicator*. It measures the *rate* at which the market is rising or falling. That is, when a market rallies, it moves up slowly at first, picks up speed, and then, although still rising, the momentum begins to slow, suggesting that a change in direction is imminent. The trend momentum indicator is a helpful tool in this respect.

The rule for rephasing the cycle when you use the trend momentum indicator is simple: *each time the trend momentum indicator changes direc-*

tion, the cycle is rephased. Rephasing involves going back ten days and taking the lowest low as the new L-day (Buy Day) and then counting ahead, L-day, S-day, SS-day, and so on.

How is the trend momentum indicator calculated? This is the rule: *take today's close and subtract the close two days previous.* Thus: close on day 3 — close on day 1 = momentum indicator number. The number generated is then *compared* to the two previous trend momentum numbers. The last number will then have one of three patterns in terms of the previous two as follows:

1. Trend momentum indicator number more positive than two previous trend momentum indicator numbers = UP trend

2. Trend momentum indicator number more positive than one of the previous two numbers but more negative than the other number = SIDEWAYS trend

3. Trend momentum indicator number more negative than two previous trend momentum indicator numbers = DOWN trend

Listed below, you will find several consecutive days of closing prices. In the columns to the right, you will find the trend momentum indicator number and the UP, SIDEWAYS, DOWN designation for each. Note that you cannot have a designation until you have at least three trend momentum indicator numbers.

Day	Close	Trend Momentum Indicator #	Trend Momentum Indicator
1	189.25	—	—
2	189.75	—	—
3	187.90	−1.35	—
4	187.40	−2.35	—
5	188.05	+.15	UP
6	188.35	+.95	UP
7	188.45	+.40	SIDEWAYS
8	188.75	+.40	SIDEWAYS
9	187.90	−.55	DOWN

As long as the TMI number is more positive than the two previous numbers, you'll have an UP designation. Note that on day 6, the +.95 is more positive than both +.15 and −2.35—hence the UP designation. But on day 7, the +.40 difference is more negative than day 6 but more positive than day 5—hence the SIDEWAYS designation. Day 8 is considered unchanged, because the +.40 number is not more negative than the previous day's. Lastly, at −.55 on day 9, the designation turns DOWN, because it is more negative than the two previous numbers.

It is important to note that the designation does *not* determine the direc-

264 WINNING IN THE FUTURES MARKET

tion of the market, only the *rate* at which it is moving up or down. Look at the close on day 7. The close is higher, but the indicator has turned from UP to SIDEWAYS. Again, on day 8, the close was higher while the designation was still SIDEWAYS. By day 9, the designation had turned to DOWN and the market had finally turned lower. The indicator tends to lead the market, but it is not used to pinpoint buying or selling opportunities. Rather, the change in the designation signals *the rephasing of the cycle*.

Often, the cycle will remain the same despite rephasing. For instance, you might have a low that occurred seven or eight days ago, and that designation may have changed several times since then. Each time, you go back and rephase the cycle. In each instance, the lowest low remains the same and the cycle stays intact. In time, however, a new, lower low will be established and the change will indeed change. When this occurs, you base tomorrow's anticipated cycle day on the *new rephased day*. For instance, let's say that before rephasing, today was designated as a Short Sale Day (SS-day); after rephasing, following today's close, however, today's SS-day becomes an L-day, or Buy Day. Hence, tomorrow's anticipated cycle day is the following day in the cycle, the S-day, or Sell Day.

To see how rephasing might change the three-day cycle, we need to look at an example which is first not rephased, and then, after calculating the trend momentum indicator, in the second example, the cycle is rephased. See how one compares with the other.

Standard & Poor's 500—June 1985

Unrephased Three-day Cycle

Day	Open	High	Low	Close	Indicator Number	Trend
Mar 21 - Thur	182.85	184.55	**182.60	183.20	−.50	DOWN
Mar 22 - Fri	183.45	*183.50	181.95	182.40	−.90	DOWN
Mar 25 - Mon	182.30	*182.40	181.15	181.60	−1.60	DOWN
Mar 26 - Tues	181.70	183.05	*181.40	182.30	−.10	UP
Mar 27 - Wed	182.20	**183.85	181.95	183.10	+1.50	UP
Mar 28 - Thur	183.35	*184.20	182.50	182.80	+.50	SIDEWAYS
Mar 29 - Fri	183.45	183.55	*182.65	183.35	+.25	DOWN
Apr 01 - Mon	183.70	**184.20	183.00	184.10	+1.30	UP
Apr 02 - Tues	184.00	*184.85	182.60	182.95	−.40	DOWN
Apr 03 - Wed	182.90	183.15	**180.80	181.25	−2.85	DOWN

Note: * indicates highs and lows made first during a trading session

** signifies a high or low made last during the trading session

In the unrephased three-day cycle shown above, the L-day, or Buy Day, repeats every third day.

Standard & Poor's 500—June 1985

Rephased Three-day Cycle

Day	Open	High	Low	Close	Indicator Number	Trend
Mar 21 - Thur	182.85	184.55	**182.60	183.20	−.50	DOWN
Mar 22 - Fri	183.45	*183.50	181.95	182.40	−.90	DOWN
Mar 25 - Mon	182.30	*182.40	181.15	181.60	−1.60	DOWN
Mar 26 - Tues	181.70	183.05	*181.40	182.30	−.10	UP
Mar 27 - Wed	182.20	**183.85	181.95	183.10	+1.50	UP
Mar 28 - Thur	183.35	*184.20	182.50	182.80	+.50	SIDEWAYS
Mar 29 - Fri	183.45	183.55	*182.65	183.35	+.25	DOWN
Apr 01 - Mon	183.70	184.20	*183.00	184.10	+1.30	UP
Apr 02 - Tues	184.00	184.85	**182.60	182.95	−.40	DOWN
Apr 03 - Wed	182.90	*183.15	180.80	181.25	−2.85	DOWN

Note: * signifies a high or low made first during a trading session
    ** indicates that the high or low was made last during a session

The cycle is rephased each time the momentum trend indicator changes in the second rephased version. (Note: for the days shown, the lowest low occurred on Monday, March 18, at 180.00, the L-day). As a result, the cycle remained intact on the close on March 26. Again, on March 29, the rephased cycle remained intact. The cycle was rephased again on Tuesday, March 26, when the momentum indicator changed from DOWN to UP. New rephasing then occurred on Friday, March 29, and Monday, April 1, and Tuesday, April 2. On each day, the dropping of the day ten days back resulted in a *new* L-day, or Buy Day, and a *new* three-day cycle. On Wednesday, April 3, the cycle was *not* rephased, because the Trend remained DOWN.

The rephasing attempts to relocate the three-day cycle when the highs and lows don't occur as expected. Very often, a simple technique to find the "correct" cycle is to push it ahead one day. For example, let's say today is the SS-day, and the pattern to expect is high made first and then lower prices. But let's say you have the L-day pattern occurring, low made first followed by higher prices. By pushing the cycle ahead one day, you can often find the pattern you are looking for. This, by the way, is one reason why you shouldn't give up when selling into a rally in hopes of capturing a down move. Let's say the market rallies on you and prices move higher. You must take the loss. But chances are, you were simply a day too early. Sell the next day in anticipation of capturing the SS-day high-to-low pattern. You'll find that this works even in bull markets.

Once you find the correct pattern, you can expect two or three cycles of winning trades.

Look at the SS-day that occurred on Monday, March 25. You go in expecting a nice break and sell right at the open. Prices are up a mere .10 points over the open, and down they go. It would be hard to lose by selling short on such a day. Since the pattern seemed reliable at that point, it makes sense to stay with the three-day cycle. The next day, the L-day, you expect the reverse: low made first and rallying prices. You buy at the open or—ideally—on a reaction down from the open. Sure enough, March 26 proved an excellent day to buy, since the market rallied off the low early in the day.

Once the market goes into one of its rephasing stages, it often pays to stand aside for three or four days until it finds the cycle once again. Consider, for a moment, what happens when a market breaks. You will have day after day of successive lows. As a result, each time the cycle is rephased, today's new low becomes the Buy Day, or L-day. This leaves the least reliable day, in terms of its market direction, the S-day, as the following day. Sooner or later, the actual low—the Buy Day low—will occur, and then, typically, the three-day cycle will again become evident. Consider the following table of prices and you'll see why standing aside when the market is rephasing often makes sense.

Standard & Poor's 500—June 1985

Rephased Three-day Cycle

Day	Open	High	Low	Close	Indicator Number	Trend
May 23 - Thur	189.20	*189.60	188.55	188.75	−1.15	DOWN
May 24 - Fri	189.05	**189.40	188.85	189.25	−.10	UP
May 27 - Mon			HOLIDAY			
May 28 - Tues	189.90	190.25	**187.60	188.10	−.65	SIDEWAYS
May 29 - Wed	187.85	188.60	*187.50	188.45	−.80	DOWN
May 30 - Thur	188.25	188.90	*187.40	188.40	+.30	UP
May 31 - Fri	188.25	**190.55	188.05	189.65	+1.20	UP
Jun 03 - Mon	190.85	*190.90	189.30	190.10	+1.70	UP
Jun 04 - Tues	190.20	190.75	*189.65	190.30	+.65	DOWN
Jun 05 - Wed	190.75	*191.15	189.85	189.95	−.15	DOWN

Right after the Memorial Day holiday, the market became rather choppy and the cycle was thrown out of synch. First, the L-day low made first on Tuesday, May 28, failed. Instead, the SS-day pattern—high to low —occurred. Here you could have pushed the cycle ahead a day. There was the L-day pattern the following day, Wednesday, May 29. But the momentum trend indicator, which had been quite choppy, going from DOWN to UP to SIDEWAYS to DOWN in four consecutive days, pinpointed Thursday, May 30, as the S-day, or Sell Day. It was wrong. After rephasing on May

30, the *real* Buy Day, when the low was made first, occurred and the market rose 3.65 points in four days.

You can see the benefit of rephasing. Looking back on the numbers *after* the cycle has occurred makes the selection of the Buy Day low an easy one. The problem, however, is spotting the Buy Day low at the same time it is occurring. This particular cycle was a difficult one to find. At the real ten-day low, on Thursday, May 30, most traders were probably selling. Why? Because the market sold off .85 points from the open and took out the two previous lows by two and four ticks, respectively. This is not an accident. What happened was that a great many traders who, in retrospect, had indeed seen the bottom coming, had the misfortune to place their stops right under the market. So they were right—but wrong! The market was driven down to get the stops—and only then did it soar upward! Note how, after the close, the market received an UP designation. The upward move carried all the way to 191.95 on Friday, June 7.

In summary, the LSS 3-day Cycle Method rephases each time the momentum trend indicator changes designations. Rephasing serves to help you find the correct three-day cycle. In addition, when the anticipated day's pattern doesn't occur as expected, it often pays to push the cycle ahead one day. Remember, there's no rule you have to buy on a so-called L-day or sell short on an SS-day. The names of the days are simply to help you identify the pattern.

Calculating the Envelopes

Now that we've covered the discovery of the three-day cycle pattern and discussed the rephasing of the three-day cycle, it is time to identify support and resistance. Where do you think the market will stabilize or encounter price resistance?

One method that has proved to be quite effective is to design two separate envelopes for each trading day. There is a buying envelope, where support can be anticipated, and a selling envelope, where you should expect resistance. As a rule, it is exceedingly difficult to forecast tomorrow's high or low *before* the market opens. Computer studies have shown that this, and other systems, can occasionally approximate these areas, but, in general, this kind of forecasting method doesn't lend itself to picking two or three key numbers.

What *can* be accomplished, however, with a high degree of accuracy is the identification of trading zones within which support and resistance should occur. Moreover, once the market is open and you have new data to work with, the *range* of these two zones—namely, the buying and selling envelopes—can often be highly accurate, often within one or two ticks.

Let's begin with the buy envelope. What constitutes the buy envelope? As we've defined it, the buy envelope is an area where support should be found in tomorrow's market. Remember, the buy envelope is calculated daily after the close for tomorrow's market. Hence, we only have past data to work with in calculating the numbers. What are the numbers we want to examine? To calculate the buy envelope, we want to look at the following:

1. *The previous day's low.* By previous day, we mean today, the day just finished. If this is Tuesday and the low of the day was 186.00, we want to make note of this number in calculating the buy envelope for Wednesday. Lows are significant because they identify points in the market where the sellers couldn't push prices lower without buyers willingly taking everything the sellers wanted to sell.

2. *The trend reaction buy number.* We have covered the calculation of this number in a previous section. This number represents support.

3. *The average of recent Decline numbers.* Here's where tracking the numbers comes into play. Remember, the Decline column measures the distance between a high and the next day's low. It measures how far a sell-off carried before support was found. As a result, if you could *average* recent Decline column numbers, and *subtract* from the previous day's high, you might very well have a ballpark figure on where support could be found. This is where the LSS system has improved Taylor's original concept. It is important to average *recent* Decline column entries, because the market can change over time.

4. *The average of recent Buying Under numbers.* The Buying Under number reflects how far under yesterday's low a market carried. If it didn't penetrate the low, the BU number is expressed as a negative number. Again, by averaging the BU entries and subtracting from the previous day's low, you can arrive at a good support level.

The selling envelope is the mirror image of the buying envelope. To calculate the sell envelope, consider the following:

1. *The previous day's high.* In calculating tomorrow's sell envelope, you take today's high as the point where resistance will be encountered. This concept is borrowed from Taylor, who maintained that resistance will always exist at the previous day's high.

2. *The trend reaction sell number.* This number is valuable as a point where resistance will be encountered. The calculation was discussed in an earlier section.

3. *The average of recent Rally numbers.* When added to the previous day's low, the average of the Rally numbers signifies a resistance area where selling should overcome buying.

4. *The average of recent Buying High numbers.* This average is *added* to the previous day's high. Remember, the BH number is the amount by which the day's high exceeded the previous high. If the last high did *not* exceed the previous high, the BH number will be negative. By averaging a series of BH numbers, you achieve a consensus that pinpoints a resistance area.

Now, taking both the buy and the sell envelopes, you should have four numbers in each. Since the previous high and low are self-explanatory and the trend reaction numbers have already been discussed, let's look at several examples utilizing the D, R, BH, and BU columns for generating buying and selling numbers for the buy and sell envelopes.

The Decline column. The Decline column measures the range in prices from high to low over a two-day period. Let's consider an actual example in which three consecutive D-column entries were averaged and subtracted from the previous day's high.

First, the target day, which, in our illustration here, we'll assume has yet to take place, is Thursday, January 10. The most recent data, therefore, are for the previous Monday through Wednesday. The Decline column entries for those three days were as follows:

Day	Decline Column
1	.40
2	1.90
3	.50

The average of these three entries is about .95 points after rounding. You then take the previous day's high and subtract the *average of the previous three Decline columns* to arrive at a number you can use in the buying envelope. The previous day's high was 169.15. By subtracting .95 points, you arrive at a support level of precisely 168.20. Now remember, this calculation was made following the close on Wednesday, January 9. The previous day's low? Precisely 168.20. Right on the money! Obviously, this was only a coincidence. The likelihood of selecting the exact low using this method is not that great. What's more, once you factor in the other numbers in the envelope, the overall buy number would have been somewhat lower. But this does illustrate how recent price behavior tends to suggest how the market might trade in the near future.

The Buying Under column. Buying Under measures the penetration of the previous day's low. How far under the previous low did the market trade? Obviously, if no penetration occurred, the number would have to be negative, since you will be subtracting a larger number from a smaller one. On Wednesday, January 9, the low of the March S&P contract was 167.10. The previous day's low was 166.35, hence the BU entry will be −.75. The two previous entries were +.60 and −.95. Here are the three BU entries in column form:

Day	Buying Under Column
1	−.95
2	.60
3	−.75

The *average* of the last three entries, therefore, is *minus* .35 points when averaged. When you *subtract* a negative number from a number, you add. Therefore, the previous low at 167.10 *plus* .35 points equals 167.45. This is the entry in the buy envelope as the Buying Under number. As we indicated above, the *low* on the following target day was 168.20—so this number was a bit low.

The reaction trend number. The reaction trend buy and sell number is derived from the formula provided earlier in the book. The high, low, and close for the day just finished were 169.15, 167.10, and 168.60 respectively. Add them up and divide by three to derive the average; then multiply by two. Subtract the high of 169.15 and obtain the reaction trend buy number, 167.45.

The buy number. The buy number is the average of the four numbers in the buy envelope. The four numbers in the example we've just covered are as follows:

BUY ENVELOPE

D-column number   = 168.20
Reaction number   = 167.45
BU-column number = 167.45
Previous low   = 167.10

Average of four   = 167.55 buy numbers

Now that you know how to derive the buy number, you must know one other rule: *you don't buy at the buy number.* Rather, the buy and sell numbers are best used to calculate the *anticipated range,* which we will describe in a moment, as soon as we cover the sell envelope.

The Rally column. The Rally column measures the difference between yesterday's low and today's high, or the range from low to high over the past two-day period. By averaging the magnitude of the rallies, you attempt to anticipate resistance in the market.

Using the data for the March S&P contract for the three days of January 7, 8, and 9, we find that the numbers were as follows:

DAY	RALLY COLUMN
1	2.25
2	.65
3	2.80

The average of these three entries was 1.90 points. When *added* to the low of the last day of trading—namely, January 9—the Rally column sell number is 169.00. Indeed, the market on the subsequent day carried far above that number—the top occurred at 172.15. But this number, like the others, only suggests where resistance should occur—not where one should necessarily sell. This is an important point to keep in mind.

The Buying High column. The Buying High column measures the penetration of the last high over the previous high. In the example we are considering, the penetration occurred during the last two out of three sessions. Hence, a negative number was entered on one session. Here's what the columns looked like.

DAY	BUYING HIGH COLUMN
1	.90
2	−.65
3	1.55

The average of the three is, therefore, .60 points. When *added* to the previous day's high of 169.15, the BH-column entry is 169.75.

The reaction trend number. This is the same formula you used to derive the reaction trend buy number. The only difference is that you subtract the *previous low* to achieve the sell number. If you do the calculations, you'll see that the reaction trend number is 169.50.

The sell number. The sell number is the average of the four numbers in the sell envelope. The four numbers in the example we've just covered are as follows:

SELL ENVELOPE

BH-column number	= 169.75
Reaction number	= 169.50
Previous high	= 169.15
R-column number	= 169.00
Average of four	= 169.35 sell number

Here again, you do *not* use the sell number to sell. Rather, you use both buy and sell numbers to establish the *anticipated range.*

The anticipated range. The anticipated range is the difference between the buy number and the sell number. In the example above, the buy number was 167.55 and the sell number was 169.35. The anticipated range, therefore, is the difference between the two, or 1.80 points. The anticipated range is used to pinpoint profit-taking points once an intraday high or low is established.

There are two ways the anticipated range can be used. In the first, you await the establishment of an intraday high or low and then you add or subtract the anticipated range in order to project a high or low for the day. This high or low is known as the *target sell* or *target buy* respectively. Quite often, this method is very accurate in predicting the high or low of the day.

For example, let's consider an actual trading situation. For Thursday, January 17, 1985, an L-day with a DOWN designation, the anticipated range of the March 1985 S&P 500 contract was 1.60 points. The buy number was 172.55 and the sell number was 174.15. On Thursday's open, at 173.80, the market rallied two ticks, to 173.90. This was the intraday high. By taking the intraday high and *subtracting* the anticipated range, you reach a target buy (cover) number of 172.35 (173.90 − 1.55 = 172.35). The actual low of the day proved to be 172.15. On the close, the market rallied to 172.60.

Another way to use the anticipated range is to *double* the number and then add to the low or subtract from the high, depending upon your initial position. In designing the LSS system, many variables were tested as profit-taking points. At first, the testing concentrated on generating many, many winners. To achieve this high probability of winning, small profits were taken—starting with just 50 percent of the range as the target buy or sell. But this soon proved to have its drawbacks. For instance, if you take just 50 percent of the anticipated range and add it to the low or subtract it from the high, you will surely increase the number of times the anticipated range number is reached. After all, if the anticipated range is one point, isn't there a higher likelihood that the market will mount at least a half-point move? Certainly. But the enhanced number of profits will be offset by the inevitable occasional losses, a half-point profit offset by a half-point loss. What's more, by taking just 50 percent of the anticipated range, you will find you often leave too many dollars on the table. After many tests, the results proved that *doubling* the anticipated range maximized the profitability. The reason: on those occasional days when the market really runs, the system will capture the entire move. More often than not, the doubling of the anticipated range means the target buy or sell number is *not* hit. Since the LSS system is designed for day trading only, you must then *exit your position on the close.* Typically, this is best achieved by using a market on close (MOC) order.

The advisability of doubling the range is shown by an example. On February 13, 1985, the March S&P contract had an anticipated range of 2.05 points. On the opening, which turned out to be the low of the day, the market mounted a rally. By doubling the anticipated range and adding it to the low of 181.35, a target sell number of 185.45 was established. The actual high of the day proved to be 185.55, just two ticks above the anticipated sell number. The range on the day was over four points—almost double the typical range for the time period. How did the system correctly anticipate the move? It didn't. Rather, it simply allowed the trader to capitalize on the occasional move of four or five points when the market really runs. On the following day, the market reverted to its more normal range, about two points.

The Overbought/Oversold Indicator

Should you buy or sell? One of the most reliable aspects of the LSS system is a simple overbought/oversold indicator that pinpoints when prices have advanced just a little too much during any given trading session, suggesting the reverse action on the following day. Like the "Bullish Consensus" percentages, the overbought/oversold indicator pinpoints when either buyers or sellers gain command of the market. And, like contrary-opinion trading, the LSS system tries to capitalize on the situation by trading *against* the short-term trend.

Thus, when you have a market that begins near the low and rallies, you will have a high reading on the overbought/oversold indicator; when the market opens near its high and trades lower, a low reading will occur. As a rule, you want to *sell high readings* in the indicator which measures 70 percent or higher and you want to *buy low readings* at 30 percent or lower. The reading is taken each day following the close of trading. The reading applies only to the next day's price action.

Here's the formula for the overbought/oversold indicator:

$$\frac{(High - open) + (close - low)}{2 \times range} = \begin{array}{l} \text{overbought/oversold} \\ \text{indicator} \\ \text{percentage} \end{array}$$

Let's take an example to illustrate how the overbought/oversold indicator works. We'll look at prices after the close on Thursday, June 13, 1985, in the June S&P contract. The prices at the close that day were as follows:

JUNE S&P—THURSDAY, JUNE 13
Open = 187.10
High = 187.60
Low = 185.50
Close = 185.60

To calculate the overbought/oversold percentage reading, we rely on our formula as follows:

$$\frac{(187.60 - 187.10) + (185.60 - 185.50)}{2 \times (187.60 - 185.50)}$$

$$= \frac{.50 + .10}{2(2.10)} = \frac{.60}{4.20} = 14\%$$

With a low reading of 14 percent, a buying opportunity presents itself on the following day. Note that, on Thursday, the high was made first and the market declined, setting up a buying opportunity as the market closed near its low.

On the following day, the June S&P contract traded down from its open and then rallied toward the close. The prices were as follows:

JUNE S&P—FRIDAY, JUNE 14
Open = 186.50
High = 187.15
Low = 185.70
Close = 187.05

The overbought/oversold indicator can also be used as a confirming signal for the three-day cycle. Remember, we recently discussed the advisability of occasionally pushing the cycle ahead a day when the ideal pattern can't be ascertained. This is the precise scenario that occurred here. Thursday, June 13, was an S-day with declining prices throughout the trading session after the initial morning bulge that occurred on the open. Instead of challenging the highs on the previous day—Taylor's Buy Day—the market had been in retreat for two consecutive days. The selling was overdone and the market was due to start rallying. Instead of the three-day rally pattern that the classical Taylor trader would expect, the market was trending downward. The third day was indeed the next day, the SS-day. Instead of selling into a rally, however, the S&P trader had to shift his thinking 180 degrees and *buy* the break. Where was a good place to buy? Right where Taylor said there would be support: above the previous day's low. The previous day's low was 185.50. The market found support at 185.70 the next day. By using the overbought/oversold indicator together with the three-day cycle, you could have made a very successful and virtually risk-free trade.

The overbought/oversold indicator works equally well when you have a rising market and you are looking to sell. In a recent three-day cycle that occurred during August 1985, the L-day pattern occurred as forecast, moving from a low made first to a high made last, followed by a second rising market on the following S-day. The pattern was ideal for a short sale on the third day.

Here are the prices for the September S&P contract for the S-day, Thursday, August 8:

SEPTEMBER S&P—THURSDAY, AUGUST 8
Open = 188.50
High = 189.45
Low = 188.25
Close = 189.10

The calculations for the overbought/oversold indicator are as follows:

$$\frac{(189.45 - 188.50) + (189.10 - 188.25)}{2 \times 1.20}$$

$$= \frac{1.80}{2.40} = 75\%$$

With the overbought/oversold indicator at 75 percent, the market was ripe for a short sale on the following day. Not only was it the third day up in the three-day cycle, but the overbought/oversold indicator percentage was pointing toward lower prices. Taylor's rule to sell near the previous day's high proved right on the money! Here are the results for the following day:

SEPTEMBER S&P—FRIDAY, AUGUST 9
Open = 189.40
High = 189.50
Low = 188.45
Close = 188.70

The 70-30 rule obviously doesn't prove accurate every day. But when used in conjunction with other signals, it is a valuable contribution to selecting the right trend of the day.

There will be many days when the percentage falls between 70 and 30 percent. How do you use the indicator when the percentage is in the middle? When this occurs, the LSS system turns toward another signal. When a balance exists between buyers and sellers, the balance is reflected by stationary or, at least, sideways price movements. The market may be up in the morning and down in the afternoon and close just about unchanged. On such days, the overbought/oversold indicator will reflect this indecision by registering a neutral reading—say, a 50 percent, or even a 45 or 40 percent, reading. Because the lack of market direction provides no clue to subsequent price action, you have to look elsewhere for a confirming tool that prices are headed higher or lower.

One good place to look is at the price action during the first hour of trading on the following day. The range which is established during this first hour of trading, we call the *intraday range*. The high and low registered during the first hour are known as the *intraday high* and the *intraday low* respectively. All but the most thinly traded futures will have some range after an hour of trading, even if the underlying cash index or commodity is virtually unchanged.

So you will have this range to work with. During the first hour on such a day (namely, when the percentage falls between 30 and 70 percent), you should make it a point to stay out of the market. What you are looking for *after* the first hour is over and the intraday range is established, is a *violation of either the intraday high or the intraday low*. Once this violation occurs, you want to *fade the move and go the other way*.

That is, *if the intraday high is violated, look to sell; if the intraday low is violated, look to buy*. These are very simple rules, but over a year's time they will return you thousands of dollars in profits.

You can be sure that this is the exact opposite of what most traders are doing—and this, incidentally, is why it works so well. When the market rallies, for instance, several things happen. One, the stops of the short sellers (who have now become buyers) are hit; this, in turn, generates more buying as the latecomers, who've been watching the market for some clue to direction, decide to jump aboard. More buying. Unfortunately for them, they are too late.

These "engineered" rallies—which are called "sucker rallies"—exist solely to fool the unwary. This is the classic Taylor rally, the very paradox that makes the Taylor *Book Method* and the LSS system so profitable. Essentially, the market is taken up in order to generate a fresh source of buyers for the sellers to sell to; the reverse, of course, is true on the down- side. When you think about it, what better time to move the market around a little bit than when the balance between buyer and seller is almost equal? There is no "reason" for the market to rally, so why not create a modest "technical rally" to get the ball rolling?

There could be a million and one excuses that will be credited for the false rally—the Fed was loosening credit, rumors of tight crop, or what- ever—but you can be sure that, regardless of the reason, the smart money will profit and the uninformed will lose.

There is a reason, of course. But not the one you'll find broadcast on the TV or radio news. The reason is that the insiders wanted to create a good selling opportunity, and they could accomplish this feat only by panicking the hapless short sellers into buying at an unadvantageous price. You have to remind yourself that there's always a buyer for each seller, and vice versa. Typically, those who engineer the early-morning false breakout know exactly what they are doing. Join their ranks and see how profitable it can be.

Using the Opening Price to Buy or Sell—the Level 1 Trade

Statistical studies have shown that the opening and closing prices are often near one end of the day's range. Typically, the opening will fall near one end of the range and the close near the other. This is not to suggest that the key to beating the market is to simply buy on the open and sell on the close, however.

The LSS system relies on using three levels of prices to initiate positions. One of these levels, which is known as Level 1, relies on buying or selling at a fixed variable, away from the morning's opening price. For obvious reasons, the variable will be different for different futures contracts. The volatility of the market, the size of the daily range, and the market's ten- dency to retrace its initial intraday range will all determine what the vari- able should be.

The move away from the opening price serves two key functions. On the one hand, a move of x points away from the open suggests the market is experiencing normal volatility and it may again soon reverse its direction; on the other hand, a larger move, of y points, in the same direction means that a reversal is highly unlikely.

Let's look at this idea in terms of an actual market experience.

Several years ago, when moves of $20 and even limit moves of $25 an ounce were not uncommon in gold, I learned an interesting statistic. A trader who had run tests on the gold market told me that if gold prices were headed lower, the *rise* from the opening price would exceed $3 only 30 percent of the time and that it would exceed $4 only 12 percent of the time. That meant that if gold was going to trade lower on any given day, it would *not* rise above $4 over the opening price 88 percent of the time. I took this to mean that I could safely sell gold on a rally from the open and place a relatively close stop to protect my position. As prices gathered strength and rose about a $4.00 premium over the opening price, I would then take losses on any short position and look for an opportunity to begin purchasing gold futures contracts. It wasn't long before I realized precisely what valuable information this was. When buying, I would wait for a decline in prices *under* the open. If, for example, gold opened at $570 an ounce, I would often buy it at $567 and watch the market. If it went more than a dollar or two against me, I promptly got out. More often than not, however, the market found support at the level and rallied, generating profits.

In the Standard & Poor's 500 index contract, extensive computer tests revealed that the same type of pattern was evident. The market could easily move x points away from the open if it was headed in the reverse direction; but once it went y points, that was the direction in which it would likely trend—*not*, however, necessarily right away.

At first, during the early volatility of the contract, .40 or .50 points seemed the ideal spot to place an entry order away from the open. But as more data became available, .30 points above the open when selling, or .30 points below the open when buying, became the logical entry point. For one, using a smaller variable when entering will get you into more positions. For another, over time this greater number of positions tends to enhance your profits.

It is important to note that these so-called Level 1 trades will be taken as soon as you have some clue as to market direction—that is, as soon after the open as possible, in most instances. In many cases, the opportunity to buy .30 points under the open or .30 points above the opening on days in which you have selected the correct direction, may exist for only a moment. For this reason, you must be quick to enter your order as soon as the opening price is known. Figures 53 and 54 illustrate the Level 1 trade.

Let's look at ten consecutive trading days in which you are buying or selling at the .30 point variable above or below the open. These are actual trades that have been verified by computer. When the position was stopped out, the table indicates by showing a loss in the position.

Standard & Poor's 500—December 1984

Ten Consecutive Trading Days—Level 1 Trades

Date	Initiate Bought/Sold	Time	Liquidate Bought/Sold	Time	Gain/Loss
09/05/84	Buy 3 @ 167.70	10:38*	Sell 3 @ 168.10	3:14**	+$ 600
09/06/84			no trade		
09/07/84			no trade		
09/10/84	Buy 3 @ 166.30	9:31	Sell 3 @ 168.40	3:14	+$ 3,150
09/11/84	Sell 3 @ 169.35	9:02	Buy 3 @ 167.05	3:14	+$ 3,450
09/12/84	Buy 3 @ 167.15	9:04	Sell 3 @ 168.35	3:14	+$ 1,800
09/13/84	Sell 3 @ 169.30	12:21	Buy 3 @ 169.70	12:55	−$ 600
09/14/84	Sell 3 @ 174.40	9:11	Buy 3 @ 172.75	3:14	+$ 2,475
09/17/84	Buy 3 @ 172.25	9:03	Sell 3 @ 172.95	3:14	+$ 1,050
09/18/84			no trade		
09/19/84	Buy 3 @ 172.10	9:01	Sell 3 @ 174.30	1:09	+$ 3,300
09/20/84	Buy 3 @ 170.65	9:20	Sell 3 @ 171.55	3:14	+$ 1,350
09/21/84	Sell 3 @ 170.80	9:03	Buy 3 @ 170.50	2:11	+$ 450

Total Profits: $17,025

* central daylight saving time
** 3:14 signifies MOC order

For the ten days shown, the Level 1 buying/selling strategy returned an average of $1,672.50 per day using just three contracts on each trade. You should note that, for the thirteen trading days, three days had no Level 1 trade. This is because the market did not trade up .30 from the open on selling or down .30 points from the open on buying. On some days, however, no trade, either buying or selling, is indicated and the LSS system calls for standing on the sidelines.

Eight out of the nine trades were taken during the first thirty-one minutes of trading. Seven out of ten trades were exited on the close using a market-on-close order. One trade was stopped out with a loss. Significantly, this trade was taken relatively late in the day and was stopped out after only thirty-four minutes. In the two other examples, the profit point was reached. This illustrates the importance of placing orders early in the day, preferably right after the open, when the day's market direction is unknown, and exiting late in the day, preferably on the close.

The open is often the best time of day to initiate trades. You'd do well to watch the open carefully and enter your orders as soon after the opening price is known as possible.

The Retracement of the Intraday Range—the Level 2 Trade

Known as the Level 2 trade, the retracement trade is based on the tendency of a market to mount a countertrend before taking its natural upward or downward course during the day. The *intraday range* is defined in the LSS system as the range of prices after one hour of trading. The retracement trade price is determined by taking the intraday range and multiplying the range by .618. The resultant product is then *added to the intraday low when buying,* or *subtracted from the intraday high when selling.* (See Figures 55 and 56.)

For example, on November 1, 1984, the intraday high and the intraday low for the December 1984 S&P 500 contract was 169.85 and 169.30. The intraday range was the difference between the numbers, or .55 points. Multiplying by .618, the result is .35 points. This amount is then *subtracted* from the intraday high to achieve the Level 2 buying price at 169.55. The market indeed traded at that price and three contracts were purchased at a price of 169.55. They were sold on the close at 170.45, resulting in a profit of $1,350 for the day. The maximum adversity on this trade was very little, since the low of the day was only .30 points below the entry point.

In the following table, we have listed ten consecutive trading days of Level 2 trades.

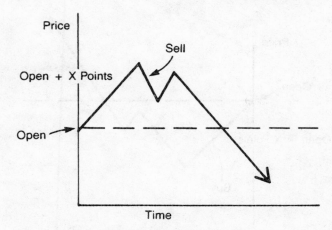

Sell at x points above the open

Figure 53. The Level 1 Sell Trade.

Standard & Poor's 500—December 1984

Ten Consecutive Trading Days—Level 2 Trades

Date	Initiate Bought/Sold	Time	Liquidate Bought/Sold	Time	Gain/Loss
09/05/84	Buy 3 @ 168.05	10:04*	Sell 3 @ 168.10	3:14**	+$ 75
09/06/84			no trade		
09/07/84			no trade		
09/10/84	Buy 3 @ 166.45	10:11	Sell 3 @ 168.40	3:14	+$ 2,925
09/11/84	Sell 3 @ 169.50	10:07	Buy 3 @ 167.05	3:14	+$ 3,675
09/12/84	Buy 3 @ 167.45	1:59	Sell 3 @ 168.35	3:14	+$ 1,350
09/13/84	Sell 3 @ 168.75	12:11	Buy 3 @ 169.70	12:55	−$ 1,425
09/14/84	Sell 3 @ 174.05	10:00	Buy 3 @ 172.75	3:14	+$ 1,950
09/17/84	Buy 3 @ 172.60	10:19	Sell 3 @ 172.95	3:14	+$ 525
09/18/84			no trade		
09/19/84	Buy 3 @ 172.05	10:00	Sell 3 @ 174.30	1:09	+$ 3,375
09/20/84	Buy 3 @ 170.85	11:16	Sell 3 @ 171.55	3:14	+$ 1,050
09/21/84	Sell 3 @ 171.90	11:53	Buy 3 @ 170.50	2:11	+$ 2,100

Total Profits: $15,600

* central daylight saving time
** 3:14 signifies MOC order

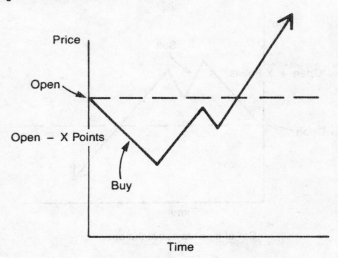

Buy at x points below the open

Figure 54.   The Level 1 Buy Trade.

The profits on the Level 2 trades almost mirror those on the Level 1 trades for the same time period. The profits are a little less: $15,600 as compared to $16,725. But they are still quite respectable.

You should note that no Level 2 trades are ever taken during the first

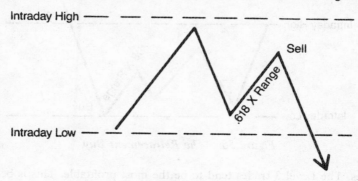

Figure 55.   The Retracement Sell.

hour of trading. By definition, a Level 2 trade can be taken only after the intraday high and the intraday low are established.

The Penetration of the Intraday High or Low— the Level 3 Trade

The Level 3 trade is taken only when the intraday high or the intraday low is penetrated by a given amount. When selling, the Level 3 trade is taken upon the violation of the intraday high. When buying, the Level 3 trade is taken upon the violation of the intraday low. The variable to use in determining the amount of penetration in placing the buying or selling price of the Level 3 trade is 15 percent of the day's anticipated range. Thus, if the anticipated range in the Standard & Poor's contract is 2.00 points, the penetration number will be .30 points above the intraday high (if selling) or .30 points below the intraday low (if buying). Figures 57 and 58 illustrate the Level 3 buy and sell trade.

Let's consider an example. On July 6, 1984, the anticipated range for the September 1984 S&P contract was 1.50 points. Fifteen percent of this amount is 22.5, so we'll round the penetration number to .25 points. The intraday high was 154.10 and the intraday low was 153.70. Since we are buying on this day, we would place an order to purchase September S&P contracts at a price of 153.45 after one hour of trading.

At precisely 10:11 that morning, just eleven minutes after the establishment of the intraday range, three contracts were purchased at that price. They were sold at the close at 154.15. The profit: $1,050. Because Level 3 trades are only taken upon a penetration of the intraday high or the intraday low, there are far fewer of them than of the Level 1 and Level 2

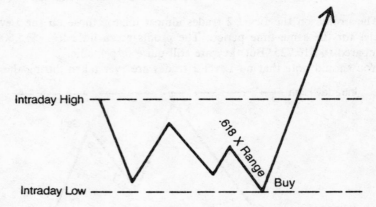

Figure 56.   The Retracement Buy.

trades. The Level 3 trades tend to be the most profitable. This is because they are placed at the highest price when selling and the lowest when buying. For this reason, the Level 3 trade is a difficult one to take for most traders. Typically, the stops are being run at the time the position is initiated and you are selling strength or buying weakness.

In the table below, you will find listed the Level 3 trades for the ten consecutive trading days shown in the previous tables. Note that there are only two trades—and only one winner.

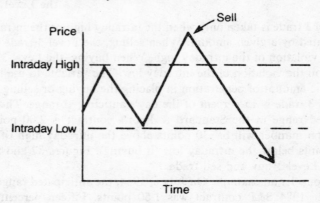

Sell at x points above the intraday high

Figure 57.   The Level 3 Sell Trade.

Standard & Poor's 500—December 1984

Ten Consecutive Trading Days—Level 3 Trades

Date	Initiate Bought/Sold	Time	Liquidate Bought/Sold	Time	Gain/Loss
09/05/84		no Level 3 trade			
09/06/84		no trade			
09/07/84		no trade			
09/10/84		no Level 3 trade			
09/11/84		no Level 3 trade			
09/12/84		no Level 3 trade			
09/13/84	Sell 3 @ 169.25	12:23*	Buy 3 @ 169.70	12:55	−$ 675
09/14/84		no Level 3 trade			
09/17/84		no Level 3 trade			
09/18/84		no trade			
09/19/84		no Level 3 trade			
09/20/84		no Level 3 trade			
09/21/84	Sell 3 @ 173.15	10:20	Buy 3 @ 170.50	2:11	+$ 3,975

Total Profits: $3,300

* central daylight saving time

For the ten days on which trades occurred, the LSS system gained over $35,000 when the three trading levels are taken together. On only two of these days would a maximum of nine contracts have been traded.

The LSS Worksheet

At the heart of the LSS system is the worksheet. Comparable to Taylor's *Book Method,* the worksheet contains all the important data you'll need to calculate the buying and selling envelopes, the cycle, the overbought/oversold, the trend, and the rallies and declines—in short, everything you'll need to trade the LSS system effectively and profitably.

Purchasers of the LSS software will find that much of the calculating is performed by their personal computer. The only requirement for PC users is to enter the daily price data as well as answer the questions requested by the program. To provide the correct trading signals, the software program will require you to enter the morning's opening as well as the intraday high and the intraday low. Once this information is known, however, the software will do the rest.

The LSS trading system is also available in the form of a Hewlett-Packard 41 hand-held calculator that has been preprogrammed. Here again, the user will be responsible for entering correct price data and answering the respective questions concerning opening price and intraday

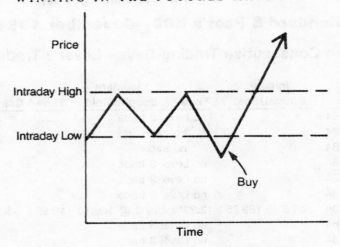

Buy at x points below the intraday high

Figure 58.   The Level 3 Buy Trade.

high and low. The calculator will then perform all the mathematical calculations associated with generating the trading signals.

For users who would prefer to do all the calculations manually, the accompanying worksheet should provide a guideline. Note that the open, high, low, and close are entered every day. Once this information is available, you can then enter the momentum trend number and the momentum trend indicator. The overbought/oversold percentage can also be calculated from these numbers, as can the trend reaction numbers and the Decline, Rally, Buying High, and Buying Under numbers. Finally, the buy and sell envelopes and the respective buy and sell numbers can be calculated.

It is important to track this vital market information daily. Unless the price data are entered daily, the correct trading cycle will be lost, as will be other important information.

Even a cursory glance at the table following should help you immediately make some decisions for the next trading day, Friday, June 14. One would anticipate the next day's cycle day as an SS-day, or the third day in the three-day pattern with the normal SS-day cycle pattern of high made first and low made last. But, in this instance, you can see from the overbought/oversold indicator that the 14 percent reading suggests the reverse: a buying opportunity on the next day's open.

Here's what happened. The June 1985 S&P 500 contract opened at 186.50. The LSS system immediately signaled a buy at the open minus .30 points, or 186.20. This trade was taken during the first hour of trading.

After one hour of trading, the intraday high and the intraday low were

Standard & Poor's 500
June 1985

Date	Open	High	Low	Close	Ovbt/ Ovsld	T#	T	D	R	BH	BU	Pivot NR	Buy	Sell
June 06 Th	189.75	***191.70	189.55	191.60	93%	+1.30	U	1.60	1.85	.55	.30	190.20-B 192.35-S	189.95	191.80
07 F	191.50	191.95	**189.50	189.55	10%	−.40	D	2.20	2.40	.25	.05	188.75-B 191.20-S	189.55	191.75
10 M	189.35	***190.05	188.85	189.95	71%	−1.75	D	3.10	.55	−1.90	.65	189.15-B 190.35-S	188.55	190.15
11 T	189.85	*190.05	188.85	189.25	25%	−.30	U	1.20	1.20	0	0	188.75-B 189.95-S	188.50	189.95
12 W	189.20	189.35	**187.65	187.85	10%	−2.00	D	2.40	.50	−.70	1.20	187.25-B 188.95-S	187.25	188.80
13 Th	187.10	*187.60	185.50	185.60	14%	−3.65	D	3.85	−.05	−1.75	2.15	184.90-B 187.00-S	184.95	186.85

Note: *means that the highs and lows were made first during the trading session

**signifies a high or low being achieved last during the trading session

known. The intraday high was 186.50, the opening price, and the intraday low was 185.70, which proved to be the low of the day. By taking this intraday range and multiplying by .618 and then subtracting the product from the intraday high, the Level 2 buy signal was generated at 186.00. This price, however, was never reached again during the trading day. The Level 3 buy signal, which would have been at 185.40 on a penetration of the intraday low, was not hit either.

The positions were sold on a market-on-close order for a profit of $1,275 for the day. The open, high, low, and close were as follows:

S&P 500—June 1985

Friday, June 14

Open = 186.50
High = 187.15
Low = 185.70
Close = 187.05

Note also that the trend reaction sell number was 187.00 and the actual high proved to be 187.15. Also, the sell number in the selling envelope was 186.85, just .30 points off the high of the day. By holding the position until the close, however, the LSS system realized a slightly better selling price on the day.

Some other observations on the use of the LSS worksheet are shown in the table. The overbought-oversold percentage worked four days out of six. Using this indicator alone would have had you selling on Friday, June 7; buying on Monday, June 10; selling on Tuesday, June 11; and buying on Friday, June 14. These were all winning trades. Moreover, using the Level 1 trades alone, the maximum adversity from the entry point would have been remarkably small.

For instance, on Friday, June 7, you would have sold the Level 1 position at 191.80, and the high of the day proved to be 191.95, three ticks higher. On Monday, June 10, the Level 1 buy occurred at 189.05, and the bottom was 188.85, four ticks away. On Tuesday, June 11, the Level 1 trade was missed by just two ticks (although the Level 2 trade would have proved profitable); and, finally, the winning trade on Friday, June 14, would have been taken at 186.20, resulting in a maximum adversity of .50 points prior to the move into profitability. Note also that the Level 1 sell on Friday, June 7, was confirmed by the selling number (191.80) being at the same exact price. The profit on the Level 1 trade on that day was $3,375 using just three contracts.

How Profitable Is the LSS System?

The LSS system was tested by obtaining the tick-by-tick data available from the Chicago Mercantile Exchange and then running the computerized LSS program against the data. It is important to note that the computer looked at every tick of every day in doing its analysis of how the system would work under actual market conditions. Most computerized systems, by contrast, are tested only against high, low, close data, which is far less accurate as a testing model. What's more, actual real-time testing with real dollars in the market since the development of the system suggests that the computerized simulation tracks the real-time record closely.

As a day-trading method, the LSS system carries no positions overnight. All the profits and losses that occur in the system are realized on a single-day basis. Stops are used every day, and losses are never allowed to overwhelm the user. As a result, the system adheres to the well-known dictum to "cut your losses and let your profits ride." Whenever the profit-taking point is not reached, all positions are liquidated with a market-on-close order.

The system was tested on one period of time and then run against a significantly longer period. All the testing occurred in the most active month of the Standard & Poor's 500 contract. The LSS system may very well work equally as well or better on a number of other futures contracts, but there are difficulties in obtaining data to test other contracts. For example, none of the New York exchanges had tick-by-tick data available. Much of the data available at the Chicago Board of Trade were incomplete or downright inaccurate. As a result, Chicago testing was limited to the S&P 500 and other futures traded at the Merc. However, the introduction of new stock index contracts, which haven't traded long enough to have price data histories, should prove good candidates for the LSS 3-day Cycle Method.

Now let's turn toward results. Over a thirty-two-month period, the LSS system, using just three contracts at each of the three price levels, returned a gross profit of $408,075.50. This was on a purely mechanical basis, taking the trades and using the stops and profit points just as has been spelled out in this chapter. During this period, the market had trended both up and down as well as sideways. The maximum drawdown averaged just 12 percent, a healthy number by almost any standard, and the so-called Shape Ratio, by which many analysts judge a system, was 3.89. A reading of 2.00 or higher is considered a good ratio for most systems. About half of all trades resulted in profits. Significantly, the average profit was much higher than the average loss.

How to Obtain the LSS Software

Software designed to run on the Macintosh, the IBM, and other IBM-compatible computers, is available now from:

> Turner Data Systems
> 17885 "K" Sky Park Boulevard
> Irvine, California 92707
> (714) 261-5094

A preprogrammed HP-41 hand-held calculator is also available from the same source on the LSS system.

A sample of the information the LSS software might generate for your computer screen is shown below. Note that the first two instructions ask the user for the intraday high and intraday low. Once this information is entered into the computer, the software provides the selling and profit-taking points.

LSS 3-Day Cycle Method
Enter Intraday High   18900
Enter Intraday Low   18840

LEVEL 3			LEVEL 2		
PENETRATION		BUY Day	SELL Day		
High	Low	Retrace	Stop	Profit	Retrace	Stop	Profit
18925	11815	18865			18875	18970	360

SELL 1 Unit at 18925 (Level 3)
SELL 1 Unit at 18875 (Level 2)
SELL 1 Unit at 18895 (Level 1)

The Profit Point is Equal to the Day's HIGHEST Price LESS 360 Points

---

For More Information on the LSS System

The LSS system, as briefly outlined in this chapter, is continually being refined, tested, and updated against the new contracts introduced in the futures markets. For additional information on the LSS system, readers are urged to write the author in care of the publisher.

Rules for the LSS System

The LSS system is a mechanical day-trading method that does not require interpretation or judgments during market hours. Because it attempts to capture a single move during a trading session, the system works best on volatile futures such as the stock indexes or the currencies. Despite its mechanical nature, however, the LSS system can be improved by employing certain judgments and intuitive reasoning. The rules that follow can help you trade the system successfully.

RULE NUMBER 1. *Track the cycle every day.* To use the LSS system, you must keep track of the daily price data and the three-day cycle. This also involves doing the calculations every day. Without the calculations and the phasing of the cycle, you cannot determine the anticipated range or other essential measurements for trading the system. Fortunately, the math is relatively simple. But the trader must be willing to put in the time to follow the market on a day-to-day basis. The software or an HP-41 preprogrammed calculator can help make this task easier.

RULE NUMBER 2. *Minimize commission costs.* With the trend toward discount brokerage services, this shouldn't be a hard rule to follow. Moreover, it makes sense. Why pay two or three times as much in commissions when you can get the same service without paying the higher fees of many brokerage houses? The LSS system generates, on average, about ninety to a hundred trades a month. This translates into more than a thousand round-turn trades a year. A savings of even one dollar per trade, therefore, will result in another thousand dollars in profits that you'll have to keep.

As a rule, you shouldn't have to pay more than $20 per round-turn at today's rates. And, depending on the size of your account and the volume, you should be able to negotiate a significantly lower commission.

An alternative to discount brokerage for the serious trader is to purchase a membership on one of the commodity exchanges. If you become a member, your costs will fall significantly. Depending on whether you trade for your account on the floor of the exchange or over the phone through a broker, your cost as a member will be as low as one dollar per trade or as high as $4.00 or $5.00—still a significant savings below the rates charged to public traders.

RULE NUMBER 3. *Act on the trading signals.* The system won't help you unless you learn to take the trades as they occur. The best trades, unfortunately, rarely present themselves for a long period of time. Typically, the best price of the day occurs shortly after the open. The system is designed to help you find this trade. But unless you have the quick-wittedness to place the order without hesitation, the market will likely get away from you, and your only alternative will be to chase the market—a risky strategy at best.

The serious money in the futures market is made by those fortunate traders who aren't afraid to fade the short-term trend. Trust the signals and place your orders before the prices are hit. In this manner, your order will be filled and you'll be earning profits right from the start.

RULE NUMBER 4. *Pay attention to the buy and sell numbers and envelopes.* Although the buying and selling levels are clearly spelled out in the LSS system, the serious trader can enhance his trading skills by watching for key support and resistance areas within the buy envelopes and sell envelopes respectively. When the numbers in both the buying envelopes and selling envelopes match those of the three levels generated by the system, the trade is apt to be a good one. What's more, once the key support or resistance is broken by having prices fall out of the bottom of the buy envelope or soar out of the top of the selling envelope, the trend is likely to persist. At this point, you might do well to use a stop-and-reverse order. Some traders make it a policy to double up and reverse when their position is stopped out. But you must be careful where you do this. Typically, the best opportunities for reversing occur early in the day. A violation of the buy envelope or sell envelope is often a sign that the trend is going in the direction of the penetration of the envelope.

RULE NUMBER 5. *Don't be afraid to take losses quickly when you are wrong.* Good trades tend to go your way almost from the very start. Bad trades, on the other hand, have a way of going against you and staying that way. It won't hurt to take a loss and then try to take the same position later if the situation warrants. Otherwise, you run the risk of burying yourself and overstaying a losing trade.

This is *not* to suggest that you shouldn't add to a loser. Under some circumstances, you want to take another trade when the stops are being run against you. Typically, despite the temporary adversity, the market will soon begin to move in your favor. But once you get behind and the market doesn't seem to want to go your way, you should be willing to take the loss and get out of the market. Never, never hold a losing—or winning —position overnight. You could take an occasional winner overnight, but never a loser. There's a reason why day trading is attractive: safety. Don't attempt to second-guess the market by staying overnight. You are only inviting trouble when you hold on to losing trades.

RULE NUMBER 6. *Don't trade too many different commodities or financial futures.* The LSS system was designed primarily with the Standard & Poor's 500 contract in mind. It is unlikely that it will work as well with other futures contracts, although there is some evidence that it has a good track record in the pork belly market and the soybean market. One reason for good profitability is high volatility. Unless you are in a market that moves, you are going to have trouble making significant profits. What's more, by following too many markets, you are likely to miss an occasional trade. Good trading requires concentration. The closer you follow one or two markets, the better your trading will be.

RULE NUMBER 7. *When the cycle seems out of synch, push it ahead a day.* The rephasing is designed to help you find the correct cycle as quickly as possible. But a simple rule is to look for the reverse to occur on the following day. For example, if you are looking to sell today with the high made first and the low last, and the reverse occurs, look for the selling pattern tomorrow. After all, now you have the market rising and the longs will have profits. To take those profits, they will need to sell.

Typically, the larger traders prefer selling into rallies. The morning bulge on the opening on the next day typically signals the imminent break in prices. For buying opportunities, of course, the reverse is true.

14

Should You Trade Commodity Futures?

UNDERSTANDING YOURSELF IS THE FIRST STEP TO SUCCESSFUL SPECULATION

Whether you have the makings of a successful speculator in commodity futures remains to be seen. No book can teach you this demanding skill. Nor can a book make the key decision to trade or not, for this decision must be made by you alone.

Most outsiders think that commodity futures trading is not for the typical investor—whoever that may be. But as with so many popular impressions, this one is apt to be false. True, commodity futures trading is not for everyone. But there are many would-be speculators with the potential for success in the commodity markets who have held back because they just haven't been exposed to commodities or have considered them too complicated to understand.

Apart from a knowledge of the mechanics of the market, however, the requisites for trading success are not all that rigorous. Certainly, an adequate supply of risk capital is necessary. But money alone cannot ensure your success. There's a saying about the markets that one sure way to make a small fortune trading commodities is to start with a large one. And not a few well-financed traders have confirmed the truth of this statement. But your psychological makeup is perhaps the single most important factor in determining whether you will be successful at trading futures contracts. Your attitude toward your risk, your ability to admit a mistake, your independence in making your own market judgments apart from the crowd—will all have a vital impact upon your trading results.

The importance of your own psychological makeup cannot be overstated. For this factor will decide whether you fall victim to one of the many pitfalls in the way of commodity futures traders. One of the most devastating pitfalls, incidentally, is opinions. Everybody has them, especially in commodity trading; and, to paraphrase Humphrey Neill, when everybody has the same opinion, everybody is likely to be wrong. Let's consider an example of the speculator who has recklessly lost money in futures trading. If he gets wind of your notion to trade commodities, is he going to tell you of his mistakes in the market? No, indeed. You are going to hear that making money in commodity futures is an impossibility. It can't be done. In a sense, he may be telling you the truth; it probably can't be done—by him. But what about you? Are your temperamental factors identical to his? Are you likely to make the same mistakes? How about your attitude toward risk? your knowledge of the futures markets and your grasp of the strategies we have discussed in these pages? your determination to win? All these factors may be different. So don't let someone else's lack of accomplishment stop you if you feel up to the task. If you let yourself be swayed, you will only have yourself to blame. The easily discouraged don't belong in such a high-risk, high-gain game as futures trading anyway. W. Somerset Maugham, the distinguished author, used to make it a practice to discourage any would-be writers who came to him for advice about the writing profession. "I always try to discourage them," said Maugham, adding, "and if they are any good they never listen to me." The same could be said of good speculators. They don't rely upon someone else's judgment to tell them what to do. They know what they want. And they know how to get it. Futures trading is simply the vehicle they use to advance themselves along their chosen avenue of success.

Your Goals

Before you decide one way or another about futures trading, you should take a hard look at your personal goals. For unless you consider where you want to go, it may be hard deciding how to get there. There are investments and speculations available for practically every pocketbook and lifestyle. You have to look at the vast array of opportunities—from savings accounts to securities, antiques to diamonds—to decide which one will satisfy your needs. And when you look at the various investments competing for your discretionary dollars, you must be aware that each has its advantages and disadvantages in terms of safety and growth of principal and equity. Barring some unforeseen economic disaster, savings accounts are reasonably safe places to keep funds, but how will your investment fare in the light of continued inflation? Real estate tends to provide a good return on investment, but it is not as liquid as stocks. Diamonds are presently fashionable, but will buyers be willing to pay higher prices in five years? What about buying silver and gold bullion? Or storing your wealth in a harder currency than American dollars, such as Swiss francs in a foreign bank account? These are just a handful of the considerations that a thinking investor or speculator must make. What's more, the typical middle-income investor will have an army of salesmen pitching him on everything from insurance to income property as the ideal way to guarantee his future against the possibility, if not probability, of absolute ruin if he doesn't get out his checkbook and close the deal immediately. Commodity brokers, of course, are no exception. Amid all the clamor, one sometimes does and sometimes doesn't make the right choice.

Commodity futures do offer one advantage (or disadvantage, depending upon how you look at it) that makes them unique. And that is leverage. By trading contracts with margin requirements as low as 5 percent of the total value of the underlying commodities, the speculator avails himself of an asset worth twenty times the value of his capital. This means that $5,000 can control a commodity worth $100,000, whereas $50,000 will margin commodities worth $1 million. As a result of this incredible leverage, futures trading represents one of the few ways in which you can take a relatively modest amount of money and turn it into a significant amount of money. This is the singular advantage of futures trading that distinguishes it from nearly any other type of investment. If this is one of your goals, then futures trading might be for you.

Your Attitude Toward Risk

Unless you are comfortable in taking risks, you are going to be unsuccessful as a futures trader. For futures trading is the art of taking prudent risks in the pursuit of profit. Knowing how to take risks is a difficult process to master, however. Most people are poor risk takers. They want a sure thing with a predictable outcome before they are willing to take a chance. Unfortunately, the two are mutually exclusive. Where there is no risk, there is no opportunity. Indeed, in the commodities markets, opportunity is commensurate with risk. Seasoned traders know this, and they wouldn't have it any other way. Cognizant of the risks involved, the experienced commodities speculator will proceed with caution. The inexperienced speculator, however, will wait until he has a "sure thing" and then proceed with abandon.

The difference in temperament between risk averters and risk takers is significant. A risk averter, waiting for a sure thing, will allow a market to go up and up before he decides the market is indeed headed higher. He then finds himself buying at the top—at the same time, of course, that the risk taker, a contrarian by nature, is selling short in the final rally. It isn't hard to see who wins in this situation. Risk takers acknowledge the likelihood of failure; risk averters do not.

Risk takers plan for losses, even welcome them (assuming they are kept to a minimum) and thus have the advantage over those with no margin for error. They know that you can lose many battles in the struggle for profits and still win the speculative war. If their judgment is proved wrong in the market—and it frequently is—they simply cut their losses and abandon their positions immediately. They don't agonize over taking a loss and perhaps stay with a losing trade that could then grow truly significant. They accept reality as it is. Knowing they will be wrong more often than they are right, they play the commodity game as it was intended to be played—with agility, shrewdness, and speed. They thrive on the pace and competitiveness. And if they have a losing series of trades, they accept them. They also know how to walk away from the markets for a while in order to refresh their mental outlook and return in a winner's frame of mind. They have an attitude toward risk that is not common among investors.

Risk Capital

Your attitude toward risk will be influenced by your attitude toward the money you use to trade with. To begin, you must have risk capital in order to trade successfully. Risk capital is not money you need to purchase necessities. It is not money you need to pay the mortgage. It is not money you need to pay for your child's education. It is money you can afford to lose. Your attitude toward the money you use to trade with will affect the way you trade. As we have already mentioned, if you wait for a "sure thing" to come along, you are almost certain to lose. Experienced speculators know the difference between risk capital and money needed for everyday expenses. They never substitute the latter for the former.

Some have suggested that if you already have all the financial resources that a conservative-minded commodities speculator should have, you don't need the additional funds that futures trading could provide anyway. This is a good point. After all, if you have the mortgage taken care of, if you have a conservatively managed stock and bond portfolio, substantial savings, income property, tax shelters, and the rest, why trade commodities? It comes down to a question of values. These well-heeled speculators might very well enjoy futures trading. On the other hand, the not-so-well-heeled speculator might very well be willing to forgo some current consumption or degree of security he could achieve—by, say, purchasing bonds—in order to trade commodities. Your definition of risk capital, therefore, depends upon your personal circumstances.

Discipline

Every speculator who hopes to succeed at the difficult art of trading commodity futures must exert a rigorous discipline over all his trading activities. He must be judicious in selecting commodities to buy and sell, and he must not overtrade. He must be mindful of commission costs and losses and never risk more than a small portion of his total trading capital on a single position. Ideally, he will have a trading plan that covers his money-management techniques, and he will stay with his plan until it becomes clear to him that another method of trading would be more desirable.

The disciplined trader has an edge on others in the markets because he is immune to the emotionalism that characterizes the trading activities of his fellow speculators. He knows what he will risk by going into a trade, and he knows what his profit objective will be. Should the market then surprise him and perform more impressively than he had suspected, he will use a method of trailing stops to exit the market. But he will never move his stops to expose himself to greater risk once he decides on his predetermined level.

The disciplined trader knows that losses are inevitable. Because of this knowledge, he decides in advance how much adversity he will absorb before he calls it quits. He will use either actual or mental stop-loss orders and be precise in placing his trading orders when he initially enters the market. He follows the market closely and keeps his charts and other technical indicators up to date. The disciplined trader may be quite independent in his judgment, but his strongest commitment is to understanding the realities of a situation. He knows how to read the "footprints" of a market and ride with it—not against it. Above all, the trader who is successful weds his discipline to his intuitive thinking process. He knows that the time-honored adage that you should "run away to fight another day" is nowhere more applicable than in futures trading. He is strong yet pliable. He knows when to press and when to relent. And, like all successful traders, he knows that his consistent, disciplined manner will bring him profits over time.

Knowledge

There is no substitute for having a comprehensive knowledge of the commodities you trade and the mechanics of the commodity game. Surprisingly, a great many speculators lose money because they don't know what they are doing. A book like this one can go a long way in supplying you with some of the information you need to trade commodities, but there is much more that you can learn on your own.

If you trade an agricultural commodity, acquaint yourself with the seasonal influences on price. Many commodities adhere to a rather rigid seasonal pattern, deviating only during years of abnormal supply-and-demand conditions. For instance, pork bellies have a decided seasonal tendency to rally in July and August. Pork belly traders acquainted with this tendency, which occurred eleven out of twelve times in recent years, will be a step ahead of those who are unaware of this seasonal pattern. Do you know when your commodity is harvested? the impact of various weather conditions on your crop? Orange juice traders are always looking for an untimely hurricane or sudden frost to send their market limit up. A lumber trader might be more interested in seeing the statistics on housing starts. A multitude of information is available for the speculator who wants to research his commodity. The important thing is to be knowledgeable in your area of specialization.

The Future

Today's commodities speculator is a new breed of investor. A few years ago, he wouldn't have considered abandoning the stock market for such a risky venture as futures trading. But in these days of economic uncertainty, many former stock market investors are finding the futures market more to their liking.

Together with the stock option markets, which, after all, are only futures markets for stocks, the commodity futures exchanges have attracted a significant portion of the speculative participation that once flourished in the securities markets. Drawn by the leverage, opportunity for profits, and pace of the commodity game, the new speculator is rapidly adapting to the demands made by these competitive markets.

But is futures trading for you?

Again, the decision is yours. We have outlined some of the pitfalls and some of the advantages of commodity trading in this book, with a special emphasis on strategies designed to win you profits. It is my hope that some of these guidelines will be useful in helping you decide whether you should speculate in commodity futures. Surely, for some, futures trading will be inappropriate; others, however, will find this speculative medium ideal. Because we live in uncertain times, however, the present commodity boom is not likely to diminish. And as any opportunity-minded investor will tell you, commodities are the genuine articles—the essentials of life, the real money.

Glossary

ACCOUNT EXECUTIVE   The person who deals with customers and their orders in commission house offices.

ACREAGE ALLOTMENT   A voluntary limitation on the number of acres farmers plant to a given crop, established under the federal farm program to stimulate production of certain crops of limited supply and curtail production of others in ample supply.

ACTUALS   The physical or cash commodity, as distinguished from commodity futures contracts.

APPROVED DELIVERY FACILITY   Any stockyard, mill, store, warehouse, plant, or elevator that is authorized by the exchange for delivery of exchange contracts.

ARBITRAGE   The simultaneous purchase of one commodity against the sale of another in order to profit from distortions in usual price relationships.

AT THE MARKET   Orders which are intended to be executed immediately by the floor broker at the best obtainable price.

BASIS   Point difference over or under a designated future at which a cash commodity of a certain description is sold or quoted. A most important term for those who hedge.

BID   An offer to buy a specific quantity of a commodity that is subject to immediate acceptance.

BREAK   A more or less sharp price decline.

BROKER   A person paid a fee or commission for acting as an agent in making contracts or sales.

BROKERAGE   A fee charged by a broker for execution of a transaction; an amount per transaction or a percentage of the total value of the transaction, usually referred to as a commission fee.

BUOYANT   Describes a market in which prices have a tendency to rise easily with a considerable show of strength.

BUYING HEDGE   A hedge that is initiated by taking a long position in the futures market equal to the amount of the cash commodity which is eventually needed.

CARRYING CHARGE   The cost to store and insure a physical commodity.

CFTC   Commodity Futures Trading Commission.

CHART   Futures prices (and sometimes other statistical trading information) plotted in a way that the chartist believes gives insight into futures price movements. Several futures markets are regularly influenced by buying or selling based on traders' price chart indications.

CHICAGO BOARD OF TRADE   The world's largest futures exchange, it was founded in 1848.

CHICAGO MERCANTILE EXCHANGE   The world's largest livestock exchange, it traces its origins to a group of agricultural dealers who formed the Chicago Produce Exchange in 1874. It was given its present name in 1919.

CIF   Price (including the cost, insurance, and freight) for delivering a commodity to a specified location.

CLOSE   A period of time at the end of the trading session when all orders are filled within the closing range.

CLOSING RANGE   A range of closely related prices in which transactions take place at the closing of the market; buying and selling orders at the closing might have been filled at any point within such a range.

COMBINATION ORDERS   Two orders, with the cancellation of one contingent upon the execution of the other.

CONTRARY-OPINION THEORY   A theory which holds that the majority are wrong at the major turning points in the market. Contrary-opinion traders believe that in order to be successful, it is necessary only to determine what majority opinion is and then go contrary to it.

COUNTRY   Refers to a place relatively close to a farmer where he can sell or deliver his crop or animals.

COVER   To buy futures contracts in order to offset previous selling.

CRUSH   The process of reducing the raw, unusable soybean into its two major components, oil and meal.

CRUSH MARGIN   The gross profit that a processor makes from selling oil and meal, minus the cost of buying the soybeans.

CRUSH SPREAD   A futures spreading position in which a trader attempts to profit from what he believes to be discrepancies in the price relationship between soybeans and their two derivative products.

DAY ORDER   An order that expires on the close of trading if not filled during that day.

DAY TRADING   A purchase and a sale of the same futures during the trading hours of a single day.

DELIVERY NOTICE   A notice of a clearing member's intentions to deliver a stated quantity of a commodity in settlement of a futures contract.

DIFFERENTIALS   Price differences between classes, grades, and locations of the same commodity.

DISCRETIONARY ACCOUNT   An account in which the customer authorizes another person to make full trading decisions.

FILL OR KILL ORDER   An order that must be filled immediately or canceled.

FIRST NOTICE DAY   The first day on which notice of intentions to deliver actual commodities against futures contracts can be made.

FLOOR BROKER   A member who executes orders for the accounts of other members on the trading floor.

FLOOR TRADER   An exchange member who fills orders for his own account by being personally on the floor. Normally called a "local."

FUNGIBILITY   The characteristic of total interchangeability. Future contracts for the same commodity and delivery month are fungible due to their specifications for quality, quantity, delivery date, and delivery location.

FUTURES COMMISSION MERCHANT   An intermediary who stands between the brokers in the pits (and subsequently the clearinghouse) and the nonmember speculating and hedging public. Every brokerage house must be a futures commission merchant in order to do business with the public.

FUTURES CONTRACT   A firm commitment to make or accept delivery of a specified quantity and quality of a commodity during a specific month in the future at a price agreed upon at the time the commitment was made.

GOOD TILL CANCELED (GTC) ORDER   An open order that remains in force until the customer explicitly cancels the order, until the futures contract expires, or until the order is filled.

HEAVY   A market in which there are apparently a number of selling orders overhanging the market, without a corresponding number of buying orders.

HEDGE   To use the futures market to reduce the price risks inherent in buying and selling cash commodities. For example, as an elevator operator buys cash grain from farmers, he can hedge his purchases by selling futures contracts; when he sells the cash commodity, he purchases an offsetting number of futures contracts to liquidate his position.

HEDGING   The sale of futures contracts in anticipation of future sales of cash commodities as a protection against possible price declines, or the purchase of futures contracts in anticipation of future purchases of cash commodities as a protection against the possibility of increasing costs.

INTERMARKET SPREAD   A spread between commodities that are traded on more than one market. For example, a typical intermarket spread might be made between Chicago wheat and Kansas City wheat.

LAST TRADING DAY   The final day in which trading may occur for a particular delivery month. After the last trading day, any remaining commitment must be settled by delivery.

LIMIT ORDER   An order in which the trader sets a limit to the price, as contrasted with a market order on which no limit is set.

LIQUIDATION   The closing out of a previous position by taking an opposite position in the same contract.

LONG   A position established by owning the actual commodity unhedged or by purchasing futures.

MARGIN   A good-faith deposit a speculator gives to his broker prior to initiating his first trade.

MARGIN CALL   A demand by a broker for additional funds sufficient to raise your deposit on a commodity futures contract above the minimum acceptable level.

MARKET IF TOUCHED (MIT) ORDER   An order that may be executed only if the market reaches a specified point.

MARKET ORDER   An order that is to be filled as soon as possible at the best possible price.

MOMENTUM   The rate of acceleration in price or volume expansion, best noted by developing gaps in velocity figures, or gaps in an on-balance volume series. Upside momentum is greatest just short of price maturity, and downside momentum tends to reach a peak at or near an important bottom.

NEW YORK MERCANTILE EXCHANGE   Founded in 1872 as a market for cheese, butter, and eggs, its principal commodities today include heating oil and petroleum products.

NOMINAL PRICE   Declared price for a future month—sometimes used in place of a closing price when no recent trading has taken place in that particular delivery month; usually an average of the bid and the asked prices.

OFFER   An indication of a willingness to sell at a certain price, as opposed to a bid.

OMNIBUS ACCOUNT   An account carried by one futures commission merchant with another in which the transactions of two or more persons are combined, rather than designated separately, and the identity of the individual account is not disclosed.

ON-BALANCE VOLUME   The result reached after subtracting all the volume on the downside from the volume on the upside. Readings can be either positive or negative.

OPEN INTEREST   The total number of futures contracts entered into during a specified period of time that have not been liquidated either by offsetting futures transactions or by actual delivery.

OPENING RANGE   Range of closely related prices at which transactions took place at the opening of the market; buying and selling orders at the opening might be filled at any point within such a range.

PIT   The area on an exchange floor where futures trading takes place.

POOLING OPERATION   A business similar to an investment trust or syndicate, which solicits, accepts, or receives from others funds for the purpose of trading in any commodity for futures delivery.

PREMIUM   The excess of a cash commodity price over a futures price or over another cash commodity price, or the excess of one futures contract price over another.

PRICE LIMIT   The maximum price advance or decline from the previous day's settlement price permitted for a commodity in one trading session by the rules of the exchange.

PRIMARY MARKET   Important centers at which spot or cash commodities are originally accumulated for movement into commercial channels.

PYRAMIDING   The practice of using accrued paper profits to margin additional trades.

RALLY   Quick advance in prices following a decline.

RANDOM WALK   Name given to the theory that price movements have no memory and occur each day completely at random.

RANGE   The difference between the highest and lowest prices recorded during a given trading session, week, month, or year.

REPORTING LIMIT   The maximum number of contracts you can hold net long or short without notifying the CFTC. Beyond this number, you must make daily reports stating the size of each position larger than the reporting limit. Pertains to speculative positions only.

RISING BOTTOMS   A bullish formation that reveals the ability of a futures contract to turn up above each preceding important low point. To be complete, however, there should also be an accompanying series of rising tops. Rising bottoms (by definition) precede rising tops and are, thus, the first technical requirement that must be met if a situation is to be termed bullish.

RISK CAPITAL   Money which, if lost, would not materially affect one's living habits or deny one the necessities and comforts of a normal life.

SELLING HEDGE (OR SHORT HEDGE)   Selling futures contracts to protect against possible decreased prices of commodities which will be sold in the future.

SETTLEMENT PRICE   The price at which the clearing house clears all transactions at the close of the day.

SHAKEOUT   A healthy technical correction of an overbought situation, characterized by a comparatively short but sharp decline in prices.

SHORT   A trader who has sold futures, speculating that prices will decline.

SHORT SQUEEZE   A situation in which "short" futures traders are unable to buy the cash commodity to deliver against their positions, and so are forced to buy offsetting futures at prices much higher than they'd ordinarily be willing to pay.

SPECULATION   Buying or selling in hopes of making a profit.

SPECULATOR   One who is interested in profiting from a price change in a commodity futures contract. Speculators may trade from the floor of an exchange if they are members, or through a broker if they are not.

SPOT DELIVERY MONTH   The nearest delivery month among all those traded at any point in time. The actual contract month represented by the spot delivery month is constantly changing throughout the calendar year as each contract month reaches its last trading day.

SPOT PRICE   The price quoted for the actual commodity; same as cash commodity price.

SPREADS AND STRADDLES   Terms for the simultaneous buying of futures in one delivery month and selling of futures in another delivery month.

SUPPORT   Any barrier to a price decline.

TOPPING OUT   A term employed to denote loss of upside energy at the top after a long price run-up.

TRADING RANGE   The amount that futures prices can fluctuate during one trading session—essentially, the price "distance" between limit up and limit down.

VOLUME   The number of purchases and sales of a commodity made during a specified period of time.

WAREHOUSE RECEIPT   Document guaranteeing the existence and availability of a given quantity and quality of a commodity in storage; commonly used as the instrument of transfer of ownership in both cash and futures transactions.

Index